TRUTH AND MEMORY

TRUTH AND MEMORY

The Church and Human Rights in El Salvador and Guatemala

Edited by Michael A. Hayes and David Tombs

First published in 2001

Gracewing
2 Southern Avenue, Leominster
Herefordshire HR6 0QF

All rights reserved. No part of this publication may be reproduced, stored in a retrieval system, or transmitted in any form, or by any means, electronic, mechanical, photocopying, recording or otherwise, without the written permission of the publisher.

Compilation and editorial material © Michael A. Hayes
and David Tombs
Copyright for individual chapters resides with the authors.

The right of the editors and contributors to be identified as the authors of this work has been asserted in accordance with the Copyright, Designs and Patents Act 1988.

ISBN 0 85244 524 5

Typesetting by Action Publishing Technology Ltd,
Gloucester, GL1 5SR

Printed in England by
MPG Books Ltd, Bodmin PL31 1EG

Contents

Acknowledgements — vii

Foreword — viii

Abbreviations — ix

MICHAEL A. HAYES AND DAVID TOMBS — 1
Introduction

PART 1: OSCAR ROMERO AND JUAN GERARDI

SCOTT WRIGHT — 11
Oscar Romero and Juan Gerardi: Truth, Memory and Hope

MICHAEL CAMPBELL-JOHNSTON SJ — 44
Martyrdom and Resurrection in Latin America Today:
Archbishop Oscar Arnulfo Romero

JUDITH ESCRIBANO — 59
The Cook, the Dog, the Priest and His Lover: Who Killed
Bishop Gerardi and Why?

KEVIN F. BURKE SJ — 81
Memory and Martyrdom: The Theological Contributions of
Ignacio Ellacuría

MARTIN MAIER SJ — 90
The Theology of Martyrdom in Latin America

PART 2: HUMAN RIGHTS AND THE COMMITMENT TO LIFE

MARCELA LÓPEZ LEVY — 103
Recovery: The Uses of Memory and History in the Guatemalan
Church's REMHI Project

RUTH GIDLEY AND HANNAH ROBERTS 118
Memory and Monuments in Guatemala: Remembering the
Dead and Solidarity with the Living

JON SOBRINO SJ 134
Human Rights and Oppressed Peoples: Historical-Theological
Reflections

PART 3: A THEOLOGY OF TRUTH AND MEMORY

MARY GREY 161
A Theology for the Bearers of Dangerous Memory

DERMOT A. LANE 175
Memory in the Service of Reconciliation and Hope

DAVID TOMBS 194
'He is not here': Disappearance, Death and Denial

PART 4: THEOLOGY AND THE QUEST FOR LIBERATION

MARÍA PILAR AQUINO
The Liberating Vision of Medellín in Feminist Theology 213

JASON GORDON 240
Truth, Memory and 'New World' Theology: In Search of
Interpretative Tools

ANDREW BRADSTOCK 265
Towards a Theology of Solidarity

List of Contributors 274

Index 277

Acknowledgements

The editors wish to acknowledge the help of the many different people who helped to organize the original conference and produce this collection. Particular thanks to Heather Ferguson-Gow for her secretarial assistance, Anna Keane who translated at the conference and to John McCarthy and Christopher Hamilton who have translated the Chapters by Jon Sobrino and María Pilar Aquino (Spanish) and Martin Maier (German) for this volume. Thanks also to Jorge Díaz Cintas who assisted us as a consultant on the Spanish. The poem *Country of My Skull* by Antjie Krog (1998), quoted on p. 174 of the text, has been reproduced by permission of Random House, Johannesburg. Finally, we are particularly grateful to Tom Longford for this opportunity to publish with Gracewing.

Foreword

This volume was born out of wanting to remember the contribution of Archbishop Oscar Romero of El Salvador and Bishop Juan Gerardi of Guatemala to truth and human rights. It is also an attempt to keep alive the significance of their work for Latin America and for the world. These bishops spoke the truth and were silenced as a result. A key principal that informs Christian theology is the Gospel's axiom 'the truth will set you free'. A theological appraisal of how we use 'memory' and a reconstruction of what it means to hope can offer the language and tools to put into practice this axiom. The paradox for the Christian is that in the presence of annihilation, destruction and radical evil, hope comes into its own. The volume grew out of a conference held at the University of Surrey Roehampton on 25 March 2000 under the title 'Truth and Memory: The Church and Human Rights in El Salvador and Guatemala'. One of the constituent colleges of the University, Digby Stuart College, used the opportunity to rename one of its buildings *Romero Court*. The conference was sponsored by the Faculty of Arts and Humanities, Digby Stuart College, CAFOD, and the Society of the Sacred Heart. Particular gratitude also needs to go to the Guatemala Solidarity Network and the El Salvador Network for providing our guest speakers from Central America and also to the El Salvador Solidarity Committee for their promotional support. Some of the chapters presented here were delivered at the conference, others have been added. I would wish to congratulate Michael Hayes and David Tombs the editors of this volume for organizing the conference and bringing together social experience and theological reflection in such a mutually illuminating way. This volume offers the fruits of this work to a wider audience.

Dr Bernadette Porter
University of Surrey Roehampton

Abbreviations

ARENA	*Alianza Republicana Nacionalista*, Nationalist Republican Alliance,
CHRLA	Centre for Human Rights Legal Action, (see also CALDH)
CDF	Congregation for the Doctrine of the Faith
CEG	*Conferencia Episcopal de Guatemala*, Guatemalan Bishops' Conference
CEH	*Comisión de Esclarecimiento Histórico*, Commission on Historical Clarification
CELAM	*Consejo Episcopal Latinoamericano*, Latin American Bishops' Conference
CELEP	*Centro Evangelico Latinoamericano de Estudios Pastorales*, Latin American Evangelical Centre for Pastoral Studies
CIIR	Catholic Institute for International Relations
CALDH	*Centro para la Acción Legal en Derechos Humanos*, Centre for Human Rights Legal Action (CHRLA)
CONAVIGUA	*Coordinadora Nacional de Viudas Guatemaltecas* National Coordination of Guatemalan Widows
COPAZ	*Comisíon de la Paz*, Peace Commission
CRISPAZ	Christians for Peace
ECA	*Estudios Centroamericanos*, Central American Studies (journal, El Salvador)
EGP	*Ejército Guerrillero de los Pobres*, Guerrilla Army of the Poor
EMP	*Estado Mayor Presidencial*, Presidential High Command
EN	*Evangelii Nuntiandi*
FAR	*Fuerzas Armadas Rebeldes*, Rebel Armed Forces
FMLN	*Frente Farabundo Martí para la liberación Nacional*, Farabundo Martí National Liberation Front
FDNG	*Frente Democrático Nueva Guatemala*, New Guatemalan Democratic Front
FRG	*Frente Republicano Guatemalteco*, Guatemalan Republican Front

GS	*Gaudium et spes*
GSN	Guatemala Solidarity Network
GRICAR	*Grupo Internacional de Consulta y Apoyo al Retorno*, International Consultation and Support Group to the Returns
LAB	Latin America Bureau
MINUGUA	*Misión de Verificación de las Naciones Unidas en Guatemala*, United Nations Verification Mission in Guatemala
NACLA	North American Congress on Latin America
NGO	Non Governmental Organisation
ODHAG	*Oficina de Derechos Humanos del Arzobispado de Guatemala*, Human Rights Office of the Archdiocese of Guatemala [also ODHA]
OECD	Organisation for Economic Cooperation and Development
ORPA	*Organizacíon Revolucionaria del Puebla en Armas*, Revolutionary Organisation of the People in Arms
PACs	*Patrullas de Autodefensa Civil*, Civilian Self-Defence Patrols
PGT	*Partido Guatemalteco de Trabajo*, Guatemalan Workers' Party
REMHI	*Recuperación de la Memoría Historica*, Recovery of Historical Memory
UCA	*Universidad Centroamericana*, Central American University
UN	United Nations
URNG	*Unidad Revolucionaria Nacional Guatemalteca*, National Revolutionary Union of Guatemala
WFP	Witness for Peace

Introduction

For you will know the truth and the truth will set you free.
(John 8.32)

In the 1990s struggles over human rights and the politics of truth and memory were at the heart of social transitions in El Salvador and Guatemala as both countries strove to come to terms with their legacies of violence and build new and more democratic societies.

During El Salvador's peace process (1990–92) a UN sponsored Commission on the Truth was established to investigate and report on cases of serious violence from the years of conflict and turmoil (1980–91).[1] To build on people's hopes for the new era the Commission's mandate was to seek, find and publicize the truth on the years of madness. Recognising and remembering the years of terror was a necessary step to rebuilding a society based on truth, freedom and justice.[2]

When the Commission's report was presented on 15 March 1993 it highlighted the extreme imbalance between the abuses committed by guerrillas and the abuses committed by the government, military and right-wing paramilitaries. The sweeping amnesty law that the Salvadoran government rushed through the Assembly less than one week after the presentation of the report was a response to this. The government claimed that the amnesty was to aid 'reconciliation' but it

---

[1] Report of the United Nations Truth Commission, *From Madness to Hope: The 12-Year War in El Salvador*, New York: United Nations, 1993. Provisions for the Truth Commission were part of the Chapultepec (Mexico) Peace Accords signed on 16 January 1992. Prior to this there had been a lengthy series of UN sponsored talks (beginning with the Geneva Accord in April 1990) which finally culminated in the New York agreement on 31 December 1991 to sign the Peace Accords.

[2] The Commission began its examination of events in July 1992 and submitted its report on 15 March 1993. For further information on the Salvadoran Truth Commission and the difficulties of peace and reconciliation in El Salvador, see M. Popkin, *Peace Without Justice: Obstacles to Building the Rule of Law in El Salvador*, University Park PA, Pennsylvania State University Park, 2000, especially pp. 105–162.

was widely seen as yet another attempt to prevent further investigation into responsibility. Many of El Salvador's military and political leaders were determined that the past should be forgotten and responsibility for it should never be confirmed. In attempts to discredit the search for truth they hypocritically proclaimed concern for 'reconciliation' as a reason to forget the past.

In Guatemala, those who opposed the truth rejected even the term 'Truth Commission'. The Commission established through the Accord of Oslo in June 1994 went by the name 'Commission on Historical Clarification' and its brief was to clarify the human rights violations and acts of violence connected with the years of armed confrontation.[3] However, this did not stop the report from being an unflinching record of the period 1962–96. When the report was published on 25 February 1999 it showed, amongst other things, that the 'armed confrontation' in Guatemala had been an entirely one-sided affair amounting at times to genocide against the indigenous peoples.

Peace and reconciliation in El Salvador and Guatemala will require more than truth and memory. Economic and political justice is urgently needed and for this many social structures must be radically reformed. However, any attempt to build just societies without the foundations of truth or memory can only be illusory and because of this progressive sectors within the Church have been at the forefront of human rights documentation in both countries. In both countries the Church had documented and denounced many of the abuses as they had occurred and the Archdiocesan offices for human rights in San Salvador and Guatemala City could therefore provide excellent foundations on which the UN Commissions could draw. Furthermore, the Church's own reports and publications could go beyond the narrow brief enforced on the UN Commissions and raise wider questions on the meaning of peace and justice.

The difficulties and risks that the Church faced in this work are exemplified in the lives and deaths of Archbishop Oscar Romero and Bishop Juan Gerardi. The murders of these prophetic church leaders – coming just before the start of the Salvadoran civil war 1980–1992 (Romero, d. 24 March 1980) and just after the end of the Guatemalan conflict 1960–96 (Gerardi, d. 26 April 1998) – mark the years of horror in an especially vivid way. Romero and Gerardi dedicated themselves to peace in cultures of violence and sought to speak the truth in societies of lies. Ultimately they paid the price for their prophetic courage and pastoral solidarity. The violence that they exposed was

---

[3] United Nations Commission on Historical Clarification [CEH], *Guatemala: Memory of Silence*, Guatemala, United Nations, 1999, available in translated summary at http://hrdata.aaas.org/ceh/report/english and as a complete Spanish text *Guatemala: Memoria del Silencio* at http://hrdata.aaas.org/ceh/index.html.

brought down on their own bodies and ended their lives. However, their memory lives on across Central America and across the world. This book is dedicated to that memory and to their vision of peace and justice in El Salvador and Guatemala.

The general format of the book reflects the belief that engaged theological reflection on human rights and social justice should begin with contextual situations of oppression and liberation. The first part of the book presents three chapters on Romero and Gerardi and two chapters on a theology of martyrdom that point to the theological significance of their deaths alongside Latin America's crucified peoples. Scott Wright begins the sequence with 'Oscar Romero and Juan Gerardi: Truth, Memory and Hope' as an overview of the two bishops and their legacy of hope. Wright describes how and why they staked their lives – and by extension the life of the Church – with the victims of the violence and oppression and shows how defending the lives and the rights of the poor was central to their understanding of the Church's mission. Wright records their parallel journeys to the heart of the people by which they restored the dignity of justice. After their deaths they are remembered and loved by the Salvadoran and Guatemalan people who recognize their lives as their own.

Michael Campbell-Johnston's chapter on 'Martyrdom and Resurrection in Latin America Today: Archbishop Oscar Arnulfo Romero' picks up on the life of Romero in more detail. He identifies the essence of martyrdom as giving witness to the truth through the offering of one's life and identifies three models of persecution against the Church: first, the historic model of a Church seeking to establish itself in non-Christian societies; second, the persecution of the Church in the socialist and communist countries by totalitarian states demanding complete allegiance; third, the relatively new situation in Latin America of persecution that comes from governments that not only proclaim themselves Christian but also seek to maintain good relations with the institutional church and sometimes even claim to be acting in its name. He highlights the influence of the 1968 Second General Conference of Latin American Bishops (CELAM II) at Medellín in Colombia and its call for a 'preferential option for the poor' and also Romero's own conversion to listening to the voice of the people, to becoming a defender of the oppressed, 'the voice of those who had no voice' and the conscience of a nation. As a result, at aged sixty, Romero went back to school and his teachers were the uneducated peasants of his diocese. He saw as his duty to identify, unmask and denounce modern idols of society: the absolutization of wealth and private property, the absolutization of national security and the absolutization of political organisations.

In 'The Cook, the Dog, the Priest and His Lover' Judith Escribano looks at the political motives behind Gerardi's murder and offers a detailed account of the slow legal process and attempted cover-up that ensued. She shows why the REMHI project – which Gerardi headed until he was murdered just two days after he presented its formal report on 24 April 1998 – provoked the wrath of the Guatemalan military and how this led to his murder.[4]

Kevin Burke explores how the theme of truth and memory has a resonance and power with the reality of martyrdom. Martyrdom and remembrance have an implicit connection – the one who witnesses is remembered, while the one who remembers re-witnesses. He brings into the discourse a third contemporary martyr – Ignacio Ellacuría – who was murdered at the University of Central America in El Salvador on 16 November 1989 along with five other Jesuit priests, a seminary cook, and her fifteen-year-old daughter. Together with Jon Sobrino, Ignacio Ellacuría was a trusted theological consultant to Archbishop Romero. Burke finds in Ellacuría important reflections on and a striking witness to the search for historical truth and also draws attention to the moral and religious imperative to remember. It is the intrinsic connection between martyrdom and the very doing of theology that Burke grapples with. He introduces the sacramental character of martyrdom in relation to the theme of memory; then sketches Ellacuría's theological method which leads into the place of martyrdom in that theological method. He shows this practice of theology as unfolding as a threefold process comprising of reflection, ethical option, and praxis. He concludes remarking on the sacrament of remembering our martyrs through the doing of theology – the original witness of the martyr becomes a sacrament of resurrection faith for those who come into contact with the martyr's story.

Martin Maier opens his chapter 'The Theology of Martyrdom in Latin America' by referring to Pope John II's axiom 'return of the martyrs'. That the twentieth century has seen more martyrs of faith than any other century and that the majority have been in Latin America is significant. Maier cites El Salvador as a microcosm of not only all the misery and suffering, but also of all the hopes of Latin America. In developing a theology of martyrdom, Maier writes of liberation theology reflecting on martyrdom as rooted in the lived experience of Latin America and not taking its starting point from a

---

[4] Recovery of Historical Memory Project (REMHI), *Guatemala: Never Again!* The Official Report of the Human Rights Office of the Archdiocese of Guatemala, trans. Gretta Tovar Siebentritt; Maryknoll, NY, Orbis Books, London, Latin America Bureau and Catholic Institute of International Relations, 1999. Abridged from Spanish original *Guatemala: Nunca Más* (Informe proyecto interdiocesano de recuperación de la memoria histórica, 4 vols., Guatemala, Oficina de Derechos Humanos del Arzobispado de Guatemala, 1998).

canonical-dogmatic definition of martyrdom. The phenomenon of martyrdom in Latin America represents a challenge for the canonical understanding of martyrdom as often those murdered are given locally the title 'martyr' prior to any official procedure for canonization, Romero for example, had declared the first two priests who were murdered in El Salvador as 'two true martyrs'. These contemporary martyrs become a theological point of reference.

The second part of the book on 'Human Rights and the Commitment to Life' opens with Marcela López Levy's discussion of the REMHI report itself and its background. She shows how the report was intended to do more than document the abuses suffered by innocent Guatemalans during the reign of terror. It was a new style of report that took the investigation out to the countryside and actively involved the communities in a process of recovery. This allowed the project to explore how survivors felt and how they coped with their grief. It was often the first time that these experiences had been voiced and recorded. However, the project did more than give voice to the victims, it also recorded a small but very important number of testimonies from perpetrators. REMHI's section on the 'methodology of horror' draws on some of these testimonies for a chilling exposé of the perverse but coherent 'method' in the madness.

Ruth Gidley and Hannah Roberts draw on their advocacy work with the London-based Guatemala Solidarity Network (GSN) to describe the significance of monuments to remember the dead and express solidarity with the living. They show how the construction of monuments functions at a popular level to challenge Guatemala's systematic amnesia and the silence that reigned for so long. They also emphasize the spiritual dimension to the monuments which are rooted in the Mayan cosmovision. The monuments provide a focus for anniversaries and social rituals that mark the passing of the dead and help communities give proper recognition to the dead and disappeared. The monuments also help the community to reconstruct their own lives, giving space for the grieving process and promoting a new political awareness and activism.

The third chapter in this section, 'Human Rights and Oppressed Peoples: Historical-Theological Reflections', was originally written in 1998 in Spanish to mark the fiftieth anniversary of Universal Declaration of Human Rights by the internationally renowned liberation theologian Jon Sobrino. Sobrino considers the historical and theological significance of human rights from the perspective of 'crucified peoples' and contrasts the idealistic rhetoric of human rights against the realities of the Third World struggle between life and death. He examines the failure to universalize human rights and advocates partiality – the option for the poor and oppressed – in the understanding and defence of human rights.

The third part of the book explores how the politics of truth and memory and the horror of human rights abuses in El Salvador, Guatemala and elsewhere might impact on contemporary theological work. Mary Grey begins her chapter 'A Theology for the Bearers of Dangerous Memory' quoting Rachel's lament for her children in Jeremiah (31.15) and the weeping Mary of Magdala at the tomb of Jesus in John's Gospel (20.12). These texts do not allow theologizing about witness and martyrdom to gloss over the brutality and unacceptability of what has happened in El Salvador and Guatemala. The task of theology is to discover within an ecclesial tradition of remembering and witnessing a space where truth is heard, honoured and witnessed to. Calling it a 'new trajectory for theology', Grey outlines the origin and meaning of a theology of *dangerously remembering* and then explores the *praxis* of it for the Christian community today as a sacred task. She shows how dangerously remembering can express a poetics of resistance and contribute to a process of repentance which includes the ancient biblical ministry of lament and the central act of the Church in remembering, the eucharistic *Anamenesis*.

Dermot Lane reviews some of the debates that have taken place in the last few hundred years about the place of memory in history. He clarifies what is meant theologically by the appeal to memory and seeks to overcome some of the ambiguities surrounding the use of the word memory. He makes an appeal to retrieve the importance of memory within Judaism and early Christianity. Furthermore, he brings into the theological discourse the tension between memory and forgetfulness and the delicate relationship between memory and reconciliation.

'"He is not here" Disappearance, Death and Denial' by David Tombs gives a re-reading of the Easter story in the light of Latin American 'disappearances'. He draws on various Latin American human rights reports – especially Guatemala's REMHI report – to describe the impact of disappearances on the families of ordinary Latin Americans and how these disappearances create an on-going trauma of disruption amongst friends and relatives. He then shows how awareness of disappearance as a tool of state terror might shed light on the traumatic events told in the Easter narrative. While the term 'disappearance' is not used in the gospel narratives the events described have parallels with disappearance in Latin America. He suggests that what Peter feared at the arrest in Gethsemane and what the women feared at the empty tomb was officially sanctioned disappearance and denial. In this context, the drama of the tomb-side announcement 'He is not here' is to be understood.

The chapters in the final part of the book relate this theological reflection to wider issues in theology and the quest for liberation since the breakthroughs of the late 1960s. María Pilar Aquino records the slow but steady gains of feminist theology in Latin America in its struggle for the rights of women. Aquino uses feminist analysis of 'kyriarchy' (rule of the Lord) to show how feminist criticism can address the wider framework of social and class hierarchies within patriarchy. Although the Latin American bishops failed to incorporate the analytical categories of feminism in their famous Second General Conference (CELAM II) at Medellín (Colombia) in 1968 Aquino argues that the meeting nonetheless provided a vital legacy for feminist theology. Medellín's liberating vision of a commitment to the poor broke with traditional ecclesial kyriarchy and provided a foundation on which feminist theology in Latin America has developed and it still provides important challenges for the future.

Jason Gordon explores truth and memory from the perspective of 'New World' theology. He suggests that we need to investigate our interpretative framework when recalling the memories of Archbishop Romero and Bishop Gerardi and contends that theology starting with a commitment to liberative praxis is in the service of truth and memory. Gordon reflects critically upon the interpretative framework of theology that has emerged in the 'New World' in the post-Medellín era, tracing the early development of this theology and its later fragmentation into multiple interpretative frameworks. Exploring the act of interpretation is, for him, an attempt to ground the truth claims of this theology. Furthermore, he explores a historiography that pushes theology beyond the fragmentation of our interpretative tools. His conclusion is that this investigation of the interpretative tools provides a new reading of the facts, highlighting interconnections in the world system and its various cycles.

Finally, Andrew Bradstock reflects from a First World perspective on the challenges of solidarity. He draws on his experience of Nicaragua solidarity work to characterise solidarity as a long-term commitment to the accompaniment of those who struggle for social change. In Central America, this means staying with the people who continue to suffer even when popular interest wanes and when the media move on because nothing they deem newsworthy is happening in the region any more. He explores how this might happen either through physical accompaniment or 'accompaniment from distance' and then offers different biblical models of solidarity – from Simon of Cyrene and Joseph of Arimethea to Christ as the incarnation of God – to illustrate the varied forms that solidarity might take.

As editors we have sought to ensure that each chapter can be read either as part of a connected work or entirely on its own. Inevitably this means that many of the same issues and occasionally some of the same material are shared in different chapters. However, even when some overlap occurs, it is remarkable how each contributor treats the issues in their own distinctive way and sets shared material in his or her own personal framework. We are grateful to all of them for the opportunity to bring this collection together in memory of Romero and Gerardi and the people of El Salvador and Guatemala.

Part 1:

Oscar Romero and Juan Gerardi

Oscar Romero and Juan Gerardi: Truth, Memory and Hope

SCOTT WRIGHT

The truth of Auschwitz remains hidden in its ashes. Only those who lived it in their flesh and in their minds can possibly transform their experience into knowledge.[1]

Memory is the key word. To remember is to create links between past and present, between past and future. To remember is to affirm man's faith in humanity and to convey meaning on our fleeting endeavors. The aim of memory is to restore its dignity to justice.[2]

But – after Auschwitz, hope is necessary. Where can it be found? In remembrance alone.

Elie Wiesel[3]

1. Truth and Memory: Coordinates of Hope

On 21 March 2000, a remarkable, though little-publicized, event took place in Washington DC at the Holocaust Museum. There, in the heart of that building dedicated to the memory of six million Jewish victims of the Nazi Holocaust, Roberto Cabrera spoke of the work of the Recovery of the Historic Memory (REMHI) project he directs, and its attempt to document the remembrance of thousands of indigenous survivors of Guatemala's thirty-six-year-old civil war.[4] Joining him at the event was Christian Tomuschat, one of the authors of the United Nations Commission for Historical Clarification (CEH) that characterized what happened in Guatemala as 'state-sponsored genocide',

---

[1] Elie Wiesel, *From the Kingdom of Memory*, New York: Shocken Books, 1990, 'Trivializing Memory,' p. 166.
[2] Ibid., *'When Memory Brings People Together,'* p. 194.
[3] Ibid., p. 196.
[4] Recovery of the Historic Memory Report, *Guatemala: Never Again!* Maryknoll, NY, Orbis Books, 1999.

placing the number of victims at 200,000.[5] The titles of both reports are evocative, as they allude to the boundaries of human speech: *Guatemala: Never Again!* and *Guatemala: Memory of Silence* – the cry of the victims and the silence of the dead.

I choose to begin this reflection with this event, and with several quotations from one of the survivors of the Holocaust, Elie Wiesel, precisely to draw attention to the claim that the victims have upon us the living. Wiesel writes and speaks passionately in the voice of the survivor about remembrance, and he links memory to truth, justice and hope. My intention is to present the testimony of the Church in El Salvador and the Church in Guatemala and their defence of human rights through the figure of their leaders and now martyrs, Archbishop Oscar Romero and Bishop Juan Gerardi. In doing so, I hope to weave into the narrative the elements of memory, truth, justice, and hope previously mentioned.

At the same time, by focusing on the words and witness of Romero and Gerardi, I hope to make clear their deepening conversion to share the suffering of the poor and to speak out even more boldly in defense of their most basic rights – especially the right of the poor to life itself. They were, by their privileged position as bishops, in a position to speak out; and they became, by opening their hearts to the suffering of their people and to the grace of God, the voice of the voiceless. Because they were not willing to forget the suffering of their people, they chose to remain in solidarity with the poor and to speak the truth, demand justice, and offer hope to their people in return. Now, after their martyrdoms, it is the Salvadoran and Guatemalan people who remember their words, their lives, and their witness as their own.

'*The truth of Auschwitz remains hidden in its ashes.*' There are plenty of ashes in El Salvador and Guatemala. One need only recall the victims of El Mozote, in El Salvador, where 767 men, women and children were massacred on 11–13 December 1981 by the Atlacatl Battalion of the Salvadoran army.[6] One person, Rufina Amaya, witnessed the cries of her four young children as they were led away to be slaughtered, and she survived to tell the world about what happened, despite denials by the Salvadoran government and the US Embassy and State Department that the massacre ever happened. Only ten years later, as the exhumation teams began to uncover the skeletons of adults and children, did the world begin to pay attention.

The United Nations Truth Commission confirmed the results,[7] and

---

[5] United Nations Commission for Historical Clarification, *Guatemala: Memory of Silence*, New York, United Nations, 1999, pp. 38–41.

[6] Mark Danner, *The Massacre at El Mozote*, New York, Vintage Books, 1993.

[7] Report of the Commission on the Truth for El Salvador, *From Madness to Hope*, New York, United Nations, 1993, pp. 114–121.

The New Yorker picked up the trail and made it its cover story.[8] The truth hidden in the ashes had been exposed to the light of day. Official estimates of the total number of victims during the twelve-year conflict in El Salvador put the number at 75,000.[9] According to the Truth Commission, 85 per cent of the cases were attributed to agents of the State, paramilitary groups allied to them, and to the death squads; 5 per cent were attributed to the FMLN guerrillas.[10]

In Guatemala, the truth is even more macabre, and the ashes even more tragically strewn across the land. According to the REMHI report, the number of massacres carried out by the military or paramilitary groups against indigenous communities numbers 422,[11] while the Historical Clarification report places the number at 626.[12] In one two year period, between September 1981 and August 1983, the REMHI report documents between 4,000 and 5,000 people were killed in the single municipality (town and surrounding villages) of Rabinal, in Baja Verapaz, out of a total of 22,733 inhabitants.[13] Similar testimonies have been documented for other regions of Guatemala.[14] According to the REMHI report, the army, police forces, civil patrollers, military commissioners and death squads were responsible for 89.65 per cent of the violence; while 4.81 per cent was attributable to the URNG guerrillas.[15]

The cruelty of the Guatemalan military defies comparison: 'In the majority of massacres there is evidence of multiple acts of savagery, which preceded, accompanied or occurred after the deaths of the victims. Acts such as the killing of defenceless children, often by beating them against walls or throwing them alive into pits where the corpses of adults were later thrown; the amputation of limbs; the impaling of victims; the killing of persons by covering them in petrol and burning them alive; the extraction, in the presence of others, of the viscera [internal organs] of victims who were still alive; the confinement of people who had been mortally tortured, in agony for days; the opening of the wombs of pregnant women, and other similarly atrocious acts.'[16]

---

[8] *The New Yorker*, 6 December 1993, 'The Truth of El Mozote'.
[9] *The New York Times*, 16 March 1993, Editorial, and *The Washington Post*, 18 March 1993, Editorial. Both use the figure 75,000 dead.
[10] *From Madness to Hope*, p. 43.
[11] *Guatemala: Never Again!* pp. 142–151.
[12] *Guatemala: Memory of Silence*, pp. 34–35.
[13] *Guatemala: Never Again!* p. 238. See also Equipo de Antropologia Forense de Guatemala EAFG, *Las Masacres en Rabinal*, Guatemala, EAFG, 1995.
[14] Ricardo Falla, *Massacres in the Jungle: Ixcan, Guatemala, 1975–1982*, Boulder, Westview Press, 1994. Falla documents between 1,000 and 1,200 deaths in the Ixcan jungle between 1975–1982. He later accompanied the communities of population in resistance during the 1980s in this region.
[15] *Guatemala: Never Again!* p. 290.
[16] *Guatemala: Memory of Silence*, p. 34.

The point of describing these cruel and savage acts is to contrast such darkness and inhumanity with the courage and dignity of the victims and survivors who bear witness to the truth. For it is, in Wiesel's words, 'only those who lived [such cruelty] in their flesh and in their minds [who] can possibly transform their experience into knowledge' and, I would add, light and hope for the future.

'The aim of memory is to restore its dignity to justice.' It is precisely through the witness of the victims in El Salvador and Guatemala – and those, like Oscar Romero and Juan Gerardi, who chose to defend them – that justice is restored to the people. It is through their tenacity *to remember* – to not forget the suffering of their people, or their aspirations for life – that justice is restored to the victims. Such remembrance means being truthful about reality, about what is really happening to the poor, about who is responsible for the violence, about how unjust economic and political structures generate violence and exclude the poor and indigenous. By staking their lives, and by extension, the life of the Church, with the victims of violence and oppression, Oscar Romero and Juan Gerardi could speak the truth with power and to power with a credibility that endeared them to the poor and ultimately cost them their lives.

In the witness of Romero and the witness of Gerardi, the judgement of the poor is eloquent: 'They were killed because they spoke the truth!' And it is precisely the victims and the martyrs that lay claim to the truth today. They are the seal of credibility, both in the sense of bearing witness to what actually happened, but also in the sense of demanding of us the living that it never happen again. Justice is a hope yet to be realized, though the struggle for justice in itself gives dignity back to the victims and to the survivors. It dignifies those who take part in the struggle for justice, and it bears witness to the truth, the reason people were killed, and the dreams and aspirations for life which they bore in their hearts.

'But – after Auschwitz, hope is necessary. Where can it be found? In remembrance alone.' We are, ultimately, people of faith, we believe in truth, we believe in justice, we hope for the future. We believe that life, not death, has the last word. In the words that another twentieth century martyr, Martin Luther King, liked to quote, 'We shall overcome because the arc of a moral universe is long, but it bends towards justice. We shall overcome ... because truth crushed to earth will rise again. ... We shall overcome ... because truth forever on the scaffold, wrong forever on the throne, yet that scaffold sways the future, and behind the demon known, stands a God within the shadow, keeping watch above his own.'[17]

---

[17] Martin Luther King, *A Testament of Hope: The Essential Writings of Martin Luther King, Jr.*, edited by James M. Washington, New York, Harper and Row, 1986, 'Remaining Awake Through a Great Revolution', p. 277.

If this were not so, we would not care about what happened in El Salvador and Guatemala; we would not be concerned about justice being restored to the victims; we would be afraid of the future. Sadly, that describes many of us, but the blame is not entirely our own. We need to help awaken hope for life, and in no small measure the victims and martyrs of El Salvador and Guatemala do just that: they help us to be better human beings, they help us to hope for the future – *by remembering*.

What follows is a reflection on the Church of El Salvador and the Church of Guatemala and their commitment to remember and bear witness to the truth of the Gospel, as exemplified by the witness and martyrdom of their bishop-martyrs – Oscar Romero and Juan Gerardi. Ultimately, for people of faith, truth is the truth of a God who calls us to act justly, to love compassionately, and to walk humbly with our Creator. And for Christians, that truth is incarnated in the life, death and resurrection of Jesus Christ. The poor of El Salvador, and the indigenous poor of Guatemala, bear witness in no small degree to this truth. Those of us who have been touched by their lives owe a debt of gratitude to them. In this spirit, I hope what follows may contribute to pointing to the light and salvation that the martyrs offer to a world torn by violence and in search of hope.

2. Journey to the Heart of the People

a. Oscar Romero and the Passion of Aguilares

Much has been made of the 'conversion' of Oscar Romero to the poor upon the death of his friend, Father Rutilio Grande, only weeks after his installation as Archbishop of San Salvador. Romero's conversion might also be likened to a call to share more deeply in the suffering of the poor and the Good News of God's love for his people.

Following Grande's death, Romero began to proclaim the Gospel in such a way that it became enfleshed in the conflictive history of El Salvador and gave hope to the poor, announcing the fullness of life and denouncing the poverty, repression and death of so many of his beloved people. Romero illuminated the conflictive reality of El Salvador from the perspective of God's plan of salvation, and called on his people to participate in bringing to fullness the life, peace, and justice that are signs of God's reign. And he did so with a coherence and credibility that in the end he became the Good News that he proclaimed.

The first three months Romero served as Archbishop of San Salvador laid the foundation for the remaining three years of his pastoral ministry, until his martyrdom on 24 March 1980. The death of

Rutilio Grande, instead of being the occasion to draw back and reconsider options that placed the Church – and indeed his own life – in danger, became instead the defining first step in a journey that would lead finally to Romero's martyrdom.

As Romero said in Rutilio Grande's funeral Mass in Aguilares, 'This is not the moment to speak about my personal relationship with Father Grande, but rather to gather from this cadaver a message for all of us who continue the pilgrimage.' And he would add, 'Let us not forget. We are a pilgrim church, exposed to misunderstanding, to persecution; but a Church that walks peacefully because we carry within us the force of love.'[18]

Romero made an exceptional decision to cancel all other Masses in the Archdiocese the following Sunday, and to invite all the faithful to celebrate a single Mass in the cathedral of San Salvador. There he made public his support for all priests who were in danger of persecution: 'Whoever touches one of my priests, touches me.' And there he received the public acclamation of the people who, in a gesture that would become the hallmark of his Sunday homilies in the cathedral, enthusiastically applauded his words:

> Thank you. This applause ratifies the profound joy I feel in my heart in taking possession of the Archdiocese: just to know that my weaknesses, my inabilities find their complement, their strength, and their courage in a unified priesthood.[19]

Strengthened by this relationship to his people, Romero began to define the mission of the Church in the midst of a conflictive social reality in the weeks that followed. On Holy Thursday he told the people:

> You are prophets in the world.... You have to announce like the prophets – like a prophetic people anointed by the Spirit that anointed Christ – the wonders of God in the world, to encourage the good that is done in the world and also to energetically denounce evil.[20]

He called on the people not to be spectators, but to allow their hearts to enter deeply into the tradition of the Church and to find their home there, a sentiment that would one day be etched on his tomb in San Salvador: 'Sentir con the Iglesia.'

> The Word of God has a religious mission ... and a human mission:

---

[18] Oscar Romero, *Monseñor Oscar A. Romero: Su Pensamiento,* 8 Volumes, San Salvador, Imprenta Criterio, 1980–1989, 14 March 1977 homily.
[19] Ibid., 20 March 1977 homily.
[20] Ibid., 7 April 1977 homily.

> To love our neighbour [means] to be concerned about their needs, their concrete situation; and, like the Good Samaritan, to help the poor fallen by the roadside.[21]

Already Romero was beginning to define the signs that would characterize his passionate defense of human rights: to announce the Good News means also to denounce what is evil in the world; to love our neighbour means concretely to come to the aid of the poor who have fallen by the roadside and to denounce the cause of their affliction. His prophetic witness would be one closely linked to the conflictive reality of El Salvador, and incarnated in the life of the poor and their struggle for life.

This commitment to the poor was precisely that which provoked the death of so many Christians in El Salvador. Rutilio Grande did not hesitate to denounce the oppression of the poor by wealthy landowners, or to empower poor peasants to organize and defend their rights so that they would not continue to be assaulted but break free from their bondage – that's why he was killed.

In the weeks that followed Rutilio Grande's death, Romero began to define the marks of a church that defends the life of its people:

> The Church is concerned about the rights of people ... and about life that is at risk.... The Church is concerned about those who cannot speak, those who suffer, those who are tortured, and those who are silenced. This is not getting involved in politics.... Let this be clear: when the Church preaches social justice, equality, and the dignity of people, defending those who suffer and those who are assaulted, this is not subversion, this is not Marxism. This is the authentic teaching of the Church.[22]

And, Romero added, 'The Church cannot remain silent. It has to speak out.'

In the months following Rutilio Grande's death, however, the violence escalated. On 11 May, a second priest, Alfonso Navarro, was assassinated. Also in May, the Army occupied Grande's parish in Aguilares, killing the sacristan, expelling a foreign priest, and turning the church into a military barracks. In June, Romero returned to Aguilares to reclaim the parish. There he told the nervous crowd that had gathered in the church:

> Today it is my responsibility to assemble this Church. This sanctuary has been profaned, the tabernacle for the Blessed Sacrament has

[21] Ibid.
[22] Ibid., 8 May 1977 homily.

been destroyed, and the people have been humiliated and sacrificed in such an undignified manner.... I bring you the Word Christ sends you: a word of solidarity, a word of encouragement and orientation, and, finally, a word of conversion.[23]

Once again Romero reaffirmed the commitment he had made to the poor of El Salvador at the Mass in the cathedral three months before. In a phrase that would characterize the paschal character of his spirituality, he referred to the poor who had gathered in the parish of Aguilares as a crucified people:

> You are the image ... of Christ, nailed to the cross and lanced by the spear. You are a symbol of every town, like Aguilares, that will be struck down and trampled upon; but if you suffer with faith and give your suffering a redemptive meaning, Aguilares will be singing the precious song of liberation.[24]

Romero pointed to the redemptive significance of the suffering of his people, not in a passive way – as victims, but rather as inspired Christians participating with the Spirit of the Gospel in the liberation of their people:

> Let us be firm in defending our rights, but with great love in our hearts, because to defend our rights in this way we are also seeking the conversion of sinners. This is the vengeance of the Christian.[25]

For the next three years, until his martyrdom 24 March 1980, Romero would continue to be a prophetic voice in defence of human rights in El Salvador. Already, by the time of his death, the violence had escalated to nearly 1,000 assassinations a month. Military incursions in the rural areas were frequent, and death squads were the order of the day.

b. Juan Gerardi and the Passion of Santa Cruz del Quiché

At the same time that Oscar Romero accompanied the passion of his people following the assassination of Rutilio Grande in March 1977 and the reclamation of the parish in Aguilares in June, Juan Gerardi and the people of his diocese of El Quiché were enduring a similar passion. In 1975 and 1976, military operations had claimed their first victims among Catholic Action members in the northern part of the Quiché

---

[23] Ibid., 19 June 1977 homily.
[24] Ibid.
[25] Ibid.

diocese. These events are reflected in Gerardi's 1977 Lenten message to the people of his diocese:

> For some time now our diocese, especially in the northern part of El Quiché, is living a climate of tension and violence. We see with sadness and pain the very things the bishops of Guatemala recognized in our message ... a situation of institutionalized violence, marked by unjust social structures, where oppression is evident, and the marginalization of the great majority cause them to live under an insupportable tension ...[26]

Santa Cruz – indeed all of El Quiché – like Aguilares, was a region marked by a profound disparity between a wealthy landowning elite who held political power and a poor indigenous majority who struggled to survive as landless peasants and farmworkers without any political participation. Worse, when the poor had organized, with the encouragement of the Church, to demand their rights, their protests were met with the cruelest military repression:

> Effectively, it appears that respect for the dignity of human persons and the recognition of their most fundamental and inalienable rights has been lost. Instead, persecution has been unleashed against citizens ... and in some cases the vile use of torture and the detention and imprisonment of people without sufficient cause has been confirmed.[27]

Gerardi went on to characterize this situation, in the light of the Gospel, as 'a decomposition of society ... a radical change of values ... a sinful situation that contradicts, opposes and makes difficult the implantation of the Gospel values of the Reign of God.' The reasons for this sinful situation are many, but among them are 'the thirst for riches, injustice, the desire for power.' And in words that would later be echoed by Romero, he added:

> We want our word to be one of encouragement and comfort for all those who suffer. We also want this word to be the *voice of the voiceless* [italics added] so that they are able to make their necessities heard and denounce the injustices that they suffer.... We want to direct our word to the great and powerful – who consider themselves and call themselves Christians and Catholics, daughters of the

---

[26] Juan Gerardi, *Monsenor Juan Gerardi: Testigo fiel de Dios*, Guatemala, Conferencia Episcopal de Guatemala, 1999, 'Mensaje para la Cuaresma, Diocesis del Quiche,' p. 53.

[27] Ibid., pp. 53–54.

church – to take note of their responsibilities for the suffering of the people, and the obligation and possibility they have to alleviate that suffering and reestablish true relationships of justice.[28]

Again, like Romero, Gerardi quotes Paul VI's Apostolic Exhortation *Evangelii Nuntiandi* to lend strength to his pastoral message: 'Evangelization brings with it an explicit message, adapted to and actualized in diverse situations and circumstances, about the rights and duties of every person ... [including] peace, justice, development ... and an especially vigorous message in our days about liberation [EN 29].'[29]

And even though many were tempted to accept the actual situation of injustice and confusion as inevitable or without solution, Gerardi urged upon his people the conviction that 'reconciliation requires sacrifice, requires the cross, requires the shedding of blood to the point of death ... but reaches its glorious fullness in the resurrection.... Christ is the great defender of human rights. He is the great liberator of all people and the great reconciler of people with God and with each other.'[30]

Over the next three years, the repression of indigenous peasants and catechists increased exponentially. Already by November 1997, just eight months after Gerardi's Lenten message, 143 Catholic Action catechists had been abducted and murdered in El Quiché. With the election of General Romeo Lucas García in July 1978, a new wave of state-sponsored terror swept Guatemala, culminating in the death of thirty-nine indigenous people, many of them from El Quiché, when they were burned to death by the Guatemalan police on 31 January 1980, after they occupied the Spanish Embassy to protest the repression.

Once again Gerardi responded, together with the clergy and religious of the diocese, to condemn the repression. This time, the tone and the judgement of the letter was even more urgent and unequivocal in its denunciation:

> As human beings and as Christians, we cannot but raise our voice in protest against the intolerable situation that has led to the death of our sisters and brothers.... For four years, a situation of extreme violence weighs upon us in El Quiché, aggravated by the military occupation of the northern part of the department and other measures that strike our people and benefit a minority. We find the fundamental cause of this in a system of economic, social and political

[28] Ibid., p. 55.
[29] Ibid.
[30] Ibid., pp. 55–56.

development, supported by a doctrine of national security, that doesn't take into consideration the interests of the poor, forcing people to live under a reign of terror.[31]

The violence in El Quiché continued unabated. The REMHI report documents no less than twenty-seven massacres in El Quiché during 1980 alone.[32] And the church was targeted for persecution as well. In June, Father Jose Maria Gran was assassinated in Chajul, and in July, Father Faustino Villanueva was killed in Joyabaj. In addition, Bishop Gerardi narrowly escaped assassination.[33]

On 19 July Bishop Gerardi, together with the clergy and religious of the diocese, took the extraordinary decision to 'temporarily withdraw' from El Quiché until more favourable conditions of security could be restored. The decision was controversial. While Gerardi intended the withdrawal to be a means to protest the violence, others saw it as the Church abandoning its mission. The gravity of the decision echoed the gravity of the situation of violence in the diocese:

> The current year 1980 has been a Calvary for the Catholic people of the diocese.... On various occasions, the Diocese of Quiché has raised its voice, demanding justice in the face of the flagrant violations of the most basic human rights. It was our duty, as human beings, as Christians, and as Guatemalans ...
>
> In addition to the death of two priests, the attack on convents, and the threat against the bishop ... we add to these terrible cases of examples of blood and violence the tragedy of so many poor families in our diocese who mourn the loss of their spouses, parents or children, and the death threats against several priests and religious who remain in the department ...
>
> The conclusion at which we have arrived, in this tragic moment in the history of Guatemala, is that it is no longer possible to offer any kind of spiritual attention in the Diocese of Quiché and, for that reason, a temporary withdrawal is necessary. The bishop, priests and religious women have decided to leave the Diocese with the hope [of finding] the minimal favourable conditions to return.[34]

While this withdrawal of the church from El Quiché was meant to be temporary, the diocese would remain without a resident bishop until

---

[31] Ibid., 'Comunicado de la Diocesis del Quiche con ocasion de los sucesos de la Embajada de Espana el 31 de enero de 1980', pp. 60–61.

[32] *Guatemala: Never Again!* pp. 142–151.

[33] Diocese of El Quiche, *Y Dieron la Vida por El Quiche*, Guatemala, Nuestra Imprenta, 1992, pp. 80–96.

[34] Ibid., 'Al Pueblo Catolico de la Diocesis del Quiche', pp. 64–65.

1985, when the current bishop of El Quiché, Julio Cabrera, would be named as the new bishop. Juan Gerardi's return, however, would be ever further delayed. Gerardi was denied entry into Guatemala upon his return from the Vatican in November 1980, and went into exile in Costa Rica for two years. When he did return to Guatemala, he was named Auxiliary Bishop of the Archdiocese of Guatemala, Vicar General of the Archdiocese, and Director of the Archdiocesan Human Rights Office (ODHAG). Meanwhile, the church of Quiché had been forced to bear witness to its faith in the catacombs:

> The Catholic Church has lived through difficult circumstances, persecution, deaths and misunderstandings throughout its two thousand years of existence. As Catholics we are aware of this and we live with hope. Christ has overcome the world, passing through a painful Good Friday to arrive at the glory of the Resurrection. Nothing will undermine the Christian spirit, inspired by the blood of martyrs and saints. We ask Catholics to remain firm in their faith, to keep the light of hope and the flame of the love of God and neighbour lit.[35]

Inspiring words, they would be costly ones as well. Of the 422 massacres documented by the Recovery of the Historic Memory (REMHI) project that Bishop Gerardi initiated in 1995, 209 of these occurred in his former diocese during a three-year period (1980–1982). While Aguilares and the death of Rutilio Grande brought Oscar Romero closer to the heart of his people's suffering, the events of El Quiché and the withdrawal of the church meant for Juan Gerardi a long and painful separation from the people of his diocese. He did not return to El Quiché until more than fifteen years later, with the birth of the REMHI project.

3. The Church and the Defence of Human Rights

a. Oscar Romero: The Voice of the Voiceless

In a homily given just eight days before his death, Archbishop Romero spoke of the sacredness of life:

> Nothing is as important to the Church as human life, the human person, especially the lives of the poor and the oppressed.... Jesus said that whatever is done to the poor is done to Him. This bloodshed, these deaths, are beyond all politics. They touch the very heart of God.[36]

[35] Ibid., p. 66.
[36] *Monseñor Oscar A. Romero: Su Pensamiento,* 16 March 1980 homily.

Romero was also the great defender of the poor, the victims of the repression and the disappeared. In addition to the 75,000 who were killed during the war, 7,000 people were forcibly detained by the death squads at night and disappeared, dumped in such infamous places as El Playon and La Puerta del Diablo where vultures ruled over the decaying cadavers.

Romero supported the families of these disappeared, especially the mothers, empowering them to speak out in defense of their loved ones:

> No one can understand as well as a mother the value of the person, especially when this person is her own child. Why did they torture him? Why did they make her disappear? The presence of a mother who weeps for the disappeared is a presence that denounces; it is a presence that cries out to heaven for the appearance of her disappeared child.... This is the voice of justice, this is the voice of love, this is the cry that the Church gathers up from so many abandoned homes to say, 'This should not be!'[37]

Like the cry of the Suffering Servant, the cry of the poor requires an advocate, somebody 'who will plead their cause': the cause of the disappeared who were silenced; the refugee women and their children who were fleeing to the mountains for safety; the cause of an entire people who were struggling for justice and being so cruelly killed.

Already by 1978, with the publication of his third pastoral letter, 'The Church and Popular Political Organizations', Romero had formulated a defence of his people's right and obligation to organize and plead their own cause for justice:

> The Church has a mission to serve the people.... The Church's role is to defend the cause of the poor, and all that is human in the people's struggle. The Church identifies with the poor when they demand their legitimate rights. In our country the right they are demanding is hardly more than the right to survive, to escape misery.[38]

Romero's defence of popular organizations was not only, or even primarily, a political option, but an essential part of evangelization. He quotes Paul VI's Apostolic Exhortation, *Evangelii Nuntiandi,* to make this point:

> The Church has the duty to proclaim the liberation of millions of

[37] Ibid.
[38] Oscar Romero, *Voice of the Voiceless: The Four Pastoral Letters*, Maryknoll, NY, Orbis Books, 1985, p. 97.

human beings, many of whom are its own children, the duty of assisting the birth of this liberation, of giving witness to it, of ensuring that it is complete. This is not foreign to evangelization.[39]

This defence of popular organizations in El Salvador meant that 'faith and politics ought to be united in a Christian who has a political vocation, but they are not to be identified. . . . Faith ought to inspire political action, but not be mistaken for it.'[40]

Romero's concern, however, was not limited to the Church. True to the spirit of the Second Vatican Council, he found the Spirit active within as well as beyond the visible structures and witness of the Church:

There is a more fundamental connection, based on faith, between the Church and popular organizations, even if they do not profess to be Christian. The Church believes that the action of the Spirit who brings Christ to life in human beings is greater than itself. Far beyond the confines of the Church, Christ's redemption is powerfully at work. . . . The Church tries to see [the popular organizations] in this way in order to purify them, encourage them, and incorporate them, together with the efforts of Christians, into the overall plan of Christ's redemption.[41]

In his fourth and final pastoral letter, 'The Church's Mission Amid the National Crisis', written in 1979, Romero reminds us that the mission of the Church is:

To be the voice of the voiceless, a defender of the rights of the poor, a promoter of every just aspiration for liberation, a guide, an empowerer, a humanizer of every legitimate struggle to achieve a more just society, a society that prepares the way for the true Kingdom of God in history.

This demands of the Church a greater presence among the poor. It ought to be in solidarity with them, running the risks they run, enduring the persecution that is their fate, ready to give the greatest possible testimony to its love by defending and promoting those who were first in Jesus' love.[42]

Romero was willing to run the risks required to defend the poor. In the end, he, too, became a martyr. But his word has not been silenced; on

---

[39] Ibid., quoting *Evangelii Nuntiandi*, No. 30.
[40] Ibid., p. 100.
[41] Ibid., p. 105.
[42] Ibid., p. 138.

the contrary, like the blood of the martyrs, his witness is his most eloquent word.

> Our world in El Salvador is not an abstraction.... It is a world which, in its vast majority, is composed of poor and oppressed men and women. And it is the same world of the poor that provides us the key to understand our Christian faith.... The poor tell us what our world is like, and what the mission of the Church should be.[43]

Seven weeks before his death, Archbishop Romero was invited to give an address at the University of Louvain, in Belgium. There he gave in a concise manner what we have described as the four marks of his spirituality: the centrality of the poor, the Gospel as Good News to the poor, the defense of life in the midst of a conflictual history, and the testimony of martyrdom.

Romero entitled his address at Louvain, 'The Political Dimension of Faith'. It may be well to note that Romero speaks of a political 'dimension' of faith. There is a political dimension to spirituality, just as there is a political dimension to the Gospel, that cannot be ignored without truncating either.

He began his address at Louvain by differentiating between the world of most people living in developed countries like Belgium and the United States, and 'the world of the poor' living in Third World countries like El Salvador, or in pockets of misery in the First World:

> Far from distancing us from our faith, these harsh realities [of poverty] have moved us to incarnate ourselves in the world of the poor. In this world we have found the real faces of the poor. Peasants without water or electricity in their poor dwellings, without medical assistance when the women give birth, and without schools when the children begin to grow up. There we found workers with no labor rights, workers at the mercy of the economy's cold calculations. There we found mothers and wives of the 'disappeared' and political prisoners. There we met the people who live in hovels where misery exceeds the imagination, and nearby mansions constitute a permanent insult.[44]

Romero's spirituality is characterized, then, in the first instance, by the centrality of the poor to our faith. And this encounter with the poor of El Salvador revealed both the structural dimension of their poverty, as well as the conflictual nature of their oppression.

---

[43] Oscar Romero, *La Voz de los Sin Voz*, San Salvador, UCA, 1987, 2 February 1980 address at the University of Louvain.
[44] Ibid.

Romero's spirituality was profoundly marked by the Gospel that he proclaimed every Sunday from the cathedral of San Salvador:

> This is my greatest concern: to try to build with Christ a Church according to his heart. . . . For that reason I ask you to focus not only on the weekly events that the prophetic mission of the Church obliges me to illuminate, but also on the light that illuminates, on the attempt of this poor pastor to build a Church according to the heart of God.[45]

Here we come to the second sign of Romero's spirituality: his fidelity in proclaiming the Gospel as Good News to the poor. The key to his proclamation, again, is the centrality of the poor, but especially the poor as seen from the compassionate heart of God.

He proclaimed the Gospel as one who knew the world of the poor, saw the world from their eyes, and shared their sufferings and hopes; and as one who knew the heart of God and God's compassion for the poor, as one who spoke on their behalf and defended their lives:

> The Church has Good News to announce to the poor. Those who have heard the bad news in a secular context and have lived even worse realities, are now listening through the Church to the Word of Jesus: 'Blessed are the poor, for the Reign of God is yours.' And then there is the Good News to announce to the rich: Be converted to the poor and share with them the goods of the Reign of God.[46]

Moreover, 'the encounter with the poor has enabled us to recover the central truth of the Gospel: the Word of God urges us to a conversion,' a conversion to the poor. The poor are the key to 'what the world is really like,' and to 'what the mission of the Church should be.'

Conversion to the poor means, then, to see the world from the eyes of the poor, and to work so that the poor have dignity and life. And it means to see the Church from the eyes of the poor, and to work so that the glory of God may be made visible in the poor. Rephrasing the words of St Irenaeus, Romero said: 'The glory of God is the poor fully alive.'

The spirituality of Oscar Romero cannot be understood apart from the life-and-death struggle of the poor for justice, and the context of conflicting interests in Salvadoran society. Consequently, the Gospel

---

[45] *Monsenor Oscar A. Romero: Su Pensamiento,* September 3, 1978 homily. See also Miguel Cavada Diez, *Predicacion y Profecia: Analisis de las Homilias de Monsenor Romero*, San Salvador, UCA, 1993, Master's Thesis.

[46] *La Voz de los Sin Voz,* 2 February 1980 address at the University of Louvain.

that Romero proclaimed to the poor was never 'an opium of the people', but 'the very heart of God in a heartless world'. His heart, in turn, was profoundly moved by the sufferings of the poor:

> The Church has not only incarnated herself in the world of the poor and given them hope, but also has committed itself firmly to their defence. The poor of our country are daily oppressed and repressed by the economic and political structures. The terrible words of the prophets of Israel are still applicable in our country. In our midst there are those who sell the just person for money, the poor person for a pair of sandals.[47]

In his address at the University of Louvain, Oscar Romero spoke of defending the poor as a necessary consequence of incarnating the Church in the world of the poor and proclaiming the Gospel as Good News to them. This option, which came to be characterized as the Church's 'preferential option for the poor', was not merely a political option devoid of any content of faith. It is at the heart of the Church's mission, and comprises the political dimension of our faith:

> Incarnation in the sociopolitical world [of the poor] is the place to deepen our faith in God and in His Christ. We believe in Jesus, who came to bring life in its fullest, and we believe in a living God, who gives life to humankind and wants all to live in truth. These radical truths of the faith become truths – radical truths – when the Church inserts herself in the midst of the life and death of the people.... It is there that the Church is presented with the most fundamental option of faith: to be in favour of life or in favour of death.[48]

Romero had a keen sense of the demonic power of sin that permeated the dominant economic and political structures of Salvadoran society. These structures, like the 'principalities and powers' cited by St Paul in his Epistles, demanded absolute obedience:

> It is not mere routine that once again we denounce the existence of sinful structures in our country. They are sinful because they produce the fruits of sin: the death of Salvadorans – the rapid death of repression or the slow death, but no less real, of structural oppression.... For that reason we have denounced the idolatry that exists in our country. Wealth is made a god, private property is

[47] Ibid.
[48] Ibid.

made an absolute by the capitalist system, national security is made the highest good by the political powers who institutionalize the insecurity of the individual.[49]

What was at stake was not only the life and death of the poor, but also the very credibility of the Church:

> There is no doubt whatsoever that here there is no room for neutrality. We are either at the service of the life of Salvadorans or we are accomplices in their death. And it is here that we are faced with the most fundamental reality of the historical mediation of faith. Either we believe in a God of life or we serve the idols of death.[50]

That meant that the proclamation of the Word had to be accompanied by both words and deeds, by annunciation and denunciation, by pastoral response and prophetic action, by personal compassion and structural transformation. What was at stake was nothing less than the life and death of the poor:

> We are dealing with a true option for the poor. This means that the Church incarnates herself in the world of the poor, proclaims the Good News, gives hope, inspires a liberating praxis, defends the cause of the poor and participates in their destiny. This option for the poor is at the root of the political dimension of our faith, and is its most fundamental characteristic.[51]

For Romero, then, the world of the poor is, above all, the very place in which God is revealed. In the face of the poor he saw the face of Christ, in the crucified and tortured bodies of his people he saw the crucified body of Christ. But also in the signs of life and aspirations for liberation he found signs of Christ's resurrection and signs of the Spirit, Lord and Giver of Life:

> Where the poor begin to live, where the poor begin to liberate themselves, where men and women are able to sit down around a common table and share, there is the God of life.... That is why, when the Church inserts itself in the sociopolitical world in order to cooperate in bringing about the emergence of life for the poor, it is not undertaking a mere subsidiary task or something outside of

---

[49] Ibid.
[50] Ibid.
[51] Ibid.

its mission, but is witnessing to its faith in God and is being an instrument of the Spirit, the Lord and Giver of Life.[52]

The poor are not only central to the spirituality of Romero and the mission of the Church, they are the key to what the world is really like and what the mission of the Church should be:

> The world of the poor teaches us how Christian love should be. It should certainly seek peace, but unmask false pacifisms, resignation, and inactivity. It should certainly be free but must seek historical efficacy. The world of the poor teaches us that the magnanimity of Christian love must respond to the demand of justice for the majorities and not flee from honest struggle.... Liberation will occur not only when the poor become recipients of government or Church benefits, but when they themselves become authors and protagonists of their struggle and their liberation.[53]

In the final part of his address at the University of Louvain, Oscar Romero bore witness to that which first brought El Salvador to the world's attention: the testimony of the martyrs and the reality of persecution. Here we come full circle to the last of the signs of Romero's spirituality: the testimony of the martyrs. Like the other signs – the centrality of the poor, the Gospel proclaimed as Good News to the poor, a faith that defends the life of the poor in the midst of history's conflicts – the witness of the martyrs is intimately linked to the poor.

> In this situation of conflict and antagonism, in which the few have economic and political control, the Church has put herself on the side of the poor and has taken up their defence.... For defending the poor, the Church has entered into grave conflict with the economic oligarchies, the political powers, and the military. This defence of the poor in so conflictive a world has occasioned a new reality in the recent history of our Church: persecution.[54]

The testimony of martyrdom is, in one sense, a tragic consequence of the conflict in El Salvador, and the cost paid by those who were faithful to the demands of the Gospel, taking sides with the poor, and offering their lives out of a fundamental option of love. But behind the death of the six priests killed in El Salvador during his lifetime, Romero saw the vulnerability of the poor:

[52] Ibid.
[53] Ibid.
[54] Ibid.

> If the most visible Church representatives have been treated thus, you can easily surmise what has happened to the simple Christian people, to peasant farmers, to catechists and delegates of the Word, to Christian base communities. It is here that the number of threatened, captured, tortured, and assassinated reaches to the hundreds and thousands. And it is poor Christians who are persecuted the most.[55]

And while martyrdom is a sign of the Church's fidelity to the Gospel, its deepest significance is that it reveals precisely what being faithful to the Gospel means in a world in which the life of the poor is so much at risk:

> While it is clear that our Church has been the victim of persecution these last three years, it is even more important to observe the reason for the persecution. It is not just any priest or any institution that has been persecuted. It is that segment of the Church that is on the side of the poor and has come out in their defence that has been persecuted and attacked. The persecution comes about because of the Church's defence of the poor, for making the destiny of the poor its own.[56]

The testimony of the martyrs, then, is intimately linked to the poor, to proclaiming the Gospel as Good News to those who have only known bad news, and to defending the life of those whose lives are most at risk. Because the Church in El Salvador has placed the poor at the heart of its identity and its mission, it was persecuted. But that is its glory. That is the way Romero saw it. In the end, he became the Good News that he proclaimed to the poor:

> As a pastor, I am obligated by divine commandment to give my life for those I love ... even for those who would assassinate me.... For that reason I offer God my blood for the redemption and resurrection of El Salvador.... Martyrdom is a grace that I don't believe I merit. But if God accepts the sacrifice of my life, may my blood be the seed of liberty and sign that this hope will soon become a reality. May my death, if it is accepted by God, be for the liberation of my people and a testimony of hope in the future.[57]

In his life and in his death, Oscar Romero bore witness to the ancient wisdom of the Church, expressed by Tertullian: 'The blood of the martyrs is the seed of new Christians.'

[55] Ibid.
[56] Ibid.
[57] *La Voz de los Sin Voz*, March 1980, p. 461.

b. Juan Gerardi: Faithful Witness to God

When we turn to the witness of Bishop Gerardi, we find a social and ecclesial context in Guatemala very similar to the one in which Romero lived. In both countries, social structures marked by injustice had oppressed the poor and increased the disparities between a rich elite and poor majority; when the poor organized and demanded changes, the response in both countries was a cruel and systematic repression. This in turn provoked a popular rebellion against the government in El Salvador and Guatemala, and an all-out war by the government against the civilian population characterized by massacres and, in the case of Guatemala, genocide against the indigenous population.

In both countries, too, the Church played a prophetic role in denouncing violations of human rights and calling for negotiations leading to peace and structural changes in the political, social and economic structures of the nation. Though deprived of the diocese in El Quiché, Gerardi returned to Guatemala in 1982 and was named Auxiliary Bishop of the Archdiocese of Guatemala where he served as Vicar General, Vicar of Pastoral Work, and eventually the Director of a newly created Archdiocesan Human Rights Office out of which was born the Recovery of the Historic Memory project in 1995.

Like Romero, Gerardi was before all, a pastor. In 1989, when he was invited to speak on the topic of 'The Response of the Catholic Church in Guatemala to the Processes of Social and Political Change', he introduced his remarks as follows:

> I am sure in my exposition that you do not want to hear the voice of a politician or social scientist, neither of which I am, but the voice of a pastor, which is what I am; and in some measure, throughout my pastoral mission, it has fallen to me to share the pain and sorrow of an oppressed and mistreated people, such as my own.[58]

Gerardi went on to characterize the period of greatest violence in Guatemala (1979–1982) as 'the most cruel and bloody repression that has been seen in Latin America.' Faced with such a challenging context, Gerardi characterized the mission of the church in Guatemala in this way:

> The Church took up a prophetic attitude of denunciation and condemnation of human rights violations, especially against the most poor and marginalized who, given the characteristics of insurgency

---

[58] *Monseñor Juan Gerardi: Testigo Fiel de Dios*, 'Respuesta de la Iglesia Catolica, en Guatemala, Frente a los Procesos de Cambio Sociales y Politicos', p. 70.

and counterinsurgency at play, were the ones who were punished the most, condemned to pay a social and human cost and to bear the bitter and painful consequences of the conflict.[59]

The Church, however, did not simply limit itself to denouncing violations of human rights, it also accompanied the victims in the hour of their agony:

> Sectors of the Church most in contact with the oppressed and persecuted people opted, together with their bishop, with a truly ecclesial and Gospel attitude, to put into practice a pastoral work of accompaniment and solidarity with this same people, willing to risk the same fate. Inspired by their faith in the word of Jesus, they understood that the Lord called them to serve God in the poor and indigent, the persecuted and tortured. In this way ... the Church opted for the God of life and committed itself to combat death.[60]

By the end of the decade of the 1980s, however, signs appeared on the horizon of limited democratic openings and potential opportunities for a negotiated solution to the conflict in Guatemala. This in turn, opened the way for a pastoral reflection on the obligation of the Church to work to lay the foundations of peace based on justice:

> We considered that the only solution to the spiral of violence was the installation of a regime of law that guaranteed respect for human rights and a climate of participation of all citizens upon whom the enormous responsibility of building peace fell. For Christians, to build peace is a Gospel demand that we cannot refuse if we want to be known as children of God (Matthew 5.9).[61]

Among the dimensions of peace, Gerardi mentioned 'the preferential option for the poor' as that which gives a concrete identity to its pastoral work; specific attention to the urgent needs of hundreds of thousands of refugees, widows and orphans displaced by the violence; 'respect for and promotion of indigenous cultures' as the foundation for a just, participatory and pluralistic society; and 'the transformation of the social and economic structures that sustain the injustice, the discrimination and the exploitation of people into new structures of justice, equality and participation' as the foundation of a genuine democracy:

[59] Ibid., p. 71.
[60] Ibid., pp. 72–73.
[61] Ibid., p. 76.

> If we want to build a genuine and participatory democracy we have to recognize that the actual situation of injustice and violence has its origin ... in the land ownership patterns that exist in this country.... The Guatemalan bishops denounce this situation of injustice that gives rise to the harmful and profound inequalities that exist in our society, and that opposes the integral development of our people and provokes the social conflicts that we continue to live.[62]

In April 1995, the Human Rights Office of the Archdiocese of Guatemala (ODHAG), under the direction of Bishop Gerardi, created the Interdiocesan Recovery of the Historic Memory (REMHI) project as a way to contribute to the United Nations Historical Clarification Commission set in motion by mutual agreement of the Guatemalan government and the URNG guerrillas the year before. The latter commission was not formally established until July 1997, and rendered its final report, *Guatemala: Memory of Silence*, on 25 February 1999 – nearly a year after the publication of the REMHI report and the assassination of Bishop Gerardi.

Bishop Gerardi and the members of the Human Rights Office were concerned that the mandate of the United Nations Commission of Historical Clarification – Guatemala's 'Truth Commission' – was too narrow, even more narrow than the Salvadoran Truth Commission, because it did not allow for the mention by name of the perpetrators of the violence in Guatemala. So the REMHI project was established with a specific interest in insuring that the truth about the violence be told in as complete a form as possible.

According to Edgar Gutiérrez, the coordinator of the REMHI project, the first challenge faced by the REMHI team was to come up with a methodology adapted both to the specific characteristics of violence in Guatemala, as well as the cultural needs of its indigenous people. Much of the violence could not be characterized simply as 'summary executions' – in many cases civilians were forced to perpetrate violence on their own or neighbouring community members, or risk losing their own lives or the lives of their family members:

> Faced with this reality, we decided to employ a more open methodology that allowed us to draw near to the global experience of the people.... It was not just a difference in methodology, it took on profounder implications. In the first place, we committed ourselves to the history of the people. Within a pastoral context, this meant that we were concerned with the survivors, with their destiny and

[62] Ibid., p. 79.

with life-giving projects, and not first with the data that they could give us....

This was our methodological lesson: the reconstruction of recent history, whose actors are still alive, has meaning when we link it to a social project of human reconstruction. History, then, is at the service of men and women, of the community, and not vice versa.[63]

A second distinguishing characteristic of the REMHI project was the decision to involve and train local people from the communities affected by the violence in the process of collecting the testimonies of the victims. More than 800 leaders, most of them from indigenous communities, underwent an intensive training to understand the history of the conflict, something about mental health, and a technique to interview the victims. Most of the testimonies were taken in one of fifteen Mayan dialects, and in some cases entire communities participated in a collective interview. The questions themselves were equally significant:

Tell us what happened? What reasons could there be for what happened? How did you confront the situation? What do you think about this experience now? What could be done so that this never happens again? These questions concluded – once the witness had finished their testimony – with a form that asked for data concerning the identification of the victim – name, age, civil state, home, etc ... as well as details of the abuse suffered: what, how, when, where. Data about those responsible, individuals or institutions. And data that identified the witness.[64]

More than 6,500 testimonies were taken, providing data on 55,023 cases of human rights violations, including 422 massacres. Two-thirds of these testimonies were taken in one of fifteen Mayan dialects. All the testimonies were recorded on cassette tapes, of which about 15 per cent were written out. Finally, the testimonies were submitted to a team who analyzed them statistically, and drew conclusions from them regarding 'the strategies of the war and the actors', 'the mechanisms of the horror', 'the experiences of the people', 'the effects on specific sectors' (individual, family, community), and 'the demands and recommendations.'

This analysis formed the basis for the four volumes of the REMHI report, which was formally released by the Guatemalan Church on 24 April 1998 in a ceremony presided over by Bishop Gerardi. Two days later the bishop was assassinated. The REMHI project, however,

[63] *Monseñor Juan Gerardi: Testigo Fiel de Dios*, Edgar Gutiérrez, 'La Artesania de la Historia', p. 267.
[64] Ibid., p. 268.

has not concluded. Its fourth and final stage involves returning the results of the project back to the communities from which the testimonies were taken, by means of programs of peace education, and commemorative ceremonies.

In the words of Edgar Gutiérrez:

> The survivors are recovering their right to speak and to affirm their sense of dignity, a right [the military] tried to take away from them. We want to contribute to the recovery of the memory of the conflict by encouraging a process of internal healing and social construction of the communities. This process complements the models of pacification that the United Nations has promoted in many countries. We think of ourselves as instruments in search of reconciliation, beginning from the very base of society that was so destroyed.[65]

What role did Bishop Gerardi play in all this? According to those who worked with him, Gerardi played a key role in the direction of the REMHI project from its conception to the day of his death – and perhaps now an even greater role in the impact that his martyrdom has had on the Guatemalan Church. According to his friends, Gerardi 'committed himself to REMHI, he lived it, he immersed himself in it and allowed what had been his own initiative to enter into his bones.'[66]

The REMHI project was deeply important to Gerardi. In the words of Edgar Gutiérrez, Gerardi had 'a debt to pay with respect to his own history',[67] and that was to return to the diocese of El Quiché that he had abandoned in 1980. The REMHI project gave him the opportunity to do that, both in person – which he did in 1997 – and in the Gospel sense of conversion. According to a friend who accompanied him on his return to El Quiché, 'you could see a happy face, content, just like the faces we saw of many witnesses after they had given us their testimony.'[68]

On the night of the public presentation of the REMHI report, Bishop Gerardi presided over the event held in the cathedral in Guatemala City. There he pronounced his final public address, and he publicly gave a copy of the report to Nobel Peace Laureate Rigoberta Menchú. The context of his words, spoken as they were just a short time before his assassination, call to mind Archbishop Romero's words to the Salvadoran military to 'stop the repression.' A brief selection of his

---

[65] Ibid., p. 270.
[66] Ibid., Edgar Gutiérrez, 'El Legado Historico de Gerardi: La Paz Desde Adentro y Desde Abajo', p. 259.
[67] Ibid.
[68] Ibid., p. 260.

remarks, however, now sealed in blood, illuminates in a way that no one else could, the spirit and prophetic power of the REMHI project:

> God is inflexibly opposed to evil in any form. The root of the downfall and the disgrace of humanity comes from the deliberate opposition to truth that is the radical reality of God and of human beings. It is this reality that has been intentionally deformed in our country throughout thirty-six years of war against the people....
>
> As a church, we do not have any doubt that the work we have carried out in these past few years has been part of a story of grace and of salvation, a real step toward peace as a result of justice. It has been a soft scattering of seeds of life and dignity throughout the country – and the advocates and participants in the work have been the suffering people themselves. It has been a beautiful service of veneration for the martyrs and a dignification of the victims that were the targets of the plans for destruction and death....
>
> Peace is possible – a peace that is born from the truth that comes from each one of us and from all of us. It is a painful truth, full of memories of the deep and bloody wounds of the country. It is a liberating and humanizing truth that makes it possible for all men and women to come to terms with themselves and their life stories. It is a truth that challenges each one of us to recognize our individual and collective responsibility and to commit ourselves to action so that those abominable acts never happen again....
>
> This project has made a commitment to the people that gave their testimonies, to gather their experiences in this report and to support all of the demands of the victims. But our commitment is also to return the collected memory to the people. The search for truth does not end here. It must return from where it was born and it must support the role of memory as an instrument for social reconstruction through the creation of materials, ceremonies, monuments and so forth....[69]

These words are powerful, knowing the context in which they were spoken. But it was Gerardi's closing remarks, perhaps, that provoked such a violent reaction and joined his blood with the blood of so many martyrs in Guatemala. First, he returned to the biblical image of the Suffering Servant, drawing a comparison between the servant's fate and the fate of his people:

---

[69] *Guatemala: Never Again!* 'Speech by Monsenor Juan Gerardi', on the occasion of the presentation of the REMHI report in the Metropolitan Cathedral of Guatemala City, 24 April 1998, translated by EPICA, pp. xxiii–xxv.

The thousands of testimonies of the victims and the recounting of the horrific crimes are the current day manifestations of the figure of the 'suffering servant of Yahweh', who is incarnated in the people of Guatemala. 'Behold my servant,' says Isaiah, 'Many were afraid of him. He was so disfigured, beyond human semblance, and his form beyond that of the sons of men. He has borne our griefs and carried our sorrows, yet we esteemed him stricken, smitten by God and afflicted' (Isaiah 52.13 and 53.4).[70]

Only in hindsight do we know the significance of these words to the manner in which Gerardi was assassinated – a concrete block crushing and disfiguring his face. The image of another martyr, Oscar Romero, comes to mind, as a single bullet penetrated his heart while celebrating Mass; or Father Ignacio Ellacuría, the Salvadoran Jesuit martyr, whose skull, like Gerardi's, was crushed, not by a concrete block but by the impact of a single bullet fired at close range. All three martyrs joined in a compact of blood with the thousands of Salvadoran and Guatemalan martyrs.

But it was his final words, perhaps, that sealed Gerardi's fate. The publication of the REMHI report was not, as some had hoped perhaps, the closing of a wound. Rather it was the display of an open wound for the world to see, in the hope that once seen and recognized, a process of genuine reconciliation – based on the truth, admission of the crime and a plea for pardon from the perpetrators, a willingness to forgive on the part of the victims and reparations for their families and justice in the form of transforming the structures of society – this was the hope:

> Bringing the memory of these painful events into the present leads us to confront some of the first words of our faith: 'Cain, where is your brother Abel?'
>
> 'I don't know,' he answered. 'Am I my brother's keeper?'
>
> Yahweh replied, 'What have you done? The voice of your brother's blood is crying to me from the ground.' (Genesis 4.9–10).[71]

The echo of that cry still resounds in the legacy left by Bishop Gerardi. In the words of his friend, Edgar Gutiérrez, 'His legacy is a dream still to be discovered, a fertile land to sow, a happiness to win, a country to build.'[72]

---

[70] Ibid., pp. xxv.
[71] Ibid.
[72] *Monseñor Juan Gerardi: Testigo Fiel de Dios*, Edgar Gutiérrez, 'El Legado Historico de Gerardi: La Paz Desde Adentro y Desde Abajo', p. 263.

4. The Legacy of Romero and Gerardi

a. Oscar Romero: You Have Risen in the People!

Those who worked closely with Archbishop Romero regard his memory as both Good News and challenge. Five years after Romero's death, Jon Sobrino was asked why Romero continues to be alive among his people. Sobrino replied: 'Monseñor Romero had a great love, an immense love for his people, and for that reason he continues to live among the poor.' Returning to the University of Louvain in Belgium, where Romero had given his last address, Sobrino added:

> To those who ignore the tragedy of the poor, Monseñor Romero keeps saying, 'Don't forget the millions of children of God who continue to suffer in this world.' To those who offer solidarity to the poor, he gives encouragement and thanks. To all of us, Monseñor Romero continues to offer both Good News and challenge.[73]

The first public procession in San Salvador, on the occasion of Archbishop Romero's martyrdom, occurred five years after his death. By then, the repression in the streets had subsided sufficiently for the people to process through the heart of San Salvador to the celebration of the Mass at the cathedral where Romero's tomb is located. Once again, Romero's spirit and his words continued to give life to the poor whose lives were at risk. The very symbols of the procession spoke to the heart of his spirituality:

> A huge banner was carried at the beginning of the procession: 'If they kill me, I will rise in the Salvadoran people.' Behind the banner was an immense photograph of Monseñor Romero, ten feet high ... and behind the photograph a river of people overflowing the streets of San Salvador – streets filled with the echoes of popular protests and bathed in blood ... People sang and repeated his words: 'We must demand at the very least respect for what is of greatest value: life.' 'In the name of God, I ask you, stop the repression!'[74]

Throughout the years of the war and since, the memory of Oscar Romero and his spirit in the people continues to bring light and salvation to the poor of El Salvador. Every anniversary of his martyrdom, every feast day of the Church, is an opportunity to bear witness to his resurrection in the people, and recall signs of his spirituality. 'What

---

[73] *Carta a las Iglesias*, San Salvador, UCA, No. 85.
[74] Ibid., No. 88.

happened to Jesus, happened to Monseñor Romero. That's why he lives in our people.'[75]

Not only do the passion and death of Jesus illuminate the martyrdom of Oscar Romero; Romero's life and death, in no small measure, has deepened the faith of the poor in Jesus Christ and led them back to the source of their life. The spirit of Romero, as the spirit of the martyrs before him, brings us back to the heart of the paschal mystery: 'When they killed Monseñor Romero, we were very sad because we thought everything had ended. But later we saw that his spirit gave us strength to resist oppression. For that reason we also believe more now in Jesus Christ.'[76]

What is the legacy of Oscar Romero today? In many respects – even though the war in El Salvador has ended – the following words offered by Jon Sobrino on the occasion of the tenth anniversary of Romero's martyrdom continue to ring true today:

> In El Salvador, as well as in the entire Third World ... an alarming situation still exists: inhumane poverty, cruel injustice, conflict and war, repression and the violation of human rights, disillusionment with the failures of the people, and all the suffering and darkness that this brings to the majority of the people who are poor. We all know this, but unless we are willing to deepen our awareness of it we will not be able to understand the importance of Monseñor Romero and his presence among us today.
>
> On the other hand, we continue to find creativity and hope in the struggle for liberation and the generous self-sacrifice of the martyrs, brought home to us in the recent martyrdom of the Jesuits and the commemoration of Rutilio Grande, the proto-martyr of El Salvador. The poor still have the intuition and fundamental hope that Jesus is Good News for them, and that a Church that resembles Jesus and responds as Jesus did is also Good News. Long before the Church made an option for the poor, the poor made an option for the Church.[77]

And while it is certainly true that the spirit of Oscar Romero and the remembrance of his words continue to be an effective and urgent voice for transformation in El Salvador, his presence extends beyond the borders of his country. He has become, again in the words of Jon Sobrino, 'the most universal Christian at the end of the twentieth century.'

---

[75] Ibid., No. 89.
[76] Ibid.
[77] Ibid., No. 206.

> Monseñor Romero inspires peasants and indigenous people, African Americans and oppressed, but also intellectuals, university professors, professionals, bishops, and humble catechists. Despite the passing of years, the commemoration of Romero's life has not diminished. In times of war and in times of peace, countless human beings continue to celebrate him. In Romero, that which is Christian and that which is human is very present.
>
> If this is true, then it is not at all rhetorical to affirm that Monseñor Romero has become a 'universal Christian,' and perhaps the most universal Christian of our time.... We don't say this out of any triumphalism, but with the same humility and simplicity with which Monseñor himself spoke.... How we wish that there were more Romeros in the world![78]

The spirit of Oscar Romero, then, through his memory and through his word, continues to be a prophetic presence in El Salvador, offering the poor the comfort that they are not alone, and the promise that things can change. His memory is a 'subversive' one, in the sense that the Beatitudes are subversive: they remind us that the world is not meant to be as it currently is, where the poor are excluded, the hungry forgotten, those who grieve hidden from view, and the victims blamed for their own persecution. Rather, the poor are blessed because theirs is the Reign of God. Life, not death, will have the last word.

On the occasion of the fifteenth anniversary of Romero's death, Gustavo Gutiérrez recalled this deeper truth of Romero's martyrdom as he preached in the chapel of the Jesuit martyrs in San Salvador:

> We come to this Eucharist to give thanks for Monseñor Romero, and for so many who have already been resurrected with Jesus, and who will continue to be resurrected.... The martyrs remind us of Jesus' resurrection; they recall for us the centre of our faith and of our hope. We must always remember – in communion with martyrs – that death does not put an end to our hopes and joys; life is the heart of the Christian message.[79]

Oscar Romero is important, not only because his prophetic word continues to illuminate and judge the current social reality from the perspective of God's plan of salvation; his spirit is essential today for the sake of our Christian faith. If it were not for the testimony of the martyrs – if it were not for the witness of Oscar Romero – and the power of Jesus' resurrection to which the martyrs bear witness, so

---

[78] Ibid., No. 254.
[79] Ibid., No. 326.

much suffering and death among the poor in El Salvador would have been in vain.

For that reason, the memory and spirit of Romero, like the memory and spirit of the martyrs, strengthens our faith in Jesus Christ, and in the power of the Gospel to bring Good News to the poor. This is the heart of the message that Gutiérrez proclaimed in his homily to the people of El Salvador:

> Today we celebrate a Eucharist, we recall a death, but we also know that for Christians – and Monseñor Romero and so many others have told us this with great clarity – death is not the last word of human existence; life has the last word.... They can silence our voices – and here I am thinking of Romero's own words – but 'they cannot silence the voice of hope and joy that we feel', this paschal joy that has overcome death.[80]

Nor has the memory of Romero among his people faded with the years. On 24 March 2000, on the occasion of the twentieth anniversary of his martyrdom, more than 100,000 people processed through the streets of San Salvador, their hands bearing candles that lit up the night, bearing as it were the harvest of dreams and promise of a better life that Romero had sown through his words and the witness of his life.

In conclusion, we may say that the force of the resurrection continues to be present in El Salvador, indeed, throughout the world, even in the midst of the crucifixion of the poor. That resurrection continues to judge the current historical reality from the perspective of God's plan of salvation, and to give hope to the poor that the last word will be life.

Because Oscar Romero was faithful to the poor, he joined his life to theirs and shared the same fate as the poor. Their passion became his passion, their crucifixion his cross. But because Romero was also faithful to the Gospel, he joined the passion of the poor to Christ's passion, and thus to Christ's resurrection. Just as God vindicated Jesus, and raised him from the dead, so God has vindicated the martyrs – and Oscar Romero with them – and joined their resurrection to the resurrection of Christ.

In El Salvador, a crucified people continues to announce resurrection. At moments, there seem to be more shadows than light, more poverty and violence than hope for transformation, more death than life, more cross than resurrection. But the spirit of Oscar Romero – made present in the communal act of remembrance – has marked the poor forever, binding their passion and death to the passion and death

---

[80] Ibid.

of Jesus Christ, and raising them to new life. While the present is at moments dark, the victory is assured: life, not death, has the last word.

b. Juan Gerardi – Guatemala: Never Again!

And what about the legacy of Juan Gerardi? I was privileged to be present in Guatemala at the first commemoration of his martyrdom, 26 April 1999. One hundred thousand people had gathered in the main plaza in front of the Metropolitan Cathedral, mostly indigenous people in their colourful traditional dress, survivors of more than three decades of military terror and cruelty in the countryside. From El Quiché and Chimaltenango, from the Verapaces and Huehuetenango, the people approached the centre of the city from four different directions, bearing four different colours of the Mayan cross. We joined one of the columns of people, joining our voices to theirs to cry: 'Guatemala: Nunca Más!'

And while the Guatemalan government, under international pressure, has taken steps to investigate the case the people who lived through the worst of the violence are convinced that those who murdered Bishop Gerardi are the same ones that murdered hundreds of thousands of their family members.

As we joined the sea of indigenous people in the plaza to commemorate Bishop Gerardi's martyrdom, we could hear the loud cry to put an end to this kind of impunity. The Central American bishops made it very clear that Bishop Gerardi had been killed because of his work with the REMHI project, unmasking the cruelty of the military violence and genocide during the war.

In fact, Gerardi's murder was a reason for the United Nations to present a stronger, not a weaker report. Just two months before the first anniversary of Gerardi's death, in February 1999, the UN Commission of Historical Clarification stunned the Guatemalan government and military with the bluntness of its conclusions. What occurred in Guatemala during the four decades of war, and most especially during the years of General Efraín Ríos Montt (1982–1983) was nothing less than genocide, a crime against humanity.

Today, however, the faces and the physical presence of so many indigenous people affirmed the conclusions of both the REMHI report and the Historical Clarification Commission. It was inspiring to see that sea of faces in the plaza the day of Bishop Gerardi's commemoration. As we processed to the central plaza, the memory of those dark years of repression mingled with the cries of 'Guatemala: Nunca Más!' that broke the silence of decades. The victims had become protagonists, and were taking back the streets, taking back their history, taking back their dreams and hopes and laying claim to their future, to a new Guatemala that would be 'different'.

In his homily before the 100,000 people gathered, Bishop Flores, the Bishop of Alta and Baja Verepaz, asked:

> What reasons did they have to destroy his face and skull with such incredible brutality and hatred? Surely it was because he was someone who loved justice and hated impunity, someone who was never insensitive to the suffering of his poor, humiliated and massacred people. It was because he looked for light amidst the darkness. Those who act with evil hate the light, and so they tried to extinguish the brightly shining torch of his life. It was because he endeavoured to build peace, to build a different country in which the people would no longer be the victims of the terror sown by a few.[81]

In a country where truth has been another casualty of war, the words spoken this day brought hope, and the Gospel phrase, 'All that has been hidden will be revealed', took on a new vitality. Archbishop Oscar Rodríguez, of Tegucigalpa, Honduras, ended his talk by inviting the people to join with him in shouting, 'Guatemala: Nunca Más!' 'Guatemala: Never Again!' The plaza shook with the sound.

While the violence continues in Guatemala, though to a lesser degree, and the military continue to enjoy impunity, the 100,000 indigenous survivors of the repression who gathered on this day in the central plaza were very clear about the authors of this violence. The people who killed Bishop Gerardi were the very same military who killed their loved ones, burned their villages, and created a reign of terror in Guatemala for four decades. Bishop Gerardi's assassination was an attempt to silence the people who had begun to speak up through their testimonies in the REMHI report, but their attempt backfired.

Much work remains to be done. But the foundation for a new Guatemala, based on the truth presented by the Recovery of the Historic Memory report and the United Nations Historical Clarification Commission, cannot be silenced. The reports recommend a series of reforms to be carried out, from reparations to the victims to a radical reform of the judicial system, as well as a strict definition and limitation of the role of the military and police. And while it is quite uncertain how or if these reforms will take place, the silence has been broken: 'Guatemala: Never Again!'

---

[81] *Challenge: Faith and Action in the Americas,* Spring 1999, Washington DC, EPICA, 1999, 'Restoring Justice to the Victims', pp. 3–5.

Martyrdom and Resurrection in Latin America Today: Archbishop Oscar Arnulfo Romero*

MICHAEL CAMPBELL-JOHNSTON, SJ

A month before his assassination, Archbishop Romero received a warning from the Papal Nuncio in Costa Rica that there were new death threats against him and that he should be very careful. This warning was repeated shortly afterwards by the Nuncio in El Salvador just as Romero was beginning his annual retreat with a group of priests from Chalatenango in the Passionist Sisters' retreat centre overlooking the capital city. He had planned to go with them to a Carmelite house in Guatemala but at the last moment his advisors would not let him since they considered it too dangerous. It is not surprising therefore that during this retreat, Romero tried to come to terms with the prospect of his assassination. He was clearly frightened.

He wrote in his retreat notes: 'I feel afraid of violence against my person. I fear for the weakness of my flesh but I beg the Lord to give me serenity and perseverance.'[1] And a little further on: 'My disposition should be to offer my life to God, whatever way it may end. He helped the martyrs and, if need be, I will feel him very near as I offer him my last breath.' And then comes his full acceptance: 'I accept with faith in him my death, however hard it be.' He ends with a firm act of faith 'for me to be happy and confident, it is sufficient to know with assurance that in him is my life and my death, that in spite of my sin

---

* From an address given at Westminster Abbey 8 July 1998 marking the installation of a statue of Archbishop Romero in a niche on the Abbey façade. Republished here with permission of *The Month* where it was originally published in March 1999.

[1] 'El último retiro espiritual de Monseñor Romero', *Revista Latinoamericana de Teología*, Vol. V, No. 13, enero-abril 1988, pp. 4–7.

I have placed my trust in him and shall not be disappointed, and others will carry on with greater wisdom and holiness the works of the Church and the nation.'

It was certainly the grace of this retreat and the strength Romero found through his prayer that enabled him to reply two weeks later to a Mexican journalist, who asked him if he was afraid of death in the famous words:

> I have often been threatened with death. I have to say, as a Christian, that I don't believe in death without resurrection: if they kill me, I will rise again in the Salvadoran people. I tell you this without any boasting, with the greatest humility. As a pastor, I am obliged, by divine command, to give my life for those I love, who are all Salvadorans, even for those who are going to assassinate me. If the threats are carried out even now I offer my blood to God for the redemption and resurrection of El Salvador. Martyrdom is a grace of God I don't think I deserve. But if God accepts the sacrifice of my life, may my blood be the seed of liberty and the sign that hope will soon become reality. May my death, if accepted by God, be for the freedom of my people and as a witness to hope in the future. You can say, if they come to kill me, that I forgive and bless those who do it. Hopefully they may realize that they will be wasting their time. A bishop will die, but the Church of God which is the people, will never perish.[2]

I believe these great words express the real nature of martyrdom: and not just the martyrdom of Romero but of hundreds and thousands of ordinary people who, throughout the ages, have offered their lives in defence of what they believe. For that is the essence of martyrdom: to give witness to the truth through the offering of one's life. In one of his early sermons as Archbishop, Romero explains what it means to offer one's life:

> To give one's life is not just being killed by someone; to give one's life is to have the spirit of martyrdom, to give through one's duty, in silence, in prayer, in the faithful performance of one's obligations, in that silence of daily life, to go on giving one's life, like the mother who, without fuss, with the simplicity of maternal martyrdom, gives birth, suckles her child, helps it grow and looks after it with love. This is to give one's life.[3]

---

[2] *La voz de los sin voz: La palabra viva de Monseñor Romero,* UCA Editores, 2ª Ed., 1986, p. 62 and p. 461.

[3] *Homilias,* 15 May 1977: Vol. I–II, p. 45.

What has perhaps changed in our day is the nature of the truth to which the modern martyr is called to give witness. As Karl Rahner has argued, the classical concept of martyrdom, which is fundamentally conditioned by the *odium fidei* (a hatred of the faith), needs to be widened to include those who have been killed by an *odium iustitiae* (a hatred of justice). And he cites Romero as an obvious example.[4]

For the Roman Catholic Church in Latin America, the turning point came in 1968 with the Second General Conference of Latin American Bishops at Medellín in Colombia. It was this conference that applied to the realities of the Third World the insights and directives of the Second Vatican Council which had ended only three years before. With its emphases on structural sin, institutionalized injustice, basic Christian communities and, though it did not use the expression, a preferential option for the poor, it launched large sectors of the Church on a new and mainly unchartered course. From being one of the three pillars of the establishment together with the military and the landowners, the Church in Latin America found itself, timidly at first but with increasing strength and conviction, confronting that establishment in the name of the poor and dispossessed whose 'deafening cry', as Medellín puts it, 'asks their pastors for a liberation that reaches them from nowhere else'.[5] The results were predictable: an increasing hostility from those whose vested interests were threatened, expressing itself in arrests, torture, banishment, assassination and the general persecution of a Church the wealthy and powerful no longer controlled and no longer cared to recognize.

Three Models of Persecution

A small book on *The Church in El Salvador*, published in 1982 after one of the bloodiest years of the war, distinguishes three models of persecution against the Church.[6] There is the historic model of a Church seeking to establish itself in non-Christian societies: the early Christians in the Roman catacombs or those in various mission countries such as China and Japan in the seventeenth or several African countries in the nineteenth centuries. Secondly, there is, or was, the persecution of the Church in the socialist and communist countries by totalitarian states demanding complete allegiance. The so-called 'underground' churches in China would still provide an example of this. And finally, the relatively new situation in Latin America which is unique

---

[4] Karl Rahner, Dimensiones del Martirio, *Concilium*, §183, Marzo 1983, pp. 321–324.
[5] *Medellín*, UCA Editores, 2ª Ed., 1985, p. 103: Doc 14, *Pobreza en la Iglesia*, §2.
[6] *La Iglesia en El Salvador*, UCA Editores, 2ª Ed., 1982, cf. pp. 18–20.

in that the persecution comes from governments that not only proclaim themselves Christian but also seek to maintain good relations with the institutional church and sometimes even claim to be acting in its name. For the persecution is not against the institution itself since freedom of religion and worship is still preserved, at least in theory. It is against those committed, as a direct result of their religion, to a search for greater social justice and the defence of basic human rights.

This was true not just in El Salvador but throughout Latin America where National Security States justified the use of absolute power to maintain the status quo and stamp out the so-called menace of international communism. Any call for change, especially for change aimed at helping marginalized groups take their rightful place in society, was immediately labelled subversive and ruthlessly suppressed. Wider geopolitical interests also came into play. Shortly after the Medellín Conference, Nelson Rockefeller made his famous whirlwind tour through twenty-two Latin American countries and concluded that, if the Latin American Church put into practice the agreements reached at Medellín, the interests of the United States in the region would be in danger.

Some years later this danger was spelt out in greater detail in the two Santa Fe Documents which strongly influenced US policies towards Latin America during the Reagan administrations. Liberation theology was identified as a threat to be countered, a policy of human rights should be abandoned in favour of one of political and ethical realism, and support was advocated for fundamentalist charismatic sects, often imported from the North, in order to undermine the work of the mainline churches. In the political sphere, unscrupulous dictators were maintained in power, military apparatuses financed and strengthened, corrupt elites protected, and massacres along with other human rights violations tolerated and on occasion covered up.

This was the general background against which Monseñor Romero began his three-year ministry as Archbishop of San Salvador. He was by no means the obvious choice for the job. Timid, retiring, hesitant, conservative in thought and action, his past record had not commended itself to the majority of priests in the diocese nor to his predecessor, Archbishop Chávez y González, retiring after thirty-eight years. He, and they, wanted Bishop Rivera Damas, auxiliary of San Salvador and a firm supporter of the post-Medellín Church. But Romero was the candidate of the Nuncio who had consulted the government, the military, business circles and the society ladies who felt he would be 'one of ours'.

When the announcement was made, there was an avalanche of protests and widespread dismay among the more progressive. Monseñor Ricardo Urioste, who was to become his Vicar General declared: 'I was in Chiltiupan on a course in rural development. Another priest said to me: 'Forget it! This man will put an end to all this!' I rushed back to San Salvador. I sent a telegram to Monseñor Chávez. Of farewell. And another to Rivera. Of sympathy. It was he we were hoping would be archbishop. To Monseñor Romero I sent nothing, I didn't congratulate him, it would not have been sincere on my part. I was profoundly disgusted.'[7] A well-known Jesuit, also destined to work closely with him later, did send a telegram of just two words: 'Lo lamento, Ibáñez' – 'I regret it, Ibáñez'.[8]

A Turning Point

The story of Romero's conversion, though he himself preferred to speak of rediscovering his roots, is well known but bears repetition. While its importance should not be exaggerated, the assassination, three weeks after Romero had taken over as Archbishop, of Rutilio Grande, a young Salvadoran Jesuit priest, together with an old man and a fifteen-year-old boy, as they were on their way to celebrate Mass in the small village church of El Paisnal some thirty miles north of the capital, had a profound and lasting effect on him. Romero and Rutilio had come to know each other ten years before when both were living in the diocesan seminary, Romero as secretary to the Bishops' Conference and Rutilio as teacher and prefect of the students.

As soon as he heard of the assassination, Romero left the city and went to the church in Aguilares where they had laid out the three bodies. There he celebrated Mass with the Jesuit Provincial and then, with peasants who had come in from many surrounding villages, spent part of the night in prayer and part seeking advice on what should be done. As he recounted afterwards, that night he read the Gospel message anew through the eyes of the poor and oppressed. He began to understand what Jesus has to say, and therefore what he as Archbishop should also be saying, to the despised, the persecuted and the underprivileged. As he put it later to César Jerez, the Jesuit Provincial: 'When I looked at Rutilio lying there dead, I thought: if they killed him for doing what he did, then I too have to walk the same path'.[9]

When morning came, he returned to the capital, summoned his priests and advisers and decided after long and sometimes difficult discussions, to boycott all state occasions and meetings with the president until an official investigation into Rutilio's death was carried out.

---

[7] María López Vigil, *Piezas para un Retrato*, UCA Editores, 3ª Ed., 1995, pp. 75–76.
[8] Ibid., p. 76.
[9] Ibid., p. 149.

It never was, and Romero all the time he was Archbishop never attended any state occasion, not even the swearing-in of the new president. He also decided to close all Catholic schools for three days, inviting both pupils and teachers to reflect on what had happened.

Finally, in the face of strong ecclesiastical opposition from the Papal Nuncio, he decided to suspend all Masses in the capital the following Sunday and celebrate just one Mass in the cathedral with all his priests, both as a sign of protest to the Government and of solidarity with Rutilio and the cause for which he died. Over one hundred and fifty priests concelebrated the Mass which was attended by an estimated 100,000 people, one of the biggest crowds ever seen in the country. And in the streets around the cathedral, long lines queued up to go to confession. For many, and not just Romero, it marked a turning point.

The rest, as the saying goes, is history. The pamphlet on *The Church in El Salvador*, already quoted above, speaks of 'a miracle which lasted three years'.[10] Romero, visibly growing in strength and conviction, became the defender of the oppressed, 'the voice of those who had no voice', the conscience of a nation. His Sunday sermons in the cathedral, which towards the end lasted one and a half hours, were, when the diocesan radio station was functioning, listened to by friend and foe alike throughout the country and by many abroad. By his enemies he was called an agitator, a communist, a false priest, an ambitious schemer out for himself. Some of the attacks, and this hurt him most, came from his fellow bishops. He recounts in his diary how Bishop Rivera came to tell him the other four bishops were preparing a secret document denouncing him to Rome in which they 'say I am politicised, accuse me of promoting a pastoral work with erroneous theological grounding – a whole series of accusations that completely impugn my ministry as a bishop'.[11] But he adds:

> In spite of how serious this is, I feel great peace. I acknowledge my deficiencies before God, but I believe that I have worked with goodwill and that I am not guilty of the serious things of which they accuse me. God will have the last word on this.

But Rome also lent an ear to the accusations. No less than three apostolic visitors were sent to examine him in a little over a year while the Congregation of Bishops, under Cardinal Baggio, seriously considered imposing on him an apostolic administrator with full powers to run the diocese. And it is common knowledge that, whereas he felt confirmed in his ministry after meeting Pope Paul VI, his first encounter with

---

[10] *La Iglesia en El Salvador*, op.cit., p. 35.
[11] *Archbishop Oscar Romero: A Shepherd's Diary*, Cincinnati, OH, St Anthony Messenger Press, 1993, p. 229: 18 May 1979.

Pope John Paul II left him sad and disheartened.

To the government and the military, Romero was a permanent threat, a thorn in the side, a subversive voice that had to be silenced. The radio station was twice blown up and repaired, I am happy to say, by contributions from Christians in the United Kingdom. But, in the end, the powerful and wealthy saw no other solution but to silence him for good. He was shot on the evening of Monday 24 March 1980 while offering Mass in the small chapel of the Divine Providence hospital where he lived, just a day after he had made a strong appeal to the ranks in the army and police forces to listen to their consciences and stop obeying immoral commands from their officers to torture and kill fellow Salvadorans.

The official investigation into the crime was a farce that was never even completed since the judge in charge of the case resigned and had to flee the country after an attempt was made on his life in his own home. But the Truth Commission, set up by the United Nations in accordance with the Peace Agreements, placed the blame squarely on Major Roberto D'Aubuisson, proven coordinator of death squads who later became President of the National Assembly and founder of ARENA, the current ruling political party in the country. Little did those responsible realise that Romero's voice and presence would live on and that today his word and example still give hope and courage to thousands of Salvadorans and to people all over the world like ourselves gathered here this afternoon.

'A Saint Within Our Grasp'

I have often asked myself what it is that makes Romero such an attractive and compelling figure. We discussed this in my parish on the eighteenth anniversary of his assassination. We spoke of his humility, his ordinariness, his humanity, his transparent honesty, his courage. We felt that here was a saint within our grasp or, as one put it, almost at our own level. He himself said about his appointment:

> I came to you weak and fearful. God knows how hard it was for me also to come here to the capital. How timid I have felt before you, except for the support that you, as a church, have given me! You have made your bishop a sign of Christianity.[12]

Monseñor Urioste has explained how Romero, at the age of sixty, went back to school. But his teachers were not university professors or

---

[12] *Homilias*, 5 February 1978: Vol. III, p. 191.

professional theologians. They were the simple uneducated peasants who flocked into his office from all over the country to explain their situation to him and seek his understanding and support. Coralia Godoy, who occasionally helped him as secretary, explains what confusion this caused both in the office and with his timetable. She tried to bring some order by introducing a new system but he eventually rejected it, saying:

> That won't work because I also have my priorities. I am always going to receive first any peasant who comes here, whatever the day or hour, whether I am in another meeting or not.... My brother bishops all have cars. The priests can take the bus and have no problem waiting. But the peasants? They have come walking for miles, in great danger, and often without eating.[13]

Another engaging trait in Romero was his readiness to admit mistakes. A notable example were two visits he made to the Christian community in Zacamil, a poor district on the city outskirts. The first, in 1972 when he was auxiliary in San Salvador, was at the invitation of Pedro Declercq, a Belgian missionary, ostensibly to celebrate Mass but really to discuss a statement of the Bishops' Conference, signed by Romero, which condoned the sacking by the army of the national university in which huge damage was done, many people beaten and some eighty killed.[14] Mass began but at the moment of homily the discussion started on the university, Father Pedro and the people condemning the violence and injustice, Romero defending the army's action because of communist infiltration among the students and quoting a conservative Chilean bishop in his support. The discussion became very heated with accusations flying. Romero eventually said: 'The work you do here is political, not pastoral. You didn't invite me to a Mass but to a subversive meeting.' At this point, Fr Pedro took off his alb and stole, and threw them on the altar saying: 'We cannot celebrate Mass in these conditions. There will be no Mass.' Romero gathered up his documents and left unaccompanied.

Six years later, as Sister Noémi recounts, he returned for a welcome celebration prepared for him as the new archbishop.[15]

> Nobody thought to say a word about the previous occasion but he started straight off with it. 'You remember, we couldn't even celebrate the Eucharist that day for the row there was between us.' We

---

[13] *Piezas*, op.cit., pp. 139–140.
[14] Ibid., pp. 43–46.
[15] Ibid., pp. 249–250.

remained silent, holding our breath. The music was turned off and the man opening the soft drinks dropped a bottle. He went on: 'I remember it well and today, as your pastor, I want to tell you I now understand what happened and that I publicly admit before all of you my error. I was mistaken; you were right and you gave me that day a lesson in the faith, a lesson in what the Church is. Please forgive me for what took place.' We burst into tears, young and old alike, and then tremendous applause. The music was turned on and the festivities continued.

Personal hesitations and Romero's reliance on others for advice and guidance, in no way diminished the coherence or power of his message or the fact that it was *his* message. He himself decried 'a preaching that doesn't get under anyone's skin ... very nice, pious considerations that don't bother anyone'.[16] The true preaching of Christ should awaken, enlighten and discomfort the sinner. 'Naturally,' he goes on: 'such preaching must meet conflict, must spoil what is miscalled prestige, must disturb, must be persecuted. It cannot get along with the powers of darkness and sin.'[17] He was acutely conscious of his role as a prophet, or rather as spokesman of a whole people that was prophetic, whose task is to let the spirit speak through them and him. Hence, in addition to consulting with many and listening to the voices of the poor, he spent hours on his knees, preparing his homilies in the presence of God during the small hours of the morning. Describing one of the early sermons, a witness reports: 'At the beginning of Mass, I noticed Monseñor Romero nervous, pale, perspiring. And when the homily started, he seemed slow, without his usual eloquence, as if doubting to enter the door history and God were opening for him. But after five minutes, I felt that the spirit of God had descended on him.'[18] This was the reason Romero had such confidence that: 'though my voice will disappear, my word, which is Christ, will remain in the hearts of those who have wished to receive it'.[19]

Preferential Option for the Poor

What was the core of his message? As he repeated many times, it was no more but also no less than the call of the Latin American Bishops at Medellín, a call they confirmed in their Third General Conference at

---

[16] *Homilias*, 16 April 1978: Vol. IV, p. 162.
[17] Ibid., 22 January 1978: Vol. III, p. 164.
[18] *Piezas*, op.cit., pp. 108–109.
[19] *Homilias*, 17 December 1978: Vol. VI, p. 41.

Puebla in Mexico, which he himself attended in 1979. He fully identified himself with their call for:

> The conversion of the whole Church to a preferential option for the poor with a view to their integral liberation.[20]

It was a call he once described as 'the subversive witness of the Beatitudes which have turned everything upside down'.[21] In a country torn by violence and bloodshed, Romero saw quite clearly where the root of the problem lay: 'I will not tire of declaring that if we really want an effective end to the violence, we must remove the violence that lies at the root of all violence: structural violence, social injustice, the exclusion of citizens from the management of the country, repression. All this is what constitutes the primal cause, from which the rest flows naturally.'[22] Hence, he concluded, it is the duty of the Church and all its members:

> to know the mechanisms that generate poverty, to struggle for a more just world, to support the workers and peasants in their claims and in their right to organise, and to be close to the people.[23]

It follows that a preferential option for the poor is an invitation not only to the Church as a whole, but to every follower of Christ, rich and poor alike. He declared:

> This is the commitment of being a Christian, to follow Christ in his incarnation. If Christ, the God of majesty, became a lowly human and lived with the poor and even died on a cross like a slave, our Christian faith should also be lived in the same way. The Christian who does not want to live this commitment of solidarity with the poor is not worthy to be called Christian.[24]

For, he argued:

> the poor have shown the Church the real way to go. A Church that does not join the poor in order to speak out from the side of the poor against the injustices committed against them is not the true Church of Jesus Christ.[25]

---

[20] *Puebla: La evangelización en el presente y en el futuro de América Latina*, UCA Editores, 3ª Ed., 1985, p. 233:§1134.
[21] *Homilias*, 11 May 1978: Vol. IV, p. 226.
[22] Ibid., 23 September 1979: Vol. VII, p. 294.
[23] Ibid., 6 August 1979: vol. VII, p. 153.
[24] Ibid., 17 February 1980: Vol. VIII, p. 240.
[25] Ibid., 17 February 1980: Vol. VIII, p. 233.

Romero recognized that his own brief as Archbishop followed directly from this: 'If I denounce and condemn injustice, it is because this is my duty as pastor of an oppressed and downtrodden people. The Gospel enjoins me to do this and, in its name, I am ready to go before the courts, to prison and to death.'[26]

Three 'Idols of Society'

Clearly such a stand means conflict. The voice of those who have no voice can hardly avoid being a voice against those who have too much voice. In his Fourth Pastoral Letter, Romero identifies three modern 'idols of society': the absolutization of wealth and private property, the absolutization of national security, and the absolutization of political organizations.[27] It is the duty of the Church to unmask and denounce these idols in the name of the Gospel, a task that will necessarily provoke opposition. And he warns: 'A Church that suffers no persecution but enjoys the privileges and support of the things of the earth – beware – it is not the true Church of Jesus Christ.'[28]

In fact Romero was able to rejoice that priests and religious were being killed alongside workers and peasants since it was a sign of authenticity, of God's blessing.

> I am glad, brothers and sisters, that our Church is persecuted precisely for its preferential option for the poor and for trying to become incarnate in the interest of the poor and for saying to all the people, to rulers, to the rich and powerful: if you do not become poor, if you do not concern yourselves for the poverty of our people as though they were your own family, you will not be able to save society.[29]

And, of course, Romero himself gave the outstanding example of this option. At an important moment in his life, he made a public vow of fidelity to the people: 'I want to assure you – and I ask your prayers to be faithful to this promise – that I will not abandon my people but together with them I will run all the risks that my ministry demands.'[30] So, when the military came to offer him personal protection, he was able to reply: 'The shepherd does not want security when they give no security to his flock.'[31]

[26] Ibid., 14 May 1978: Vol. IV, p. 247.
[27] *La voz de los sin voz*, op.cit., pp. 145–149: §42–51.
[28] *Homilías*, 11 March 1979: Vol. VI, p. 190.
[29] Ibid., 15 July 1979: Vol. VII, p. 79.
[30] Ibid., 11 November 1979: Vol. VII, p. 432.
[31] Ibid., 22 July 1979: Vol. VII, p. 112.

The years have passed. Romero, like so many other martyrs in Latin America, but perhaps more so than most, has truly risen again in the hearts of the people who have long since canonized him as St Romero of the Americas. Today the situation is different and his country is no longer at war. But the poor are still poor, still marginalized, still suffering, and more numerous than ever. The experts estimate that 170 million Latin Americans are living below the poverty line and a further 170 million in what they describe as 'chronic poverty' or 'misery'. And most Latin American countries are now caught up in neo-liberal models of development which rely on globalization, privatization and deregulation. The wealthy countries, represented by the Group of Seven and the international financial institutions they control, impose harsh structural adjustment programmes on debt-ridden and defenceless nations who have no option but to accept and endeavour to implement them, even though knowing full well that most of their own citizens will be the first to suffer.

The results are predictable: the dehumanizing of people, of workers, of the marginalized; the cutting back of essential social services especially in health and education; the preferring of safety nets to comprehensive programmes; the submission of morality to the dictates of the market; the promotion of individualism, consumerism and structural unemployment. It is argued that in the long run the lot of the people will improve. But, as Lord Keynes once pointed out, in the long run we are all dead.

Relevant and Divisive Message

Romero's message is therefore just as relevant today as it was twenty years ago. Unfortunately it is also just as divisive. Though hard to credit, Bishop Revelo, once his auxiliary, declared in the presence of the Pope during his visit to El Salvador in 1996, that Romero was responsible for the death of 70,000 Salvadorans. And there are those who seek today, as his canonization process slowly grinds through Roman wheels, to water down his message, to weaken his image. But, as Bishop Juan Gerardi's recent and cruel assassination in Guatemala has shown so clearly, the same forces of evil are still present and active in Latin American society. Like Romero, Bishop Gerardi was an uncompromising defender of human rights, seeking to expose the truth about the long and horrific persecution of indigenous peoples at the hands of the armed forces, a persecution he himself had witnessed and suffered as Bishop both in Verapaz and Santa Cruz del Quiché. Once again a voice that knew too much had to be silenced by those willing to murder with impunity if they considered their own personal interests at stake.

And, to mention only El Salvador, things were no different in the case of the six Jesuit martyrs of the UCA together with their housekeeper and her daughter, of the three American sisters and the lay missionary who worked with them, of Bishop Joaquin Ramos and eleven diocesan priests, and, as Jon Sobrino has put it, of

> many other pastoral ministers and lay missionaries, delegates and ministers of the Word, catechists and sacristans, Caritas workers and human rights groups; many Protestant brothers and sisters, pastors and ministers, deacons and preachers; countless campesinos and Amerindians, workers and students, teachers and journalists, nurses, doctors and intellectuals; all persecuted and murdered for the reign of God.[32]

Responding to the Pope's invitation in his Letter on the Third Millennium, Christian communities and parishes throughout the country, and doubtless in many other countries too, are presently engaged in drawing up lists of their martyrs with the idea of compiling a twentieth-century Martyrology to be presented in official celebrations planned for the year 2000.[33] The motive is neither revenge nor recrimination, but a recognition that *Sanguis martyrum, semen christianorum*[34] ('The blood of martyrs is the seed of Christians'). As the second millennium draws to a close, the Church has again become a church of martyrs whose blood will give birth, hope and guidance to the Christians of a new millennium. Of this vast array of modern martyrs, most of whom will remain largely unknown and never be formally canonized, Romero stands out as a sort of proto-type or model. Jon Sobrino again writes:

> In this life he was the voice of those without voice. In his death, he is the name of those who have no name.[35]

'He Belongs to Us All'

The fact that the Anglican Church has decided to honour a Roman Catholic bishop in what is one of its central and most venerable shrines is proof that Romero has now become the common property of all, a universal saint for our time. A visitor from France told us: 'I have bad

---

[32] Jon Sobrino, *Spirituality of Liberation*, Orbis Books, Maryknoll, New York, 1988, p. 88.
[33] See *Tertio Millennio Adveniente*, Pope John Paul II, §37.
[34] *Apologeticus*, Tertullian, §50.
[35] *Monseñor Romero*, Jon Sobrino, UCA Editores, 3ª Ed., 1995, pp. 63–64.

news for you. Romero is no longer yours. He belongs to us all.' And it is true that today his memory is revered by Christians of every denomination, by non-Christians, marxists and even agnostics. His official canonization by the Roman Catholic Church will confirm what is already a world-wide recognition that here was an honest and upright man whose life and death have much to say that our modern world needs to hear.

I hope and pray that his statue, now gracing the west façade of this great abbey, will recall not just his person or the sacrifice of his life, but what he has to say about being a genuine follower of Christ today. I believe his message is for all of us. He doesn't mince his words. 'It is inconceivable to call oneself a Christian without making, like Christ, a preferential option for the poor.'[36] And again: 'A Christian who defends unjust situations is no longer a Christian.'[37] Or: 'The wealthy person who kneels before his money, even though he goes to Mass, is an idolater and not a Christian.'[38] And a warning: 'It is a caricature of love to cover over with alms what is lacking in justice, to patch over with an appearance of benevolence when social justice is missing.'[39] And finally a pertinent question:

> Do you want to know if your Christianity is genuine? Here is the touch-stone: Whom do you get along with? Who are those who criticise you? Who are those who do not accept you? Who are those who flatter you? Know from that what Christ said once: 'I have come not to bring peace, but division'. There will be division even in the same family, because some want to live more comfortably by the world's principles, those of power and money. But others have embraced the call of Christ and must reject all that cannot be just in the world.[40]

Because of his forthright stand, the example he gave and the sort of person he was, the poor in El Salvador and many other countries still look to him as their saviour, their father. I would like to end this brief talk, in which I have tried to bring Romero's spirit to life through his own words, with the testimony of a witness who went into the cathedral early one morning to pray at his tomb.

> One winter's morning, the sky dark with rain, a man in rags, covered in dust, his shirt in shreds, was carefully cleaning Romero's

---

[36] *Homilias*, 9 September 1979: Vol. VII, p. 236.
[37] Ibid., 16 September 1979: Vol. VII, p. 262.
[38] Ibid., 11 November 1979: Vol. VII, p. 426.
[39] Ibid., 12 April 1979: Vol. VI, p. 276.
[40] Ibid., 13 November 1977: Vol. I–II, p. 323.

tomb, using one of his rags. It was barely light but he was already active and awake. And though the rag was filthy with grease and age, he was giving a polish to the stone. On finishing, he smiled contentedly. At that early hour he had seen no one. And no one had seen him except me. When he went out onto the street, I felt I had to speak with him. 'You, why are you doing that?' 'Doing what?' he replied. 'Cleaning Monseñor's tomb.' 'Because he was my father.' 'How was that?' 'I'm no more than a poor beggar. Sometimes I'm a carrier in the market with a cart, other times I beg, and sometimes I spend everything on liquor and lie senseless in the gutter. But I never lose hope. I had a father. He made me feel somebody. Because people like me, he loved and didn't turn up his nose. He spoke to us, touched us, asked us questions. He trusted us. He let it be seen the love he had for me. Like the love of a father. That's why I clean his tomb. As a son would.'[41]

---

[41] *Piezas*, op.cit., p. 398.

The Cook, the Dog, the Priest and His Lover: Who Killed Bishop Gerardi and Why?

JUDITH ESCRIBANO

1. Introduction

Bishop Juan Gerardi was killed on 26 April 1998, just two days after presenting the Catholic Church's truth commission report, *Nunca Más*.[1] During the presentation ceremony, Bishop Gerardi said:

> The report has a pastoral aim, it is a service of the Church to society and to the victims [of human rights violations and the civil war]. . . . We want to contribute to the building of a new and different country. For that reason, we are recovering the memory of the people. The path has been, and continues to be, full of risks, but the construction of the Kingdom of the Lord is risky, and can only be built by those who have the strength to confront those risks.[2]

Since Bishop Gerardi's assassination, the Catholic Church has faced many risks, but has maintained the strength to continue its pastoral and human rights work. If killing Bishop Gerardi was intended to silence the Church, the assassins were not successful.

Despite various allegations, leads, arrests, autopsies, exhumations and suggested motives, three years on, there has still been no convic-

---

[1] For more information on *Nunca Más*, see Chapter 6 by Marcela López Levy and the English summary of REMHI's report *Guatemala: Never Again!* Maryknoll, NY, Orbis Books, London, Catholic Institute for International Relations and Latin America Bureau, 1999.

[2] See Gerardi's final speech on 24 April 1998 at Guatemala City cathedral in J. Gerardi, *Monseñor Juan Gerardi: Testigo Fiel de Dios*, Guatemala City, Conferencia Episcopal de Guatemala, 1999, pp. 182–183 (own translation).

tion for the brutal assassination. The nature of Gerardi's human rights work and the timing of the assassination point to a political killing. However, many in positions of authority – the public prosecutors, the government, the police and the army – have consistently come up with alternative theories, in an attempt to prove that the murder was a common crime.

We may speculate as to who killed Gerardi and why, but given the long history of impunity in Guatemala, we may have to accept that – as with the assassination of Archbishop Romero of El Salvador (24 March 1980) – we may never see the convictions of those responsible. This chapter details some of the theories about who killed Bishop Gerardi and why. The more I investigated the life of Bishop Gerardi, the more I wondered how he had been allowed to live for so long.

Within Guatemala, the Catholic Church is one of the major pillars of power, along with the private sector and the army: statements made by Catholic bishops criticising government policy make national headlines. In a thorough introduction to the social and political culture of Guatemala, author Trish O'Kane states:

> Throughout the 1990s, the social vocation of the Catholic Church was demonstrated in its pioneering work defending human rights through the Archbishop's Human Rights Office (ODHAG). The [Guatemalan] Bishops' Conference has been a prominent promoter of social justice and active in the peace process....[3]

Given that Gerardi was a representative of the Catholic Church, headed ODHAG, often criticized government policy and took part in the peace process, it is no wonder that he became a target for assassination.

Bishop Gerardi had a long history of working in the Catholic Church – '... he believed what he preached and practised what he believed'.[4] For the vast majority of his pastoral ministry, his work centred on the defence of human rights of peasant workers and indigenous peoples. It was said of him: '... his commitment to the Gospel, the Church and the people did not waiver in his fifty-two years as a priest. In short, he gave his life for the Gospel and for the people.'[5]

Throughout the thirty-six-year civil war in Guatemala (1960–1996), Bishop Gerardi dedicated his life to defending the social, economic and human rights of poor communities; the majority indigenous population

---

[3] Trish O'Kane, *In Focus: Guatemala – A Guide to the People, Politics and Culture*, London, Latin America Bureau, 1999, p. 60.

[4] Grupo Internacional de Consulta y Apoyo al Retorno and World Council of Churches (GRICAR and WCC), *The Assassination of Monsignor Gerardi*, Special Report I, 4 May 1998, Guatemala City, GRICAR/WCC, 1998.

[5] Ibid.

and the unarmed innocent civilians caught up in the middle of the conflict. Those who wished to maintain the status quo – such as large landowners, the military and the government – would often resort to violence to get rid of those who stood in their way. To those in power, Gerardi was a threat to the status quo and an obstacle that needed removing.

2. Biography and History

Juan Gerardi Conedera was born on 27 December 1924, the son of Laura Conedera and Manuel Gerardi. His grandparents were Italian immigrants. He was ordained a priest in 1946 and was assigned various parishes in the metropolitan area of Guatemala City until 1967.

From 1967–1974, Gerardi was the Bishop of Baja and Alta Verapaz in the centre of Guatemala. He worked closely with indigenous peoples, learning about their cultures and helping to train them to become community leaders by means of the first Indigenous Pastorate, which he created. His aim was to understand the indigenous people to whom he had been sent; to get to know the worlds of the Q'eqchí, Pokonchí, Kichí, and Ixil. He believed that by studying their diverse situations and needs, he would be much better suited to developing a work and pastoral plan with them.

At the same time, the guerrilla movement was starting to mobilize within Guatemala, while outside the country, the Second Vatican Council (1962–65) and the Latin American Bishops' meeting (CELAM II) in Medellín in 1968 had been held. Such meetings were characterized by impassioned debates about liberation theology: vocal sectors of the progressive church reinforced the 'preferential option for the poor' and were outspoken in their demands for social justice.

In 1974, Pope Paul VI named Juan Gerardi as the Bishop of Santa Cruz del Quiché, at this point in the civil war the most impoverished and violent region in the country. From 1978, the country was ruled by the virulently anti-Communist, brutal assassin, General Lucas García. Within the context of the military government's counter-insurgency operations, Lucas García's targets were not only civilians – who were seen as potential supporters of the guerrilla movement – but also certain sectors of the Catholic Church, whose belief in the 'preferential option for the poor' was considered a threat to the status quo. Gerardi tried to reason with the military, asking them to cease their attacks against the local population, but they would not listen.

Following countless massacres and forced disappearances targeting the civilian population and the assassination of thirteen priests and catechists in just one eighteen-month period in 1979–1980, Gerardi was forced to close the diocese of Quiché in June 1980, shortly after escaping an attempted ambush. On leaving Quiché, Gerardi said: 'It is not possible to work here anymore. They will kill all of us.'[6] Writing twenty years later, the Archbishop's Human Rights Office stated that through this move: 'Bishop Gerardi's heart was broken in two through anxiety and pain. He was seen to cry several times; not only during the burial of martyred priests, but also when he had to leave Santa Cruz del Quiché'.[7]

Bishop Gerardi was widely respected within the Catholic Church in Guatemala: he was named President of the Guatemalan Bishops' Conference (CEG) from 1972–74, again from 1974–76, and it was in this capacity that he attended the Synod on the Family in the Vatican in August 1980. While there, he took the opportunity to inform Pope John Paul II about what was happening in Quiché and throughout Guatemala. Horrified, the Pope decided to write a letter of support to the CEG. The Pope's language was more direct than usual. He spoke of the dramatic 'scale of suffering and death that presses down, giving no sign of letting up, upon so many families and church communities, deprived not only of many catechists, but also of priests who have died in obscure circumstances, at times in vile and treacherous ways.'[8] Pope John Paul II also decided that the population of Quiché would be best served and protected if Bishop Gerardi were to return to serve the people, so he sent Gerardi back to Guatemala with the letter for the CEG.

By the time Bishop Gerardi arrived at Guatemala City airport, General Lucas García had already been warned about the content of the letter. Offended that the Pope was questioning his authority, he prevented Gerardi from entering the country. Gerardi was forced to spend the next four years in exile, mainly in Costa Rica. While this gave him the opportunity to continue condemning successive military governments from a relatively safe distance, Gerardi was disappointed not to be able to serve his people from within Guatemala itself.[9] ODHAG described Gerardi as representing: 'a part of the Church which ... does not flinch from telling the truth and which awakens the conscience of Christians to injustice, deception, death and exploitation.'[10]

When conditions were safe for his return – following democratic elections in 1984 – Gerardi returned to Guatemala. He was named one of the Auxiliary Bishops of Guatemala City; helped create the

---

[6] Philip Berryman, *Christians in Guatemala's Struggle*, London, CIIR, 1984, p. 54.
[7] 'Monseñor Gerardi, su vida y sus obras', in ODHAG, *Antecedentes*, Guatemala City, ODHAG, nd. (own translation).
[8] Berryman, *Christians in Guatemala's Struggle*, p. 55.
[9] General Lucas García (1978–1982) was overthrown by General Ríos Montt (1982–83), who was also overthrown in a military coup by General Mejía Victores (1983–84).
[10] 'Monseñor Gerardi, su vida y sus obras' (own translation).

Archbishop's Human Rights Office, and was then named its Coordinator. During the early 1990s, he was delegated by the CEG to participate in the peace talks between the government and the guerrilla forces. And in 1995, ODHAG asked him to head the Catholic Church's truth commission investigations, REMHI (the Recovery of Historical Memory Project). Meanwhile, Gerardi continued to condemn civilian governments in Guatemala for human rights violations against its own people at the annual UN Commission for Human Rights in Geneva.

It was Bishop Gerardi's belief that: 'democracy is impossible where hunger and misery are present.'[11] He also believed that the Church had a moral obligation to act on behalf of marginalized people; to assist those living in poverty; to condemn human rights violations; and to be prepared to suffer the same fate as those who suffered any form of injustice.

On 24 April 1998, Bishop Gerardi presented REMHI's report *Nunca Más*, which attributed 80 per cent of the crimes committed during the civil war to the military. Two days later, he was bludgeoned to death.

3. Assassination and Investigation

The 26th of April had just been like any other day – Bishop Gerardi had lunch with the REMHI team to celebrate the report's success, but also to warn Edgar Gutiérrez, the coordinator of REMHI and Ronalth Ochaeta, the Executive Director of ODHAG, to take care, since they had received anonymous threats as a result of their work. He had dinner with his family. Given that Gerardi had also received threats, his family members followed his car home to make sure he arrived safely. They waited for him to enter the garage and then left. Little did they know, the assassins were waiting inside.

The force of the blows of the cement block was so severe, it was the equivalent of being knocked down by a vehicle travelling at 100 km per hour.[12] Juan Gerardi's face was so disfigured, he could only be identified by the Bishop's ring on his finger. There were abrasions on his left thumb, illustrating that he had tried to defend himself. After being knocked unconscious, he had been dragged some five metres further into the garage, where he was hit seventeen times in the face with the same piece of concrete. The assassin, or assassins, entered Gerardi's home and ransacked Gerardi's office, although later it was reported that nothing had been stolen.

First reports suggested that the body was discovered two hours later

---

[11] 'La construcción de la paz en Guatemala a partir de los temas de negociación' (Speech by Bishop Gerardi in Guatemala in 1994) in *Monseñor Juan Gerardi: Testigo Fiel de Dios*, Guatemala City, CEG, 1999, p. 99.

[12] 'Agonizó dos horas', *Al Día*, 28 April 1998.

by Father Mario Orantes, the parish priest with whom Gerardi shared the house. He claims to have woken up and seen that the light in the garage was on. On discovering Gerardi's body, he telephoned a fellow church member who arrived at the scene of the crime with two other people. They then called the police, who arrived minutes later. The Public Ministry was placed in charge of investigations.[13]

Juan Gerardi's telephone bill showed that a phone call had been made to the Presidential High Command (EMP) just minutes after the supposed time of the crime.[14] Although they originally denied it, it was later revealed that at least two members of the EMP also appeared on the scene just minutes after the police arrived.[15]

Although the crime was made to look like the result of a botched burglary, no item of value was taken: Gerardi's wallet and ring were left untouched. At the scene of the crime, there was complete lack of control by the responsible authorities: firemen, police, journalists, private individuals, human rights activists, EMP members and the public prosecutor all arrived on the scene, but the area was never properly cordoned off; hence vital evidence at the scene of the crime was disturbed.

In the hours and days immediately after the crime, there was widespread national and international condemnation of Gerardi's assassination, with the majority of people suspecting that it had been due to the Bishop's work with REMHI. The European Union – with the UK holding the presidency – issued a declaration on 30 April 1998, expressing condolences and encouraging 'all Guatemalans not to let the murder distract them from full implementation of the peace accords.'[16]

Pope John Paul II sent a special letter to be read at Bishop Gerardi's Mass. As well as condemning the assassination as an act of violence against peace, against the Gospel and against the nation, the letter held out hope that the assassination would have some redeeming purpose for

---

[13] The Public Ministry (Ministerio Público/MP) is the state prosecutors' office; it appoints prosecutors to criminal cases. It is a notoriously inefficient part of the judiciary. At the time of writing, three prosecutors had been appointed to this case and still no conviction had been made.

[14] The Presidential High Command (Estado Militar Presidencial/EMP) is a military intelligence unit attached to the presidency. It was supposed to have been abolished as part of the 1996 Peace Accords, but – at the time of writing – is still in existence. The current president, Alfonso Portillo, claims that he will abolish it and has refused to use them as bodyguards during official events.

[15] The house is in the San Sebastián parish of Zone 1 of Guatemala City, just three blocks from the main square and even less from the National Palace, the official presidential residence and accompanying military installations, including the EMP.

[16] Declaration by the NGO Unit of the European Union, issued on 30 April 1998 (received in an internal Christian Aid memo on 18 May 1998 from the Programme Funding and Support Team, which works with the EU).

the nation: 'I hope that this crime – which has cost the life of a true servant of peace and an untiring ambassador for harmony among Guatemalans - will clearly show the uselessness of violence'.[17]

Like Archbishop Romero before him, Bishop Gerardi had been the voice of the voiceless. For those who had been afraid to speak out, the Catholic Church and the REMHI investigation had guaranteed anonymity and a chance to tell their own story; an opportunity to recall their memories; a chance to gain some kind of relief and reconciliation by telling the truth – it was the first step towards justice. Through his assassination, Gerardi became - like Archbishop Romero – the named of the nameless and a martyr to the cause.

Almost immediately after the initial condemnation of the killing and accusations of political assassination, the state apparatus kicked into gear – the public prosecutor, the police and the military all appeared determined to prove that this was merely a common crime. The Mayor of Guatemala City (from the ruling political party), Oscar Berger, told the press that 'this is not a political crime, this is nothing more than the product of a sick mind'.[18] Meanwhile, the Minister of the Interior, Rodolfo Mendoza, stated that: 'I cannot qualify this as a political crime.'[19]

President Alvaro Arzú formed a special commission made up of government representatives to investigate the assassination and invited CEG and ODHAG to each send two representatives to the commission. However, the bishops refused to participate, stating that it was 'not the mission of bishops, nor would [it] be good for the strengthening of democracy'.[20] Meanwhile, ODHAG announced that it would employ its own investigative and legal team to ensure a thorough investigation, which would hopefully lead to an independent prosecution.

As early as 28 April 1998, the Guatemalan press suggested that 'retired military officers who took part in the internal armed conflict between 1978 and 1984' were responsible for the crime.[21] In an apparent attempt to protect the military's impunity, the government authorities instead pointed the finger of blame at the cook, the dog, the priest and his lover.

Anxious to be seen to be doing something concrete, the police were swift to arrest the first of many suspects. Two homeless men who were camped nearby Gerardi's house on the night of the murder identified Carlos Vielman, an alcoholic man who sometimes slept in the park near

---

[17] Pope John Paul II quoted in GRICAR/WCC, 'The Assassination of Monsignor Juan Gerardi'.
[18] 'Gobierno condena el asesinato de Gerardi', *El Periodico*, 28 April 1998.
[19] GRICAR/WCC, 'The Assassination of Monsignor Juan Gerardi'.
[20] GRICAR/WCC, 'The Assassination of Monsignor Juan Gerardi'.
[21] 'Militares retirados, en la mira' in *Siglo XXI*, 28 April 1998.

the Bishop's house. Although Vielman had no motive for killing Gerardi, and the only evidence was the witness reports of these two men, the public prosecution maintained that they had their man.

However, Bishop Gerardi was killed by a blow to the head with a large cement block and Vielman had a disability in his right arm making it impossible for him to lift heavy objects. Furthermore, Gerardi was 1.85 metres tall and Vielman 1.55 metres tall, making it virtually impossible for him to strike the Bishop's head with a heavy object. Vielman also had an alibi – at the time of the assassination, he was seen drinking in a bar in another part of the city until he fell asleep there.

However, the public prosecutor, Otto Ardón, detained Vielman for ninety days – the maximum period allowed without prosecution – before releasing him without charge. Days later, with 150 heavily armed policemen in tow, Ardón arrested the priest with whom Juan Gerardi had shared a home.

Father Mario Orantes, was arrested for murder: the alleged motive being 'a crime of passion'. It was suggested that Bishop Gerardi and Father Orantes had been having an affair – Gerardi had wanted to end it, so Orantes killed him. It was also rumoured that the Bishop had caught the priest in bed with a male lover and they had killed the Bishop in order to prevent him from telling anyone. There is no evidence to suggest that Bishop Gerardi and Father Orantes were having an affair or that Juan Gerardi was homosexual.

The public prosecutor also arrested the cook, Margarita López, who had worked at the parish house for twenty-two years. She was arrested as an accomplice, having swiftly cleaned up the scene of the crime before the police had a chance to complete their initial investigations. López originally claimed that she was ordered to do so by a representative of the Public Ministry. In a later plea, she claimed that she had been ordered to clear up the scene of the murder by Father Orantes.

And so on to the dog. Baloo, a German Shepherd belonging to Father Orantes, was also arrested as an accomplice to the crime. Otto Ardón suggested that Father Orantes had trained Baloo to stand up on its back legs in order to bite Gerardi to death, despite the fact that Baloo had arthritis in its back and tests proved that it could not stand on its hind legs alone. Undeterred, Ardón drafted in an expert, the Spanish anthropologist Dr José Reverte: 'We will bring a wise man from Spain because they can't accuse him of partiality nor of being in favour of one or the other groups'.[22] This 'wise man' insisted that

---

[22] GRICAR/WCC, 'The Gerardi Case: The Continuing Crisis of Human Rights in Guatemala' (Special Report III, 17 October 1998; Guatemala City, GRICAR/WCC, 1998).

Baloo had killed the Bishop – before he had even seen the Bishop's body and before he had even set foot in the country.

In order to prove his theory Reverte insisted that Gerardi's body be exhumed. Gerardi's family and ODHAG agreed – on condition that two experts appointed by ODHAG, could observe the second autopsy. Reverte pointed out two holes in Gerardi's' skull claiming that they were consistent with Baloo's teeth marks. He even produced a cast of the dog's jaw and a photo of the skull to show that the holes matched the dog's teeth.

However, one of ODHAG's experts – an expert on photographs and animal bites – pointed out that a dog could not bite with its top teeth only and showed that there were no marks consistent with a bottom row of teeth. Furthermore, he illustrated that Reverte had blown up the photo of the skull by twenty-five per cent, while leaving the cast of the teeth the original size.

ODHAG then publicly stated what they had known all along, and what they had quietly tried to warn the prosecutors – Reverte's evidence could not be trusted nor could it be seen as impartial. He had originally been invited to participate in the investigations by President Cristiani of El Salvador, who was anxious to prove that his security forces had not committed atrocities against innocent civilians. But he had been removed from the investigations into the massacre of El Mozote in El Salvador in 1993, since he alone maintained that the army could not have carried out the massacre.

An ageing and infirm Baloo was eventually released into the care of Father Orantes' parents. Car stickers declaring 'Free Baloo' can still be seen on the streets of Guatemala.

Guatemala City Auxiliary Bishop, Mario Ríos Montt – who replaced Gerardi as head of ODHAG – stated: 'It is time to put an end to this soap opera'.[23] Fortunately, a new public prosecutor and a new judge were appointed and they appeared to be determined to investigate the more plausible political motivation theory. In order for us to do the same, we must remember the contents of Gerardi's biography and the historical context within which Gerardi's life is set.

4. Chronicle of a Death Foretold

Bishop Juan Gerardi had been an outspoken defender of human rights in Guatemala throughout his pastoral career. He spoke up for those who dared not speak and he angered those in power. And he was killed.

---

[23] Paul Jeffery, 'Little Headway Made in Bishop's Murder', *Latinamerica Press*, Vol. 30 No. 32, 3 September 1998.

It is difficult not to make a connection between these facts. Just a few days after the assassination, Mauricio López Bonillo, former assistant to the Minister of Defence (and now retired from the military) stated: 'Curiously, common crime has eliminated prominent Guatemalans in historic moments that put those in power in jeopardy, a curiosity that the law of probabilities would discard as impossible without thinking twice.'[24]

It is also difficult not to see Gerardi's assassination as a threat to the peace process: throughout the thirty-six-year civil war, not one bishop had ever been murdered in Guatemala. And yet, once the peace accord was signed, a bishop who had spent his life pleading for peace was brutally assassinated. While Archbishop Romero was killed at the height of the repression in El Salvador, Gerardi was killed after a negotiated settlement had been reached between the government and the guerrillas. The assassination of Bishop Gerardi, therefore, could be seen as a bitter blow for efforts to establish truth and reconciliation in the wake of the civil war. British journalist Jeremy McDermott suggested: 'It is feared that Right-wing elements are trying to undermine the peace settlement and destabilize the country.'[25]

Did those who opposed the peace process want to halt it? While such high level murders remain unsolved, Guatemala's fragile peace process hangs in the balance, threatened also by the country's highly unequal distribution of wealth and rise in violent crime. According to official estimates, seventy-five per cent of Guatemala's ten million population live below the poverty line. Furthermore, the socio-economic power structure – one of the root causes of the war – remains virtually unaltered: sixty-five per cent of productive land continues to be owned by only 2.2 per cent of the population.[26] The 36-year civil war was concluded in 1996 with the signing of a Peace Accord between the government and guerrilla forces. However, many suggest that the absence of war does not mean peace in Guatemala and until the root causes of the conflict – the unequal distribution of wealth and land, the corrupt judicial system, impunity for those in positions of power and the denial of minority rights – are addressed, there will never be real peace or democracy in the country. Since he was a participant in the peace talks, and a tireless advocate of addressing the root causes of the conflict, Gerardi's assassination could also be seen as symbolising a serious obstacle to the peace process.

[24] 'Un crimen con significado político' *Siglo XXI*, 27 April 1998 (own translation).
[25] Jeremy McDermott, 'Pope Condemns Bishop's Murder', *The Daily Telegraph*, 29 April 1998.
[26] Judith Escribano, 'The Victim who said Never Again', *The Catholic Herald*, 30 October 1998.

Did those who had committed human rights abuses during the civil war wish to punish all those who had dared to tell the truth through the REMHI report? In his final speech, during the presentation ceremony of the REMHI report, Bishop Gerardi acknowledged the difficulty of finally telling the truth:

> Years of terror and death have ... reduced the majority of Guatemalans to fear and silence. 'Truth' is the primary word, the serious and mature action that makes it possible for us to break this cycle of death and violence and to open ourselves to a future of hope and light for all.[27]

Immediately after his assassination, CEG issued a communiqué stating: 'We fear that this assassination could be linked to the presentation of the results obtained by REMHI'.[28] The Guatemalan daily newspaper *Siglo XXI* reported that sources within ODHAG had indicated that Gerardi had a premonition of a hostile reaction from the military. Shortly after finishing the formal presentation of the REMHI report, Gerardi said: 'the hard-line elements of the army will react to the accusations'.[29] Gerardi even mentioned the name of one particular retired military officer as an example of someone from whom he expected an adverse reaction.

Did those who had committed human rights abuses fear prosecution for those crimes? The REMHI report accused three generals – Lucas García, Ríos Montt and Mejía Victores – of genocide and torture, crimes not covered in the amnesty laws within the peace accords. Although the 1996 Peace Accords had also mandated a United Nations-sponsored truth commission – the Historical Clarification Commission (CEH) – neither the CEH or the REMHI reports were supposed to be used as evidence for prosecution. However, it was long-suspected that human rights groups would use evidence within them to bring genocide charges against former military leaders.[30]

[27] Bishop Gerardi's final speech on presenting the REMHI report in the cathedral of Guatemala City, for an English version see *Guatemala: Never Again!*, (xxiii–xxv); for the Spanish version see *Monseñor Juan Gerardi: Testigo Fiel de Dios*.
[28] 'Comunicado de la Conferencia Episcopal de Guatemala', fax sent to (former) President Alvaro Arzú of Guatemala and copied to various national and international NGOs on 27 April 1998 (own translation).
[29] GRICAR/WCC, 'The Assassination of Monsignor Juan Gerardi', (Special Report II, 26 May 1998; Guatemala City: GRICAR/WCC, 1998).
[30] The Centre for Human Rights Legal Action (CHRLA) has accused Generals Lucas García and Ríos Montt of genocide and torture, aiming to take them to court in June 2001. Meanwhile, indigenous leader, the Menchú Foundation (named after Rigoberta Menchú, who was awarded the Nobel Peace Prize in 1992 as a representative of the 500 years of resistance campaign) brought cases of genocide and torture against eight military officers through the Spanish courts.

Did the military wish to show that they were still in control of the country – despite twelve years of civilian rule? According to the non-governmental organisation (NGO), the Guatemalan Alliance Against Impunity: 'There is a governmental policy of obstructing justice, especially in cases in which there are military involved.... Increasingly, the Executive is the prisoner of the military. If it were not so, there would not have been the pressure that there is in cases where the military is involved'.[31]

Did they wish to send out a clear signal: stop your accusations, or you will suffer the same fate as Bishop Gerardi? One of the people who gave their testimony in the *Nunca Más* report clearly highlighted the fear that people felt:

> ... when you realize just how many people have been murdered, then you share this sorrow. And you know that it is a moral obligation, a duty too [to tell your story], not only for the voiceless, but also for the whole society that has been terrorized. Because that psychology of terror is part of the abductions, right? Since they took so and so, they are also going to take others who were his friends.'[32]

In Guatemala, it has long been a counterinsurgency strategy to carry out both indiscriminate massacres and high profile indiscriminate assassinations in order to sow the seeds of terror, leaving people in a constant state of fear for their lives. Edgar Gutiérrez, the coordinator of the REMHI project, suggests: 'They physically killed their victim Monsignor Gerardi. And they aim to kill the legitimate supporter base of his pastoral work, ODHAG and REMHI.... Symbolically, destroying the face of Monsignor Gerardi means destroying the face of the church.'[33]

Did they wish to show how the apparent untouchables and defenders of others could easily become victims themselves? Following the assassination, ODHAG has attempted to carry out its own investigations into the crime and to organise commemorative events – but has suffered as a consequence. Many members of ODHAG and the REMHI team have received death threats. On 16 April 1999, armed men broke into the house of Ronalth Ochaeta, the Executive Director of ODHAG. They searched the house and threatened the housekeeper who was looking after Ochaeta's four-year-old son. Although they did not take

---

[31] GRICAR/WCC, 'The Gerardi Case: The Continuing Crisis of Human Rights in Guatemala'.

[32] Case 5449, Guatemala City, 1979, in *Guatemala: Never Again!*, p. 10.

[33] Edgar Gutiérrez, 'El Complot y el Paraguay', article written by for the Guatemalan press on 10 August 1998, sent by email by the Centre for Human Rights Legal Action (CHRLA), Guatemala City.

anything away, they did leave behind a box disguised as a bomb with a piece of brick inside, an apparent allusion to the cement block used to batter Bishop Gerardi to death.

Did they hope to frighten the Catholic Church in Guatemala in the same way that it had been frightened in El Salvador, following Archbishop Romero's death? ODHAG's initial reaction was to classify the killing as 'a disgraceful attack against the Guatemalan Church ... and the whole population ... and a severe blow to the peace process'.[34]

Did they hope that by killing Gerardi – who was the visible face of REMHI – the public's attention would shift from the *Nunca Más* report to the murder investigation instead? Several analysts have identified the timing of Gerardi's assassination as a direct threat to the United Nations-sponsored truth commission, the Historical Clarification Commission (CEH), which was due to publish its results.

Human rights activist, Frank La Rue, of the Guatemalan NGO, the Centre for Human Rights Legal Action (CHRLA) concludes that Gerardi's assassination symbolized a number of different things: 'It was an attack against the Catholic Church for developing their prophetic mission to record the testimonies of communities that had suffered as a result of the armed conflict.... The murder is a clear attack against the peace process, against those who highlight the truth and against the attempts that are being made to establish the rule of law.... This crime was surely planned and ordered by those who were responsible for the most serious atrocities detailed in the REMHI report, and those who oppose Guatemala's transition on the road to exercising democracy in peace and with justice. Guatemala has once again been thrown into mourning by those sectors with economic and political power, who wish to maintain impunity, under-development and economic misery in the country.'[35]

There are countless theories that point to Gerardi's assassination as being a political killing, and yet very little was done to follow up those leads during the initial investigations.

5. Impunity Versus Truth, Memory and Reconciliation

a. Judge and Public Prosecutor (1)

Ever since Gerardi's assassination, the Catholic Church, through ODHAG, has suggested that military personnel were responsible.

---

[34] 'Indignación por Asesinato de Monsenor Gerardi!', email sent by ODHAG on 27 April 1998 to various national and international NGOs and press agencies (own translation).
[35] 'Mártir de la verdad' (Martyr of truth), a declaration by CHRLA published in the Guatemalan newspaper *El Periódico*, 28 April 1998.

More specifically, they have suggested that Colonel Lima Estrada and his son Captain Lima Oliva headed a secret military team within the EMP that investigated REMHI.[36] It is alleged that the colonel and the captain wished to kill its most prominent figurehead since they were angered by the contents of its report *Nunca Más*. Within days of Gerardi's assassination ODHAG claimed this father and son team were responsible for the murder North American journalist, Paul Jeffery – who has been following the Gerardi case closely from within Central America – states: 'The two officers reportedly are members of a hard-line sector of the military that is displeased with the peace accords and what it views as government concessions to the former guerrillas.'[37]

Despite ample evidence behind this and other political-motivation theories, valuable time was wasted while public prosecutors followed up such implausible leads as the cook, the dog, the priest and his lover. Indeed, the first judge and public prosecutor were adamant that the assassination was merely the result of a common crime, or a crime of passion, and refused to follow up any leads that suggested political motivation. ODHAG requested that the public prosecutor Otto Ardón be replaced, claiming that he was negligent and incompetent. However, their request was overturned, since the Public Ministry maintained that he was doing a good job. 'The question is, a good job for who?' asked ODHAG.[38] Guatemalan Archbishop Prospero Penados del Barrio called Ardón 'Simply a puppet, who appears to lack the character to take real action.'[39] ODHAG then suggested that Ardón should be removed due to a conflict of interests, given that he had family members in the military and since he had himself previously received a salary from the military. But the Public Ministry also rejected this allegation.

Eventually, the judge was forced to resign after widespread condemnation of his work, and surprisingly, public prosecutor Otto Ardón resigned claiming that his honour had been offended by ODHAG's accusations of partiality and incompetence.

---

[36] Colonel Lima Estrada was known as a *'tough fighter'* under General Lucas García and the Director of Military Intelligence at the EMP under former President Alvaro Arzú. Captain Lima Oliva was a member of a United Nations Multinational Force and Chief of Security within the EMP under former President Alvaro Arzú.

[37] Paul Jeffrey, 'Little Headway Made in Bishop's Murder', *Latinamerica Press*, Vol. 30 No. 32, 3 September 1998.

[38] ODHAG, 'Monseñor Gerardi, su vida y sus obras', *Antecedentes*, (Guatemala City: ODHAG, nd), (own translation).

[39] 'Focus on Faith', BBC World Service report on Bishop Gerardi, broadcast on 5 November 1998.

b. Judge and Public Prosecutor (2)

The next judge in the case, Henry Monroy, was more open to suggestions that the crime could have been politically motivated. He demanded the release of Father Orantes. The Public Ministry said that Orantes would remain the prime suspect in the case and suggested that the Catholic Church would have to be responsible for guaranteeing that he did not flee the country. However, Judge Monroy ruled that this was illegal and demanded his unconditional release.

Accompanied by the new public prosecutor, Celvin Galindo, the case seemed to be making headway. On 13 October 1998, Galindo even agreed to investigate six members of the armed forces, including the father and son team from the EMP who had been named as prime suspects by ODHAG. At this point, however, military arrests were not made.

In an unprecedented move, Guatemala's new Defence Minister, General Marco Tulio Espinoza and two other top military officers,[40] were accused of masterminding the murder of Bishop Gerardi by a judge who claimed to be acting independently. The accusations took ODHAG by surprise, leaving them wondering whether this was yet another more ingenious attempt to deflect attention away from the true perpetrators of the crime. 'The accusation has been made by a former judge, Juan Carlos Solís Oliva. But he has family ties with the two men – an army captain and a colonel – whom the archdiocese has long regarded as the suspects.'[41]

Judge Solís Oliva's charge came shortly after ODHAG had arranged DNA tests on an exhumed corpse without head or hands. The unidentified body was found one month after Gerardi was killed: its DNA was to be matched with blood found at the scene of Gerardi's murder. It was suggested that the man may have been involved in the crime and later killed by his fellow conspirators. Public prosecutor Galindo, told reporters that analyses of bloodstains at Bishop Gerardi's parish residence were positively matched up with DNA samples taken from Father Orantes, while tests taken from military officers – thought to be linked to the crime – were still inconclusive.

On 7 March 1999, Judge Monroy ordered a reconstruction of the events of the night of the crime. The reconstruction did not lead to a clear resolution of the case, but it did eliminate some possibilities and open up others as well as clarify certain aspects of the case. It was demonstrated, by testimony, that at least two members of the EMP – Major Andrés Villagrán and Dario Morales – were present at the scene of the crime and there were several witnesses who testified that Morales was taking video footage inside the crime area, and

---

[40] Colonel Rudy Pozuelos, head of the EMP, and Major Juan Escobar, also of the EMP.
[41] 'Did Guatemala's New Defence Minister Kill Bishop?', *The Tablet*, 10 July 1999.

not just observing from a distance, as they had claimed.

Shortly after the reconstruction, Judge Monroy fled the country, claiming lack of support from the Public Ministry and acts of intimidation against himself and his family. Public prosecutor Galindo lamented the loss of Monroy indicating that he had been a very effective judge who had advanced the case significantly.

On 7 October 1999, Galindo himself resigned and fled to the United States to seek political asylum after receiving repeated death threats. In an interview with a Guatemalan radio station, Galindo said he was 'frustrated at not reaching the end – but I believe that, in reaching the end of the case, I would run a very great risk.'[42] The death threats had apparently increased after Galindo told reporters that he was awaiting the results of DNA tests of twelve military officers and five other people against blood samples found at the murder scene. An angry Bishop Ríos Montt – the Auxiliary Bishop of Guatemala City who replaced Gerardi as head of ODHAG – stated: 'Government officials have their hands and feet tied by bands of untouchable assassins who can do what they want, and the government is incapable of touching them'.[43]

c. Judge and Public Prosecutor (3)

When the Public Ministry appointed Leopoldo Zeizzig as the new prosecutor in October 1999, ODHAG demanded that the government give him the support necessary to continue the investigation. Zeizzig had worked as an assistant to Galindo for five months and was keen to follow up leads that suggested military involvement.

On 26 December 1999, Alfonso Portillo was elected President of Guatemala. Portillo was the official candidate of the right-wing Guatemalan Republican Front (FRG) political party – founded by military strongman, General Efraín Ríos Montt.[44] It was feared that Portillo would merely be the puppet of the former general, but he has surprised many in his determination to solve the Gerardi case: 'The current president Alfonso Portillo has made a lot of offers in relation to clarifying the case of the murder of Monsignor Gerardi. Promises went beyond electioneering because he took them up again in his acceptance speech.'[45]

---

[42] 'Fear for safety – further information on UA 139/98', Urgent Action letter (AMR 34/37/99) issued by Amnesty International on 11 October 1999.

[43] Paul Jeffery, 'Gerardi Murder Still a Puzzle', *Latinamerica Press*, Vol 31 No. 44, 29 November 1999.

[44] The general himself had been barred from standing due to a constitutional ruling that prohibits former coup leaders from becoming presidential candidates. Ríos Montt is, however, President of Congress.

[45] 'Proyecto: Conmemoración del Segundo Aniversario, Martirio de Monseñor Juan Gerardi', Guatemala City, ODHAG, April 2000.

Portillo has also surprised observers in other ways. He announced that he would hire private security, rather than use the EMP, during his inauguration ceremony and has said that he will disband the EMP – as laid down in the 1996 Peace Accords.[46] Furthermore, on 14 January 2000, Alfonso Portillo announced the forced retirement of seventeen brigadier generals, two major generals and one vice admiral, as they were all of higher rank than the newly appointed Minister of Defence, Colonel Juan de Dios Estrada Velásquez.[47] This was an act without precedent in Guatemalan history; but more was yet to come – Portillo then announced that the colonel's appointment would only be temporary, since he intended to appoint a civilian to the post of Defence Minister.

In order to highlight his commitment to the resolution of the Gerardi case, President Alfonso Portillo even appointed Edgar Gutiérrez, former Coordinator of REMHI, to head the governmental Secretariat of Strategic Analysis (SAE), making him personally responsible for investigating Gerardi's assassination. On 24 January 2000, when Gutiérrez searched the files for information on the case, he found the Gerardi file was empty, its contents removed by former staff members of the SAE. On 2 February 2000, he fired eighty-six members of the Secretariat's staff, including several military officials. Gutiérrez said that joining the SAE was not an easy decision for him to make, but finally agreed to it once he had talked things over with people in the Church, in civil society and in the international community. He stated his belief that he would be able to make changes from within the government, rather than from outside.

The investigation of the case picked up following testimony from a homeless man who slept on the streets around the area of the crime. The new judge in the case, Flor de María García Villatoro ordered the arrest on 21 January 1999 of father and son team Colonel Lima Estrada, Captain Lima Oliva and former military adviser, Obdulio Villanueva, and accused them of Gerardi's murder.[48] Father Mario Orantes was re-arrested and also accused of murdering Bishop Gerardi.

---

[46] The international community contributed towards the cost of training of a civilian guard; but once they had completed the training, Portillo then claimed not to have enough money to pay the severance pay and pensions of the EMP officials. Human rights lawyer, Frank La Rue of CHRLA has stated: 'Portillo depends on the EMP. No government will be truly civilian until the president breaks away from the EMP' (Central America Week Conference, Bristol/UK, 24 March 2001).

[47] Military officials cannot take orders from a lower ranking officer.

[48] Villanueva's lawyers tried to get the charges against their client dropped on the grounds that he had been in prison (for the murder of a man who had allegedly tried to kill President Arzu) at the time of Gerardi's assassination. However, a fellow prisoner claimed to have seen Villanueva leave the prison on the very night of Gerardi's assassination and then return hours later.

Father Orantes denies the charges: 'I didn't see anything, I didn't hear anything, I didn't do anything.'[49]

Once again, the cook has been accused of covering up the crime. An address book was found in her room with the names and numbers of some of the members of the EMP – she claims it was given to her as a present.

Baloo was not re-arrested. He had died of natural causes in September 1999.

At the time of writing, the connection between the two sets of people has not been made public, but it has been suggested that Father Orantes – who lived just three blocks away from the EMP building – was having a homosexual affair with at least one member of the EMP and that he collaborated with them in the murder in return for a promise not to reveal the affair(s). Some reports have suggested that one of the officers arrested was planted to win over Orantes' affections in order to gain access to Gerardi's home.[50]

Having vociferously condemned the public prosecution the first time the priest was arrested and implicated in Gerardi's murder, the Catholic Church then decided to reserve judgement, stating that 'He as a human being, could have committed an error or a sin. In the Church, we have all kinds of people, some faithful, others unfaithful.'[51]

There now appears to be no doubt in anyone's minds – nor any attempt to cover up the fact – that this was a political assassination. An editorial in the Guatemalan daily newspaper, *Prensa Libre* was explicit in its condemnation of the assassination of Bishop Gerardi:

> You have to not want to see to say that this assassination is just one more case of common crime. It is a political crime. He was assassinated because he was the Coordinator of the section of the Archdiocese responsible for investigating human rights. It is that simple and clear.... This cowardly and vile assassination should make us reflect on the unexpected consequences of intolerance. You cannot directly accuse the government of having participated, but neither is it possible to affirm that it might not be the case that some state institution, without any authorisation and acting independently, decided to end the life of the Bishop.[52]

---

[49] 'Priest Denies Murdering Bishop', *The Universe*, 9 April 2000.
[50] Paul Jeffery, 'Priest Latest to be Charged with Guatemalan Bishop's Killing', *ENI*, 10 February 2000.
[51] 'Ex-seguridad de Arzú fue detenido', *Prensa Libre*, 23 January 2000.
[52] Guatemalan newspaper *Prensa Libre* editorial quoted in GRICAR/WCC, *The Assassination of Monsignor Gerardi*, (Special Report I, 4 May 1998; Guatemala City, GRICAR/WCC, 1998) (own translation).

5. What were the Unintentional Results of Killing Bishop Gerardi?

There are consequences of Bishop Gerardi's assassination from which we can draw hope, so that we can take comfort that his death was not in vain.

Following his assassination, the REMHI report *Nunca Más* gained worldwide attention. ODHAG was originally going to print 3,000 copies of the report; shortly after Gerardi's assassination, it decided to print 20,000 copies. ODHAG also translated versions into English, German and French and produced a shorter version in popular style for Guatemalans who do not have advanced reading skills. It is unlikely this would have happened without the worldwide coverage Bishop Gerardi's assassination granted. Furthermore, the criminal investigation – which has been in the national newspapers nearly every day for three years – keeps the REMHI report alive.

Despite receiving constant threats, the Archbishop's Human Rights Office has not been silenced. In fact, it is determined more than ever to continue its human rights work; to uncover the truth; to allow survivors to recall and retell their memories. Although some people have questioned Edgar Gutiérrez's wisdom in accepting a post in Portillo's government, he claims that he did so in the belief that it would be much easier to influence the investigation from within, rather than from the outside. The resolution of the case now at least looks possible.

Just before Gerardi's assassination, the UN Human Rights Commission had removed Guatemala from the blacklist of countries of human rights violators that require the UN Commission's observation. The UN's Verification Commission in Guatemala (MINUGUA) quickly condemned Gerardi's assassination in April 1998 and said that it hoped the case would not result in impunity. MINUGUA's mandate was extended until the end of 2000.

Although Gerardi's assassination seemed to signal a temporary halting of the peace process, representatives from civil society seem more determined than ever to keep it going. They have even buried their differences to join together in a fifty-eight-strong coalition of civil society organisations known as *Convergencia Guatemala, Nunca Más* (Guatemala Convergence, Never Again) in order to demand a thorough investigation of this murder – and other high-profile political assassinations – and to demand that the government fulfil its obligations to the people of Guatemala, as laid down in the 1996 Peace Accords.

Thousands turned out on the streets to follow the funeral cortege and to attend mass. Bishop Gerardo Flores – the current Bishop of Alta Verapaz – spoke at the funeral mass: 'Gerardi's voice will go on, an eternal echo in every corner of our nation. They did not silence his voice, they made it more powerful.... He fought for real peace ... for peace based on justice and truth. For that he gave his life and for that they wanted to silence him.'[53] However, following Gerardi's assassination, Guatemalan people seem to have found the strength to be more vocal. The people of Guatemala have not been cowered into silence. It is hoped that organizations, such as *Convergencia Guatemala, Nunca Más,* and demonstrations of public support will continue to contribute to ending the cycle of fear and violence which has characterised Guatemala for so long.

Although Gerardi's assassination could serve as an example to other countries of how fledgling and fragile peace processes can falter, it is also an illustration of how something so horrific can galvanize public feeling and motivate people to act. *Nunca Más* should serve as a fitting epitaph to the life of Bishop Gerardi. It is hoped that his death – which has inevitably turned him into a martyr for the cause of peace, truth and reconciliation – will ultimately serve some useful purpose. Never again should someone be assassinated for their beliefs; never again should the justice system protect the guilty and persecute the innocent; never again should a priest or bishop or archbishop be martyred for the cause of his people.

Following Gerardi's assassination, Dennis Smith from the Guatemalan branch of the Latin American Evangelical Centre for Pastoral Studies (CELEP), produced the following reflection:

Curious how they killed our brother Juan Gerardi.
Did his assassins think that
by crushing his skull,
disfiguring his face,
they could stamp out his ideas,
his identity,
his commitment to the Gospel?

It doesn't work that way.
Those who tried to silence Jesus tried the same thing:
Jesus rose from the dead.
Because Jesus rose again, Juan Gerardi lives.
Not just symbolically,
but in the Gospel, deeds, words, attitudes and commitments
that flourish among the Guatemalan people.

---

[53] 'Thousands Attend Slain Guatemalan Bishop's Burial', AFP article sent by email on 30 April 1998.

Please take note:
we hereby dedicate ourselves to be unconditional accomplices
to the Gospel of Jesus Christ,
the same Gospel lived and preached by our brother, Juan Gerardi.

We are accomplices in building a new Guatemala
filled with justice, tenderness and solidarity,
a Guatemala big enough for all her sons and daughters.
We are accomplices in telling the truth,
practising repentance and pardon,
defending the dignity of each person.
We are accomplices in the mission of Jesus:
abundant life for all.
We join all those calling for the prompt clarification of this crime,
and for the capture and trial of the material and intellectual authors
of Monseñor's death –
not in pursuit of vengeance,
but because impunity lessens the humanity of all Guatemalans.

In the meantime, thank you, Monseñor,
for teaching us how to value every human life,
for pointing us down the path of the Gospel.
Thank you for continuing to accompany us on our journey...
Jesus said to her: 'I am the resurrection and the life;
those who believe in me, even though they die, will live.'
(John 11.25)[54]

If Gerardi's assassination can be seen to have had positive consequences, we can say that it has made visible that which had previously been covered up; it has granted a voice to the voiceless; and it has named the nameless. If we look at the cover of the *Nunca Más* report, we see a man covering his mouth, his eyes and his ears: in the final picture he shouts out loud. Juan Gerardi's face was so battered that his eyes, ears and mouth were unidentifiable – there can be no doubt that this was an intentional atrocity. There is still a lot to be done before the perpetrators of political crimes are convicted; before impunity becomes a thing of the past; before the Peace Accords are fully implemented; and before the unjust distribution of land and wealth is addressed. However, the REMHI report and Gerardi's assassination have at least allowed the people of Guatemala to see, to hear and to cry out: *Nunca Más, Never Again!*

---

[54] 'Muchas Gracias, Monseñor' in *Monseñor Juan Gerardi: Testigo Fiel de Dios*, CEG, 1999, Guatemala City, p. 342 (own translation).

Postscript

Up to March 2001, the number of people who fled the country following death threats to themselves or their family rose to nine. This includes six witnesses, one judge and a prosecutor. Furthermore, Public Prosecutor Leopoldo Zeissig, Judge Flor de Mara García and two journalists covering the case have also received death threats and complained about being followed by unmarked cars.

The start date of the trial was also delayed by difficulties in finding a judge to hear the case. The first judge resigned amidst accusations of incompetence; his successor resigned after receiving death threats; then a further judge – Alexis Caldron – resigned on 4 June 2000 amid accusations that he was not impartial. Judge Calderón had ruled in favour of Obdulio Villanueva, one of the accused, in a previous trial. Villanueva was convicted of killing a milk delivery driver who accidentally drove too close to the then president Alvaro Arzú. At the time of that case, Bishop Gerardi publicly questioned Calderón's independence and said that Villanueva's sentence was too light.

There then followed a debate over whether the military officers should be tried separately in a military court, but eventually it was decided that all five should be tried in a civilian court. The start date for the trial was finally set for 23 March 2001. On that day, Colonel Lima Estrada claimed to be too sick to stand trial; and a grenade was thrown into the house of the judge due to hear the case. The case was suspended yet again.

Finally, on 8 June 2001, in an unprecedented court ruling, Byron Lima Oliva, Byron Lima Estrada and Jose Obdulio Villanueva were sentenced to 30 years in prison for murdering Bishop Gerardi. The officers are the highest ranking soldiers to be convicted of human rights abuses.

Father Mario Orantes was found guilty of acting as an accomplice and given a 20-year prison term. The bishop's cook, Margarita Lopez, was found innocent of the same charges.

The court said it based its ruling largely on the testimony of the key prosecution witness, Ruben Chanax, a homeless man who claimed he had been hired by the army officers. Chanax said that he had been told to spy on Gerardi and to alter the scene of the crime before the police arrived.

In a case that has lurched from tragedy to farce, but may transform the country's political landscape, there has been a final twist to the plot. The Catholic Church's lawyers believe that former President Alvaro Arzu was involved in planning the killing, and have requested that the judges order an investigation. Arzu had used his parliamentary immunity to avoid testifying.

Memory and Martyrdom: The Theological Contributions of Ignacio Ellacuría

KEVIN F. BURKE, SJ

The theme of this volume, 'Truth and Memory: The Church and Human Rights in El Salvador and Guatemala' gains much of its resonance and power from the reality of martyrdom. In particular, it draws upon the witness of Archbishop Oscar Romero of El Salvador and Bishop Juan Gerardi of Guatemala, two great Christian martyrs of our day. In my reflections I focus primarily on Bishop Romero and the situation in El Salvador. I also draw a third contemporary martyr into our conversation, Ignacio Ellacuría. A Jesuit priest, university president, and philosopher-theologian, Ellacuría was the main target of the ghastly massacre that took place at the University of Central America (UCA) in El Salvador on 16 November 1989. An elite battalion of soldiers operating under direct orders from the high command of the Salvadoran Army murdered him in the middle of the night along with five other Jesuit priests, a seminary cook, and her fifteen-year-old daughter. My choice of Ellacuría is not arbitrary. For one thing, he worked closely with Archbishop Romero. In fact, he and Jon Sobrino, another UCA Jesuit who only escaped the massacre because he was out of the country when it occurred, were two of Romero's most trusted theological consultants.[1] But beyond this direct association with Romero, I consider Ellacuría an important resource for this volume, dedicated to truth and memory, because of the distinctive and profound contribution he makes to liberation theology. Indeed, I could have explored this

---

[1] Ellacuría and Sobrino provided significant help in the writing of Romero's influential pastoral letters. In many other ways they helped him formulate a theological vision for the Church of San Salvador during an agonizing civil war. Thus, becoming acquainted with Ellacuría is a way to remember Romero. I will return to this point at the end of this essay.

contribution by focusing my remarks on the theme of truth, for one finds in Ellacuría important reflections on and a striking witness to the search for historical truth.[2] However, I intend to draw from the other side of our theme, the theme of memory, of the moral and religious imperative to remember. For the moral and religious imperative to remember our martyrs is inextricably linked to the vital task of keeping liberation theology alive, this is, of keeping alive a theological faith praxis dedicated to 'bringing the crucified peoples down from their crosses', to quote Ellacuría.

Archbishop Romero was gunned down on 24 March 1980 while celebrating Mass in the chapel at the Divine Providence Hospital where he lived. The twentieth anniversary of his death in March 2000 prompts us to remember and reflect upon his witness; we also give voice to our own Christian desire to be in solidarity with the Church in El Salvador and everywhere in the world where Christians celebrate the memory of Archbishop Romero. Like us, Ellacuría was profoundly aware of the rich theological meaning of Romero's martyrdom. But the heart of Ellacuría's contribution to our conversation springs, in my view, *not* from his having constructed a formal theology of martyrdom, but rather in having articulated the intrinsic connection between martyrdom and the very doing of theology, in having drawn martyrdom into the very dynamics of theological method.[3] This has profound implications for our understanding of both martyrdom and theology. It impels us to explore what could be called the sacramental character of martyrdom. It impels us to remember – a key dimension of sacrament. And it impels us to do theology in the service of liberating faith – to do theology as a praxis that keeps the memory of our martyrs alive. I develop these reflections in four steps. First, I introduce what I mean by the sacramental character of martyrdom in relation to the theme of memory. Second, I sketch Ellacuría's theological method and briefly justify my characterization of it as contextually embedded. Third, I identify the place of martyrdom in Ellacuría's method. Fourth, I conclude with a few remarks on the sacrament of remembering our martyrs through the doing of theology.

---

[2] As a citizen of the United States I feel an urgent sense of responsibility to press for the truth about my country's relations with the nations of Central America. During the civil war in El Salvador, for example, the United States subsidized the Salvadoran government and military – the very ones directly responsible for the assassination at the UCA, and closely linked to the death of Archbishop Romero – to the tune of $5 billion dollars. A similar need for US accountability towards Guatemala and other countries of Central America exists as well.

[3] Indeed, this point could be extended to include the connections between martyrdom and the praxis of philosophy, as well as the link between martyrdom and the purpose of the university.

1. The Sacramental Character of Martyrdom

The word 'martyr' comes from the Greek word for *witness*. From very early in the history of Christianity, it took on the specific meaning of *bearing witness unto death*, of bearing witness with one's life. And from very early in our history, the Christian church proved to be a church of martyrs. The sacramental implication of this can be intimated in the lapidary phrase of St Tertullian, who saw *the blood of the martyrs* as *the seed of the church*. Archbishop Romero drew on this same agricultural-ecclesial metaphor image when he said, just days before his own death:

> Martyrdom is a grace of God that I do not believe I deserve. But if God accepts the sacrifice of my life, let my blood be a seed of freedom and the sign that hope will soon be reality. Let my death, if it is accepted by God, be for my people's liberation and as a witness of hope in the future.[4]

In this quotation, too, we catch a whiff of the sacramental character of martyrdom. Martyrdom, according to Bishop Romero, is a grace and a sign of real hope. It is, I might add, a forceful grace and an efficacious sign, central attributes of all sacraments. It mediates resurrection faith and does so in a way that nothing else can. 'If I am killed,' Bishop Romero added, 'I shall arise in the Salvadoran people.'[5] Finally, martyrdom plants a seed of freedom. It generates a liberation that mediates salvation. It yields the hope that mediates the future. This is the heart of the matter.

Remembrance is implicit in the very notion of martyrdom. The one who witnesses is remembered, while the one who remembers re-witnesses. The witnessing occurs *to* and *through* the remembering. It occurs *in* the memory of the martyr's community, in response to the command to 'do this in remembrance of me'. But what kind of remembrance are we talking about? It is not something private. By it's very nature it involves a community, a people in solidarity with the martyr. Moreover, it is not nostalgia. It is not some sentimental journey into the past, some romantic flight back to 'the heady days of the revolution', for example. In fact, remembering martyrs is not primarily centered on the past at all. The Christian sacrament of remembrance – the *memoria passionis* that gives birth to the Christian movement – has everything to do with fidelity in the present and hope for the future. Rightly does Johann Baptist Metz call this constitutive Christian event a 'dangerous memory' that interrupts all our tidy constructs and

---
[4] Quoted in James Brockman, *Romero: A Life*, Maryknoll, NY, Orbis, 1989, p. 248.
[5] Brockman, *Romero*, p. 248.

romantic flights.⁶ In the eucharistic language of St Paul and the Synoptic Gospels, we embody our present identity and embrace our future hope precisely when we 'do this' – break bread, proclaim the word, heal the sick, forgive sinners, reconcile enemies, liberate the oppressed, love God's poorest ones, whatever it is we do – *in remembrance of Jesus*. Memory, remembering, remembrance, as I am using these words, thus refer to both a process and a content, a remembering and a remembered. What do we remember when we remember martyrs like Archbishop Romero and Father Ellacuría? We remember their commitment to God's cause and God's people. In so remembering, we come into the proximity of hearts afire with love for God's reign, hearts aching for the sufferings of the poor, hearts yearning for the liberation of the oppressed. When we remember, we reawaken the martyrs' dreams, that is, the *future* that they dreamed for their people. Paradoxically, therefore, when we remember in the specifically Christian, sacramental sense of remembrance, we remember the future. Martyrdom – both as an original act of witnessing-unto-death and as a re-witnessing, an act of remembrance that keeps the martyr alive – thus functions as an eschatological sacrament of resurrection faith. Keeping in mind this anamnestic connection between martyrdom and faith, allow me to address what links martyrdom to theology.

2. Ellacuría's Contextually Embedded Theological Method

In his brilliant essay, 'The Church of the Poor, the Historical Sacrament of Liberation', Ellacuría gives us a striking definition of liberation theology. He writes: 'The theology of liberation understands itself as a reflection from faith on the historical reality and action of the people of God, who follow the work of Jesus in announcing and fulfilling God's Reign.'⁷ This definition is characteristic of Ellacuría's theological vision. In his view, the practice of theology unfolds as a threefold process involving reflection, ethical option, and praxis. The first dimension, the noetic moment, corresponds to the image of theology as *reflection* from faith, the object of which is the Reign of God which Jesus proclaimed and served. This reflective moment logically entails the second dimension, what Ellacuría calls the ethical moment.

---

⁶ See Johann Baptist Metz, *Faith in History and Society*, London, Burns & Oates, 1980, trans. by David Smith. See also J. Matthew Ashley, *Interruptions: Mysticism, Politics and Theology in the Work of Johann Baptist Metz*, Notre Dame, IN., Notre Dame Press, 1998, pp. 161–162.

⁷ Ignacio Ellacuría, 'The Church of the Poor, Historical Sacrament of Liberation', in Ignacio Ellacuría and Jon Sobrino, eds., *Mysterium Liberationis: Fundamental Concepts of Liberation Theology*, Maryknoll, Orbis Books, 1993, p. 543, trans. by Margaret Wilde.

What is at issue here is the place of theology *[lugar teológico]* and the fundamental ethical *option* to do theology from this as opposed to that historical place. In the definition of theology I just cited, this dimension appears in with the reference to 'the historical reality' – that is, the concrete situation – of the people of God. The third dimension is likewise intimately connected to the noetic and ethical moments. It is theology as *praxis*. It appears as the 'historical action of the people of God,' the historical action of the disciples of Jesus who continue in history his effort to announce and fulfil God's Reign.

This threefold characterization of theology is not arbitrary. Ellacuría carefully traces the connections between these considerations and the practical imperatives that orient humans in historical reality.[8] His theological method springs from a 'philosophy of historical reality' which details the contextually rich, historically conditioned human encounter with real things. It is important to note that these three dimensions of the encounter with reality do not unfold in a temporal sequence. They occur as completely integrated and simultaneous. This has important implications for theology. It means that theology does not first conceptualize a faith content, then take up an ethical stance on the basis of that conceptualization and only then, as a final step, adopt a pastoral praxis in response to these first two. Nor does it invert this schema – as some superficial explanations of liberation theology would have it – and begin with praxis, move to an ethical stance, and from there conceptualize the faith. Rather, Ellacuría's method starts from the integral human encounter with historical reality and a philosophically rich description of the dynamics of that encounter. When confronting the problems of living in and among realities, the three dimensions of human intellection – intelligent apprehension, ethical stance, and historical praxis – operate in dynamic tension. Likewise, every act of theological reflection and production is simultaneously a noetic exercise, a deployment of one's

---

[8] These three considerations correspond to the practical imperatives which orient humans in reality. Ellacuría weaves them together in a passage famous for its density and untranslatable wordplay. He writes that the 'act of confronting ourselves with real things in their reality' involves the noetic dimension of intelligence, that of 'realizing the weight of reality' *[el hacerse cargo de la realidad]*, the ethical dimension, 'shouldering the weight of reality' *[el cargar con la realidad]*, and the praxis-oriented dimension, 'taking charge of the weight of reality' *[el encargarse de la realidad]*; see Ignacio Ellacuría, 'Hacia una fundamentación filosófica del método teológico latinoamericano', in E. Ruiz Maldonado, ed., *Liberación y cautiverio: debates en torno al metodo de la teología en América Latina*, Mexico City, August 11–15, 1975, 626. For an exegesis of this dense passage and a fuller treatment of the foundations and operations of Ellacuría's threefold theological method, see my book, *The Ground Beneath the Cross: The Theology of Ignacio Ellacuría*, Washington, D.C., Georgetown University Press, 2000, pp. 99–149. For Ellacuría's most important philosophical work, see Ignacio Ellacuría, *Filosofía de la realidad histórica*, Madrid, Editorial Trotta, 1990.

fundamental ethical stance, and a historically real praxis. Hence, my characterization of Ellacuría's method as contextually embedded. As a context-sensitive, praxis-oriented reflection on faith, theology can align the universal character of its assertions with the critical exigency generated by historical consciousness. In my view, this represents one of Ellacuría's greatest contributions to contemporary theology. To educe his concrete relevance for reflection on truth and memory in Latin America, I now probe this method in view of the logic of martyrdom.

3. Theological Place and Martyrdom

The ethical dimension of the encounter with reality requires, in Ellacuría's phrase, 'that we take upon ourselves what things really are and what they really demand.'[9] This option is not primarily cognitive. It involves the whole person in all of his or her personal, social, and historical dimensions. It requires a discernment regarding where I locate myself within historical reality. It asks, from what place can I most fully grasp what is in fact going on? The place of theology proves crucial because human intellection can only apprehend reality in the concrete realities it encounters. In other words, what one knows and who one becomes depend on where one puts one's body, one's energy, one's life. Likewise, because one's fundamental stance toward reality exists in a mutually conditioning relationship with the place from which reality is encountered, one's theology is intrinsically conditioned by one's theological place.[10] Thus, theological reflection and the social-historical location of the theologian exist in circular relation to one another.

Ellacuría sets out to discover the place most capable of manifesting God's revelation and call to conversion (the ethical dimension), the place most likely to inspire a living faith in Jesus and a corresponding praxis of discipleship (the praxis-oriented dimension), and the place most apt to stimulate a lively, authentic theological understanding of faith (the noetic dimension).[11] He finds that place among the poor. He

---

[9] Ellacuría, 'Hacia una fundamentacíon filosófica', p. 626.

[10] Ellacuría distinguishes theological place *(lugar)* and source *(fuente)*, taking as '"source" or deposit that which in one form or other maintains the contents of the faith.' However, he notes that this distinction must not be applied in a way that views the two as mutually exclusive. 'In a way, the place is a source insofar as the place makes it possible for the source to present one thing or other, so that, thanks to the place and by virtue of it, certain specific contents are actualized and made really present,' Ignacio Ellacuría, 'Los pobres, "lugar teológico" en America Latina,' in idem *Conversión de la Iglesia al Reino de Dios: Para anunciarlo y realizarlo en la historia* (CIRD), Santander: Editorial Sal Terrae, 1984, p. 168 trans. mine; originally published in *Misión Abierta* (No. 4–5, 1981), pp. 225–240; hereafter cited as 'Lugar teológico'.

[11] See 'Lugar teológico', pp. 165–168.

writes, 'The poor of Latin America are theological place insofar as they constitute the maximum and scandalous, prophetic and apocalyptic presence of the Christian God and, consequently, the privileged place of Christian praxis and reflection.'[12] The ethical dimension of the encounter with reality thus gives rise to and corresponds with liberation theology's most distinguishing feature: its commitment to the principle of mercy through its preferential option for the poor.[13]

Drawing on his experience of the *Spiritual Exercises* of St Ignatius Loyola, Ellacuría associates this preeminent *lugar teológico* with the place at the foot of the cross. Loyola instructs the believer, kneeling before the crucified, to ask, 'What have I done for Christ? What am I doing for Christ? What ought I to do for Christ?'[14] Ellacuría adapts this prayer, urging us to place our 'eyes and hearts upon these peoples who are suffering so much, some from misery and hunger, others from oppression and repression, and then, before this people thus crucified, to ask, What have I done to crucify them? What am I doing in order to uncrucify them? What ought I to do so that this people will be raised?'[15] The crucified people: their story and reality represent the preeminent place of theology.

A corollary attends the Christian discernment which places theology – as well as the ecclesial praxis that theology serves – at the service of history's victims. Because historical reality is divided by oppression, interpreting it in the light of God's Reign and, above all, actively transforming reality into that Reign, necessarily implies unmasking and fighting against the anti-Reign. Stated bluntly, a genuine theological commitment to the realization of the Reign of God almost inevitably leads to conflict, it often brings on persecution and, in the extreme, it sometimes ends in martyrdom. In the praxis of Christian faith, the logic of martyrdom appears intrinsically linked to the iconic gesture of Christian blessing, the sign of the cross. Likewise, the Christian theologian, as a person of faith really affected by the negativity of historical reality, must incarnate theology in a very specific gesture or praxis. This

---

[12] 'Lugar teológico', p. 163.

[13] On the 'preferential option for the poor' see Gustavo Gutiérrez; *A Theology of Liberation: History, Politics and Salvation*, trans. by Caridad Inda and John Eagleson, Maryknoll, Orbis, 1973, 1988; 'Theology from the Underside of History', in *The Power of the Poor in History*, Maryknoll, Orbis, 1983, pp. 169–214; 'Option for the Poor', *MLT*, pp. 235–250; Juan Luis Segundo, *The Liberation of Theology*, trans. by John Drury, Maryknoll, Orbis, 1976; 'The Option for the Poor: Hermeneutic Key for Understanding the Gospel', in *Signs of the Times: Theological Reflections*, Maryknoll, Orbis, 1993, pp. 119–127.

[14] Ignatius Loyola, *The Spiritual Exercises of Saint Ignatius*, No. 53, trans. and ed. by G. Ganss, St Louis, Institute of Jesuit Sources, 1992.

[15] Ellacuría, 'Las Iglesias latinoamericanas interpelan a la Iglesia de España', *Sal Terra* (No. 826, 1982) trans. mine, p. 230.

is why Ellacuría insists that theology incarnate itself in the place of the crucified people. This is why he focuses on the action of taking them down from their crosses. This is what his companion and friend, Jon Sobrino, means by 'the principle of mercy'. Sobrino writes: 'Theology becomes converted in its very task and not only in the contents which it offers, into soteriology. It becomes compassionate reason.'[16] Thus, to the traditional understanding of theology as *intellectus fidei*, faith seeking understanding, Sobrino adds the image of theology as *intellectus amoris*, love seeking understanding. He argues further:

> There are not only limitations and tragedies in reality, but there exists *sin*, personal and structural, as a form of death.... Reality *qua* sin fights against anyone who wants to transform it into grace. In the language of the Synoptic Gospels, the anti-Reign fights against the Reign. So sin is not only there, but it lashes back, and it presents theology with the dilemma of taking on this backlash in the form of persecution and martyrdom, of 'shouldering the weight of reality' or 'allowing oneself to be carried along by reality'.[17]

In the case of Ellacuría, the implications of theology as *intellectus amoris* appear with stunning clarity. As a theologian, he articulated the connections between perceiving, shouldering, and transforming historical reality. As a martyr, like Bishops Romero and Gerardi, he incarnated those connections.

4. The Sacrament of Remembering Our Martyrs

The original witness of the martyr becomes a sacrament of resurrection faith for those who come into contact with the martyr's story. Two things are at work here: the *memory* of the martyr, and the *story* that keeps the memory alive and gives it historical flesh. Let me say a word about the story, about the sacrament logic of the narrative dimension which communicates the transformative memory of the martyr. I will do this by telling a story that I first encountered in Johann Baptist Metz, who got the story from Martin Buber, who learned the story from an old Rabbi, whose grandfather first told this story. Buber writes, quoting the old rabbi:

> My grandfather was paralyzed. Once he was asked to tell a story

---

[16] Jon Sobrino, 'La teología y el "principio liberación"', *Revista Latino americana de Teología*, No. 35, 1995, p. 127. See also, Jon Sobrino, 'Theology in a Suffering World: Theology as *Intellectus Amoris*', in *The Principle of Mercy*, Maryknoll, Orbis Books, 1994, p. 29.

[17] Sobrino, 'La teología y el "principio liberación"', p. 134, author's emphasis.

about his teacher and he told how the holy Baal Shem Tov used to jump and dance when he was praying. My grandfather stood up while he was telling the story and the story carried him away so much that he had to jump and dance to show how the master had done it. From that moment, he was healed. This is how stories ought to be told.[18]

In his reflections on this little narrative, Buber adds, 'The story is itself an event and has the quality of a sacred action.... It is more than a reflection. The sacred essence to which it bears witness continues to live in it. The wonder that is narrated becomes powerful once more.'[19] Metz adds his own commentary. 'Buber's text points to an inner relationship between the story and sacrament ... in which the unity of the story as an effective word and as practical effect is expressed in the same process.'[20]

Let me pick up on this point with a few concluding remarks. What is theology? It is, to use Metz's phrase, the 'effective word.' Its task is to mediate between the dangerous memory of the martyrs, on one hand, and the practical implications of remembering the future for which they died, on the other. This task of theology, this vocation, if you will, shows up with special force in liberation theology, in the liberation theology of witnesses and rememberers like Ignacio Ellacuría and Jon Sobrino. This is why liberation theology is still quite relevant and, more than relevant, why it is essential for the Christian churches, why it is vitally necessary. This theology listens to the 'voices of the voiceless', as Bishop Romero says. This theology reminds 'non-persons' that they are persons, to quote Gustavo Gutiérrez. This is a theology of mercy as well as justice, a theology of the crucified people, the body of Christ in history, a theology of historically real and transformative salvation. We need to recognize the correlation between declarations that would bury and forget about liberation theology, and the desire to bury and so forget the martyrs. Likewise, while deliberate efforts to actively suppress liberation theology function like deliberate campaigns to discredit the martyrs, the careless tendency to forget what liberation theology has taught us goes hand in hand with a tendency to romanticize the martyrs or trivialize the reasons for their deaths. The active or passive suppression of liberation theology is, in the final analysis, one more way to actively or passively forget martyrs like Archbishop Romero, Bishop Girardi, and Father Ellacuría. But we cannot forget our martyrs any more than we can stop doing theology that is historically conscious and socially responsible.

[18] Martin Buber, *Werke* III, Munich, 1963, 71, quoted in Metz, *Faith in History and Society*, pp. 207–208.
[19] Ibid.
[20] Metz, *Faith in History and Society*, p. 208.

The Theology of Martyrdom in Latin America*

MARTIN MAIER, SJ

1. Return of the Martyrs

In his Papal Communication 'Tertio millenio adveniente' of 10 November 1994 Pope John Paul II speaks of a 'return of the martyrs': 'At the end of the second millennium the church has once again become a church of the martyrs. The persecution of believers – priests, monks and nuns, and the laity – has led in various parts of the world to a great many being martyred. To bear witness to Christ to the point of shedding blood has become the common heritage of Catholics, Orthodox, Anglicans and Protestants.... So far as possible this testimony must not be lost to the Church' (No. 37). In saying this, the Pope was adverting to an indisputable fact: In no century before in the Church's history have more people borne witness to their faith through giving up their lives than the twentieth century. And even though, from a quantitative point of view, the number of martyrs should not be overestimated, one can nonetheless say that in no other continent have as many Christians been persecuted and killed on account of their commitment to faith and justice as in Latin America. Jon Sobrino speaks of the Latin American Church as a 'Church of martyrs'.[1]

The general public usually only reacts to atrocities that have occurred, and continue to occur, in Latin America when well-known personalities are murdered, such as, for example, Archbishop Oscar Romero in El Salvador on 24 March 1980, or the six Jesuits of the Central American University on 16 November 1989. The last bishop murdered in Latin America was Juan Gerardi: on 26 April 1998 he was beaten to death with a stone in Guatemala, two days after he had presented in public a report

---

* Translation from the German by Christopher Hamilton.
[1] Cf. J. Sobrino. 'Los mártires latinoamericanos. Interpelación y gracia para la Iglesia', in *Revista Latinoamericana de Teología*, 48 (1999), 307.

on the worst violations of Human Rights in Guatemala during the years of the civil war. This white paper, which consists of over 1,400 pages in three volumes, carries the title 'Recuperación de la memoria histórica' – 'Recovery of Historical Memory' (REMHI). Bishop Gerardi was thus called the 'martyr for the memory of a people'. These 'well-known' martyrs stand in for many unknown ones: they are in death, just as they were in life, the voice of those who have no voice.

That there are so many martyrs in Latin America is a consequence of the new direction which the Church has taken, a direction which itself stems from the first postconciliar meeting of the Latin American Bishops Conference of 1968 in Medellín, Colombia. The bishops sought there to translate into a Latin American context the epoch-making events of the Second Vatican Council. What the Council saw as an opening of the Church to the modern world became in Medellín an opening of the Church to the world of the poor which was later expressed as the 'option for the poor'. This involved a fundamental change of position for the church in Latin America. Aside from a few notable exceptions, it had, in the centuries following the violent conquest of Latin America, stood on the side of the powerful and rich. Now it gave up this alliance – at least to some extent – and became the defender of the poor and their rights. This was bound to lead to conflict.

2. The Example of El Salvador

In hardly any country in Latin America was the impetus of Medellín as enduringly effective as in El Salvador. Indeed, El Salvador can serve as an example for the whole subcontinent since, despite all its peculiarities, the country unites as in a microcosm not only all the misery and suffering, but also all the hopes, of Latin America. This small country has a long history of repression and exploitation. In 1932, after a military coup, the army put down a revolt by peasants and agricultural workers, the infamous 'Matanza', killing 30,000 people in a few weeks. Until 1979 military dictatorships held sway, seeking to conceal themselves behind a threadbare democratic façade.

In the 1960s, however, the people of El Salvador started to become restive. They could simply no longer acquiesce in the extreme social divisions and the unequal distribution of land. New social movements, unions and left-wing parties emerged. The Catholic Church with the then Archbishop Luis Chávez y González also supported the predominantly landless peasants in their attempts to organise themselves. In 1976 the Christian Union of Peasants and Agricultural Workers FECCAS-UTC (Federción Cristiana de Campesinos Salvadoreños-Unión de Trabajadores del Campo) played an important role in supporting a planned land reform which was, however, eventually subverted by the oligarchy. This increasingly led to those in power viewing socially committed Christian groups as opponents: repression and persecution followed.

The new direction signalled by Medellín was put into practice by the Jesuit priest Rutilio Grande in the *campesino* village of Aguilares. He impressed upon the impoverished peasants the idea that Christian belief in no way required them simply to accept their fate. On the contrary, the Bible showed them the way in which they could demand justice and recognition of their human dignity from their oppressors. In his sermons he often said: 'God doesn't lie around in heaven in a hammock: he is right here among us.'

Rutilio Grande encouraged the *campesinos* to organise themselves into a union. The reaction of those in power was, however, not long in coming: Rutilio Grande was the first priest murdered in El Salvador in 1977. Shortly before that, Oscar Arnulfo Romero had been appointed Archbishop of San Salvador. Romero was considered a deeply pious but, until then, rather timid and conservative man of the Church. He was the favoured candidate for the archbishopric among the oligarchy which dominated the country and conservative circles in the Church. However, the murder of Rutilio Grande released an inner conversion in Romero. He himself now put into practice the change of direction for the benefit of the poor and oppressed as this had been envisaged by the Latin-American bishops in Medellín. Thanks to his sermons, which were broadcast on the radio and in which he protested against the violations of human rights by the military regime, he became the person in El Salvador whose voice was most in evidence.

On account of his prophetic defence of the poor Oscar Romero was increasingly treated with hostility and threatened with death. He found particularly painful the opposition of some of his own bishops. At least at first even Pope John Paul II failed to understand him. On 24 March 1980 Romero was shot during the celebration of Mass by a hired army marksman. The instigator of the murder was Roberto D'Aubuisson, a major in the army and later founder of the extreme right-wing ARENA party. Since then, Romero has become a symbol throughout the world of a socially and politically committed Church which takes its inspiration from liberation theology and the option for the poor. Members of other denominations and even atheists see him as an example to all. In 1998 a statue of Romero was unveiled over a portal in Westminster Abbey in London where he is to be seen with nine other martyrs of the twentieth century, including Dietrich Bonhoeffer, Martin Luther King and Maximilian Kolbe.[2]

---

[2] See the chapter in this volume by Michael Campbell Johnston.

3. Expansion of the Theological Concept of Martyrdom

In his memoir of Archbishop Oscar Romero Jon Sobrino writes that Romero asked him to reflect, in the light of the persecution of the Church and of martyrdom in El Salvador, on the theological meaning of such events. Sobrino noticed that there were few texts which threw theological light upon persecution and martyrdom of the kind which took place in El Salvador. Indeed, in European theology the topic of martyrdom appears only as a side issue.[3] On the other hand, for liberation theology in Latin America, which takes historical realities as a point of departure, martyrdom has become a central topic. Thus the Bolivian theologian Victor Codina writes: 'Whereas martyrdom seems to play no role any more in modern European theology, liberation theology has, as result of the persecution of the Church in the last few years in Latin America, made of this topic a focal point of concern.'[4]

Liberation theology begins its theological reflections on martyrdom, not from the canonical-dogmatic definition of martyrdom, but from the lived experienced of Latin America. Thus Sobrino writes at the start of his investigation of a theology of martyrdom: 'I had to begin a theological argument with reality'.[5] In this it became clear that the reality of martyrdom as it appeared in Latin America was not to be grasped from the usual theological and canonical perspective. This reality led to further theological developments, starting from historical facts in order to expand the conceptual and systematic resources of theology. Jon Sobrino expresses it thus: 'There are new motives for murdering Christians and in such high numbers, and this lays on us the obligation to rethink the definition of martyrdom since anything else would issue in the paradoxical situation that many Christians suffer a violent death yet cannot be considered martyrs. And whatever the official definition of martyrdom might be this would be something that neither common sense nor faith itself can accept'.[6]

A good account of the traditional concept of martyrdom is to be found in an article by Otto Semmelroth in the theological encyclopaedia *Sacramentum Mundi*.[7] Semmelroth distinguishes here between the

---

[3] Cf. L. Weckel, *Um des Lebens willen. Zu einer Theologie des Martyriums aus befreiungstheologischer Sicht* Mainz, 1998.

[4] V. Codina, *Parabolas de la mina y el lago. Teología desde la noche oscura* Salamanca, 1990, p. 178.

[5] J. Sobrino, 'Mi recuerdo de Monseñor Romero' in *Revista Latinoamericana de Teología* 16 (1989), p. 25.

[6] J. Sobrino, *Jesucristo liberador. Lectura histórica-teológica de Jesús de Nazaret*, San Salvador, 1991, p. 442; ET *Jesus the Liberator: A Historical – Theological View*, Maryknoll, Orbis, 1993, p. 266.

[7] O. Semmelroth, 'Martyrium' in *Sacramentum Mundi*, Vol 3, Freiburg 1969, 363–367.

material aspect, that is, martyrdom as the suffering of a violent death; and the formal aspect, that is, martyrdom as an expression of love and for the sake of a life in imitation of Jesus. If a death is to be recognized by the Church as martyrdom this presupposes both that it is freely accepted and neither that it occurs in the course of armed struggle nor that the victim is killed involuntarily. The martyr bears witness to the meaning and correctness of his belief. An important element in this is the 'odium fidei', the hatred of Christian belief. Martyrdom presupposes an inwardly affirmed and freely-given renunciation of life. It is the highest fulfilment of love in a unity of love of God and of one's neighbour. Martyrdom means a 'loving sacrifice of oneself as the Thou of God that is affirmed in faith'. Martyrdom is a potent testimony for others. From a christological point of view, it is a shaping of one's own life consonant with that of Christ and a 'participation though grace in the death of Christ and in its achievement'. In addition this confers on martyrdom a soteriological quality.

From a historical point of view the concept of martyrdom is an analogous concept which has changed in the course of history and has been adapted to new realities. An example of this is John Paul II's Papal Edict of 25 January 1983 'Divinus Perfectionis Magister' in which the ecclesiastical procedure with respect to canonization was put on a new footing. Here the suffering of a violent death is recognized by the Church as a martyr's death when it takes place 'in aerumnis carceris', that is, 'in the misery of the dungeon'. This opened the way for the possibility of recognizing those people who have died as a result of incarceration and maltreatment, for example in the Nazis' concentration camps, as martyrs. The Church has thus altered and expanded its understanding of martyrdom.

Karl Rahner is one of the few European theologians who have concerned themselves more intensively from a theological perspective with the topic of martyrdom. Shortly before his death he appealed in an essay 'Aspects of Martyrdom', which was published in the journal *Concilium* in 1983, for an extension of the classical concept. The point of departure for him in this essay is the question whether the concept of martyrdom can be applied to the case of a person who has been killed in active struggle. He points out that 'the "passively suffered" death of Jesus was the consequence of Jesus' struggle against the religious and political rulers of his time'. Jesus' death must not, therefore, be seen in isolation from a life which included a struggle against social and religious suppression and exploitation. With this proclamation of the Kingdom of God and of the way of life which this brings with it Jesus came into conflict with the rulers of his time. Interestingly enough, Rahner casts a glance in this context in the direction of El Salvador and asks: 'But why, for example, should Archbishop Romero, who died in the struggle for justice in society, a struggle which he derived from a profound Christian faith, not be a martyr?'[8]

The phenomenon of martyrdom in Latin America represents also a challenge for the canonical understanding of martyrdom. The official procedure for canonization runs, as is well known, slowly and laboriously. Yet in Latin America many who have been killed as Christians are honoured by their communities as martyrs without further ado. Hence Archbishop Romero said of the first two priests who were murdered in El Salvador that they were for him 'two true martyrs':

> It seems to me that they are martyrs as the people understand things. Of course, I do not mean in a canonical sense, where to be a martyr presupposes a process involving the supreme authority of the Church which then proclaims a person a martyr before the universal Church. I respect that law and I will never claim that our murdered priests are canonized. But they are certainly martyrs as the people see things, they are men who preached precisely this kind of involvement with poverty....[9]

4. The Conflictual Nature of Reality

Martyrdom in Latin America is an integral part of the social and political conflict which has dominated, and continues to dominate, most of the countries of the subcontinent. It is true that the period of military dictatorships is over, yet the problems which led to repression and civil wars have not therewith disappeared. Martyrdom thus reflects the conflictual and dialectical structure of reality.

In liberation theology this dialectical and conflictual character of reality found expression in the opposition between the God of life and the idols of death.[10] It was Archbishop Oscar Romero who spoke anew of idols as a wholly genuine reality: the idolisation of wealth, of power and of the ideology of national security, which is posited as an absolute and in whose name people are sacrificed. In one of his sermons he expressed it in the following terms: 'I denounce, above all, the absolutisation of wealth. This is the great evil of El Salvador: wealth, private property as absolutely sacrosanct, and woe to him who touches the high tension wire: he will burn his fingers!' (sermon 12 August 1979).[11]

---

[8] K. J. Rahner, 'Dimensionen des Martyriums: Plädoyer für eine Erweiterung des klassischen Begriffs' in *Concilium*, 19 (1983) 175.
[9] Sermon of 23 September, 1979.
[10] Cf. *La lucha de los dioses. Los ídolos de la opresión y la búsqueda del Dios liberador*, San José, 1980.
[11] Sermon 12 August 1979.

The conflictual nature of Christian belief is thus connected with the conflictual nature of reality. The idols have an active presence in reality, and Sobrino connects this with that which he calls an 'anti-kingdom'. The martyrs 'make clear that there are victims and victimizers, justice and injustice, grace and sin. They make clear the Kingdom of God and the Anti-Kingdom, the God of Life, Abba, and the gods of death. They make clear that Jesus is the truth and the life and that the Devil is a liar and murderer'.[12]

Martyrdom in Latin America reveals itself to be the result of the prophetic criticism which the Church and theology have directed at these idols. As long as the Church limited itself to works of charity it was never considered to be disturbing or threatening. Yet as soon as the Church began to enquire about the causes of poverty and injustice it was persecuted. Archbishop Helder Câmara from Brazil articulated this in the well-known sentence: 'When I give the poor bread, they call me a saint. But when I ask why the poor have nothing to eat I am cursed and called a communist'.[13]

It is important to see that the Church is not persecuted as an institution. Rather, only that part of it is, which has put into practice the option for the poor. This means that the Church is internally divided. This could be seen when Oscar Romero was Archbishop of San Salvador in the division in the Bishops' Conference – for himself personally a painful episode. Societal division led to a division within the Church itself.

In Latin America martyrdom comes not primarily from an 'odium fidei' but an 'odium iustitiae'. This comes to the fore in that it is, in general, Christians who kill other Christians. In Thailand, directly after the murder of his comrades, Jon Sobrino was asked in astonishment: 'Are there really Catholics in your country who kill priests?' Because the martyrs were killed on account of their work for justice and the human dignity of the poor, martyrdom in Latin America is fundamentally bound up with the option for the poor.

The memory of the martyrs in Latin America is also an integral part of the conflictual character of reality. This memory is a concrete example of what Johann Baptist Metz has called 'dangerous memory'. At the beginning of the eighties, after the murder of Archbishop Romero, it was dangerous for the poor even to have a picture of Romero hanging in their hut. A picture of Romero was enough in some cases for someone to be considered 'subversive' and to 'disappear' if the hut was searched by army officers.

---

[12] J. Sobrino, 'Los mártires jesuánicos en el tercer mundo', in *Revista Latinoamericana de Teología*, 48 (1999) 249.

[13] Quoted in L. Kaufmann, *Damit wir morgen Christ sein können. Vorläufer im Glauben*, Freiburg, 1984, p. 99.

5. Theology of Martyrdom

Having given a somewhat descriptive account of the reality of martyrdom in Latin America it is appropriate to show by briefly sketching an example of Jon Sobrino's how it is that martyrs cast light on the central concepts of theology. Of prime importance here are Christology, Ecclesiology and Soteriology.

a. Christology: 'Jesuanic Martyrs'

Sobrino calls the martyrs in Latin America 'jesuanic martyrs' because they were killed in imitation of Jesus, and for the same reason. Thus he is able to say: 'The martyrs are, historically existentially, the highest introduction into the mystery for Christology'.[14] The martyrs in Latin America represent for Sobrino the jesuanic face of Christianity and lend it credibility. The most important point of reference in the Latin-American understanding of martyrdom is the practice of Jesus.

Martyrs are witnesses for that which most concerned Jesus: The Kingdom of God for the poor. In practical terms, to preach the Kingdom of God is to identify with the poor, with those who own nothing, with the disenfranchised. This exposes the prophet and the mediator of the Kingdom of God to danger, for it leads him or her into potential conflict with the powerful. Even in the Gospels persecution is a sign that men and women of the Church are truly following Jesus. For the willingness to give up one's own life is a condition of the imitation of Jesus:

> To be a martyr is not only to die because of Christ, but to die for the cause of Jesus. Martyrdom is, then, not only death for the sake of fidelity to some demand of Christ's, which, speaking hypothetically, could even have been in some way arbitrary, but rather as a faithful imitation of the death of Jesus.[15]

When martyrdom is thus understood as a participation in the death of Jesus the death of martyrs and the cross of Jesus illuminate each other:

> Let us also say that the cross of Jesus refers to all crosses that exist, but that these in turn refer to that of Jesus and that they are historically the great hermeneutics towards understanding why Jesus was killed. They find theological expression in the unfathomable question of why Jesus dies.[16]

---

[14] Sobrino, 'Los mártires jesuánicos', p. 250.
[15] Sobrino, *Jesucristo liberador*, p. 444; cf *Jesus the Liberator*, p. 267.
[16] Ibid., p. 310; *Jesus the Liberator*, pp. 195-96.

b. Ecclesiology: Martyrdom as the Sign of the True Church

Martyrdom in Latin America has an ecclesiological dimension. Archbishop Romero understood persecution as one of the signs of the Church: 'Persecution is a typical sign of the authenticity of the Church. A Church which does not suffer persecution, but rather enjoys the privileges and the support of worldly things is not the true Church of Jesus Christ'.[17] In its persecution Romero saw a sign that the Church was fulfilling its mission.

For this reason he could utter the astonishing words:

> It makes me happy, brothers, that our Church is persecuted precisely on account of the option for the poor and because it is committed body and soul to the concerns of the poor. The Church speaks to the whole people, the rulers, the rich and the powerful. If there are no poor, if we do not concern ourselves with the poverty of our people as though they are our own family, we shall not be able to save society.[18]

The Church in Latin America also found itself confronted by the reality of 'collective martyrdom'. This refers to the massacres in, for example, El Salvador and Guatemala, during which sometimes hundreds of people, predominantly women and children, were simply butchered by army units. These massacres often took place in the context of communities in which a theology of liberation in the spirit of the Medellín documents was being put into practice. In these cases the people did not give up their life of their own volition, and neither did they display the virtues which are necessary for canonization. Nonetheless, the Church has to find a way of approaching such cases from a theological point of view. In this context Romero coined the concept of the 'crucified people' which came to be of central importance for the theology of Ignacio Ellacuría[19] and Jon Sobrino. Sobrino applies the concept of martyrdom in an analogous sense to the 'anonymous mass of innocent people who have been murdered' and he identifies them with the servant of God of the prophet Isaiah. He describes them as 'crucified peoples' and a people of martyrs.[20]

---

[17] Sermon 11 March 1980.
[18] Sermon 15 July 1979.
[19] Cf. I. Ellacuría, 'El pueblo crucificado, ensayo de soteriología histórica' in *Revista Latinoamericana de Teología* 18 (1989), pp. 305–333.
[20] Cf. *Jesucristo liberador*, pp. 440ff; *Jesus the Liberator*, pp. 254 ff.

c. Soteriology: The Significance of Martyrdom for Salvation

The significance for salvation of a death suffered violently for the sake of others is spoken of in the Bible in the songs of the servant of God in the prophet Isaiah where it is said that the suffering servant became the justification of many (Isaiah 53.11) and the light for all people (Isaiah 49.6). In the New Testament one of St Paul's comments in the Epistle to the Colossians became important for the meaning of suffering for the nature of salvation. He writes: 'I am now rejoicing in my sufferings for your sake and in my flesh I am completing what is lacking in Christ's afflictions for the sake of his body, that is, the church (Colossians 1.24). Sobrino applies this thought to the martyrs who in an analogous way accordingly complete through their body that which is still lacking in the suffering of Christ.

Ignacio Ellacuría has distinguished between the historico-political level and the level of faith in the meaning which a martyr's death has for salvation. Yet the two are surely connected with one another. What kind of meaning would the Christian belief in salvation have if absolutely nothing of this meaning could be established in historical reality?

The martyrs show that death and sin are indisputable facts of history. They come to light in that they illuminate the truth that this world is a world of victims. Yet they also show that mercy and resurrection are a reality of history. The martyrs call for solidarity and a renewal of life. They evangelise. The most well-known example is that of Rutilio Grande for Archbishop Romero. The martyrs open up new space for living. They demonstrate love and solidarity as an alternative to the prevailing attitudes of violence and suppression. They show that it is possible to live and die in this world as a human being and a Christian.

Archbishop Romero, too, often spoke of the soteriological meaning of suffering:

> As a minister and a citizen of El Salvador it makes me deeply sad that the organized elements of our people are still being massacred simply because we go out onto the street in an orderly manner to ask for justice and freedom. I am quite certain that so much blood spilt and so much pain inflicted on the families of so many victims will not be in vain. This blood and suffering will rain down and bring up again and again new and more numerous seeds of Salvadorians who will become aware that they have the responsibility of building a more humane and fairer society, a society which will grow with the realization of the bold structural reforms, urgent and radical, which our country needs'.[21]

---

[21] Sermon 27 January 1980.

The old understanding of martyrdom as a baptism of blood, as a death with Christ in order to be resurrected with him, is being reactivated in Latin America in a new way. The martyrs are present in history as ones who are resurrected, something which is expressed in the call 'Presente' at memorial services for the martyrs. Shortly before his murder Romero said, with presentiment: 'If they kill me, I shall be resurrected amongst the Salvadorian people'. A few weeks after the murder of the fellow members of his community Sobrino wrote in one of his very personal reflections:

> All the martyrs will be resurrected in history, each in his own way. The case of Monsignor Romero is exceptional and cannot be repeated. Yet Rutilio Grande is also present in numerous peasants, the nuns of North America live on in Chaltenango and La Libertad, Octavio Ortiz in El Despertar, and all the hundreds of martyred peasants live on in their communities.

6. Conclusion

The martyrs in Latin America who have lived right to the last as followers of Jesus are not only witnesses of a lived Christian faith in modern times, but also a source of understanding for theology of the first importance. They are 'signs of the times' in the sense that *Gaudium et spes* has defined the signs of the times: 'Signs in which the presence of God and his plans manifest themselves in history' (GS 11). The martyrs make real the life, cross and resurrection of Jesus. They confront the Church and theology with the urgent nature of being a Christian. Thus they become a 'locus theologicus', a theological point of reference, which Jon Sobrino describes in this way: 'In these martyrdoms, reality has pronounced the last word, not only with respect to the things which lie on the surface, but on life and death, the horror of sin and the fascination of grace'.

PART 2:

HUMAN RIGHTS AND THE COMMITMENT TO LIFE

Recovery: The Uses of Memory and History in the Guatemalan Church's REMHI Project

MARCELA LÓPEZ LEVY

> ... *we are collecting the people's memories because we want to contribute to the construction of a different country. This path was and continues to be full of risks.*
>
> Monsignor Gerardi[1]

Truth and Power

A bloodstained lump of concrete lay blatantly on the garage floor. There was blood everywhere. A dead man lay on the floor, his face utterly disfigured by numerous blows to the head while too many people trampled the scene of the crime, obscuring possible leads.[2] The death of Monsignor Gerardi could not have been more laden with symbolic intent to terrorize. He was the head of the Catholic Church's effort to reclaim the hidden truth of victims of terror; his was the mind behind the work of many hundreds, listening to many thousands, to defend human rights in Guatemala. The apparatus of death showed it was intact, even though the thirty-six-year-old war was officially over, by murdering the most senior member of the church to perish in the conflict.

The killers attempted to obliterate the work of years, based on a

---

[1] Speech by Monsignor Gerardi on his presentation of the REMHI Report at Guatemala City Metropolitan Cathedral on 24 April 1998 in REMHI, *Guatemala: Never Again!* The Official Report of the Human Rights Office, Archdiocese of Guatemala, London, Latin America Bureau and CIIR, 1999, p. xxiii. Where the REMHI report is quoted in this chapter, it refers to the English abridged edition, published in North America by Orbis Books and in Europe by the Latin America Bureau and CIIR, 1999. The full work comprises four volumes and is currently only available in Spanish.

[2] Resumé of the Case of the Murder of Monseñor Juan José Gerardi Conadera compiled by the Human Rights Office of the Archdiocese of Guatemala, personal communication, November 1999.

life alongside the poor and indigenous majority of Guatemala. They aimed to silence the population, again. If a prominent clergyman could be killed (with assumed impunity), nobody was safe. Nobody could speak out. The restricted spaces which had been opening in Guatemala to challenge the structures of terror were made starkly vulnerable.

The forces which seemed to have retreated out of the public light proved they believed the country belonged to them, and with it, the truth. That the truth which had been unveiled two days previously in the REMHI report would not be countenanced, would not be allowed to have a place in the national discourse. Truth was being denied to those whose lives had been taken, with the death of yet another.

Yet against all odds, hundreds of thousands of people poured onto the streets to prove them wrong. Mourning was done publicly, in thousands' strong marches and demonstrations which were also wake and funeral. To show that there is another Guatemala, which belongs to the people who have suffered most, that their truth is real, and different from the official history; that the silent Guatemala will be so no more, will not allow itself to be silenced again, *Never Again!*

It is a mark of the chilling degree of control the state machinery of terror feels it retains that it did not think it was creating a martyr, but silencing a society. In a war which has left over 200,000 dead and disappeared, there are so many martyrs for so many Guatemalans, that there has not been a single unifying figure whose death in the struggle could mobilize the divided country and international opprobrium. The murder of Monsignor Gerardi, two days after his presentation of the unofficial, but crucial, church truth commission, put the memory of the war at the forefront of everyone's mind. The power struggle for truth, and with it the future of Guatemala, continued.

Recovery of Historical Memory Project (REMHI)

The REMHI initiative was born of frustration at the lack of scope and mandate agreed for the official Truth Commission, (CEH)[3] in the Oslo

---

[3] The Commission for the Historical Clarification of the Violations of Human Rights and Acts of Violence which have Caused Suffering to the Guatemalan Population, known by the Spanish acronym CEH, *Comisión de Esclarecimiento Histórico* was agreed at Oslo Accord signed as part of the Peace Process in 1994, 'charged with investigating and elucidating the human rights violations and violence connected with the armed confrontation and recommending measures to promote peace and national harmony'. *Guatemala: Memoria del Silencio*, (Guatemala, United Nations, 1999). The CEH can be found in its entirety at http://hrdata.aaas.org/ceh/index.html

Accord signed by the government and the URNG[4] in 1994. It was made explicit that the CEH could not 'individualize responsibility, nor have any legal implications'.[5] Moreover, the commission was to have an impossibly short time to collect testimonies and other evidence of thirty-six years of violence. REMHI was to contribute to the CEH with research over a longer period of time, coupled with the unequalled reach of the church into the rural areas of the country, and significantly, was to provide names of both victims and perpetrators.

REMHI was coordinated by the Human Rights Office of the Archdiocese of Guatemala, and directed by auxiliary Bishop Juan Gerardi. The task was described by him in these words: 'as a church, we collectively and responsibly took on the task of breaking the silence that thousands of war victims have kept for years.' (*Guatemala: Never Again!* p.xxiv) The primary objective, was 'to know the truth which will set us all free', he said, quoting from John 8.32 (ibid.). Yet REMHI aimed to go much further. From the beginning, the work of collecting testimonies was rooted in the communities where they were gathered, to be returned, to support 'the use of memory as an instrument of social reconstruction' (ibid. p. xxv). Previous truth commissions, in other countries, have contained the hope, at the level of national society, that truth can bring about reconciliation. The strength of REMHI is that it also fulfilled this hope at the level of individual named communities as they sought justice, and to bury and remember their dead with due respect and ceremony.

REMHI was important to the Church as a visible sign of its human rights ministry, a public commitment to the dignity of the people, and a statement about the contribution it could make to the construction of a different country. The Church in Guatemala had solid foundations on which to base such forthrightness; although it has contained conservative elements, and up to the 1970s these were predominant, from that time on it has placed itself consistently on the side of the poorest, those with least voice in Guatemalan society. The rural networks which make REMHI a unique gathering of testimonies are a testament to the long-standing presence of the Church in the distant highlands. To take a truth commission to those who cannot come to the cities, due to lack of resources, marked a bias towards those whose silence has been

---

[4] The Unión Revolucionaria Nacional Guatemalteca, or Guatemalan National Revolutionary Unity, was the united front created in 1982 by the three guerrilla movements, the FAR (Rebel Armed Forces), EGP (Guerrilla Army of the Poor) and ORPA (Revolutionary Organization of the People in Arms) and the PGT (Guatemalan Workers' Party).

[5] Quoted in R. Wilson, 'The Politics of Remembering and Forgetting', in R. Sieder (ed.), *Guatemala After the Peace Accords*, London, Institute of Latin American Studies, 1998, p. 184.

deepest, those who have had the least access to a hearing. In parallel, people cooperated with the project because they recognized the Church which suffered the ravages of repression along with them in the 1970s and 1980s. Bishop Gerardi was forced in 1980 to close down the parishes he worked in in Quiché due to the repeated attacks and threats to priests, religious and lay catechists; religious and lay people were killed, at a time when being a catechist was synonymous with guerrilla to the army.

The Protagonists

There was a cathartic benefit to those who gave their testimony, a sense of weight being lifted, as well as the awareness of becoming part of history: 'Now I am content because the testimony I have given will become part of history ... now I have released my pain by giving my testimony' (ibid. p.xxxii).

The focus of REMHI on the communities, the strong emphasis on their priorities for rehabilitation and justice arises from the evidence of the extent the armed forces's counterinsurgency strategy included 'community destruction' as an aim; the effects are laid bare, as one in five testimonies reported it. The most extreme form of such devastation were the 422 documented massacres of entire villages;[6] the majority of massacres recorded took place in Quiché (263 compared to 63 in Alta Verapaz, the next worst-affected department). The number of instances were communities were attacked, burnt and pillaged are much higher. The militarization of communities, which meant 'people's lives were transformed into a battleground' (ibid. p. xxxiii) is tackled as another facet of the military's assault. The most concerted effort to alter power relations within and between communities was achieved by the forced recruitment into the Civilian Self-Defence Patrols (PACs),[7] which at their height numbered some 900,000 men across the country; although they have officially been disbanded, the PAC authority structures continue to affect community relations. For many hundred of thousands of highland inhabitants, exile or displacement were the only ways of surviving these concerted attacks; for some, it took the form of forcible displacement into military-controlled 'model villages' to be 're-educated' and kept under close surveillance.

The bottom-up nature of the work gives REMHI much of its power.

---

[6] REMHI uses two definitions of 'massacre', one related to community destruction as quoted here; the other refers to multiple killings of three or more people, of which they documented 1,090. These accounted for over 60 per cent of all deaths (*Guatemala: Never Again!*, pp. 295–6).

[7] Patrullas de Autodefensa Civil, PAC.

The interviews were carried out by some seven hundred volunteers, who spoke the local languages of the region they worked in. They gathered over 6,000 testimonies which accounted for more than 55,000 victims. The open-ended questions were not meant only as a way of gathering information, but as one tool in the process of hearing, actively, what survivors of the violence had to say. The seven general questions underline the commitment to seeing from the speakers's point of view: Who was the victim? What happened? Who did it? Why did it happen? What did you do to cope with the situation? What effect did the event have on you and your community? What needs to be done so that it doesn't happen again?

There are many layers to the impact of these questions. We have already touched on the fact that having an outsider, in the name of the Church, come to a community and request testimonies to establish the truth, *their* truth, is already to begin changing the power dynamics in a rural context which has received mostly neglect and violence from external agents.

The questions not only focus on the memory of specific acts of violence, but also inquire after the effects on the individual, the family and community. Beyond that, they acknowledge the capacity for individuals and communities to deal with their experience by seeking to know how they have coped – this last element is a powerful recognition that people are more than simply victims. Human rights information gathering[8] can easily reinforce the helplessness felt by victims of arbitrary violence, yet REMHI's questions contain the intent to value people's own resources as the only possible starting point to subsequent 'reconstruction'.

The report reflects the complexity of relating the levels of effects while portraying the specific violence targeted against different social groups. Violence against children deserves special treatment, as testimonies record an upcoming generation of young people who at the very least have witnessed and absorbed terror in the less differentiated way characteristic of childhood, and who at worst have been direct victims, been left orphaned, or been displaced. Because children were often to be found near their mothers, there is significant overlap between violence aimed at women. Although men make up the majority of victims, women were subjected to brutality made more extreme by their greater vulnerability; the atrocities against defenceless civilians take

---

[8] For an illuminating discussion on the way in which human rights work constructs particular ways of understanding often chaotic events with limited information, see R. A. Wilson 'Representing Human Rights Violations: Social Contexts and Subjectivities' in R. A. Wilson (ed.), *Human Rights, Culture and Context: Anthropological Perspectives*, London, Pluto Press, 1997. Wilson's reflections are also apt when discussing the conclusions drawn as to the causes of the conflict (see below).

unbearable proportions when the rape of young girls is recounted in testimonies, or the hacking of pregnant women. Although REMHI could not find documented evidence of a planned assault on women, one testimony sums up how it felt:

> I think that the counterinsurgency policy was very detailed, thought out, and calculated in the case of women. Because women definitely are a symbol, the symbol of life, of the perpetuation of life. In other words, to kill a woman is to kill life. Like in the case of old people, the idea was to kill the people's wisdom, their historical memory, their roots (ibid. p.80).

The questions used by the parish workers not only enabled the gathering of specific requests for memorials, support in initiating exhumations or seeking judicial process; it also meant bringing rural communities, the most numerous victims of violence, into the national consciousness, going to them to recognize their centrality to the Guatemalan national experience. Two-thirds of the testimonies were collected in Mayan languages, a concrete sign of change in Guatemala, to hear the excluded majority in their mother tongue; to hear those whose history and memory are known among themselves, but did not form part of the collective history of Guatemalans. Moreover, the not unproblematic traditional role of the church in promoting forgiveness and reconciliation enabled REMHI to reach perpetrators, a significant, if tiny, breach of the wall of impunity.

The testimonies of perpetrators of the crimes are not many numerically, but their weight is significant nevertheless. They approached REMHI workers themselves, desperate to unburden themselves of their guilt and horror at what they had seen and participated in. Every one of the men cried before they could begin to speak; all of them feared retribution if identified. Most could not recount what they had been involved in in the first person, but described events they claimed to have witnessed; these men who cannot recognize themselves in the brutality of what they have lived and done are the first signs of an admission of guilt which is a necessary step in recovery, personally, and socially.

Reaching perpetrators has provided a key breakthrough in other countries. In Argentina, notwithstanding a respected truth commission report which became a best-selling book[9] and the only trials of their kind in the continent, against the military junta generals, it was not until the public confession of one naval captain driven to alcoholism by

---

[9] *Nunca Más*, Informe de la Comisión Nacional sobre la Desaparición Personas, Buenos Aires, Eudeba, 1984.

his part in the dirty war that the 'process of national reorganization'[10] truly began to unravel for the majority of Argentinians. Adolfo Scilingo was an ex-Navy officer who in March 1996, exactly twenty years after the coup which began the dirty war, confessed his part in throwing drugged prisoners from a helicopter into the river Plate, alive. In the thirteen years of democracy which had elapsed, the military had consistently denied the 'flights of death', while Scilingo told of how those participating were rotated to ensure all officers were implicated and compromised. Then president Saúl Menem called Scilingo a 'crook and a liar' when he first spoke up, and the military succeeded in blackening his character in the media; he was eventually imprisoned in Spain, mostly for his own protection. His confession opened the floodgates which forced the head of the armed forces to make a formal apology to the victims of the *proceso* in 1998.

In the case of REMHI, those who needed to unburden themselves of their actions could not, for their own security, reveal their identities or rank. From their accounts, it is possible to assume that most held lower ranks or were civilians forced into service. The relevance of their status is clear because although we learn more about the specific means of training for absolute obedience and the steps to creating a torturer and a murderer, these confessions have not rocked the repressive boat. The carefully constructed conspiracy of silence, where all are implicated in a true blood pact, has safeguarded the apparatus of terror, so far. While leaden control remains a reality, the chances of any of the intellectual authors of Guatemala's horror repenting are dim. Yet until some form of repentance is forthcoming, the balance of power, where the military believe they were in the right and continue to have the power to make their truth prevail, will be tipped against the Guatemalan people. Clearly, justice should not wait for the culprit to admit their guilt; but in Guatemala the judiciary is so weak that it cannot as yet force those responsible to face judgement. The Guatemalan military responsible for over ninety per cent of grave violations of human rights still believes it fought a necessary war. A turning point in understanding the conflict is required for justice to be served. The Chilean writer Ariel Dorfman faced the same problem with Augusto Pinochet: days after the ex-dictator's arrest in London in 1998, Dorfman was interviewed live on British TV and asked what he wanted from Pinochet, what he would say to the man himself. His response was to look straight into the camera, and speaking in Spanish, he said: *'General, arrepiéntase'* (General, repent). The effect was electrifying.

The abridged REMHI report, aimed at a wider audience, begins with

---

[10] This was the title given by the first military junta to their aims for society during their rule.

the reactions of those who have suffered violence, their coping mechanisms, and their contributions to ensuring Never Again is a meaningful call. Only after a reflection on how to prevent a recurrence of the horror lived, are we guided through analyses of the strategies and methodologies of terror.

The Method in the Madness

The section entitled the Methodology of Horror begins by outlining the institutions of the armed forces and the state dedicated to the planning and intelligence work required for the horror to be carried out to maximum effect. The detailed research into the 'intelligence behind the violence'[11] achieves one of REMHI's important aims: it names names. The CEH may not do so, but the church's report brings together years of investigations carried out by human rights activists at great personal risk, which put the testimonies gathered into their proper context. Violations were not random acts of brutality, but carefully planned and ordered police, military, and paramilitary missions.

We have known since the studies which followed the Holocaust[12] that obedience to authority can lead any 'normal' person to harm others knowingly. It is easier to be shocked by the duress which can be brought to bear, seen in the trajectory of one man from Jesuit and guerrilla collaborator to an advisor of the intelligence services and the Presidential General Staff (EMP)[13] which shook the church in Guatemala: in 1981, Luis Eduardo Pellecer Faena was abducted in Guatemala City, with witnesses testifying that he was wounded in the process; he is assumed to have been tortured to the degree that he literally 'lost' his mind. It is much harder to accept how sophisticated the military understanding of psychology was so that they could incorporate and control hundreds of thousands of men to a war without quarter.

The report calls the training of soldiers 'an education in violence' (*Guatemala: Never Again!*, p. 127), and it sets out just how regulated and thought-through the ways of imposing terror were, to affect the perpetrators as well as the victims. Although Guatemala holds the

---

[11] *Guatemala: Never Again!*, Chapter Seven, p. 105

[12] See S. Milgram, *Obedience to Authority*, London, HarperCollins, 1983, for the best overview of psychology research on this topic, including a thorough argument for why 'following orders' cannot be accepted as a valid defence.

[13] The EMP was a key institution in the counterinsurgency war, although it acquired even more political power after the March 1982 coup and particularly during the civilian presidencies after 1985. For more detail, see J. Schirmer, *The Guatemalan Military Project: A Violence Called Democracy*, Philadelphia, University of Pennsylvania Press, 1998, pp. 175–179.

woeful distinction of having been the first country to use disappearances on a massive scale, none of the methods described in their painful bleakness are novel. They form part of the corpus of counterinsurgency training given across the continent by US advisors;[14] in particular cases in Guatemala, the direct influence of Argentinian military personnel, among others, is documented. The savagery analysed underlines the continuity of horror in the twentieth century, and leaves no element beyond our comprehension.

Disappearances merit a much longer discussion than in possible here (see David Tombs' contribution in this volume). It is an ongoing violation, and as such is near impossible to grieve fully and recover from. Disappearances remain legally an open case, and for those left behind, an open wound, until the person is confirmed dead or reappears alive. When REMHI testimonies were gathered, the last known forced disappearance had taken place in 1993. In 2000, however, another case has been denounced by the human rights community, rekindling too familiar fears.

The experience of other countries in relation to challenging the perpetrators of the crimes brought to public light is that in the immediate aftermath of the conflict they are near untouchable. In Guatemala, the weakness of the judiciary, and the party in power since 1999, the Frente Republicano de Guatemala (FRG), the vehicle for ex-dictator Ríos Montt, both uphold impunity, politically and legally. In spite of a strong response from civil society following Monsignor Gerardi's death, in the course of 2000 a climate of fear has returned to haunt those working for social change, as threats and violence become a reality once more.

Recommendations

The recommendations made in the report reflect directly the cumulative input of those who shared their painful testimony: reparations, humanitarian assistance, collective memory, investigation of murder and disappearances, honouring victims, exhumations, and restoring memory to the people. The Church also calls for wider social change to ensure peace: demilitarization, freedom to an individual and collective cultural identity, and land distribution.

On the national arena, REMHI was successful in contributing to the

[14] See M. McClintock, *The American Connection, Volume Two: State Terror and Popular Resistance in Guatemala*, London, Zed Books, 1985, for an excellent historical overview of US involvement. For more current information, see the National Security Archives, (NSA) an NGO based in the US which requests declassification of state documents related to human rights abuses in other countries. The information the NSA provided for the CEH made a significant difference to their strong conclusions. Their research results can be found at http://www.gwu.edu/~nsarchiv/

results of the CEH report, which in turn produced a report that was to go beyond the expectations of many human rights advocates. As with REMHI, the CEH stresses the importance of constructing the nation on a different basis as its aim. The recommendations are similar, seeking respect for the memory of victims, reparation, exhumations, purges of the police and military, and a culture of respect and observance of human rights, democracy and justice. The impact of the CEH did not arise from these clear and strong general guidelines, but because it was able to substantiate that the overwhelming majority of abuses were carried out by the state, accounting for ninety-three per cent of cases (higher than REMHI estimated from its sample); stronger still, it accused the representatives of the state of crimes of genocide against the Mayan peoples between 1981 and 1983. Overall more than eighty per cent of victims were indigenous. The charges of genocide bypass the limitations to judicial process based on the CEH, as they are crimes against humanity which cannot have any recourse to amnesty or immunity.

Both reports operated on wider assumptions of truth commissions: that they will serve for the victims and their relatives to have their reality, their memory and history, vindicated. The social implications of such an assertion include confronting the majority of society which wanted to believe state propaganda (only dangerous guerrillas were killed) with the reality that the state is capable of genocide, murder and grave abuses of power against unarmed civilians.

The continuing power of the state forces involved in violence into the twenty-first century is evident in their silence in the face of the grave accusations levelled against them. As Monsignor Gerardi's murder shows, they feel powerful enough to protect themselves whilst they continue to sow terror. Between 1985 and 1999 the military was an acknowleged but not explicit power in the nation's politics. In 2000, with retired General Ríos Montt the President of Congress, they do not feel the need to remain in the shadows. The military were never defeated, not by the URNG, and not by civil society after the final Peace Accord was signed in December 1996. The state repressive machinery has not resorted solely to character assassination against the human rights movement, as used in Argentina against, for example, the Madres of the Plaza de Mayo, who have been disdainfully known as the *locas* (the madwomen). In Guatemala retribution is concrete: when Nobel Peace Prize winner Rigoberta Menchú took up the challenge set out in the CEH to accuse the ruling military juntas of 1981-1983 of genocide,[15] the military instructed a lawyer to take her to court, in turn, accused of treason. They are powerful enough not to accept that they

---

[15] The judicial process was set in motion in December 1999. She accused a number of generals and ex-chiefs of state of genocide, torture and state terrorism. Judge Guillermo Díaz Polanco accepted the case.

may have done wrong. The military's continued strength within the state begs the question of how *Nunca Más*, (Never Again) can be achieved, and how long it might take to construct a new country.

The Uses of Memory

> ... memory and oblivion, or remembering and social amnesia – and its institutionalized manifestation as amnesty – are an integral part of the process of building identities, both at the individual and collective levels. The are also an integral part of democratic institution-building.
> Elizabeth Jelín[16]

Memory is the process of being in the present as the sum of our past, our own and our community's, be that geographical or emotional. To recover, to restore memories which have been denied is to reinforce life in the present, to recognize the dignity of life. To apply the process to those who have been terrorized and silenced is to bring life back to the community; acknowledging the dead who have not been mourned, given proper sepulture, is to begin to reconstitute the social fabric which was rent by violence. Positively, it means mourning can take place where the dead take their appointed place, the ancestors who can be referred to, sought; yet the perpetrators also remain, sometimes in the same or neighbouring communities, and to remember the murder of loved ones is also to dwell again on the existence and presence of the murderers.

In memory we have a concept so rich that it works as shorthand to question history, which in turn brings together the personal and the political. Memory is the mechanism, although perhaps more accurately, the art, which we have found to make the contestation of history intelligible to all those who consider history academic.

Memory, in psychoanalysis, is the pathway to realization, the process through which repression of unbearable pain can be reclaimed, understood, and incorporated into a mature psyche so that it will not be held hostage any longer to past pain. It is to find a place for past traumatic experience, which allows us to live better in the present and face the future differently. As Martín-Baró expresses it: 'historical memory ... has to do with rescuing those aspects of identity which served yesterday, and will serve today, for liberation.'[17]

---

[16] E. Jelín, *The Minefields of Memory*, in NACLA, Volume XXXII No 2, September–October 1998, p. 24.

[17] I. Martín-Baró, *Writings for a Liberation Psychology*, Cambridge, Mass., Harvard University Press, 1994, p. 73. Martín-Baró was an outstanding social psychologist teaching in war-torn El Salvador. He was murdered on 16 November 1989 along with five other Jesuits, their housekeeper and her daughter, by the US-trained Atlacatl Battalion.

Individually, remembering helps set us free from the immobility caused by trauma, because it is a process of giving meaning, and to be able to create meaning is to exercise power. The power derives from our meaning being acknowledged by others: memory plays an active part in the social process. As Jelín writes, 'memory is always an intersubjective relationship based on the act of transmitting and reinterpreting. Even personal memory requires the participation of others'.[18]

Not only do each of us remember differently, but we do so as a function of who we are: our place in the world, our power in shaping reality, our gender, education, ethnicity, class. Often it is not that our versions are different from other people's, they also contradict and contest others' memories.

Collectively, memory is how we build community, over time, across generations, in spite of distance, persecution or dispersal. REMHI uses memory as a way of recognizing the mental health repercussions of violence, in the collective context of community while also strengthening memory's importance to the assertion of identity.

Memories are often encapsulated in images or feelings which may contain a strong symbolic resonance. Many memories can be painful or disturbing to retain and what remains are the deeper understandings, the narrative which gives meaning. In the REMHI testimonies, the descriptions of burning of houses, of livestock recurred. Survivors felt the loss of property and livelihood, but also conveyed that 'the burning of everyday objects linked to human life also destroys their *mwel* or *dioxil*, the principle underlying the continuity of life' (*Guatemala: Never Again!* pp. 40–41).

The report allows us to hear the voices of those who have suffered keenly, and one of the report's recommendations may seem at odds with the stated desire for justice: 'memory must avoid fixation on the past, obsessive repetition' (ibid. p. 318). In the context of conflicts, forgetting is often mentioned in relation only to the perpetrators preferring it, or what must be avoided if society is to prevent the same happening again. But it is also worth remembering that those who have suffered, at some point, need to continue living, and as Tzvetan Todorov says *'también existe el derecho al olvido'* (there must also be the right to forget).[19]

In a historical reversal of fortunes, the genocidal aim of the state to destroy the consciousness of community, at the local level, regionally, and in the political sense of organising around class interests, has created an unprecedented unity among diverse victims of state terror. It would be over-optimistic to say there is unity among the left-wing

---

[18] Jelín, *The Minefields of Memory*, p. 29.
[19] Tzvetan Todorov, *Los abusos de la memoria,* Buenos Aires, Paidósasterisco* 2000, p. 25.

political organizations which have survived the war, such as the URNG, or been created towards the end or after the final Peace Accords, such as the FNDG[20] or the ANN.[21]

However, wider sectors of progressive civil society have been brought together under the banner of human rights, as indeed has the Catholic Church. The human rights grand narrative is not unique to Guatemala, but fits within an international elaboration of human rights discourses. The local effects are not necessarily predictable, but one of them has been the joining of forces of previously distinct struggles.[22] Following through the military logic imposed, '[the] terror-inspired counterinsurgency project has had the intended atomizing effect on Guatemalan social life, it has also aimed for a simultaneous global effect, that is, the consolidation of all spheres of life – specially rural life – under the state's military and political apparatuses'.[23] The consolidation effect has also taken place at the level of *resisting* the state's power.

It is among the twenty-three Mayan ethnic peoples that the effect is most evident. From being localized identities without a common language except Spanish, the aftermath of the war has included a resurgence of Mayan activism and intellectual endevour which, among many other tasks, has set its sights on a pan-Mayan indigenous identity.[24]

---

[20] Frente Nacional Democrático de Guatemala, a political party formed six months before the November 1995 elections, the first left-wing party to go to the polls since 1954. They won six seats in Congress; two were occupied by high-profile human rights campaigners, Nineth Montenegro (of GAM, Mutual Support Group, an organization of family members of the disappeared, founded in June 1984 and the first Guatemalan human rights group to emerge and survive after the terror of the Lucas García regime) and Rosalina Tuyuc, an indigenous woman, founder member of CONAVIGUA, the National Coordination of Guatemalan Widows). FNDG's showing was specially impressive given that one third of the population of voting age were not registered to vote and this affected rural areas disproportionally.

[21] Alianza Nueva Nación, the left coalition including the URNG, which went to the 1999 elections.

[22] For a provocative discussion of the effects of human rights on specific Guatemalan rural communities, and nationally, see D. Stoll, 'Human Rights, Land Conflict and Memories of the Violence in the Ixil Country of Northern Quiché' in *Guatemala After the Peace Accords*, R. Sieder (ed.), London, Institute of Latin American Studies, 1998, pp. 42–62.

[23] This point is fully argued by F.M. Afflitto, 'The Homogenizing Effects of State-Sponsored Terrorism: The Case of Guatemala' in J.A. Sluka (ed.), *Death Squad: The Anthropology of State Terror*, Philadelphia, University of Pennsilvania Press, 2000, pp. 114–126 (124).

[24] There are a wealth of publications dealing with the direction of indigenous movements. A valuable overview is provided by D. Lee Van Cott, (ed.) *Indigenous Peoples and Democracy in Latin America*, New York, St Martin's Press, 1994. A good starting point is E. F. Fischer and R. McKenna Brown (eds.), *Maya Cultural, Activism in Guatemala*, Austin, University of Texas, 1996.

Power and Recovery

A nineteenth-century etymological dictionary admits 'recovery' is a difficult word, and hazards the guess that perhaps it comes from the Latin 'to make good again'. The more up to date Collins gives two relevant definitions, 'the act or process of recovering; in law, to obtain a right by judgement of a court'. To recover also contains the possibility of its own denial, as Mary Daly points out when she proposes new words, among them recover.[25]

Both REMHI and the CEH have taken place relatively quickly after the end of the conflict as defined. The experiences from other countries in the region suggest that assimilating the content and specially in the case of REMHI, the process, of the reports will continue into the future, for years, probably decades. The legacy of the violence is beginning to take shape, and it is not heartening. It is closer to the everyday violence of El Salvador, another long war which was ended but has not resolved the underlying social problems; it could take heed from Chile, where the army was likewise not defeated and where the process of admitting the truth by the whole of society has taken a decade longer than democracy to arrive. Guatemalans can take heart, though, from the fact that nowhere does it seem to be possible to bury the painful past and pretend it never happened. Experiences across Latin America point to the fact that even a few dedicated citizens who refuse to forget, who will not give up the hope of justice, can turn whole societies around.

In Argentina, the call for justice has taken many forms. From the original Mothers of the Disappeared[26] (there are now two organizations), has arisen a political voice which had been discredited, both by military government and by democratic neo-liberal successors: the left, the unions, the intransigent demand for change. They have encouraged an organization of the children of the disappeared, HIJOS, who have become part of the radical youthful critique of the state. And outside the political limelight, the Grandmothers,[27] who decided to go it alone, through their remarkable ingenuity and endurance have found over sixty children stolen from their parents by the military at their worst attempt to play God with people and society; as part of their search, they have also found a way to bring the same junta leaders who were amnestied by then President Menem, back to court.

---

[25] M. Daly, *Gyn/Ecology: The Metaethics of Radical Feminism*, Boston, Beacon Press, 1978, p. 24.

[26] See J. Fisher, *Mothers of the Disappeared*, London, Zed Books, 1989, for a concise history of the movement.

[27] R. Arditti, *Searching for Life: The Grandmothers of the Plaza de Mayo and the Disappeared Children of Argentina*, Berkley, University of California Press, 1999.

The true value of REMHI's work is greater than recovering the suffering of the indigenous majority in the last forty years – the ways in which it has gone about it, and the explanations of the causes for the recent conflict it has highlighted, point to an understanding of their recent victimization as continuous with their centuries-old exploitation and suppression.

The experiences of other countries in the region show that the process of using memory for political change is not linear; sometimes a step forward can be followed by setbacks. REMHI has been unafraid of arriving at conclusions which go beyond the specific cases recounted, serving as a conducting rod for unexpressed experiences across society. The climate of terror which reigned in the early 1980s, for example, is described and supported by individual case studies. From the use of savage torture as public exemplary spectacles by the army, to the less blatant sowing of distrust in communities, the report establishes the importance of psychological damage, affirming the victims' understanding of past events and their right to their grief and trauma, contesting the widespread attempts to blame the victim by the repressors.

The REMHI report and project has placed the conflict within an understanding of structural and historic problems of socioeconomic exploitation, inequality and racism. As political scientist Rachel Sieder concludes in an analysis of collective memory works and their contribution to political change: 'the commemoration of the victims of political violence also implies the symbolic revalourization and inclusion of those who were previously excluded from the national polity, and as such represents an attempt to rework the moral and political community of the nation-state.'[28]

The further change needed is a fundamental alteration of the mentality of those with power in society. A new understanding that the country is as much of the indigenous majority who since the conquest have been treated as 'dispensable', as they perish to overexploitation or in the course of counterinsurgency. The recovery sought by REMHI through its search for memory and history is a means of altering the balance of power by recognizing the power of the truth of those who have been oppressed and marginalized. The truth *Guatemala: Never Again!* offers is a means of setting the foundations for such a change in power relations.

---

[28] R. Sieder, 'War, Peace and the Politics of Memory in Guatemala', in N. Biggar, (ed.), *Burying the Past: Making Peace and Doing Justice after Civil Conflict*, Georgetown University Press, forthcoming 2001.

Memory and Monuments in Guatemala: Remembering the Dead and Solidarity with the Living*

RUTH GIDLEY AND HANNAH ROBERTS

I. Introduction

Many people in Guatemala are challenging the systemic amnesia and silence that has reigned so brutally and for so long. In this chapter we examine the legacy of Guatemala's violence and how communities are working to overcome this.

We begin by considering the role of monuments, and then look at the context and situation in Guatemala. In particular we consider the impact of the violence on a local level and how many Mayan spiritual practices were paralysed. Some communities are bravely exhuming mass gravesites and then building 'truth' monuments. These are important for individual and collective honouring of the dead. They are also a political statement, challenging the army's official version of history – a permanent reminder that the truth cannot be denied. By acknowl-

---

* Some of this article is based partly on R. Gidley, S. Kee, H. Roberts and E. Scarfe, *Guatemala: a Place for Memory*, London, Guatemala Solidarity Network, 1999. The Guatemala Solidarity Network (GSN) is supporting the construction of truth monuments in Guatemala. This includes financial contributions towards: publicity such as radio announcements, meals and refreshments for meetings and ceremonies, transport costs and the cost of the construction materials. A small amount of money can make a large contribution to a Guatemalan community – £100 ($155) is enough for an engraved plaque. Some communities have asked for larger sums to build mausoleums and even chapels for the whole community. For more information, to make a donation, to order *Guatemala: a Place for Memory* or to support solidarity work please contact us: GSN, 36, The Street, Old Basing, Hants RG24 7BX. E-mail address: gsn_mail@yahoo.com.

edging its past, communities can move towards genuine reconciliation, building a future rooted in dignity and respect, so that injustices and brutalities are not repeated. Finally, we consider the role for international support in this process.

Many monuments do not have particularly positive associations. For example, national memorials are often seen as a celebration of British power, colonization and nationalism. In contrast, monuments in many rural parts of Britain are not about imperial pride, but commemorate the deaths of local men and women, whose descendants may still live in the village. Such memorials may be treated in much the same way as gravestones in the local churchyard: well-tended and frequently adorned with flowers. In some instances, memorials serve as a communal gravestone for soldiers whose families never knew their fate or day of death. Similarly in Guatemala, monuments can have this personal and spiritual meaning to people who live nearby.

Plaques and engravings have also been used in Britain to commemorate unjust deaths and political situations. For example, to Stephen Lawrence's racist murder or to the persecution and death of religious martyrs.* Such monuments are a way of claiming territory and paying homage to unforgotten people and events. In British culture, where death is often a taboo subject, memorials give people a socially sanctioned space to address death and our spiritual and emotional needs.

As in Britain, there are numerous state-sponsored monuments in Guatemala. There are monuments to 'national heroes', and army bases often have ostentatious decorations to military 'heroism'. To many these are regarded as insignificant or offensive – a reinforcement of the state's brutality against its own people.

There are superficial tokens to peace, such as an 'eternal flame' in the central square of Guatemala City, or the statue of cupped hands placed in the presidential palace in 1999. These remain unknown to much of the population, or are felt to be only a hollow gesture – a political manoeuvre serving the government's image rather than the needs of a damaged society.

In contrast, community monuments in Guatemala are highly valued and meaningful. They allow people to address their own spiritual needs and make a political statement. Unlike the British memorials, they do not commemorate a struggle to defend the state but stand for direct opposition to state oppression. They challenge the prevailing culture of silence and denial.

For nearly 500 years, ever since the Spanish first invaded Central America (1524–1534), the Mayan peoples of Guatemala have endured repression, exploitation and elimination. Despite this they are still the

---

* *Editorial Note.* Stephen Lawrence was brutally murdered on 22 April 1993 in an unprovoked racist attack in Eltham, South East London, UK.

majority population and speak their Mayan languages, wear Mayan clothing and live life according to a Mayan cosmovision or world view.[1]

In December 1996 peace was signed in Guatemala, after thirty-six years of civil war and counter-insurgency.[2] All of these years are characterized by army control and brutality, particularly against the Mayan population. The UN-sanctioned truth commission – the Historical Clarification Commission (CEH) – declared that the state had committed acts of genocide against the indigenous Mayans. Many Guatemalans comment that 'peace is not signed, it is built'. Little has changed since the end of the conflict, and many communities remain paralysed with continuing pain, fear, intimidation and confusion.

There is a prevailing culture of silence, effectively a denial of the horrific events that took place, fostered largely by the army and state. There is still some confusion about the meaning of what took place – the view that the dead 'deserved what they got' is so strong that some survivors have actually come to believe this themselves.

Many people still live in fear, as perpetrators of the violence live locally. The Guatemalan army militarized civilians, by forming civil defence patrols (PACs), and often it was these militias that committed the tortures and killings. Thus survivors live alongside those who persecuted them, and threats and intimidation are still commonplace. Guns are easily available and the police and judicial system are largely ineffective.[3]

In this context many Guatemalans have good reason to feel that silence and ignoring the past is their only option. There is an enormous personal price to pay for this. Cancer incidence has increased, and alcohol abuse is exacerbated. Stomach problems, troubling dreams, headaches and insomnia are rife in rural communities affected by the violence. 'Sadness' is perceived as an illness.

This fear, denial, and confusion can render people and communities inactive and inward-looking. This is amplified in the neo-liberal national climate, which promotes individualistic, consumerist thinking, rather than traditional Mayan values of community. After years of government ineffectiveness and official brutality, most people are sceptical about the possibility that any kind of political action could improve things, either locally or nationally.

[1] R.Wilson, *Maya Resurgence in Guatemala: Q'Eqchi' Experiences*, Oklahoma, University of Oklahoma, 1995.
[2] R. Sieder, *Guatemala after the Peace Accords*, London, Institute of Latin American Studies (ILAS), 1998.
[3] R. Gidley, C. Kee and R. Norton (eds), *Guatemala: Thinking about the Unthinkable: Reflections and Responses to the Recovery of Historical Memory (REMHI) and Historical Clarification (CEH) Reports*, London, Association of Artists for Guatemala (AAG), 1999.

Social and political passivity and community division are also fostered by the multitude of fundamentalist Protestant churches which have won over up to a third of Guatemala's rural population. These churches, many of them based and financed in the United States, and actively encouraged by the military in the 1980s, are very different from the older established Protestant churches such as the Episcopal, Presbyterian and Lutheran, which are much more progressive and concerned with human rights and economic rights.[4]

In this context, telling the truth about the past can have a cathartic and liberating effect – personally, socially and politically. The spiritual dimension is crucial to this. Grieving and respecting the dead are universal, but are particularly significant in the Mayan cosmovision (world view). However, disappearances, secret mass graves, and threats to personal safety meant that many people did not have a chance to bury their dead properly, and to mourn. One testimony from the REMHI project said:

> My heart is heavy because of this suffering and pain. I grieve for my son but I can't do anything now. I don't know where his body and his blood might have been left. I ask God to keep him, to shine His light on him, to gather up his soul.[5]

2. Relating to the Dead

Mayan cultures involve a distinctive spiritual relationship with death, nature, and the universe. For Mayan peoples, the ancestors are part of a living tradition, and dead family members are in a sense alive and in communication with the living. Showing the deceased respect not only helps their spirit to move on peacefully, but also protects the living.[6]

Death rituals provide the dead with a safe passage to the afterlife – something that can only be achieved with the help of the living. It is important for the spirit of the dead person to depart with the body and not to linger unhappily between the two worlds, possibly causing harm and anguish to the living. On a psychological level, the rituals enable the bereaved to express their mourning in a culturally respected way, and to be comforted and supported by the community's accompaniment.

---

[4] J. Painter, *False Hope, False Freedom*, London, Catholic Institute for International Relations (CIIR), 1987.
[5] Recovery of Historical Memory Project (REMHI), *Guatemala: Never Again!* (The Official Report of the Human Rights Office, Archdiocese of Guatemala; London, CIIR/Latin American Bureau, 1999), p. 18.
[6] J. Zur, *Violent Memories: Mayan War Widows in Guatemala*, Boulder and London, Westview Press, 1998.

Customs include the wake, when family, neighbours and friends show their respect by keeping the dead person company throughout the night, and placing flowers and lighted candles around the coffin. The clothes and significant personal possessions of the deceased are placed in the coffin. The procession to the cemetery sometimes stops at places of special significance, such as the dead person's work-place, or the church. The coffin is opened at the graveside for last farewells, blessings, sprinkling holy water, and placing unlighted candles in the dead person's hands. The grave must follow the appropriate East-West orientation – some ethnic groups say that adults should be buried looking towards the setting sun, and children towards the rising sun.

Special significance is attached to commemorating the anniversaries of death and the 'Day of the Dead' (1 and 2 November). Children fly kites during November, and this is also a form of communicating with the dead. There are family visits to the cemetery and placing lighted candles, flowers, and offerings of food and drink on the graves.

These values and traditions were negated during the wave of violence that swept over the Mayan highlands in the 1980s. This is another example of the attempted ethnic genocide that the army conducted.

Corpses were destroyed, mutilated and desecrated. Some of the dead lay unburied, either because there was no one left to bury them, or because those who had killed them forbade it. Many of the dead were killed in massacres, and their bodies burnt in the homes, schools and churches.[7] For example, the exhumation at the site of the Cuarto Pueblo massacre, in Ixcán, in the western highland department of Quiché, produced forty-three sacks of ash where human remains were inextricably mixed with the ash from timber and household goods. Others were tossed like rubbish into mass graves, heaped in layers on top of one another – 'the way we throw dead chickens into a pit when there's an epidemic' – as one village woman put it as she watched an exhumation.[8]

Worst of all were the disappearances – people disappeared without trace after being detained by the police, army or intelligence services, who then denied any knowledge of them, regardless of evidence. By denying relatives access to a body, and in many cases without even knowing where they had died, the dead were deprived of loving hands to lay them in a coffin – no facing towards the setting sun.... These families have nowhere to go in November to light candles and burn incense, and share food offerings in the company of their loved ones.

Denial of such spiritual customs and needs weighed heavily on the

---

[7] R. Falla, *Massacres in the Jungle: Ixcán, Guatemala, 1975–1982*, Boulder and London, Westview Press, 1994.

[8] Guatemala Solidarity Network, op.cit., p. 9.

survivors. Many had disturbed and anguished dreams – dreams being the main form of communication between the dead and the living – that continued for years because they were unable to fulfil their familial responsibilities towards their dead. One survivor told REMHI:

> ... just a little bit of earth to be able to say there he is. There is the little cross, he is there, everything is there. There is our little bit of dust and we will go to show our respect, leave a candle ... but when are we going to light the candle? and where are we going to...? There isn't any place. I feel so much pain. Each night I get up to pray, every night. Where can we go?[9]

There have been various initiatives to help people, communities and the country as a whole to recover from these experiences, and to work on preventing the horrors from ever happening again. Some of these projects have come from communities, and some have been organized at a national level. All of them have involved the difficult and painful process of breaking the silence and remembering the violence.

One of the main motives for speaking out is to restore a sense of dignity, which is closely related to the need for the injustice of events to be acknowledged. Survivors often talk about the way that their relatives were treated as 'worse than animals'. People wanted to investigate where their kin might be interred, so they could re-bury them with proper ceremony and attention, and so bring to a close the process of grief.

Another motive is to demand justice and punishment for those responsible, who were often well-known and still living in the community.

A third reason is for the practical function of having proof of the person's death, and obtaining a death certificate. This enables people to claim inheritance and land rights, or remarry legally. This is an issue that Guatemalan human rights groups are working on with communities who have requested their assistance.

An important process linked to each of the motives for speaking out about the past is the exhumation of mass graves. The significance of the exhumation is different for different actors in the process. For the popular movement, it was vital to be able to prove that the massacres happened, that the army had killed thousands of civilians and that there were hundreds of secret mass grave sites throughout the country. All of this had been denied by the army and its supporters, and dismissed as left-wing propaganda.

The details uncovered in exhumations – earrings, necklaces, small

---

[9] *REMHI*, op.cit., p. 20.

bones, skeletons of unborn babies – can show that the victims were unarmed civilians, including many women and children. They often show the manner of death – a bullet to the back of the head, noose around neck, burnt bones, crushed skulls, women with their skirts missing, indicating that they were raped.

The human rights movement began to speak out against repression, violence, torture and disappearance in 1986, and the first calls for exhumations were perilous, since they were a direct challenge to the army.[10] It was not until 1992 that there was the political space to try and look for forensic evidence. By then, there was increased international pressure, the popular movement was much more confident, and the government was aware that it needed to put on a more humane face in order to participate in world affairs.

The early exhumations played a role in creating further political space to address issues of truth, memory and reconciliation. Community members who were active in the popular movement understood the importance of these first initiatives.

The process is as follows: the exhumation team arrives in a community, and talks at length with local people to try and piece together what happened on the day of the massacre and to ask where the grave sites are most likely to be.[11] They collect any information that might be useful in identifying individuals, such as their age, height, any illnesses or injuries that might show up on the bones, dental patterns and whether they were right- or left-handed.

The exhumation team then begins to sift painstakingly through the earth. The first bodies are often found quite close to the surface. The remains are removed in the order they were found, and then analysed back in the laboratory. Sometimes positive identification cannot be made, and the team is only able to determine the number of dead, with five long bones counting for one person. The forensic team produces a comprehensive report on its findings, bearing in mind that it could well be needed for any future court case. The bones are then released back to the family for re-burial. The long, laborious process was often hindered rather than assisted by state functionaries. Since 1992, four teams have conducted over fifty exhumations, but so far few have gone to a legal case.

Exhumations and burials are community processes, involving everyone who wants to participate. In front of others, people tell what happened to them, and they can grieve together, often for the first time.

[10] M. Sinclair, 'Faith, Community and Resistance', in M. Sinclair (ed.), *The New Politics of Survival: Grassroots Movements in Central America*, Washington D.C., EPICA/Monthly Review Press, 1995, pp. 75–106.
[11] EPICA/CHRLA, *Unearthing the Truth: Exhuming a Decade of Terror in Guatemala*, Washington DC, EPICA, 1996.

This is painful, but usually cathartic. Journalists and foreign observers might come and listen to people's experiences, and survivors begin to feel that the truth is being acknowledged.

While evidence is the most politically important aspect of the exhumation, the burial ceremony is the most significant part of the process for most people. A dignified burial place after all these years allows contact with the dead. For years, people did not know what had happened to their kin. Some did and knew that they had been tossed into a shallow grave but were too frightened to do anything about it. Others secretly visited these sites leaving flowers or making offerings to their dead in an attempt to fulfil necessary rituals.

Exhumations are not always straightforward. Sometimes people lost their special place to mourn or were left with nothing if no remains were found or could not be identified. But those who are able to rebury their dead then have a place to mourn openly and with certainty. Communities often wish to follow the whole process with a monument, a point we will return to later.

The national-level projects of the CEH and REMHI were important to people. The CEH reported:

> A witness showed us the remains of one of the victim's bones. He had these remains wrapped in plastic in a string bag: 'It hurts so much to carry them ... it's like carrying death.... I'm not going to bury them yet.... I do so want him to rest, to rest myself, too. But I can't, not yet.... This is the evidence for my testimony.... I'm not going to bury them yet, I want a piece of paper that will say to me: "they killed him...., he had committed no crime, he was innocent." And then we will rest.'[12]

REMHI in particular went beyond investigation and documentation to be a pastoral programme aimed at helping individuals and communities towards recovery and reconciliations. The key factor was the network of outreach workers, most of whom were members of the same local communities where they would receive the testimonies, or in some cases religious personnel with close links to the community. Many were themselves survivors with their own testimonies to give. Selection and training placed great importance on the mental health dimension of the project, fostering listening skills, sensitivity to the emotional impact of giving testimony, and the ability to provide basic emotional support and to recognize when people might need professional help. The testimonies needed to be handled in a way that not only recognized the pain, but also

---

[12] CEH, *Guatemala: Memory of Silence, Report of the Commission for Historical Clarification, Conclusions and Recommendations*, Guatemala, CEH, 1999, back cover. For full publication see http://hrdata.aaas.org/ceh.

rescued the sense of dignity that the violence had been used to suppress. There was an awareness that to concentrate only on the harm done would carry the risk of turning the survivors into victims.

The project was not intended to end with the publication of the report. On the contrary, it was committed to returning the collective memory to the people. This commitment was strengthened by the requests of many who gave testimony, that the history should not merely 'remain on paper'. The giving-back process is based on the following principles: firstly, history should be made available in a form accessible to all; second, this should be expressed in rituals, shrines, commemorations and monuments; third, the process should help to explain and clarify what happened, giving it context and perspective, including the lessons and conclusions extracted from the experience; fourth, this should not involve recreating the horror, but rather should affirm the dignity and identity of victims and survivors, and their communities.

The REMHI follow-up programme is being implemented in various areas, with workshops and discussion groups on historical memory, exhumations, reburials, monuments and commemorations of significant dates. As a result of the interviews, several areas now have mental health teams who work with individuals and communities.

Despite initial doubts about the CEH, its final report constitutes an official institutional version of the truth that is difficult for state bodies to belittle or deny. Its recommendations are widely respected for being fair, appropriate and specific. They provide a useful measure for dialogue with the Guatemalan government – both from within Guatemala and internationally.

However, it can be argued that the government has done little to respond to the CEH recommendations. Rather than seeing the report as a basis for on-going work, the government is seeing it as a closed chapter. Another limitation was that although the commission collected a huge amount of very detailed information, due to legal reasons this evidence is unlikely to be used for prosecution purposes.

3. Beyond the Truth

Exhumations, reburials, REMHI and the CEH have opened up a plurality of narratives, which is a step towards lessening the official stranglehold over the 'truth'. Official recognition of the wrongs of the past is a necessary first step for those who have been persecuted by the state to be included once again in their society.

Extensive and generally positive media coverage of the two major reports, as well as of exhumations, has brought the horror of the past to city dwellers, and others who claimed they 'didn't know' what was happening in other parts of the country. Others had an idea, but were stunned to confirm the scale of the atrocities. It is now widely recognized that the state was the perpetrator of most of the horrors of wartime, and people can say it out loud, in public. A public opinion which expresses abhorrence of past events is at least a step towards making it more difficult for them to be repeated.

> The memory of atrocities is an important aspect of violence prevention. Versions that justify what happened not only attempt to exonerate the authors, but also, in effect, justify the ideology and methods underlying the use of horror. Without public acknowledgement and social censure of the guilty, the perpetrators may end up strengthening their positions.
>
> The perpetuation of power structures imposed through violence have significant repercussions for the future. History contains many examples of reconstructing a distorted memory. These range from rationalizing atrocities to blaming the victims. Official versions of events frequently evoke the need to 'turn the page of history in order to rebuild society. Besides, denial of the past, or an officialized memory helps those responsible for crimes to keep their self-image intact.
>
> This intentional distortion of memory is an example of social fraud and one more humiliation for the victims. It also has long-term implications for society, including an installation of a democracy with military oversight, as has occurred in other Latin American countries that lived through military dictatorships. Memory has a clear preventative function. Preventing a recurrence of tragedy is largely dependent on dismantling the structures that made horror possible.[13]

However, little has been done officially with the truth that was recorded and analysed in the reports, or their recommendations. After the signing of 'peace', the violence of the past could be attributed to the 'war' with no further explanation. This is convenient for those who sanctioned, participated in and benefited from the violence and who still hold positions of power in government, the military, business and civil society. Not all Guatemalans want to talk about recent history, especially the wealthy. They argue that focusing on the past is damaging rather than healing. Some influential people feel threatened by the truth.

[13] *REMHI*, op.cit., p. 176.

At a village level, some areas have opened up to new possibilities of more democratic participation, but in other regions former military commissioners and ex-civil patrollers still unofficially hold significant power, and continue to impose fear and limit people's options. There are reports that some civil patrols have been informally re-established to 'combat crime', as well as rumours of ex-military commissioners being used by the army to influence rural communities on political issues. The army has played a part in fomenting divisions and conflicts within communities.

Meanwhile, at a national level, post-war changes to the military, intelligence and paramilitary structures have been insufficient, and almost entirely guided by the military themselves. Trials on wartime cases have come to court, but in virtually every case so far, guilty verdicts have been overturned and the accused set free. There is a general assumption that 'they have got away with it' and no one will be brought to legal justice.

4. Justice

The truth should not be a substitute for justice and the Guatemalan people have the right to demand justice.[14]

Some people want the perpetrators to be punished. Yet it is difficult to actually isolate exactly who should be held accountable. It is generally recognized that the foot soldiers and civil patrols who actually carried out the killings were often forced to do so. Some think that their personal suffering and anguish is enough.

In areas where civil patrollers and soldiers participated willingly in atrocities, their victims often want justice, but most survivors feel it is the intellectual authors who should be punished. This is an incredibly difficult task, given the strength of impunity. Judges and prosecutors are subject to bribery, and suffer threats and even assassination.

Traditional Mayan law, which is widely practised and respected in many rural areas, takes a different attitude to punishment than the conventional national legal system. The punishment decided by the community elders is usually an attempt to redress an act committed against the community or individuals in it, and tries to re-incorporate the crime's perpetrator into the community. For example, in one case a man who had committed a murder was ordered to provide food and

---

[14] Alvaro de Soto, UN spokesman at CEH presentation, speech made in presence of R. Gidley, Guatemala, February 1999. See also *Central America Report*, Vol.XXVI No.8, Guatemala, Inforpress Centroamericana.

wood for his victim's family until the oldest son was able to take over this duty. Mayan customary law is largely concerned with acknowledgement of the crime and finding a means of restitution. This is why truth processes are so important in encouraging people to acknowledge the truth, and why compensation has emerged as an important demand. The government has responded with token offerings that barely address the issue.

There have been several attempts to pursue justice through the national legal system, such as the trial concerning the massacre at Río Negro, Rabinal, in Baja Verapaz, which used exhumation evidence.[15] This resulted in three civil patrollers being found guilty of murder. The appeals court overturned the verdict and ordered a new trial, and in October 1999 they were again found guilty and sentenced to death. A Guatemalan human rights group – the Centre for Human Rights and Legal Action (CHRLA)[16] – is pursuing a national prosecution of a number of former high-ranking officials for genocide, using evidence from exhumations. These include General Efraín Ríos Montt, who ruled during 1982 and 1983, some of the most violent years in Guatemalan history. Nobel laureate Rigoberta Menchú is also pursuing an international case in Spain against Ríos Montt for genocide.

However, many people feel that this type of legal justice is difficult to achieve. In this absence, issues of truth and memory become even more important. Civil society and grassroots movements are working to take up the challenge of what has been described as 'memory work'. Monuments to the dead are one example of this.

5. Guatemalan Truth Monuments

'Truth monuments' have been erected by a number of communities as a permanent shrine and a comment on the brutalities suffered. The church or NGOs may help, but these are essentially community-rooted actions. People want to remember their dead, to let the truth be known about how their loved ones died, and to have it stand in stone. The process involves an examination of collective memory and a re-negotiation of power structures and practices within the community.

Monuments typically follow an exhumation – which often gives people the evidence and courage to state the truth of what happened. All those who died are listed by name and maybe something of their lives, such as what community they were from, and how many were

---

[15] R. Alecio, 'Uncovering the Truth: Political Violence and Indigenous Organizations' in Sinclair, op.cit., pp. 25–45.
[16] Known in Spanish as CALDH.

men, women or children. They state the circumstances of their death, and may also incorporate an explicit painting of the events. The monuments have been located at various positions – sometimes at the sites of mass graves, or where remains have been re-buried, or at village cemeteries. Some communities want a simple plaque or modest cross, others a large structure to shout the truth and withstand the elements and vandalism – from those who do not want the truth to be heard.

The process is crucial to a monument's effectiveness – at each stage dialogue is opened and people become more involved. Individuals donate their finances, labour and time for the good of the whole community. The villagers decide together what type of monument they want, where it will stand and what it will say. Community decision-making practices that were often corrupted and suppressed during the years of violence are used again.

The process culminates in an inauguration ceremony, often sanctifying the site with both Christian and Mayan religious rituals. Generally, these are open occasions involving as much of the community as possible, with food and drink prepared for all. Rather than individuals being isolated in their pain, the village is joined together in a dignified, respectful and profoundly meaningful occasion.

> When the people came from Guatemala City for the exhumation here I was too scared to come and talk to them even though my brother and sisters had been killed in the massacre. Then when the people were re-buried, I lit some candles and prayed, I still didn't go down to the town for the burial, but I wanted to go. A few months later there was talk in the village about building a monument and that everyone should help. I went to two meetings and heard what the men were saying. On the day the monument was finished we had a celebration. I brought some tamales and so did other women and we all shared the food and talked about what had happened to us.
> (Widow from La Puerta, Quiché)[17]

For example, in Río Negro, Baja Verapaz, the community built a large monument at the gravesite of 143 exhumed bodies. A few days later it was vandalized – probably by soldiers from the nearby military base. The community responded with defiance, building an even bigger monument that named the killers, stating that they were civil patrollers under army orders.[18]

In the nearby village of Plan de Sánchez, witnesses testified that up to 268 people were killed, but the exhumation revealed only eighty-four

---

[17] Personal interview with S. Kee, Guatemala, 1994.
[18] Guatemala Solidarity Network, op.cit., p. 18.

skeletons. There was a re-burial in a mass grave marked with an engraved plaque, the first line of which reads: 'The light of the truth cannot be hidden'. It goes on to explain how and by whom these people were killed.

In Chichupac a monument to massacre victims is planned for the municipal cemetery. Villagers feel they also want something right in the centre of their community, something they will pass everyday and remember, something children will be familiar with and learn about, in a sense reincorporating the dead into the life of the village. People also feel it is important to list the names of those whose remains have not been found. Some are unsure how their relatives died or even when they were killed, just that they disappeared.

> I feel so bad, to this day I do not know what happened, how he was killed or even where. My neighbour told me his tortured body had been seen in some nearby woodland, but I was too afraid to go and find him. A few days later when I had the courage, I went to look for him with our small daughter. But there was nothing, maybe the dogs took him. I do not know. But I want a place for him to be and for us to remember him because he is not forgotten.
> (Widow from Chichupac)[19]

There is a Mayan exhumation team working exclusively in the Quiché area. However it is unlikely to be able to carry out exhumations of all the secret mass gravesites, because there are simply too many. However, there are plans to consecrate many of these sites as sacred areas marked by monuments, plaques or crosses.

A national truth statement has been made on the cathedral in Guatemala City's main square. Its front pillars have been engraved with the names of hundreds people killed and massacres.

At Sahakok, Alta Verapaz, the monument is inscribed with the names of everybody who died locally, from all sides of the conflict – guerrillas, soldiers, civil patrollers and unarmed civilians. This is an especially impressive achievement since it was built before peace was signed. It took considerable commitment to make the pilgrimage there, eight hours from the road, up the highest hill in the area. Now a new road passes within half an hour's walk of it. Carlos Beristain, a Spanish doctor who spent many years in Guatemala, wrote about the monument in his book *Journey to Memory*:

> The elders dreamt of a cross on the hill. And today that dream comes true in Sahakok. A cross and eight marble plaques with the

---

[19] Personal interview with S. Kee, Guatemala, 1994.

names of 917 people from 28 communities. In these mountains, entire communities resisted, living on the run for five years.... That hill that is full of bones now has its own memory and meeting place.... For the ceremony and celebration, everyone brought what he or she could: a pound of beans, dough for tortillas, sugar. People who barely had anything to eat made it a party, they prepared for months, and fed the living and the dead. They made a miracle of remembering and having a place to visit the dead. In this way they contributed to building their future.[20]

6. Conculsion: From Victims to Activists

Monuments can help re-build the social fabric of a community. During the violence, almost all community activity was prohibited unless controlled by the army. People kept to themselves and when they did communicate with one another it was in whispers. Sundays and market days – the traditional days of social interaction – were heavily patrolled by the army. Working together on the monument provides a foundation for the community based on truth and respect for people's rights.

Monuments allow space for people's private pain to be acknowledged and legitimized. Even after the inauguration, they provide a focus for private and shared grieving – placing flowers, marking anniversaries and religious rituals. Rather than bearing the burden alone, the pain is in some way recognized and shared. Perpetrators may also use the site to begin to come to terms with their own actions.

By participating in the monument process, survivors benefit from the knowledge that they are contributing to making some small amount of good from the victims' deaths. Their memory is serving a common purpose. Participants in exhumations speak of wanting the reality to be known, especially by the young, and also by the wider world. Monuments are accessible to everyone, including those without formal education, or those not usually involved in community organization or activism. Monuments are also a message and an education to domestic and foreign visitors and organizations.

Monuments are a marrying of public and personal functions: they operate in cultural, social, psychological, spiritual and political spheres. By reclaiming their dead, their spirituality, their territory, their village, survivors can move from being victims frozen in pain to activists helping the community heal and develop.

Monuments are one way for individuals to grieve, heal and become

---

[20] C. Martín Beristain, *Viaje a la Memoria: Por los caminos de la milpa*, Barcelona, Virus editorial, 1997, pp. 152–153 (author's translation).

active. The process of their creation produces dialogue that helps some of the most marginalized and silenced Guatemalans to recover their voices. Communities begin examining their collective memory and identity and deal with the social legacy of conflict. The completed monument is a challenge to the dominating power structure and a reminder for current and future generations. Monuments work holistically in helping survivors reclaim not only their families, but also their history, their community, their culture and their future.

Seeking an exhumation and building a monument can be a difficult period, when people are often threatened and intimidated. International support can provide accompaniment, moral support and financial assistance. It gives out a message that there are people around the world who care about what happens and are prepared to stand up for truth and justice. We can help validate people's memories, truths, values and actions.

> But when you realize just how many people have been murdered, then you share the sorrow and you know that it is a moral obligation, a duty too, not only for the voiceless, but for a whole society that is terrorized.[21]

---

[21] *REMHI*, op.cit., p. 10.

Human Rights and Oppressed Peoples: Historical-Theological Reflections*

JON SOBRINO, SJ

Introduction: The Human Rights Paradox

I would like to make some reflections on the problem of the human rights of oppressed peoples in the context of the fiftieth anniversary of the Universal Declaration of Human Rights.

On the occasion of this celebration it is appropriate to applaud the advances made by humanity in regards to human rights. The continuing development of these historical claims means that we can now talk about various generations of human rights.[1] In El Salvador we understand very well the importance of these advances, albeit *sub specie contrarii*, as throughout the long years of oppression and repression the most fundamental rights of human beings, as far as life, security and liberty are concerned, have been violated. Those who have defended these rights have paid a high price. Marianella García Villa and Herbert Anaya Sanabria, both directors of the non-governmental Commission of Human Rights, were assassinated in 1983 and 1987. Father Segundo Montes, SJ, director of the UCA's

---

* This paper was first given on 3 March 1998 at the Universidad de Deusto, Bilbao, within the series of conferences on human rights, organized by Foro Deusto, the Vizcaya School of Lawyers and the Pedro Arrupe Institute of Human Rights of the Universidad de Deusto. The series was organized to coincide with the Fiftieth Anniversary of the Universal Declaration of Human Rights. It has been previously published in Spanish as 'Los derechos humanos y los peblos oprimidos: Reflexiones histórico-teológicas', *Revista Latinamericano de Teología*, 43 (1998), pp. 79–102. This is the first time it has appeared in English (translation by John McCarthy in consultation with Jorge Díaz Cintas).

[1] The Magna Carta (1215), Bill of Rights (1689), Virginia Declaration of Rights (1776), Declaration of the Rights of Man and the Citizen (1789, 1793).

Institute of Human Rights, was assassinated in 1989. Many others who worked for the defence of life were also killed, from Archbishop Romero to Father Ignacio Ellacuría.

We shall not, then, stress what is positive and necessary in the theoretical development of human rights, in the advance in legislation in this area and, above all, the real respect there exists for these things. But we do want to point out a paradox which, seen from places like El Salvador, seems shocking and, ultimately, scandalous. This paradox lies in the fact that there are advances in the theorization and formulation of human rights, particularly individual rights, but looking at the world as a whole, and considering life for the vast majorities, the actual condition of this life does not improve in line with theoretical advances. Not only does it fail to improve, it sometimes even deteriorates. Worse still, universal human rights can become a totally abstract set of rules that do not work in favour of the popular majorities and Third and Fourth World countries. They can even offer a spirited defence of what has been acquired or is acquirable by the strongest. This is how Ignacio Ellacuría put it, in a lecture he gave in 1989, just before his assassination:

> The problem of human rights is not only complex but also ambiguous, because within it not only does the universal dimension of man meet with the actual situation in which men's lives are lived, but it tends to be used ideologically in the service not of man and his rights, but rather in the interests of one group or another.[2]

In order to avoid these serious dangers, Ignacio Ellacuría called for an adequate historicizing of human rights and asked scholars to theorize from the point of view of the Third World and its peoples, in the same way that liberation theology had dealt with theological issues from the perspective of Third World reality, by talking about the God of life, the Church of the poor, and salvation as liberation.

By analysing human rights from the perspective of oppressed peoples, these reflections are modestly intended to contribute to the above mentioned end. In the first part, we will analyse two important elements which, in a wide sense, we might call the fundamental *epistemology* for recognizing the rights of the oppressed: (1) know how to listen to the outcry of the victims and (2) awaken from the dream of inhumanity in which the collective consciousness is submerged. The first appears clearly in the situation of *the people of*

---

[2] I. Ellacuría, 'Historización de los derechos humanos desde los pueblos oprimidos y las mayorías populares', *ECA* 502 (1990) 590.

Israel in Exodus – important for being the founding moment of the biblical tradition (less evident in the Western tradition). The second also appears clearly in what happened in the sixteenth century to the indigenous peoples of Latin America and the reaction of 'Hispaniola' – important because it determined in great measure the West's history and its ambiguous tradition of human rights.* In the second part we will analyse the present reality as a reality of *crucified peoples*, who express the ultimate truth of the human rights situation, a questioning of them and the direction they should move towards in order to become rights of the entire human race, rather than of individuals, groups or countries.

In concluding this introduction we insist that human rights be tackled as something that refers to a global reality. We will not, therefore, analyse the actual content of what is today conventionally understood by 'human rights'. Taking this as understood, we focus our attention on what is most general and central: 'the radical problem of human rights is the battle between life and death, the search for that which gives life as opposed to that which takes it away or brings death'.[3] We will see what can be learned about this from Exodus and Hispaniola.

1. The Primary Experience: Listen to the 'Outcry of the Victims'

It is clear that without the institutionalization of human rights, the first reaction in the face of the victims' reality – indignation and compassion – becomes ineffective. But, conversely, without this first experience the process of acknowledging how humans should be treated does not get under way; what is more, if this original experience is not maintained throughout the process, human rights are threatened by serious dangers: ineffectual abstraction and manipulation that works in favour of the strong and against the weak. This is why we begin with the first experience.

We, human beings, have coined, at least in the Spanish language, the phrase 'It's not right!' ('*¡No hay derecho!*'). This expresses a profound sense of injustice, whose origin lies not in an attempt to contrast reality with some set of regulations, but in a grasping of the wrong done to some human beings by others. Neither does it have its roots solely in historical claims aimed at winning some right that has

---

* *Editorial note*. The island of Hispaniola (*La Española*) – modern day Haiti and the Dominican Republic – was the first in the 'New World' to be settled by the Spanish and was the first centre for colonial administration.

[3] I. Ellacuría, op. cit., p. 593.

not yet been recognized. At the core of the human rights experience there is a more basic fact: the huge existence of victims.[4]

a. *Exodus: Dialectic and Partiality from the Victims' Perspective*

First proposition: The content of human rights is found, dialectically, in the violation of victims. These rights express, above all else, the basic necessities of life and survival; they are the rights of all people; they have to be worked for and actively defended, and those who violate them must be confronted.

i) *The Dialectic: Denied Rights and the Victims' Outcry.* The Bible does not use human rights terminology nor conceptualization in the modern sense – in fact, some of them are not even present – but it does demand the fulfilment of the fundamental right to life and vigorously denounces violations of it, as the prophetic tradition shows. The important point, as far as our object is concerned, is to know how the primary experience emerges as a notion that suggests something is owed to the human being; in other words, how the Bible *founds* these same rights. The answer seems important to us even today.

So, the reflection concerning what is due to the human being began to help in the understanding of what is done to him unjustly, that is, through the grasping of its opposite. This reflection began with the events in Egypt – whatever their basis in fact may be – the founding event of Israel. Some centuries after the events, the story's author relates it thus:

> I have surely seen the affliction of my people which are in Egypt, and have heard their cry by reason of their taskmasters; for I know their sorrows. And I am come down to deliver them out of the hand of the Egyptians, and to bring them up out of that land unto a good land and a large, unto a land flowing with milk and honey (Exod. 3.7–8).

It all began then with some cries of protest. God (or Moses) hears the cries of human beings, condemns the fact that certain men are

---

[4] The unjust oppression of some people by others, victimization, is what causes the cry 'It's not right'. But this also occurs with the inhuman management of what may be licit matters in themselves (the amount of money spent on arms, hasty amnesties, media monopolies) and before clamorous comparative injustices (the resources invested to make possible a football match, which might amount to a considerable percentage of a poor country's national budget). In these cases too the phrase 'It's not right' resounds. Whether it resounds or not is an indication of the moral health of a society.

oppressed by others, feels compassion, descends to liberate them, confronts and destroys the pharaoh. In religious language the fundamental experience is expressed here: the 'It's not right' and the practical reaction 'I have come down to liberate you'. The text expresses it clearly: God (or Moses) reacts because the *reality* is inhuman in itself, not because some previous law (or some proscription of his) has been violated, nor because the Israelites have recourse to these laws.

This means that the people of Israel did not establish human rights essentially and universally, rather historically and dialectically. It is true that in the Bible we find, in fact, the bases for such a universal founding – 'all men are created in the image of God' (Gen. 1.27)[5] – as the story of creation says, but this comes later. This way of arguing based on the human provenance is akin to the argument of the Universal Declaration: 'all men are born equal in dignity and rights' (Art. 1). This is necessary and correct, but does not make the original experience superfluous – rather the opposite: this should be present in the process of universalization.

We have stated that human rights are understood dialectically – from the violations against humanity – because this way of understanding is still fundamental today, even though our world has human rights declarations. We say it is fundamental because this very world often attempts, in clumsy or subtle ways, to obscure or smother the 'It's not right' adage that sets the whole process in motion. It is obvious that the situations in the Great Lakes, Algeria and East Timor are tragic, but neither the understanding of them nor their solution depend, essentially, in considering them through the perspective of human rights declarations, but rather through the indignation and compassion we feel before the tragedy itself. We shall return to this point in the second part, but state from the very beginning that in order to have the primary experience it is necessary to be in the victims' reality; as the Negro slave chant has it: 'Were you there when they crucified my Lord?' From outside, in as far as substantial reality and not solely the *ubi* categorial is concerned, only with difficulty can we understand what are victims and what are rights.

---

[5] In the New Testament this type of founding principle is made possible by the appearance of Christ. Paul says that *in Jesus Christ* 'there is neither Jew nor Greek, there is neither bond nor free, there is neither male nor female' (Gal 3.28), though it should not be forgotten that in Corinthians 12.13 he neglects to mention the male-female binomial caused by the social convulsion this generated at its time. This founding principle would be radicalized after the incarnation: the human, because of its nature and without additions, is assumable by God and can be divinized, by which the radicalness of human dignity is proclaimed.

ii) *Partiality: The Primacy of the 'Victims' Over the 'Whole'*. We have already said that in human rights everything begins with victims, not simply with human beings. From this perspective, then, Israel insisted on partiality, as hermeneutics, we would say today, for understanding the whole of reality.

From this standpoint God was defined from a biased perspective. 'A father of the fatherless, and a judge of widows', says Psalms 68.5. The true *confessio Dei* of Israel consists of the acclamation: 'in you will the orphan find compassion'.[6] This means that God is, above all, defender of victims, and only afterwards acclaimed creator of everything. Remembering that God was theorized from the partiality of the victims helps us to understand how the law was theorized.

In Israel and the surrounding areas, this did not emerge as a conclusion reached from a universal comprehension of human nature, but as a means of defending the victims, whom without this reality called 'law' are even easier prey to the powerful.

> When in history the role of a judge was thought up, or what later came to be called a judge, it was exclusively in order to help those who, because they were weak, could not defend themselves; the others had no need of it.... When the Bible talks about Yahweh 'judging' or of the justice whose subject is Yahweh, it is referring specifically to saving the oppressed from injustice.[7]

'The king's justice does not consist fundamentally in the issue of an unbiased verdict, but in the protection he offers to the helpless and poor, widows and orphans.'[8] Partiality, not abstract universality, which is historically biased toward the powerful, is what is found in the origin of the law of Israel. That is because it is about the defending of victims.

We recall the partiality of the law because it is, once again, a topical issue. The contemporary symbol of the impartiality of justice – the blindfolded woman to whom all are equal, would that it were so – is more Western than biblical. That is not how things are in the Scriptures. The ideal figure of the just and trusted king has his eyes open: he looks directly at the poor and oppressed in order to defend them. We know very well that in reality the law is partial only towards the powerful, as Monsignor Romero said, quoting a peasant. 'The law is like the snake. It only bites the barefooted'. As opposed to spuriously impartial partiality, the victims represent *true* partiality.

---

[6] H. Wolf, *Dodekapropheten*, 1, p. 304.
[7] P. Miranda, *Marx y la Biblia*, Salamanca, 1972, p. 140.
[8] J. Jeremias, *Teología del Nuevo Testamento* 1, Salamanca, 1974, p. 122.

iii) *The Life of a People.* Apart from dialectic understanding and partiality, Exodus offers a 'constellation' of realities alongside human rights, still important today, though, obviously, they must be placed in their historical perspective.

Primarily, Exodus considers the *basic* rights necessary for life: to be allowed to live (not to kill the male offspring of the Israelites), to be able to sustain life (in a land that enables one to do so), to live in freedom (rise above slavery). We have already said it in general terms: to promote human rights is, above all, to promote life and fight against death. To violate human rights is, above all, to promote death and fight against life. We should add that life and death refer not only to subsistence, but also to the fundamental dignity and culture of peoples.

We will come back to this point, which is fundamental in the modern world, but make it clear now. The paradigm of Egypt is evident in countries such as El Salvador, but not usually in countries of plenty, in which to talk of human rights suggests the enjoyment of political and civil liberties, liberty of expression and worship. Humanity is divided into two main groups: those who are accustomed to take life as a given and those for whom life is anything but a given. For these people, the majority of humanity, the greatest problem is life under threat, and, on the other hand, their greatest dream and right is 'this minimum which is the greatest gift of God: life', as Archbishop Romero said. It is this right to life that demands urgent historicization. In the words of Ellacuría, mere biological life:

> might be something taken for granted in the richest countries, where this right is assured..., but this is not the case in the majority of countries, where the preservation of biological life is highly problematical, whether because of extreme poverty, or whether because of violence and repression. For the greater part of humanity ... the necessary conditions to maintain biological life are absent as a result of hunger and lack of work.[9]

In the second place, Exodus considers the rights of a social group (Exodus speaks, idealistically, of a people); that is to say, they are the rights of majorities (not primarily individuals) and the rights of a people. In this viewpoint, the community and society based anthropology of more ancient peoples might be more active than the individualist variety. What is also doubtless active is the theological fact that God's relationship with a whole people is of a direct nature. But in any case, this perspective is important for understanding

---

[9] Op. cit., p. 593.

human rights from the 'logic of the majorities' and from 'the logic of oppressed peoples'.

It is bad enough that the rights of individuals are violated, but it is worse that those of an entire people or continent are violated. Not merely because of the obvious quantitative dimension of the problem, but because where the rights of peoples are concerned, the roots of their violation tend to be deeper and better concealed. In these cases, the concealment reaches such a level that the conventional language of the violation of human rights is no longer used, unless in the old communist regimes. If in Cuba, for example, an intellectual does not have freedom of expression, this is not merely considered something bad, but a violation of human rights. But when great blocks of people in the Third World lack housing, healthcare and education, when between thirty and forty million human beings die each year of hunger or related illnesses, when entire ethnic groups are denied the right to speak out, then there might be criticisms and complaints (sincere or hypocritical, depending on individual cases), but the language of human rights is not used, nobody says that the right to life of entire peoples has been infringed. In this way there is no need to call those responsible to account, nor to react with the urgency and magnitude the situation demands.

In the third place, these rights should be not only recognized but also defended – that is to say, they should be *worked* and *fought* for. Indignation is an integral part of the original experience, but so is the commitment to praxis (though in Exodus this is all very stylized, the fundamental praxis being attributed to God or Moses, without analysis of the material base of such praxis).[10]

This means that a purely theoretical concept is insufficient to grasp what a human right is, and that a theory-praxis concept is necessary. As occurs in all relationships between theory and praxis, what they consist of is grasped by considering how they are defended. In becoming actively involved in bettering the lives of the deprived and fighting against the darkness of death, one starts to understand from within – through the great difficulty of this struggle – what the right to life is and what are the rights of the poor, and how they are placed in hierarchies. There is no better way to find out what human rights are, in what hierarchy they lie and who is in most urgent need of them than to take it upon oneself to defend the lives of the poor.

In the fourth place, Exodus will remain a reference throughout Israel's history in both its credo and social legislation. It did not establish jurisprudence in the technical sense, but introduced an essential

---

[10] What should be maintained from the paradigm of Exodus is the necessity of the praxis and even of the struggle, not, clearly, the violent war-like methods used against the Egyptians which are attributed to God.

perspective and element into the legislation of Israel: 'Remember that you too were a stranger in Egypt.' (Deut. 5.6; Exod. 20). Good and evil, what one should or should not do, refer always to the original experience: nobody can be ill-treated in Israel, whether from outside or inside, because 'strangers were you in the land of Egypt'.

The conclusion of everything said in this section is that we must always return to what made us conscious that something is owed to the human being. This origin must be theorized and historicized, but should remain alongside the process to grow in humanity and to avoid the paradox of which we spoke at the beginning. In a word, there is no real progress if the original 'It's not right!' is not remembered.

b. Hispaniola: The Blindness and Self-justification of the Oppressors

Second proposition: In correlation to victims there are oppressors of entire peoples. Not only do these oppressors infringe human rights, but seek theoretical justification in order to do so with impunity. What is really serious is that they tend to form part of a structural blindness that is difficult to overcome.

i) *Peoples Destroyed*. Another important moment to take into account in the theorization of human rights is what happened five hundred years ago in what today we call America. As we concentrated in the last section on the fate of the victims, we will now focus on the oppressors and their behaviour. While we are on the subject, there was at the time a religious Christian trial.

The *fact* is indisputable. Shortly after the arrival of the Spaniards, the life of the indigenous peoples began to disappear and whole communities, along with their populations, cultures, traditions and religions were destroyed. There was a multitude of causes: wars, savage acts, imported illnesses against which the natives were not immunised, extremely hard work, suicides as the result of desperation, inhuman migrations and so on. Sometimes the indigenous themselves collaborated with the invaders in order to throw off the yoke of their local oppressors – a fact that for some historians provides fundamental evidence of the enormity of the drama. It is, then, unjust to blame what happened entirely on one particular group, but neither can the crudity of the fundamental act and those responsible for it be ignored: in the new continent an immense act of depredation, pillaging and destruction was carried out by the Spaniards and Portuguese. Some seventy years later, the indigenous population was on the road to extinction, reduced to fifteen per cent of what it had been.

This was not accidental. Although not a direct objective, the annihilation was a practical and necessary consequence of the Europeans' limitless appetite for wealth. Later, when that instrument of enrichment began to be exhausted, Africans were enslaved to substitute as new sources of energy. That was the founding factor in relations between Europeans and the populations of that New World, and explains, to a great degree, what has occurred during these past five centuries.

Hispaniola demonstrates, then, that there are tyrants. As far as the theorization of human rights is concerned, various things can be learned from Hispaniola: the slumber of inhumanity that impedes the exclamation 'It's not right!', the search for theoretical justification for the infringement of rights, and the real consequences of the original depredation.

ii) *Inhumanity's Slumber*. Long before the theoretical debates began in Spain, the primary reaction was voiced in the very place of these deeds: 'It's not right!', and there were, too, some early attempts to explain it. We record the well known reaction of Friar Antonio Montesinos, in 1511, in the island of Hispaniola:

> All of you are in mortal sin and will live and die in it for the cruelty and tyranny with which you have treated these innocent people. Say, by what right and by what law hold you in such cruel and horrible servitude these Indians? With what authority have you waged such hateful wars on these peoples who were meek and passive in their own lands? Where once they were so many, with death and unimaginable ravages have you consumed them. How is it you keep them so oppressed and fatigued, neither giving them food nor curing the sicknesses they incur as a result of their heavy toil, else die, in order to dig out your gold each day? Are these not men? Have they not rational souls? Are you not obliged to love them, as you love yourselves? Do you not understand this? Do you not feel this? How can you sleep so lethargically in so deep a slumber?[11]

The text uses implicitly the language of human rights: with what *right*, with what *justice*, with what *authority*. It lays the foundations for them: the Indians cannot be treated in this way because they have rational souls, they are human beings. Most importantly, though, the text expresses the fundamental experience: the Dominicans grasp 'the cruel and horrible servitude'. What ought to be obvious, the Spaniards either fail to grasp, disregard or conceal. It is something almost unconscious: 'How can you sleep so lethargically in so deep a slumber?'

The metaphor of 'sleep' is not used here as an excuse, but in order

---

[11] Cited in Bartolomé de Las Casas, *Historia de las Indias*, according to the BAC edition, *Obras escogidas II*, Madrid, 1958, p. 176.

to illustrate the deep roots of the problem. It expresses a quasi-physical reality, not only epistemological or moral, and is the greatest hindrance to a grasping of reality: in this case, the existence of victims produced by tyrants. To 'wake up' is necessary, but also difficult, almost impossible, and therefore epochal, as Kant proclaimed when he urged people to 'wake up from dogmatic sleep' (have the courage to think for yourself and not to delegate the task to others) in order to be simply humans. This awakening is a real change of the paradigm, a 'seeing' of things in a completely different way. And this awakening, as we shall see, continues to be a fundamental problem today.

iii) *Justification of the Infringement of Rights.* The affirmation of the existence of victims led to a theoretical debate about who had rights, the Europeans or the indigenes, and what rights each of them had. Montesinos, Las Casas and others argued for the indigenes, that is, they theorised the original experience of 'It's not right'. But the argument in favour of the rights of the Europeans was much larger and came from very diverse fronts.

The human inferiority of the Indians was established *anthropologically*, to the point where it was denied they possessed souls or humanity. The bad and perverse customs of the Indians were cited *ethically*, which not only permitted but demanded they succumb in order to become liberated from them. *Political philosophy* affirmed that there were no legitimate owners of those lands, and for that reason the Europeans could legitimately conquer them. *Ecclesiastically* the four bulls of Alexander VI, proclaimed just after 1492, were cited, in which the areas of Spanish and Portuguese dominance were demarcated – for evangelization – but a dominance nevertheless. *Theologically* it was affirmed that God had given these lands to the Spaniards, and that this had been his providence or reward for their struggles against the Infidels during the Reconquest of Spain.[12]

We must also mention that within the debate there were very different modes of arguing – something it is important to remember because, in essence, the problem may still persist today. To defend the right to wage war on the Indians, Sepúlveda used Aristotle, while Las Casas

---

[12] An anti-evangelical evangelization was also argued for. This reached scandalous extremes at times, as the following text by Parecer de Yucay, 1571, shows. 'This I say of these Indians, that one of their means of predestination and salvation were these mines, treasures and riches, because we clearly see that wherever they are found flies the gospel, and where there is not this dowry of gold and silver, there is neither soldier nor captain who desires to go, nor even minister of the gospel.... Then, the mines are a good thing among these savages because God bestowed them to bring faith and Christianity to them, and preservation through it, for their salvation'. Taken from Josiene Chinese, *Historia y Cultura*, Lima, 1970, p. 142.

retorted: 'The devil with this nonsense about Aristotle',[13] and could say it because he was an active part of the reality and affected by it. His thinking 'is the product of somebody inside that reality. And his way of being in the reality allows him to reason on matters concerning the Indians with much more logic and sureness than the Spanish theologians, whatever their celebrity and illustriousness'.[14] This is also how Gustavo Gutiérrez[15] and F. Fernández Buey[16] view him.

What we have called primary experience does not substitute for theoretical argument, but lends it authority, and without this experience the argument is not solidly founded, nor does it find a satisfactory direction. The 'being there', the knowing things at first rather than second hand, the arguing from the perspective of the reality – as we have said of the theological method – has no substitute. But it is difficult nevertheless, and not only for psychological or ethical reasons, but for other more fundamental and structural reasons. Those in the position of taking life as a given have to make an immense effort to 'be in the reality', not just looking at the concept or idea. Being in the reality of the victims it is possible to theorize about the rights of peoples because somehow, with all the analogies of the circumstance, we are among the victims. But it is structurally difficult, as the First World in general demonstrates, and that is one of Hispaniola's great lessons.

iv) *Progress and Failure in Human Rights: The Concept and the Reality.* The Dominicans of Salamanca produced the rights of peoples, but the praxis of the *Conquista* established and made normal the conquering and depredation of other peoples – a praxis which, in different forms, reaches down to today, albeit with a more advanced legislation in the matter of human rights. Since then, despite the protests of such as Las Casas and the theories of people like Vitoria, Europeans and North Americans have invaded militarily, economically, culturally and religiously – in varying degrees according to circumstances – the continents of Asia and Africa, and continue to invade Latin America. The primary experience of indignation and compassion began to pale, for which the cultures and religions of the West were to a great degree responsible.

Centuries have had to pass (for the Christians practically until Medellín in 1968) in order to see things in a different light. In the

---

[13] F. Fernández Buey, *La gran perturbación. Discurso del indio metropolitano*, Barcelona, 1995, p. 159.
[14] J. Vitoria, 'Diversidad cultural y evangelio de los pobres', *Revista Latinoamericana de Teología*, 42 (1997) p. 279.
[15] *En busca de los pobres de Jesucristo. El pensamiento de Bartolomé de las Casas*, Salamanca, 1993.
[16] Op. cit.

famous words of Ignacio Ellacuría, what happened five centuries ago has been systematically distorted and that distortion is, in my opinion, one of the important reasons for the inadequate, shrouded and in any case insufficient contemporary theorization of the human rights of oppressed *peoples*.

The discovery of 1492 was not, according to Ellacuría, America, which remained hidden, but Spain (and the Roman Catholic Church). Laid down in thesis form:

> it is the Third World that discovers the First World in its most real and negative aspects.... Today too we can say in all honesty that the First World approaches the Third, globally, in the same way and with the same intentions. It too comes in ideological clothing whose sole intention is to cloak in 'prettiness' its true intentions.[17]

The lesson is an important one. Theoretical advances concerning rights are by nature always useful, but two things should be guaranteed. One is that they should be advances from the *victims'* perspective. And the other, that these advances are not co-opted – as still happens today, at times in very serious matters – in veiled attempts to defend what has been acquired or is acquirable by the strongest. For that reason it is important to be aware of the larger reality in which the concrete advances in human rights are inscribed. Is it not an illusion to pretend that rights concerning life are advancing while, for example, an omnipresent neo-liberalism is reinforced?

2. The Necessity Today: Hear the Outcry of 'the Crucified Peoples'

Third proposition: In today's world there are important advances in the formulation of individual rights, but there are still victims, particularly in the form of 'crucified peoples'. What is more, conscience has fallen asleep, as though we had come to the end of history, and there is no one to call to account. In the face of this, human rights must be placed in a hierarchy, beginning with life; there must be a struggle to ensure they are truly universal, and, most importantly, the concept of 'human rights' must be rethought so that they have as their subject the popular majorities and the peoples.

In the present world, after two centuries of revolutions, human rights have been formulated in successive generations. The first generation

---

[17] 'Quinto centenario de América Latina. ¿Descubrimiento o encubrimiento?, *Revista Latinoamericana de Teología*, 21 (1990) 272ff.

claimed political and civil rights; the second, economic, social and cultural rights; the third – still in the process of evolving – rights to peace, to a certain quality of life, a healthy environment, freedom of information and so on. This is all well known, and has brought an improvement in the lives of many people. However, the global reality of the world, viewed from a basic 'human' perspective, the lives of the people, is a disaster. The problem is that the field of 'human rights' does not encompass sufficiently 'all that is human', and that is why defending it and making advances within it does not necessarily signify any real progress. There are, then, advances made in 'human rights', but the 'human' crisis continues, and at times even worsens. To grasp and accept this distinction strikes us as essential in order to form more effective theories around what 'human rights' means.

Two centuries of struggle should not, of course, be ignored, rather built upon and amplified. But, therefore, two things should be added. One is to *complement materially* that tradition with a consideration of the 'humane', which comprises two essential things: life and the belonging to the human race. The other is a *formal rethinking* of human rights from the perspective of the victims, including all that has been done in the three generations of the movement – the hermeneutics offered by the crucified peoples.

Continuing from that perspective and from what we have analysed in the first part, we would like to make the following reflections to help illuminate, modestly, some aspects of an appropriate theorization of human rights.

a. The Fundamental Factor: The State of the 'Humane' among the Crucified Peoples

The current expression 'crucified peoples' might surprise and even offend, because it places our century on a par with the slavery of Egypt and the outrages perpetrated in America in the sixteenth century. From a Christian perspective, though, and also from an honest historical perspective, there is no exaggeration, though we have to clarify our terms. At the end of the twentieth century there have been important advances in human rights but neither should it be forgotten that this century, as Hanna Arendt says, has been the cruellest in the history of humanity: Auschwitz, Gulag, Hiroshima, Vietnam, Rwanda, Bosnia, the massacres in Guatemala, Haiti, El Salvador, the missing of Argentina and many other examples. Once again, unsuppresably, the cry of 'It's not right' rings out. The 1948 Declaration sought to remedy the situation, but 'the cruellest century in history' continued on its course of violence – more than 130 wars after the Second World War, all of which, with a few exceptions, in the Third World, plus all the repression and terrorism – especially that of the state. And the slow violence of poverty, exclusion and underdevelopment continues and grows.

'Crucified people' is not, then, an entirely metaphorical term. Further, it is necessary and illuminating for an understanding of the state of 'the humane'. It exposes the innocent geographical language of 'Third World' and 'the south' and of cloaked euphemisms such as 'developing countries' and 'fledgling democracies'. It expresses what is essential about 'the inhumane', the cross signifying death, despicable and reserved for slaves and agitators, and that is what the Third World has been sentenced to: the slow death which is the result of unjust poverty and the violent death that befalls the poor who only want to live (the basic instinct behind almost all 'revolutions'). To this must be added, at the end of the twentieth century, death by 'non-existence', the emergence of a human sub-species that no longer counts, not even as a means of cheap labour to be exploited, as a result of which the population of the Third World is changing from a population that can be exploited into one which is surplus to requirements.[18] Geopolitically, the Third World is being assigned the role of the planet's refuse bin. It is not so inappropriate then to talk of crosses.[19]

What we have just said can be understood in itself, without the necessity of conceptualizing it in terms of human rights, and its seriousness stems from the reality itself, not from the fact that the legislation concerning human rights has been infringed. However, if we want to formulate the reality of the crucified peoples in the language of human rights, perhaps we can say the following:

i) In our world, the fundamental right (the 'meta-right' to life of oppressed groups of people) is cruelly infringed on a massive scale. Crucified peoples do not occur naturally but are produced. The relationship between poverty and wealth, between development and underdevelopment, is the result of the fact that the developed world is based on an original accumulation, made possible by the exploitation of poor countries. Even today, its progress depends in no small measure on its exploitation of underdeveloped countries. One statistic says it all: with the payment of the foreign debt poor countries have financed the rich countries to the equivalent of six Marshall plans (Susan George).

---

[18] 'The greater part of the third world's population is no longer required', F. Hinkelammert, *La crisis del socialismo y el tercer mundo*, San José, 1991, p. 8.
[19] This term is important for Christians because it refers to the type of death Jesus suffered, and this gives these people something basic in common with him. As Bartolomé de Las Casas said: 'I leave Jesus Christ our Lord in the Indies, scourged, struck and crucified, not once but millions of times, when the Spanish crush and destroy those peoples', op. cit., p. 511b.

ii) Humanity's situation is resoundingly unequal.[20] According to United Nations statistics, the relationship between rich and poor in 1960 was 1:30, and 1:60 in 1990. And the relationship between the richest of the rich and the poorest of the poor was 1:180. The resources consumed by a child in the United States are 420 times greater than those consumed by a child in Ethiopia. Eduardo Galeano expressed it graphically: 'a citizen of the United States is worth fifty Haitians'. And he wonders, as though shaking the foundations of our civilization, 'what would happen if one Haitian was worth fifty North Americans'.

This inequality between peoples and nations is in itself unacceptable, and even more unacceptable because today it is perfectly surmountable. The fact is that 'the condition of underdevelopment is in itself and in relation to states of development a flagrant violation of human solidarity, that is, of the very nature of the basis of human rights, and entails the permanent violation of human rights'.[21] The parable of the rich man and poor Lazarus describes perfectly, in Jesuitical language, the reality of our world. As far as rights are concerned there is a massive discrepancy.

iii) In addition to the lack of solidarity with the crucified peoples there is a failure to defend themselves. It is no exaggeration to say that practically all the world powers effectively ignore the crucified groups, historically seek to take advantage of them and, where necessary, tend to oppose them: oligarchies, capital and the world banking system, the armies, many governments and political parties. Neither do the media, the unions, the churches and the universities make any great efforts to defend them, if they do not belong to the above groups, although there are exceptions. There are no bodies that would grant *guarantees* of life to the peoples.

With the new geopolitical configuration of the world, the lack of protection of poor peoples is increasing even more. With the fall of the East, the Third World has been left at the mercy of capital,[22] even though John Paul II stresses in his encyclicals the superiority of work over capital. That is why the twenty-first century is no longer described in terms of east-west but of north-south. As has been written, the twenty-first century has already begun, and its basic fact is 'the north

---

[20] See Luis de Sebastián, *Mundo rico, mundo pobre. Pobreza y solidaridad en el mundo de hoy*, Santander, 1993.
[21] I. Ellacuría, 'Subdesarrollo y derechos humanos', *Revista Latinoamericana de Teología*, 25 (1992) 4.
[22] Monsignor Rivera, Archbishop of San Salvador, had some notable words to say on this subject: 'With the fall of real socialism, only the Church is left to fight for the essential welfare of the poorest of the poor', *Carta a las Iglesias* (*Letter to the Churches*) 236 (1991) 8.

against the south'.[23] To this must be added that if the 'First World' used to act as a model for the Third, showing its human side, now the capitalism of the central countries does not bother anymore – it has no necessity – to 'show any human side whatever'.[24]

b. We Continue 'Slumbering in Lethargic Sleep'

The 'slumber' of Hispaniola persists in our world for diverse reasons and in diverse forms. J.B. Metz said shortly after the euphoria that followed the fall of the Berlin Wall that 'a popular postmodernism of hearts that ignores the poverty and misery of the so called Third World in a greater faceless distancing is spreading'.[25] At the moment, a cultural, even philosophical, atmosphere (call it postmodernism, with all the defining that is necessary, 'light thinking', etc.) is expanding which, at the moment of truth, ignores the victims, or certainly does not place them centre stage, and does not refer to them in evaluating the advances and setbacks of this world.[26]

Worse still, a positive – and triumphant – language has been introjected and popularized to describe our world. Today's world is a global village and we have arrived at the end of history.[27] There is an admission, of course, that problems exist and that we have to advance. But it is as though humanity had found the definitive path, at least in as far

---

[23] X. Gorostiaga, 'Ya comenzó el siglo XXI: el norte contra el sur', *Envío* 116 (1991) 35.

[24] F. Hinkelammert, 'El huracán de la globalización: la exclusión y la destrucción del medio ambiente vistos desde la teoría de la dependencia', *Economía informa*, 255 (1997) 14. The location of the first world is still basically the north, though its correlation is no longer simply the south, but also all the excluded.

[25] 'Teología europea y teología de la liberación', in J. Comblin, J. I. González Faus, J. Sobrino (eds.), *Cambio social y pensamiento cristiano en América Latina*, Madrid, 1993, p. 268.

[26] These words of Pedro Casaldáliga suffice to describe the atmosphere of the spirit of our time. At least read from the perspective of El Salvador, they hit the nail on the head: 'There are those who think that now is the time to change our paradigms. They even think the martyrs get in the way in this post-modern or post-militant memory. In the wave of this disappointment, friends and enemies come asking three provocative questions: what is left of socialism?, what is left of liberation theology?, what option is left for the poor? I hope we will not end up asking what is left of the gospel', 'El cuerno de jubileo', *Carta a las Iglesias* 393 (1998) 8. We would add that we hope we do not end up asking ourselves 'what is left of the victims'.

[27] 'The end of history does not refer to the end of world-wide events, but to the end of the evolution of human thought in respect of guiding principles.... It is the end of humanity's ideological evolution and of the universalization of western liberal democracy as the ultimate form of government', explains Francis Fukuyama. See Hugo Assmann, *Las falacias religiosas del mercado*, abridged edition of *Cristianisme i Justícia*, Barcelona, 1977, p. 15.

as it is the only one to arrive at the objective.[28] Hugo Assmann puts forward a yet more radical thesis: the problem of the market should not be viewed moralistically – the traditional but insufficient and mistaken view of the left – but from the euphoric point of view of the right. This euphoria is expressed in the rhetoric about the market as 'Good News', 'Jubilant Gospel', 'happy discovery'. And 'when the oppressors feel themselves to be benefactors', says Assmann, 'it is because they believe in an unshakeable Gospel'.[29] Once the market has been elevated to gospel, the question of whether it is efficient – in what and for whom – can no longer be asked. All verification is removed. It is now on a par with divinity: there is no longer any need for justification.

There are other aspects of Western culture that contribute to the sleepiness. From an ideological perspective, anything that expresses conflict or radical criticism is avoided – even though the victims are forced to express it. From the cultural point of view, neither indignation nor compassion are held as primary attitudes and values – even though they constitute the primary experience in the face of the victims – as they do not converge with what now appeases: tolerance, dialogue, consensus, civilized debate. From an ecclesiastic point of view, the denunciation of social sin and injustice is declining – even though the victims are a product of them. From a theological point of view, little is spoken – with any conviction – of the God of life and justice, of the Jesus who acted for the poor against their oppressors – even though for the victims there is no other God or Christ. Neither are the idols that exist today spoken about (accumulation of capital, power and resources, in addition to nationalistic and ethnocentric movements) – even though their reality manifest itself by producing victims. The conclusion is that, the reality being more resounding, the victims are not central at the time of thinking through an adequate configuration of this world or a new world order; far more central are the market and consumption (spoken of publicly), and arms production (about which a silence is maintained). It appears that today the pathos of indignation and misery generated by the victims' experience is not 'politically correct'.

Blindness, indifference, euphoric ecstasy or lethargic sleep are recurrent in history in extremely serious contexts, and this fact still has an impact. Before the 'historic condemnation' of victims and the excluded – two-thirds of humanity – practically accepted as something natural by our world, comes to mind – at least to people of my generation – how naturally the 'eternal condemnation', of possibly millions of human beings, used to be talked about. And more, how the predestination of the

---

[28] 'As now spaces of alternative solutions apparently no longer exist, globalization and the submission to it seem like the only reality', F. Hinkelammert, op. cit., p. 11.
[29] Cf. op. cit., p. 20.

human being was defended by theological theses: to heaven and to hell. All of that reflected an idea of God, and therefore, given the ultimateness of God, reflected a 'that's how things are and nothing can be done' – which is what we are now interested in emphasizing. J. I. González Faus has recorded this, comparing the spirit of capitalism with the spirit of Jansenism:

> The brutality of the Jansenist God, who condemns those he wants and is left indifferent or satisfied by their condemnation, led Jansen to write that 'the condemned are only born and live for the usefulness and profit they provide to the chosen.' If this can be calmly said of the final and only destiny of men, what can be so strange about the vast majority of men being born into this world and living solely for their usefulness and profit to a small privileged minority? Or about this minority who, instead of bearing this biblical justice that condemns them for their inhumanity and heartlessness, cling to the capitalist claim that they are God's chosen and his defenders?[30]

This is what occurs in the presence of the crucified peoples: some metaphysical structure of reality according to which 'that's how things are' is implicitly invoked. And we still have not awoken from the slumber, because now it is no longer simply sleep – an anthropological reality of the human being – but immutable metaphysical reality. Jesus has already said it: 'neither will they be persuaded though one rose from the dead'.

c. The Fallacy of the Universality of Human Rights

Human rights in the Western world, although universally formulated, have in fact always benefited some more than others – and that is still the case today. There has, then, existed from the beginning a partiality, but of a tendency contrary to that which we have mentioned: in general, human rights are the heritage of the powerful rather than the poor. In fact, it is the oppressors who usually benefit from them more than the oppressed.[31] The conclusion is clear:

> It is not enough to be human to have the bare minimum to

---

[30] 'Veinticinco años de la teología de la liberación: teología y opción por los pobres', *Revista Latinoamericana de Teología*, 42 (1997) 232.

[31] Commenting on the achievements of the end of the eighteenth century, Ellacuría says: 'Although they are presented ideally as human rights, they are rights limited to a determined type of man (English *freemen*, white men from respectable Virginia, the French bourgeoisie, etc.). So much so that these rights were not even attributed to those who lived with them (English or French farm workers, Negroes and North American slaves, etc.), even though they were not denied their status as human beings', 'Historización de los derechos humanos', 591.

survive, a basic dwelling, resources to buy medicines for sick children, etc. One has to be North American, European, Soviet or Japanese to have adequate resources in order to survive and enjoy the resources that God, through nature and reason, put in the world for everyone. It is, in fact, more important to be the citizen of a rich and powerful country than to be a person – it gives you greater rights and more real possibilities. That's how fractured human solidarity is.[32]

Human rights are based on the proposition that the human *species* is also essentially a *family*, and that we should all do what we can to help one another in life. What we have at the moment, though, is exactly the reverse. General economic activity today is organized in an egotistical way in order to profit disproportionately the industrialized countries (Luis de Sebastián). 'Never in history has there existed, not even in the colonial era, such an extreme bipolarisation of the world'.[33]

The universality that is essential to the Western conception of human rights does not exist. One also has to ask whether its existence is possible, intentions being what they are: is it possible that *all* human beings could enjoy the right to work, freedom of information and expression, a clean environment and so many other things, without this becoming a serious threat to the established economic, military and political orders? We are afraid not. A truly universal enjoyment of human rights is, historically, a threat to the powerful groups and peoples. So, despite the prevailing rhetoric, it is logical that they are not seriously interested in the *universality* of human rights.

The lesson is that, although necessary, the advance in the theoretical formulation and foundation of universal rights is insufficient. There is a lack in the developed world of the indignation and compassion in the face of the cruelty caused or tolerated by these same countries. There is the need for a partiality of perspective in order not to confuse universality with what is in reality only twenty-five or thirty per cent of humanity. There is a need to think of human rights from the perspective of the peoples' lives, not from points of view that may be secondary to them. There is a need to be able to denounce those responsible for violations of the basic right to life. There is the need for the possibility of holding those responsible accountable for their actions.

---

[32] I. Ellacuría, 'Subdesarrollo y derechos humanos', *Revista Latinoamericana de Teología* 25 (1992) 5f.
[33] X. Gorostiaga, op. cit., p. 36.

d. Who to Hold Responsible

Human 'rights' presupposes responsibility in ways that can be guaranteed. *Accountability* is essential to human rights and the problem is who to hold to account. Simplifying things, in the area of conventional human rights this is generally the State. This can (and according to circumstances often does) guarantee first generation human rights, individual and political rights. But it does not guarantee, nor can it in the same way guarantee, the economic rights of the second generation, that is to say, it does not guarantee life – though it can help. The thing is that 'in the idea of political and civil liberties the idea of distributive justice is in no way implicit.... The law is only a means, absolutely detached from the aims of justice'.[34] The State makes itself responsible for law, but not for justice.

The social State is not inclined towards the elimination of the presuppositions of economic capitalism, but exclusively towards the correcting of the inequality of distribution of the wealth produced.... While the system of the corporations maintains the power to direct the economic process, the State is assigned the task of creating a 'social security' system with the aim of assuring greater equality in standards of living.[35]

Who, then, can be held to account? Or to put it another way, do we not fall into ambiguity by using the same term 'rights' and applying it to political and civil rights, with a body that should and is able to guarantee them, with checks to verify it is complied with, and to economic rights, with a body that, ultimately, can only regulate what others do, but without being able to demand that these others provide any guarantee of life?

These others, the economic and financial apparatus, feel no obligation to guarantee the lives of all. Moreover, they invoke rights – freedom – in order not to have to submit their procedural means to a normative that would result in a living for the majorities. And there may be worse to come. In the heart of the Organization for Economic Cooperation and Development (OECD), the Multilateral Agreement on Investments (MAI) is being formulated in absolute secrecy.[36] As far as rights and obligations are concerned, the agreement envisages a trade treaty that will authorize multinational corporations and investors to bring governments before the courts for any such action that had the effect of reducing their profits. In this agreement, the international

---

[34] Pietro Barcellona, 'Los sujetos y las normas. El concepto de Estado social', in Enrique Olivas (ed.), *Problemas de legitimidad en el Estado Social*, Madrid, 1991, p. 31.
[35] Ibid., p. 33.
[36] See Lori M. Wallach, 'El nuevo manifiesto', in *Le Monde Diplomatique*, February 1998, Spanish edition.

companies and investors reserve the rights, while governments assume all the obligations. In this way, governments have an obligation to guarantee 'full enjoyment' of investments, and investors and companies have the right to denounce any policy or government action (fiscal measures, dispositions on the environment, labour legislation, rules for consumer protection) that they consider prejudicial, and can demand compensation in cases of government intervention that restricts their profits.[37]

That is the situation we are in. If this is what is happening on national levels, how much more must be going on globally? Who can be called to account for the thirty-six million annual deaths by starvation? Who can the oppressed peoples call to account? Who can be called to account when wars break out if the security council of the United Nations controls the world's armaments?[38] And if nobody can be called to account, what hope is there for the people?[39]

Calling to account has been an important dimension in the Christian tradition. In the presence of evil, inhumanity and wrong doing, God has been called to account. It is the problem that in technical terms has been called theodicy. We will not go into that now, but merely recall the point. At times strong words have been used:

> In a world in which the reason and liberty of the human being have produced the realities of this twentieth century, to talk about the continuity between the human and the divine can only signify that the ultimate mystery of existence – God – is not a Friend of the human being but, more probably, an Enemy: God creates with destruction as his only aim.[40]

Religious language has the advantage of being able to be bold and honest at the same time, something not often found in other languages. Is not the problem with our world that the system, with all its rhetoric

---

[37] 'While countries everywhere are cutting back on their social programmes, at the same time they are being asked to approve a world-wide programme of assistance to international companies.', ibid.

[38] 'Ninety per cent of arms sold between 1988 and 1992 were sold by the five permanent members of the security council (p. 42), who, by the way, have not signed many of the pacts relating to human rights proposed by the United Nations (p. 39)', J. I. González Faus, 'La paz: nuevo nombre del desarrollo', *ECA*, 550 (1994) 830. The author comments on and quotes V. Fisas, *El Desafío de Naciones Unidas ante el mundo en crisis*, Barcelona, 1994.

[39] 'The United Nations supreme court of justice is practically unknown: in its forty years existence it has only tried sixty cases and when it ruled against the mining of Nicaraguan ports by the United States, the USA refused to recognize the supreme court jurisdiction (p. 63)', ibid., p. 830.

[40] D. Hollenbach, 'Etica social bajo el signo de la cruz', *Revista Latinoamericana de Teología*, 37 (1996) 51.

and political, economic, military discourses is not a 'friend of the oppressed'?

Returning to religious language, God can be called to account, can be criticized and rejected. According to Christian tradition, though, on the one hand God also, indefensibly, becomes a victim and is crucified. But, on the other hand, he rallies to defend the lives of the poor, brings the crucified Jesus back to life, and gives hope to the crucified peoples. Whatever the acceptance of that Christian tradition, the symbolism is important: we human beings can call to account. God will not fail to understand the reality of crucifixion, nor will God be deaf to the cries of protest. 'God' joins the other side and becomes a member of this world of victims.

This is religious language, symbolic and utopian, certainly. But the point is that the system does not, even at the symbolic and linguistic levels, bother itself with the victims' reality. It usually generates them. And it is useless to try calling it to account.

3. A Word on the Mysticism of Human Rights

We end up where we began. In today's world, the situation is paradoxical. On the one hand there are advances in specific humane areas (freedoms, guarantees etc.), especially in countries of plenty, and also, to a much lesser extent, in the 'pockets of prosperity' in poor countries. These advances have not achieved everything, but have set the humane on the right course. They have introduced a tradition of vindication and the conviction and hope that change is possible. They have introduced too, with their fallen and martyrs, the tradition of compromise and struggle. Human rights show, then, that there has been great love. But, on the other hand, all that has not substantially changed the inhuman situation of oppressed peoples and impoverished majorities. 'The inhumane', more than the enjoyment of 'human rights', is what defines the life of oppressed peoples.

This is something we have to be aware of in the present world. To give a current example, the violation of an individual's right 'to privacy in the area of information technology' cannot be compared with the fact that two-thirds of humanity live in poverty. For this reason, it is not the same thing to defend the right to this privacy as to struggle to get this world out of poverty. The conclusion is that the human rights struggle, in the conventional sense, must be integrated into the greater struggle for the lives of the poor, the majorities and the oppressed peoples.

Summing up what we have said, this struggle must recapture and maintain the phrase 'It's not right' in the face of the world situation and not allow this cry to be stifled – the most subtle way of stifling it would be the refusal to act on the grounds that it corresponds with no concrete formulation of human rights. It must make priorities of the theorization and putting into practice of human rights as *rights* – in the plural – of all *human beings* – simply for the fact they were born human and not in countries of plenty. It must guarantee and facilitate *life*, without the enjoyment of rights by a few turning into a comparative injustice. It must uncover a sleeping, drugged collective consciousness that prevents us from seeing the obvious.

Today it is notable how many civil, religious and university institutions are involved in human rights, and this is hopeful. On the one hand it shows that the bodies that should be watching out for human rights often are not, hence the proliferation of these institutions. But it also shows that there is an absolute necessity to do this, a consciousness that should be accompanied by creativity and mysticism in order not to weaken in a world that, to a great extent, is set against human rights and the humanity of the people.

Where this mysticism comes from is something worth analyzing. For my part I would like to end with some words from fifteen years ago when I was asked to write about 'the divine in working for human rights'. I did not know how to begin, and began like this, which will perhaps also help shed light today on what this mysticism is:

> Is there anything 'sacred' in today's world? Is there anything that asks of man something as an ultimatum, but presents too something promising and abundant? Is there anything that impedes him from relativizing all things on an equal basis, even though he might not know, from a theoretical viewpoint, why he should not relativize them? Is there anything that impels him to go beyond the individual and the group, even though they might be good, like the family, the party, the country or the Church itself?
>
> Throughout history there has always been this something we have called 'the sacred', in either a religious or secular way. At present there seems to be little doubt that the defence of human rights is for many something sacred, with finality, requirements and the promise of salvation. It is certainly that in Third World countries and is too, in different ways, in the First World. This sacredness is the life of the poor, the life of the victims.[41]

The mysticism of the struggle for human rights depends ultimately on relating them to life, and to the life of the majorities, the crucified

---

[41] 'Lo divino de luchar por los derechos humanos', *Sal Terrae* 856 (1984) 685. The text is somewhat modified.

peoples. What makes us rounded, 'holy' human beings – if such language appeals – what makes it possible for us to live with dignity and without shame at having fashioned a cruel world, is this struggle for the life of victims, running risks for them and participating in their reality. In this way we can enjoy the pleasure of belonging to and living among the human race.

Part 3:

A Theology of Truth and Memory

A Theology for the Bearers of Dangerous Memory

MARY GREY

*A voice is heard in Ramah
lamenting and weeping bitterly:
it is Rachel weeping for her children,
refusing to be comforted for her children,
because they are no more.*
                                    Jeremiah 31.15

*'Woman, why are you weeping?'
'They have taken my Lord away,' she replied,
'And I don't know where they have put him.'*
                                        John 20.12

These two texts are my chosen frame for this chapter because they capture *part* of the essence of its theme. In grieving for the thousands of murdered victims of the repressive regimes of El Salvador and Guatemala – their brutal deaths as well as the manner of their disappearances, the absence in so many cases of graves, of records and above all acknowledgement of the truth of these disappearances and murders, these texts offer a powerful biblical resonance and rooting. In the case of Rachel, she, the grandmother of Ephraim and Manasseh, is depicted by the prophet Jeremiah as mourning their defeat in being carried off to slavery in Babylon. Rachel's tomb, near Bethlehem, has become a poignant and cherished memory of this for the Jewish community, a memory recalled by Matthew when he evoked Rachel's voice at the slaughter of the innocent children at the time of Jesus' birth. (Matt. 2.18)

The case of Mary of Magdala is even more poignant. She is faced with the empty tomb, the vanished body of the Lord she loves and cherishes. Her grief-stricken cry, *I don't know where they have put him*, is echoed by the thousands of mothers whose stories are still being recovered and remembered. Yet the contrast is painful: Mary of Magdala's cry was followed by a joy-filled revelation of the Risen Jesus. The families of the missing ones now recalled must always live with loss and grief. In remembering the Jesuit martyrs, the courageous leadership of Archbishop Romero and Bishop Gerardi, the heroism of countless ordinary people, theologizing about witness and martyrdom can never be allowed to gloss over the brutality and unacceptability of what happened.

This is why the document, *The Recovery of Historical Memory Project,* (referred to from now on as REMHI) which cost the life of Bishop Gerardi, is of such crucial importance. For, the first task of dangerously remembering is the breaking of the official silence and hearing the voice of the victims. Secondly, the voices of the victims and the truth of the victims are heard and acknowledged to be true. And this is a dangerous recognition because it privileges the truth of the sufferers and victims, their families, all who stand with them, over and above the truth of the oppressive regimes. It is a subversive truth, a truth and memory running against the grain of the establishment. What has to be done in theology and in faith community is to create space where this truth is heard, honoured and witnessed to, placed within an ecclesial tradition of remembering and witnessing. Against regimes which systematically distort and systemically impose amnesia about the war, (as if anyone could forget!) in REMHI all groups working for human rights not only have a document giving voice to horrific accounts of torture, violation and rape, but also of the systemic ways in which a regime can turn ordinary young men into sadistic torturers and rapists.

How does theology react with its memory of a crucified and risen founder? The first task is to outline the origin and meaning of *dangerously remembering* as key motif for theology and then to explore the *praxis* of it for Christian community today.

1. A Theology of Dangerously Remembering – A New Trajectory for Theology

The theology of dangerous memory arises in the wake of brutal mass killings of the last century, although in fact it is the recovery of a much more ancient wisdom. After the Holocaust, the Shoah, of the Second World War, grief, a colossal loss of faith, a culture of silence and shame covered the memory of the Jewish survivors. Only in the last fifteen years did the Jewish community begin to speak of theologies of the Holocaust – and some would reject the attempt to find any

---

[1] See Dan Cohn-Sherbok, *Holocaust Theology*, London, Marshall, Morgan & Scott 1989; Rabbi Albert H. Friedlander, *Riders toward the Dawn*, London, Constable, 1993.

meaning.¹ The literary life of the Jewish survivor of Auschwitz, Eli Wiesel, has been described as *between memory and hope*,² as in his many novels he explores the trial of faith for the Jewish people, chosen by God, yet apparently abandoned to mass extermination in Hitler's death camps. For him, the task of dangerously remembering, keeps the spark of hope alive. As he expresses it in one of his novels, *Beggar in Jerusalem*:

> The Jews are God's memory and the heart of mankind. We do not always know this, but the others do, and that is why they treat us with suspicion and cruelty. Memory frightens them. Through us they are linked to the beginning and the end. By eliminating us they hope to gain immortality. But in truth, it is not given to us to die, not even if we wanted to. Why? Perhaps because the heart, by its nature, cannot but question memory. We cannot die because we are the question.³

It was a Jewish thinker and philosopher Walter Benjamin (1892–1940) who coined the term *dangerous memory,* in a manner foreshadowing the post-modern challenge to objectivity in history and the impossibility of capturing the 'how it really was' of an event. To recover the past means, for Benjamin, 'to seize hold of a memory as it flashes up at a moment of danger.'⁴ In a way prophetic for the theme, Benjamin thought that the historian would only be successful in fanning the spark of hope if he was convinced that *even the dead are not safe* if the enemy wins. After Walter Benjamin the theology of dangerously remembering entered Christian theology through Johann Baptist Metz, who understood it as the ground of his political theology. It is from Metz that Christian theology drew the notion of the *memoria passionis et resurrectionis Jesu Christi,* (the memory of the passion and resurrection of Jesus Christ), the dangerous memory of freedom that anticipates the future as a 'future of those who are oppressed, without hope and doomed to fail.' Hence memory 'breaks through the magic circle of prevailing consciousness', forcing us to establish a new form of solidarity, 'inasmuch as the history of suffering unites all men like

---

² This is the title of a book on his work: Carol Ritner (ed.), *Eli Wiesel: Between Memory and Hope,* New York, New York University Press, 1990. 'Hope, Despair, Memory' was the title of Wiesel's unpublished text on receipt of the Nobel Prize, Oslo, December 1986.

³ Eli Wiesel, *A Beggar in Jerusalem,* New York, Random House 1970, p. 113.

⁴ Walter Benjamin, 'Theses on the Philosophy of Memory', in *Illuminations* ed. and introduced by Hannah Arendt, New York, Schocken Books, 1969. In this section I am drawing on some ideas from my previous article, 'Liberation Theology and the Bearers of Dangerous Memory', in *New Blackfriars,* 75, 887, (November 1994) 512–524.

a "second nature".'[5] Important as this inspiration is, and continues to be, in telling us to read history from the standpoint of the conquered and the victims, there is still an element of abstraction here. This is because Metz looks beyond history, relying on a (soteriological) guarantee that 'situates the ultimate outcome of the human condition in a realm beyond history and society.'[6]

This chapter prefers to make the link between Benjamin and Elizabeth Schüssler Fiorenza's process of dangerously remembering, because both are in solidarity with concrete situations and communities of suffering and struggle.[7] They invoke no happy endings outside history. Fiorenza began her life project by refusing to read Scripture with the dominant interpretation of the Jesus movement in Palestine, but reads *against the grain*, subversively, to recover women from silence, from the shadows, margins, into being participants, agents, and even leaders in this prophetic and transforming movement. As with the stories from El Salvador and Guatemala, she casts light on not only women's suffering – as did Jeremiah with the story of Rachel, but their 'active struggles to transform their situation.'[8] The invitation is not merely to empathize with the victims and the dead: dangerous memory invites to solidarity and commitment to transform present oppressive social relations, and emancipate those still enslaved by them. This is the prophetic agenda of dangerous memory as we see with the REMHI, with the Truth and Reconciliation Committee in South Africa, the memory of slavery in the American south, and wherever the reading of history serves the interests of those in power today and hold the powerless in its grip.

2. Who Are 'We' Who Remember?

Where do we stand, we, the communities who remember? With the victims, the missing ones and those who mourn them? To stand with the bearers of dangerous memory demands honesty about our own standpoint in society. For those of us who were alive in the times of

---

[5] Johann Baptist Metz, *Faith and History and Society: towards a Practical Fundamental Theology*, (tr.) David Smith, New York, Seabury Press, 1980, p. 90, p. 105. I cite here from 'Memory, Revolution, Redemption' in Marsha Aileen Hewitt, *A Critical Theory of Religion: A Feminist Analysis,* Minneapolis, Fortress, 1995, pp. 155–157.

[6] Hewitt, ibid., p. 157.

[7] There is an irony here, as Marsha Hewitt points out: 'given Benjamin's feelings of solidarity with the oppressed classes, his representations of women contain a poignant irony ... women appear in Benjamin's writings as somewhat less than full human beings lacking agency or subjectivity. He does not consider their experience or point of view. Benjamin, moreover is aware of the limited male capacity to see the female only under two simultaneous perspectives, as a whore and as an untouchable lover.' (Hewitt, p. 162)

[8] Hewitt op cit. p. 163.

apartheid, who knew about the killings in El Salvador, Chile, Guatemala, East Timor, Palestine, who are caught up, whether we like it or not with the globalized systems which ensure that violence continues, there is a real challenge to examine our own complicity in these 'killing systems'. To stand with the memory of the 'crucified peoples' of the world is only possible within a continual conversion experience in which we are dependent on the generosity of the peoples themselves for forgiveness. The crucified peoples are never an abstract category, but are the real women and men whose stories are written in this book of pain and suffering (REMHI), the stories of the South African *Truth and Reconciliation Committee*, the women whose bodies wear the scars and bruises of abuse, the women who have been silenced forever and whose stories will never be told.

This stance of conversion, solidarity and commitment is made possible by the dynamic strand of tradition within Christianity of protest and revolution. The bearers of dangerous memory are keeping alive the very core of Jesus' project of the Kingdom of God, which of its essence must conflict with the wisdom of the kingdoms of this world. The 'we' who remember then, are committed to protest, to protest against the domestication of the Gospel and its facile assimilation into conventional religion. Secondly, the bearers of dangerous memory are committed to the wider project of re-membering the underside of history. Reading against the grain means challenging all that has been handed down to us with seal of objectivity and fact. As Bertold Brecht (1898–1956) put it:

A Worker Reads History

Who built the seven gates of Thebes?
The books are filled with the names of Kings.
Was it Kings who hauled the craggy blocks of stone?
And Babylon, so many times destroyed,
Who built the city up each time?

In which of Lima's houses
That city glittering with gold, lived those who built it?
In the evening when the Chinese wall was finished
Where did the masons go?
Imperial Rome is full of Arcs of Triumph:
who reared them up . . .
Young Alexander conquered India:
He alone?
Caesar beat the Gauls;
Was there not even a cook in his army?[9]

---

[9] Bertold Brecht, 'A Worker Reads History,' in *Collected Poems,* London, Faber, 1956

The point is clear: not only that history records the hero's victory, not those who share the effort to achieve it. But the memory of the victory and achievement is enshrined in stone, text, official chronicle, song, story and art form to ensure that the dominant memory triumphs. The bearers of dangerous memory have to hear into speech the silences of the suppressed underside, remember them in that literal sense of putting new flesh on the bones of the official story. In Europe, justice-seeking communities and human rights groups began to do this as, while the dominant intention was to celebrate the memory of Columbus's discovery of the so-called New World, we began to listen to other stories, to realize that there was no call for celebration, but rather, for a long repentance for what Europe had done in terms of exploitation and enslavement of much of Latin America.

This culture of silence shrouding the underside of history is far from being the peaceful silence of contemplation, the wordless adoration of the mystic; rather, it is engendered by shame and humiliation. While systemic amnesia may be enforced by the powers who make history, *Dangerous memory* can also be covered over by *false* memory, by distorted memory – (false memory syndrome is now well recognized). Allowing the memories of killing and rape to emerge can be too costly. It may bring too much pain. So suppression of horror is one way to cope with the truth. Terror and fear also block and distort the act of remembering. It may be too dangerous to remember the truth, especially if the status quo is unchanged. Women who try to report rape and abuse have faced a barrage of accusations: they are to blame, they provoked it, their stories are contested, the situation becomes reversed so that they are the guilty ones, not the perpetrators.

One example of this is the way African-American women have struggled to find a voice for the memory of slavery and its consequences which they bear in their own lives. Re-membering the sufferings of the past is engaged with to create new possibilities for the present, even though the racist and sexist exploitation still continues. Many readers will be familiar with the novel, (now a film) *Beloved,* by Toni Morrison.[10] It is the story of a young mother who killed her baby in order not to allow her to be re-captured into slavery. But this theme is interwoven with the dangerous memory of the mother, Sethe's own slavery experience. This very remembering is so crushing and overwhelming that it cannot be recovered as a continuous flow, but in slow, painful stabs, in burst of short tellings, where present and past are interwoven.

(permission sought). I am grateful to Professor Elaine Graham for this reference as well as for some of the insights of her article, 'Some expressive Dimensions of a Liberation Practical Theology: Art Forms as Resistance to Evil', by Elaine Graham and James Poling in *International Journal of Practical Theology* (2000) 2.

[10] Toni Morrison, *Beloved*, Pan, Picador, 1988.

The pastoral theologian, Elaine Graham, because of all these difficulties involved with remembering, writes that even if memory is unspoken or repressed,

> its 'trace' endures as the sign of its being. This makes it possible for us to wait for the echoes that remind us of the occluded others at the margins of history. There may be no absolute authority of memory as complete and definitive record of the past. Memory is never a perfect account of what has gone before, but also to some extent a fabrication. But even these recollections, as reconstructions of the imagination, can be heard and received as legitimate witness. That is why literature and art are vital to the gathering of dangerous memory.... Words are like exiles, forever wandering, forever cut off from a final resting place.... all we have are 'traces' – the vestiges and echoes of silenced voices.[11]

But when these traces are gathered together within a tradition of protest and remembering of the crucified and risen Christ, a *praxis* of dangerously remembering becomes a solid foundation for ecclesiology, for *a liberation theology of church*. I will now sketch some elements of this.

3. The Praxis of Dangerously Re-membering

The praxis of 'dangerously remembering' is work, a sacred task, *leitourgia*, (liturgy), for us, the communities who bear this dangerous memory. As the poet Adrienne Rich – whose thirty years of writing poems is marked with the painful task of remembering the past as a Jewish woman, lesbian, confronting the violence and racism of the United States, wrote:

> The past is not a husk yet change goes on ...
> Freedom. It isn't once to walk out
> under the Milky Way, feeling the rivers
> of light, the fields of dark –
> freedom is daily, prose-bound, routine
> remembering. Putting together, inch by inch,
> the starry worlds. From all the lost collections.[12]

This sacred work is a *process,* and as I said, part of the process is repentance. Repentance for the voices silenced even within the Church

---

[11] Elaine Graham and James Poling, op cit., p. 22.
[12] Adrienne Rich, 'For Memory' in *A Wild Patience has Taken me thus Far*, New York, W. & W. Norton, 1982.

herself, repentance for our cooperation with regimes of violence and torture. The process asks that this repentance is ongoing and tangible through the creation of new ecclesial spaces, which become safe spaces for remembering. (The liturgies of the Justice and Peace Conferences and the celebrations of Women Church are good examples of this). If this is not achieved, we remain in a system of exclusion and ongoing marginalization of the Other, the stranger, in the hundreds of ways in which the Other appears in our midst: asylum seekers and refugees are clear examples at the moment.

I am aware that at the moment, as part of the Jubilee events, that the Vatican has announced a time of purifying memory and of reconciliation. The areas addressed specifically are such categories as offences against Christian unity, imposing the faith by violence – for example, in the Crusades – as well as offences against Human Rights in the present – although these are not specified. I think it is important to welcome any movement toward reconciliation and redeeming the past, and to hope that this is but a first step towards redressing its wrongs and taking responsibility. But far more important is the investigation of involvement in contemporary regimes of repression, and the embarking on repentance for where the Church has taken the side of the landowner and the repressive government.

Thirdly, commitment is expressed through a poetics of resistance, a poetics of dangerously remembering. This is an ancient practice: what else was the culture of Negro spirituals but a poetics of protest and resistance against slavery in a context which offered little or no hope? (This was also the context of the rise of the Blues and Jazz). To sing 'Go down, Moses' in this context was keeping alive subversive memory in the context of the most extreme oppression, slavery, and for women in addition to this, sexual humiliation. Even though the present offered little or no hope, the faith of the slaves was a faith *in time and history*, loving Jesus meant freedom and justice in *earthly* life but maybe not *experienced*.[13] So, when they sang,

> I am a poor pilgrim of sorrow
> I'm tossed in this wide world alone
> No hope have I for tomorrow
> I've started to make heaven my home

they did not mean giving up on this life. The very strength of the oral tradition itself generated life-giving affirmations. Cheryl Kirk-Duggan writes:

---

[13] See Cheryl A. Kirk-Duggan, *Exorcising Evil: A Womanist Perspective on the Spiritual*, Maryknoll, Orbis, 1997, p. 123.

Divine justice limits exploitation and helps one make sense out of a powerless existence.[14]

Many have written on the meaning of the spirituals in keeping faith and hope alive, but the part that women have played has often been missed. Toni Morrison's poignant picture of the spiritual leadership of the old woman, Baby Suggs in *Beloved* opens another dangerous memory; Alice Walker's charting of the creativity[15] of the black women of her childhood in *In Search of Our Mothers' Gardens* is a powerful witness; many womanist theologians combine poetry, song and art in a creative remembering of silenced voices:

> O Beautiful Blackness,
> You sing with melodious voices
> On stage, at church, in fields ...
> You sing
> Only For the ears of God
> Other times before great halls of justice
> Broadcast before shuttering masses
> As deputised lynched mobs
> Lurked in the shadows.[16]

In Britain the Third World Agencies – Cafod and Christian Aid – have made the Hunger Cloths / Lenten veils (from Haiti, India, the martyrs of El Salvador and so on) part of a solidarity with this poetics of remembrance. In the Christian women's movements, quilts remembering our foremothers, quilts making visible the suffering of violated women have all become part of the poetics of resistance. There are tapestries remembering Aids victims. In ecological spirituality, a hermeneutics of remembrance creates liturgies of remembering the wounded earth, the vanished birds, animals and trees.

The fourth element of the praxis of *dangerously remembering* is the ministry of lament. It is striking that from many contexts has arisen the awareness that we have lost the prayer of lament.[17] Churches offer services that are relentlessly positive, it is said, and 'without lament,

---

[14] Ibid.
[15] Alice Walker, *In Search of our Mothers' Gardens*, London, The Women's Press, 1984.
[16] Cheryl A. Kirk-Duggan, op cit., p. 206.
[17] For example, David Power's book, *The Eucharistic Ministry: Revitalising the Tradition*, Dublin, Gill & McMillan, 1992, calls for the restoration of penitential lament to the eucharistic prayers of the Mass. Wild Goose Worship of the Iona community is engaged with much creative work on the prayer of lament, for example, a lament for a stillborn baby.

hope is still-born'.[18] Far from fostering a 'culture of complaint' and encouraging victimization, the prayer of lament stems from the voice of protest against oppressive reality. The cries of pain and suffering – of which Psalm 22's scream of abandonment, 'My God, my God why hast thou forsaken me?' is the most famous expression, were for Israel the necessary first step in order to hope. The writer Samuel Balentine puts it even more strongly. In order to be able to praise authentically, he says,

> praise must be sung back down to pain, where hope lives; to hurt, where newness surfaces; to death, where life is strangely given.[19]

In the prayer of lament, the roots of Jewish tradition are drawn on, where Job argued with God, but, even more poignantly, where God laments the disloyalty of humanity:

> O my people, what have I done to you?
> Tell me how I have wearied you; answer me this.
> (Micah 6.3)

These words entered the Christian tradition to form the basis of the Reproaches formerly sung on Good Friday. Jesus himself lamented over Jerusalem, and the whole of creation, disturbed and mourning the Crucifixion of Jesus belongs to this tradition. In the weeping daughters of Jerusalem, addressed by Jesus carrying his cross, a glimpse is gained of a marginal, almost forgotten tradition – the role of women in lamenting, especially at deaths and funerals.

So, the bearers of dangerous memory by keeping the prayer of lament alive, remain close to the sources of compassion. With remembering, so much more than the cognitive activity of western philosophy is restored, as with the prayer and ministry of lament, the reality of bodily pain and experience is kept alive, grieving is an honoured ecclesial activity, awareness of bodily experience is recognized at the heart of Christian life. I use the word 'ministry of lament' in recognition that lamenting may begin and end as prayer, but means also accompanying people in their grief, in their attempts to hold onto a fragile truth, to live with Rachel's cry that *the loved ones are not,* to live with the fact of disappearance: this is a daily ministry for the whole community.

And the final element in the praxis of dangerous memory is the

---

[18] Kathleen D. Billman and Daniel L. Migliori, *Rachel's Cry: Prayer of Lament and rebirth of Hope,* Cleveland, Ohio, United Church Press, 1999, p. 14.
[19] Cited in ibid., p. 30.

central act of the Church in remembering, the eucharistic *Anamnesis*. Many have written on the prophetic challenge of Eucharist.[20] What I want to emphasize here is the confrontation of one kind of remembering with another. The situation of torture, of murder and disappearance was the product of the distorted imagination of brutal regimes. William Cavanaugh in his book *Torture and the Eucharist* wants us to recognize that torture is an *ecclesiological* problem.[21]

> Torture plays out the dreams of a certain kind of state....
> The imagination of the state has a tremendous power to
> discipline bodies, to habituate and script them into a drama
> of its own making...[22]

Just I was not speaking of remembering purely as a mental act, so, here, he is here not speaking of imagination as a mere fanciful state. The examples Cavanaugh gives are from the oppressive regime of General Pinochet in Chile. Here the problem for the state was not so much resistance, but the lack of it:

Violence was used (in 1973) not as a response to threats
by the state, but rather to create the threats from which
the only possible protection was the state itself. This type
of terror is a mode of governance which is itself self-justifying.[23]

Already in 1986 Elaine Scarry, in her book *The Body in Pain*,[24] had made the connection between physical pain and torment and the regime. The prisoner's world, she wrote, is collapsed to the cell and her own suffering body and the reality of the torturer's voice. In a structured way, the methods of torture parody in a *demonic* way the creating of the world of the biblical story, by a deliberate un-making, of the body and the world of the victim.

But if torture, brutality and unmaking are the products of the imagination of the State, how is the Eucharist the imagination of the Church? Cavanaugh shows us how the Eucharist gives us an alternative economy of pain and the body:

---

[20] See Tissa Balasuriya, *The Eucharist and Justice*, London, SCM, 1978; M.Grey, *The Outrageous Pursuit of Hope: Prophetic Dreams for the 21st Century*, London, Cassell 2000.
[21] William Cavanaugh, *Torture and the Eucharist*, Oxford, Blackwell, 1998.
[22] Ibid., p. 31.
[23] Ibid., p. 33.
[24] Elaine Scarry, *The Body in Pain*, Oxford, OUP, 1986.

> Whereas torture is anti-liturgy for the realization of the
> state's power on the bodies of others, Eucharist is the
> liturgical realization of Christ' suffering and redemptive
> body in the bodies of his followers ... torture creates
> victims, Eucharist creates witnesses, martyrs... (p. 206)

He gives a brilliant illustration of this contrast from a novel, *Imagining Argentina*.[25] This tells the story of Carlos Rueda, who is the Director of a Children's Theatre. Both his wife and daughter have disappeared under the military dictatorship. In his sharing of the anguish of the victims he becomes aware that he possesses an extraordinary gift. He tells a boy whose father had disappeared, that this very night a colonel will visit his cell bringing food, a carafe of wine, and giving the advice to his father – (a university professor) – that he must be more careful what he says to his students. Then two soldiers will come and he will be released. This happens – and soon Carlos's garden fills up with people every evening to learn the fate of their missing loved ones. It seems that Carlos's imagination actually *makes things happen*: some people are found and walk to freedom, whereas others die. His friends, sceptical, dismiss this as mere imagination. Carlos knows the difference and realizes that the conflict is between two types of imagination – that of the state and that of its opponents. He says:

> All I've been trying to tell you is that there are two Argentinas, Silvio, the regime's the travesty of it, and the one we have in our hearts. We have to believe in the power of imagination because it is all we have, and ours is stronger than theirs.[26]

Ours is stronger than theirs. In conclusion, I want to sum up what it means, to commit ourselves to dangerously remembering in the power of Eucharistic imagination:

First, the issue of truth. Our ability to admit it, tell the truth, to keep a hold on it is fragile, given the privileging of the lie, in so many areas of society. But the Eucharist is about the *truth* of the vision of the kingdom of peace and justice: there cannot be anything to privilege over this as the realisation of *God's* vision, *God's* imagination of the new creation, the re-making of the world, where time and space are transformed, because now they offer peace to all nations, and to the myriads of life forms within the universe.

Secondly, it is remembering not only of a form of words and past

---

[25] Lawrence Thornton, *Imagining Argentina,* New York, Doubleday, 1987, p. 131.
[26] Ibid., p. 65.

action, but a commitment to protest, resistance, to the alternative ethics of the kingdom in solidarity with a long tradition of remembering the crucified and risen one. And in the memory in the Risen One we live now *threatened with Resurrection* – as the poem of Julia Esquivel put it.[27] We *practice* Resurrection in the waiting time expressed liturgically by the Holy Saturday tradition, the vigil between Crucifixion and the joy of Easter. That is how the bearers of dangerous memory re-connect with Mary of Magdala: in the grief of disappearance we were in solidarity. In the waiting time we can identity in hope with her joy at the encounter with Christ.

Building on this *in-between* theme, (the now and not yet), eucharistic imagination invites to open up the many silences, the voices still silenced when unjust structures are reproduced within the Church. It is too easy – see the earlier remark on Johann-Baptist Metz – to assume an eschatological happy-ever-after ending, while ignoring the many ways in which we collude with the State's imagination. Dangerously remembering recalls the Church herself to the body of a tortured man; dangerous memory calls to repentance where the language of rejection, exclusion and distancing from the language of the body, have been the lived truth of our own Christian communities. Dangerous memory is not about idealizing of victims/martyrs, but is the costly struggle to achieve the telling of truth, albeit if we have to hang on to traces because the total reality is unbearable: what is asked is the even more costly *continual* narration of this truth in public spaces.

And then, like the powerless groups who embodied the poetics of resistance in art, music and poetry, eucharistic communities have to transform the poetics of resistance to a *politics of resistance* – and pay the price it takes. For that is what makes it eucharistic.

But the last word for dangerous memory cannot be resistance alone. Resistance is always in service of what we try to achieve. Forgiveness and reconciliation are at the heart of eucharistic memory. It is not for the fortunate ones, who have not suffered torture, abuse and loss to persuade people to forgive. But at the root of this memory praxis I have been tracing is the prayer for forgiveness of the dying thief and the cry of Jesus, 'Father forgive them' (Luke 23.34). . . .

For that is the situation in which we are still caught. So this Chapter will end with the poem of the journalist poet, Antjie Krog, who after covering for radio the *Truth and Reconciliation Commission* in South Africa, ends her poignant book, *Country of my Skull* with these words for *all* the victims of both sides of the conflict:

---

[27] Julia Esquivel, 'Threatened with Resurrection', in Janet Morley (ed.), *Bread of Tomorrow,* London, SPCK, 1992, pp. 127–128.

174   TRUTH AND MEMORY

> because of you
> this country no longer lies
> between us but within ...
>
> in the cradle of my skull
> it sings, it ignites
> my tongue, my inner ear, the cavity of heart
> shudders towards the outline
> new in soft intimate clicks and gutturals
>
> of my soul the retina learns to expand
> daily because of a thousand stories
> I was scorched.
>
> A new skin.
> I am changed forever. I want to say:
> forgive me
> forgive me
> forgive
> You whom I have wronged, please
> take me
> with you.[28]

With this plea, I return to Mother Rachel. If those who took the children of her sorrow into captivity, if all the mothers of the missing ones, heard this plea for forgiveness of the young South African journalist, would it be heard? Would it touch the heart-ache? *There are tears of things*, said the Roman poet years ago, and some will never dry.[29] But if there was hope ahead, of *some* reconciliation with justice, would the pilgrims at Rachel's tomb find consolation in their remembering?

---

[28] Antjie Krog, *Country of My Skull*, Random House, Vintage, 1999, p. 423.
[29] *There are tears of things,* (Sunt lacrima rerum) is a quotation from Virgil's *Aeneid*.

Memory in the Service of Reconciliation and Hope

DERMOT A. LANE

I feel honoured to be associated with the commemoration of the twentieth anniversary of the death of Archbishop Oscar Romero (1980). Romero stands out in the last century not only as a witness to and a martyr for the Gospel of Jesus Christ but also as a church leader who fully appreciated the liberating dynamic of the Second Vatican Council. I am also happy to be associated with the commemoration of the second anniversary of the death of the human rights activist Bishop Juan Gerardi (1998) and the commemoration of the deeply disturbing death or disappearance of 200,000 people in Guatemala over the last thirty-six years.

I must also congratulate the editors of this collection on choosing the theme 'Memory and Truth' to commemorate these three historic realities. In selecting this theme they are drawing attention to the role of memory in arriving at the truth and bringing about reconciliation in the world. The choice of this theme coincides and resonates deeply with the remarkable visit of John Paul II to Yad Vashem in Jerusalem commemorating the victims of the Holocaust on 23 March 2000. Furthermore the theme of 'Memory and Truth' echoes some of the elements in the document 'We Remember: A Reflection on the "Shoah"' published by the Vatican Commission for Religious Relations with Jews in March 1998, the more recent document issued by the International Theology Commission entitled 'Memory and Reconciliation: The Church and the Faults of the Past' (December 1999) and of course the document produced by the human rights office of the Archdiocese of Guatemala entitled 'Recovery of Historical Memory Project' released in English by Orbis Books, New York, 1999.

In marking the anniversaries of Romero, Gerardi and the death or disappearance of 200,000 people we are seeking to keep alive the memory of those who died unjustly before their time; we are refusing to forget the outrageous manner of their deaths; we are aiming to redress these injustices of history; and we are trying to ensure that their respective martyrdoms have not been in vain but rather will influence the course of history in the future. The key to realizing these important objectives is the invocation of the much neglected human faculty of memory.

In this paper I will review some debates that have taken place in the last few hundred years about the place of memory in history. In the light of these debates I will try to clarify in part two what we mean by the appeal to memory and seek to overcome some of the ambiguities surrounding the use of the word memory. In part three I will seek to retrieve the importance of memory within Judaism and early Christianity. In a fourth part I will discuss the tension between memory and forgetfulness. In the fifth and final part I will discuss the delicate relationship that exists between memory and reconciliation.

1. Debates about History from Recent Centuries

Let me begin by outlining a very significant debate that took place in the United States after the signing of the Declaration of Independence in 1776. The motto adopted at that time, namely the 'The New Order of Ages' (*novus ordo saeclorum*), was inscribed on the seal of the monument commemorating this historical event. This new motto, in the spirit of the European enlightenment, signalled a break with the past and an indication that a new chapter in history had come into being with the foundation of the American nation.

To be new at that time meant to be rid of the dead weight of the past. This interpretation of the significance of this event in American history is spelt out in the writings of Thomas Jefferson, the third President of the United States. Jefferson believed there should be a revolution every nineteen years so that people could be fully liberated from the shackles of the past. He points out in a letter of 1816 that 'the dead have no rights. They are nothing and nothing cannot own something'.[1] In another letter of 1824 Jefferson asks: 'can one generation bind another, and all others in succession for ever? I think not. The creator has made the earth for the living, not the dead'.[2] He goes on to say that the dead have no binding powers and can make no claims upon the living.

In contrast Abraham Lincoln takes a different point of view. In his famous Gettysburg address, writing in a different context to that of

---

[1] Thomas Jefferson, 'Letters to Samuel Kercheval, July 12, 1816', *The Portable Jefferson,* New York, Viking Press, 1975, p. 560.

[2] Thomas Jefferson, 'Letters to Major John Cartwright, June 5, 1824', *The Portable Jefferson*, p. 580

Jefferson, Lincoln suggests that 'the living' must 'be dedicated here to the unfinished work in which they who fought have thus far nobly advanced'. The dead do make demands on the living and the living therefore are obliged to be 'resolved that those dead shall not have died in vain'.[3] For Lincoln profound obligations and duties link the living with the dead and the yet unborn. To achieve this unity between the past and the present, Lincoln appeals to what he calls 'the mystic chords of memory' which as he sees it unite the living with the dead in a relationship of duty and responsibility in the present.

A somewhat similar debate took place between the First and Second World War in Europe of the last century among members of the Frankfurt School of Philosophy known as critical theorists. A leading figure in this discussion was Walter Benjamin. In 1937 Benjamin wrote an article about history in which he pointed out: 'The work of the past is not closed for the historical materialist'. A colleague, Max Horkheimer, reacted by saying that 'the supposition of an unclosed past is idealistic.... past injustice has occurred and is closed. Those who are slain ... were truly slain'.[4] Horkheimer was repeating what he had said on other occasions: 'What has happened to those human beings who have perished does not have any part in the future. They will never be called forth to be blessed in eternity'. And then as if to clinch the issue against Benjamin he says: 'in the end your statements are theological'. Benjamin replies: 'The corrective for this sort of thinking lies in the reflection that history is ... a form of empathetic memory. What science has settled, empathetic memory can modify'.

Benjamin was seeking to work out a theory of history that does not ignore our unity with past generations, especially those who have been oppressed. According to Benjamin history is usually written by the victors and therefore ignores the history of the suffering of the victims. Most attempts to write history require empathy with the victor and this makes us incapable of seeing 'history as the history of the suffering of the world'. What is really needed, therefore, in the writing of history is an 'empathetic memory' that keeps alive the knowledge of how badly people have been victimized in the past. In this way Benjamin believes he can keep history open and unclosed. Refusing to go down this road because of its affinity with theology, Horkheimer admits that 'a metaphysical sadness pervades the writings of the great materialists' and these materialists are acutely aware of the 'unlimited loneliness of man'

---

[3] Abraham Lincoln, 'Address delivered at the Dedication of the Cemetery at Gettysburg, November 19, 1863', *Abraham Lincoln: Speeches and Writings,* Vol. 2, New York, The Library of America, 1989, p. 536.

[4] The appropriate references for this debate and original sources in German are available in Helmut Peukert, *Science, Action, and Fundamental theology*, Massachusetts, M.I.T. Press, 1984, pp. 206–210

because the past is indeed past. Horkheimer, with characteristic pessimism, speaks out against the idea of justice: 'it can never be ... realized in history. Even if a better society takes the place of the present disorder it will not redress the penury of the past'. According to Helmut Peukert this exchange between Benjamin and Horkheimer should 'be considered one of the most theologically significant controversies of the twentieth century'.[5]

A similar debate about history can be found in an important article by the political scientist Christian Lenhart in 1975.[6] He invites the reader to consider three successive generations: G1 as a generation of enslaved predecessors, G2 as enslaved contemporaries who emancipate themselves, and G3 as a generation of emancipated successors. What should be the attitude of the generation of emancipated successors, that is the G3? Can they enjoy life without reference to their predecessors in G1 and G2? Are G2 and G1 to be forgotten and reduced to the status of dead wood in the evolution of humanity? Is oblivion, that is forgetfulness, the precondition of bliss in the present? Would the generation of emancipated successors, G3, be really liberated if they ignored, forgot and erased the memory of the struggles of G2 and G1. The generation of emancipated successors, G3, seem to have everything and owe nothing – but if it is to live nobly it must learn that it owes everything and possesses nothing. In response to this apparent paradox, Lenhart proposes what he calls 'anamnestic solidarity', that is a solidarity with the oppressed in remembrance of the past. If the struggle for a revolutionary cause is to continue, then it must be informed by some kind of larger historical solidarity with the dead comparable to that which takes place in ancestral worship.

The red thread running through these three debates is the emphasis on memory. It is implied that memory can keep history open, that memory can effect a unity between the living and the dead, and that the memory of the past can influence the shape of the present and the future.

Perhaps even more important in these debates is the emerging view that history is not closed and finished, that perceptions of the past shape the present, and that the past can, in a qualified sense at least, be changed in the present. Some philosophers of history, especially in Germany, make an important distinction between the reality of what happened in the past (*historie*) and our changing understanding of that reality in the present (*geschichte*). What is of crucial importance in our understanding of the past in the present is the appeal to memory and the way we exercise memory. If these claims for memory are to carry

---

[5] Helmut Peukert, op.cit., p. 206.
[6] 'Ananmestic Solidarity: The Proletariat Manes', *Telos* 25 (1975), 133–154.

weight, then more work needs to be done to deepen our understanding and appreciation of the critical role of memory. Above all the marginalisation of memory within modernity and the mass-media must be overcome.

2. Clarifying the Appeal to Memory

It is quite extraordinary how little serious work has been done on the human faculty of memory within modern philosophy and theology. There are, of course, notable exceptions to this broad generalisation. These exceptions include at least the critical theorists of the Frankfurt School of Philosophy, the philosophers Paul Ricoeur and Edith Wyschogrod,[7] the German theologian Johann Baptist Metz, and more recently some psychological studies addressing the phenomenon of false memories.

Memory is one of the most fragile faculties that human beings possess and for this reason it is open to much misunderstanding and misuse. The exercise of memory can be life-enhancing as well as life-diminishing. Because memory is so fragile it is also along with imagination one of the most creative faculties that human beings possess. As fragile and yet creative the exercise of memory is ambiguous: it can imprison people whereby they become locked up in a selective memory, it can also be liberating in so far as people can be freed from fear and isolation through recourse to memory, and it can be destructive by coming up with false claims about the past. However, in the context of this book, the use of memory can be transformative in so far as it can redress the injustices and sufferings of the past.

In the last twenty years there has been gradual recovery of the importance of memory. This new appreciation of the power of memory has come from a wide variety of sources. These sources include the critical theorists of the Frankfurt School of Philosophy, renewed attention to the memories of the Jewish Holocaust, ecumenical excavations of historical divisions between the churches, the striking work of the Truth and Reconciliation Commissions around the world, and psychological studies analysing how memory, especially false memory, operates. In each of these different domains, memory has come to the fore and there is now a growing realization that humanity has a duty to remember the past.

This duty to remember is an ethical duty and derives ultimately from the debt that the living owe to the dead. The living remember the past

---

[7] The work of Edith Wyschogrod, *An Ethics of Remembering: History, Heterology, and the Nameless Others*, Chicago, The University of Chicago Press, 1998 came to my attention after writing this paper.

so that they can honour their debt to the dead. There is a variety of reasons why the living have a duty to remember the dead.

We have a duty to remember, first, because every generation is in an important sense indebted to previous generations and as seen above has inherited so much that is life-giving from the past. To be sure there is often a negative inheritance from previous generations and we will come to that question presently. The principle point here is that the present generation is what it is as Lenhart has argued so persuasively in virtue of previous generations and this debt to the dead ought to be remembered.

A second reason why we have a duty to remember the past is in order to overcome the threatened destruction by time of past achievements. We build, often quite unconsciously, on the achievements of the past and these achievements are the foundation stone of advances in the present. Without drawing on the achievements of the past there would be few successes in the present. We live all the time out of our memories of the past and this debt should be acknowledged.

A third reason why we have a duty to remember the past is in order to attend in the present to the existence of unkept promises from the past. Unfulfilled promises from the past can be reactivated in the present through the power of memory.

A fourth reason why we have a duty to remember – and this reason is by far the most important from the point of view of the theme and purpose of this book – is on the one hand to keep alive the injustices and sufferings of the past and on the other hand to redress these injustices and sufferings in the present. Here it must be acknowledged, and this is the great contribution of Walter Benjamin, that history by and large has been written up by the victors at the expense of the victims. In virtue of the ontological solidarity that exists within the human family and in the light of the empathy of the human heart with the sufferings of the victims of history, humanity has an ethical duty to remember. If we do not remember past injustices and sufferings then we will be destined to repeat such injustices and sufferings in the present. There is abundant evidence, too much evidence, within the present of the repetition of past injustices and sufferings simply because of the neglect of humanity's duty to remember. This neglect of memory can exist at two different levels. On the one hand we may neglect our duty to remember by ignoring our unity with those to whom we have done injustice. The invocation of this neglected memory may demand some form of reparation in the present in so far as this is possible. On the other hand we can neglect the duty to remember by refusing to ask forgiveness from those on whom we have inflicted injustice.

A fifth and final reason why we have a duty to remember the past arises paradoxically out of a concern and responsibility for the future.

A sense of responsibility for the future impels us to remember the past so that the negativities of the past may not be repeated in the present and the future.[8]

This duty to remember will not succeed, however, unless we can outline some of the benefits that will accrue from fulfilling this duty. Is there any point in remembering and recalling the past? Does it make any real difference to retrieve the past in the present? Is not the perceived view the right view, namely what is done is done and cannot be undone? Can the injustices of the past, at least in part, be redressed in the present? To answer these questions we need to attend to the relationship that exists between memory and human identity, memory and reason, memory and history respectively.

(a) *Memory and Human Identity*. It is fairly self-evident that the understanding of who I am depends in large measure on the store-house of memory. Self-identity is shaped by the memory of family, human experiences, relationships and community. Access to human identity requires a narrative in which memory plays a pivotal role. The human subject is a storied self, shaped by memory. On the other hand a declining memory often entails a diminished narrative of human identity.

The one who has most clearly expressed this link between self and memory is Augustine in his well-known *Confessions*. In many respects the *Confessions* is an extended narrative of Augustine's quest for self and God. In Book IX of the *Confessions* Augustine asks: 'who am I and what manner of being am I' and then in Book X he sets out in search of the self in what he calls the 'fields and palaces' of memory. This journey through 'the caves and dens'[9] of memory enables him to sum up his answer in the following way:

'The power of memory is great, O Lord. It is awe inspiring in its profound and incalculable complexity. Yet it is my mind: it is myself (*et hoc animus est; et hoc ego sum*).'[10]

In effect Augustine is claiming a close correlation between memory and identity. I am what I remember and if we find it difficult to accept this we need only note how the loss of memory entails loss of human identity. In brief, therefore, Augustine highlights that memory is not only at the centre of human identity but is in fact an important source of identity. Neglect of historical memory reduces our full sense of self identity. We depend all the time on our human faculty of memory and in truth we live our lives out of our memories. It is memory, therefore, that drives the human being in action and reflection.

---

[8] A helpful discussion of this duty to remember can be found in Paul Ricoeur, 'Memory and Forgetting', Richard Kearney and Mark Dooley (eds.), *Questioning Ethics: Contemporary Debates in Philosophy*, London, Routledge, 1999, pp. 5–11

[9] Augustine, *Confessions,* Book X, §8.

[10] *Confessions*, p. 17.

(b) *Memory and Reason*. At the time of the enlightenment there was a strong reaction against the past, especially as expressed in tradition and religion. The whole spirit of the enlightenment sought to shake off the shackles of the past so as to enable reason to stand on its own two feet. This outlook is found in Immanuel Kant's account of the enlightenment summed up in the phrase *'sapere aude'*: have the courage to use your own reason independently. It is now recognized by many commentators that within the enlightenment there was a 'prejudice against memory'[11] and that in the modern world something of a 'flight from memory' has taken place.[12] Modernity has espoused a view of reason shorn of memory and this diminished use of reason is, according to Johann B. Metz, in part responsible for the current crisis within the human sciences.[13] Metz, more than most theologians, argues very persuasively for the rediscovery of the 'primacy of a reason endowed with memory, that is, anamnestic reason'.[14] Theology today, especially in the light of the Jewish Holocaust, and the on-going holocausts in the developing worlds 'cannot maintain its historical innocence'.[15]

Metz traces this removal of reason from memory back to the Hellenisation of Christianity in the early centuries. In the view of Metz this gave rise to a timeless dogmatism and a non-historical form of orthodoxy removed from historical memory. For Metz the great difference between the biblical world and contemporary society is to be found precisely in this lack of attention to memory within the modern world today.[16] Part of the uniqueness of Judaism is its passionate commitment to the centrality of memory, especially the memory of freedom from injustice in the past and the promises of God in the present and the future.

(c) *Memory and History*. It is in working out the relationship between memory and history that we discern first of all the different forms of memory which can exist. Secondly, and perhaps more impor-

---

[11] J.B. Metz, 'Monotheism and Democracy: Religion and Politics on Modernity's Ground', in *A Passion for God: the Mystical-Political Dimension of Christianity*, New York, Paulist Press, 1998, p. 142.

[12] Vera Schwarcz, *Bridge Across Broken Time: Chinese and Jewish Cultural Memory*, New Haven, Yale University Press, 1998, 24; pp. 160-161.

[13] J.B. Metz, 'Anamnestic Reason: A Theologian's Remarks on the Crisis in the *Geisteswissenschaften*' in T. McCarthy and A. Honneth (eds.), *Cultural-Political Interventions in the Unfinished Project of Enlightenment*, Cambridge, M.A.: MIT Press, 1992, 189-194.

[14] J.B. Metz, 'The New Political Theology: the *Status Quaestionis*' in *A Passion for God: the Mystical-Political Dimension of Christianity*, p. 25.

[15] Ibid.

[16] J.B. Metz 'Freedom and Solidarity: the Rescue of Reason' in J.B. Metz and J. Moltmann, *Faith and the Future: Essays on Theology, Solidarity, and Modernity*, New York, Orbis Books, 1995, p. 76.

tant, this complex relationship between memory and history reveals the benefits and fruits that can accrue from their mutual interaction.

Broadly speaking there is the existence of collective memory and individual memory vis á vis the past. Collective memory is made up of the traces and influences that different events have upon our understanding of the past. This collective memory is usually expressed in a memory-narrative which arises out of conversations with others. More often than not, however, these memory-narratives become codified into an official historical-narrative. The difference between memory-narratives and historical narratives is that the historian seeks to establish the facts and to offer explanations of past events by searching for causes, motives and reasons. A break takes place usually in the movement from memory-narratives to the establishment of historical-narratives.[17]

However, in spite of this break between memory-narratives and historical-narratives there may remain a tension or conflict between individual memory and the established historical-narrative. This tension can arise out of the neglect of some detail or testimony in the movement towards the establishment of historical-narrative. Or, this tension may arise through the discovery of new evidence after the historical-narrative has been determined. Or, a tension may arise with the historical-narrative out of a particular subjective and/or psychological unease that an individual may have with an experience or an event of the past.[18] This persistence of memory is sometimes referred to as repetition-memory.

It is possible to address this nagging persistence of memory (repetition memory) through what Ricoeur drawing on Freud calls 'the work of recollection'.[19] The work of recollection is an exercise of memory in a critical mode, seeking to overcome the tensions that can exist between past experiences and the present official record. What is important here is to be able to reopen and to re-examine the tensions within narrative memories, in one or other of their various expressions, through the work of recollection. There is a duty and a responsibility on human beings to recover as accurately as possible what really happened in the past. When this happens, when the conflict between memory-narratives and historical-narrative is overcome, then some form of healing can begin to take place between past experience and

---

[17] See Paul Ricoeur, 'Memory-Forgetfulness-History' *ZIF: Mitteilungen,* 2/95, (Universitat Bielefeld, 1995) 3–11.

[18] Ricoeur in his article 'Memory-Forgetfulness-History' focuses principally on this latter without addressing the other two possible sources of tension with historical narrative. What Ricoeur has to say about the psychological tensions also applies to the other sources of this tension.

[19] Paul Ricoeur, 'Memory-Forgetfulness-History', *ZIF: Mitteilungen,* 2/95, 7–8.

present understanding. The work of recollection can ultimately and ideally lead to the work of reconciliation.

Certain shifts begin to take place through the influence of the work of recollection on the present. These shifts are particularly significant when the work of recollection is about exposing suppressed injustices and/or forgotten sufferings in the past. While it is true that the past cannot be undone as such, nonetheless the meaning and significance of the past in the present can be changed. This brings us to the heart of the matter. If events and experiences of the past can be interpreted differently in the present through the painstaking work of recollection, then the influence of the past on the present changes.

The work of recollection involves a revisiting of the past, a reopening of the historical-narrative and a new analysis of the data so that the official record of history can be changed. If the official record of history is reinterpreted in the present, then the meaning and significance of the historical-narrative for the present changes. After all, more than one reading and more than one interpretation of the past is possible, especially if and when new or neglected evidence comes to the fore.[20]

A number of important things begin to happen when the historical narrative is changed in the present. Foremost here is the possible alleviation, if not the transformation, of past injustices and/or sufferings in the present. Past injustices and/or sufferings can be addressed, compensated, or even put right in the present. The complex question about the extent to which this can bring about reconciliation will be addressed separately in the final section of this chapter.

Secondly, the moral debt owed by the living to the dead and to their living offspring can be lightened. This reduction of the debt of the living to the dead can happen in various ways: through the celebration of anniversaries, through the ritual of public commemoration which can be a form of protest against forgetfulness, and through the process of forgiveness.

Thirdly, the relationship between the past and the present is changed and when this happens then the relationship between the present and future also changes. Changing our understanding of the past changes our expectation of the future.

Fourthly, by reopening the past the present generation have the possibility of revisiting what Ricoeur refers to as 'the graveyard of unfulfilled promises' from the past.[21] Some of the noble but unrealised

---

[20] An example of this recently has been the 1999 Catholic-Lutheran Agreement on the doctrine of Justification. This new agreement has far reaching consequences for the relationship between Catholics and Lutherans, both in the present and the future. The interaction between memory and history was central to this new ecumenical agreement over a bitterly contested understanding of the past.

[21] Paul Ricoeur, 'Memory-Forgetfulness-History', *ZIF: Mitteilungen*, 2/95, 9.

aspirations of past generations can be reawakened and taken up in the present.

If the past remains closed forever, then there is the danger that history will become a vicious circle repeating itself in the present without any hope in the future. A future without hope can give rise to cynicism about life and a fatalism concerning the course of history. If on the other hand humanity can fulfil its duty to remember the past or at least seek to fulfil its duty to remember, then there will be some benefits in the present and real hope for the future. A close correlation, therefore, can be seen to exist between the duty to remember the past and the benefits that arise from attention to that duty – the two most important benefits being that the injustices and sufferings of the past can be redressed in the present and therefore that we can hope they will not be repeated in the future. It is against the background of these philosophical reflections on what it means to invoke memory that we can now turn to memory within Judaism and early Christianity.

3. Memory within Judaism and Early Christianity

Within Judaism it is very clear that memory plays an essential role in determining and shaping religious identity. Particular emphasis is placed throughout the Jewish religion on the importance of remembering God's covenant with God's people, the Passover experience, and the gift of the Torah to the people through Moses. What is distinctive about memory in the Bible is that it is not simply a calling to mind of some experience or event from the past. Instead, to remember the past is to reactualize the past in the present. Further memory influences the behaviour of the one who remembers in the present. Memory, for the Jew, therefore has an ethical dimension in the sense that it impacts on human actions and decisions. Basically, 'Hebrew recollections of the past means that what is recalled becomes a present reality' influencing praxis in the here and now.[22] In celebrating the Passover through the power of memory, the past is made present for those who relive it. For the Jew memory is so powerful that past history becomes a present experience. Memory in Judaism, therefore, is more than a reflection on past experience and more than a recognition of the significance of past events; instead memory has the capacity to make the past actions of God reverberate and resonate in the present and in so doing memory energizes and empowers those who remember.[23]

It should be noted that in the Bible it is not only human beings who

[22] 'Memorial, Memory' *The Interpreters Bible*, Vol. 3, 1962/1986, p. 344.
[23] Bruce T. Morril, *Anamnesis as Dangerous Memory: Political and Liturgical Theology in Dialogue*, Minnesota, A Pueblo Book, Liturgical Press, 2000, pp. 153-154.

remember but also God who remembers. In many instances God is the subject of the verb to remember. Thus we find God remembering people like Noah, Abraham, Rachel and Hannah. In addition, God is constantly remembering God's covenant with Creation and with the people of Israel (Gen. 9:15; Exod. 2:24; Lev. 26.42). There is, of course, a difference between God's act of remembrance and Israel's act of remembrance. The memory of God is not about the re-actualization of the past in the present since the action of God is not restricted by time. Instead God's memory is about the continuation of God's creation and covenant as the sources of life for Israel. In contrast when the people of Israel remember they are recalling and reactualizing the past in the present: they are making the past available in the present with a view to bringing about a new praxis. For the Jewish people memory provides a dynamic link between the past and the present.

It is God who invites Israel to remember the Sabbath Day (Exod. 20:8) and to remember to keep the Commandments (Num. 15:39, Ps. 103:18). On the other hand Moses challenges the people to remember God, to remember the deeds of God, especially the Exodus event, the return from exile and the fact that once upon a time the people of Israel were a people who lived in slavery.

The Hebrew religion, therefore, is built around memory and memory is given its fullest expression in prayer and worship. Both prayer and worship are ways of making God's activity in the past operative once again in the present. It is this invocation of memory and the powerful dynamic attached to memory that constitutes the identity of Israel and has kept that religious identity intact throughout history.

Christianity inherited and took over this rich theology of memory from Judaism in and through the life of Jesus. It hardly needs to be emphasized that it was the living memory of Jesus as the Christ that constituted what we call the Church. The memory of Jesus evokes and activates the transforming mission and ministry of Jesus in the name of the reign of God, the command of Jesus at the Last Supper, and the saving death of Jesus within present experience.

There are clear parallels between Jewish and Christian memory: both focus on the saving action of God in history, on the reality of God's promises in history, and the importance of manifesting memory in the ritual of prayer and worship. There are, however, differences also between Jewish and Christian memory. The 'object' of Christian memory is a living person and not just events in history. Further, Christian memory is specifically sustained and supported by Resurrection and Pentecostal experiences. The key difference, however, between Jewish and Christian memory is that according to Christian memory the Messiah has come in Jesus and this affects directly the content of the memory of God's action in the world. For example, the memory of Jesus as God's Messiah is embodied ritually in the Eucharistic action which has prophetic and ethical consequences for the present as well as prefiguring the future (the *Eschaton*). What happens in the celebration of the Eucharist is that the Christ-event is propelled into the present, in all its fullness, so that those now performing the Eucharistic action can participate as if present at the original event of Jesus as the Christ in his saving death and Resurrection.[24] And the key difference between Jewish and Christian memory is the Christian claim that the future has already arrived in the paschal mystery of Jesus as the Christ.

4. Memory versus Forgetfulness

It is against the background of this Jewish and Christian understanding of memory that we must now address a peculiarly modern problem, namely the propensity to prefer the political expediency of forgetfulness over and against the prophetic character of memory. To do this we must first of all summarise the prophetic character of Jewish and Christian memory and then address the arguments in favour of forgetfulness.

As seen above the invocation of memory enables us to recover the lost unity within the modern world between the past and the present. Memory has the capacity to recover the binding solidarity between the living and the dead, and to activate the moral debt of the present generation to previous generations. Further, memory has the power to piece together the scattered fragments of time which are so much a characteristic of our post-modern culture. Indeed the recovery of memory stands out as a radical critique of the individualism of modernity and the relativism of post-modernity. It is only from within this unified perspective on history opened up by the power of memory that we can plan for a better future, that is, a future that is more humane and more just.

Secondly memory has the power to call into question the record of the established historical-narrative. As Benjamin reminds us very powerfully, every work of civilisation is at the same time a work of barbarism.[25] Behind the apparent successes of history lies also a story of immense suffering. What appears as victory for some is often the violation of the human rights of others in the past. There is rarely if ever just one reading of history but several readings, or better several memories of the past. These different memory-narratives, especially

---

[24] Bruce T. Morrell, *Anamnesis as Dangerous Memory*, pp. 163–180.
[25] W. Benjamin, 'Theses on the Philosophy of History', *Illuminations,* New York, Shocken Books, 1968, p. 256.

those relating to suffering and injustice, need to be exposed, addressed and where possible healed.

A third point is that Jewish and Christian memory can prophetically interrupt the existence of continuous, homogenous, and evolutionary empty time. Memory can provoke people to move from the boredom of chronological time, *chronos,* to open up the possibility of a new kind of revelatory time, *kairos*. Without this critique of *chronos* coming from memory, the future will appear simply as a hopeless prolongation of the past, more often than not in the grip of the powerful.

Fourthly, Christian memory stands out as an important protest against the modern myth of history as progress. This progressive view of history is employed by various organizations, especially political organizations, to cover over the injustices and sufferings of the past. The so-called progressive march of history has all too often ridden roughshod over the backs of the victims in the past and continues to ride on the broken backs of the weak in the present. According to this view there is no possibility of an alternative reading of history: the progressive march of history must go on and quantitative time must prevail over qualitative time. Within this outlook optimism, namely the prospect of more of the same with progressive improvement, takes over from hope.

In making these claims for the prophetic power of Christian memory it must be emphasized that memory is not an end in itself but rather the initiation of a process, a stepping stone as it were, on the way to the possibility of healing and reconciliation. An important step towards the healing of injustices and sufferings in the past is to be able to name in word and ritual the injustice and sufferings of the past inflicted by the victors on the victims. Once named, recognized and owned, there is then a possibility of moving towards a reconciliation of the conflict between memory-narratives and historical-narratives. However, it must be acknowledged that reconciliation may take considerable time, even painful time, to effect.

If this outline of the prophetic role of memory is to gain credibility then it must be contrasted with the rival position coming from the secular world of politics, namely historical forgetfulness. The arguments against memory must be taken seriously as a possible alternative before a theology of memory will gain acceptance and acquire a new urgency. In naming the arguments against the invocation of memory we need to recognize that the political world is just as much interested in reconciliation as the world of religion. The route, however, to reconciliation within the political world is very different to that of the world of religion.

The arguments for reconciliation promoted within the secular world of politics can be summed up in the slogan 'forgive and forget'. This slogan is spelt out in different ways. Some will argue that we need to forget our past and to recognize that when all is said and done we share more than actually divides. The past is over and strictly speaking belongs to another time, another order and another culture. The battles of the past are just that – battles of the past and therefore it is now time to move on. Others, however, will suggest that we live in an era that has the potential for all to be free and that this freedom will come from the new promises of liberal democracy, the benefits of market forces, and the ever-increasing phenomenon of globalization. In the future human identities will be shaped not by memory but by the advances of science, not by history but by information technology, not by tradition but by modern politics. The final argument against memory is that raking over the past will only generate revenge, violence and recrimination. Such arguments should not be dismissed lightly because they have their own particular seductive spirit.[26]

The underlying premise within these perspectives is that forgetfulness is the way forward in the forging of a new future. There are a number of difficulties about this politics of forgetfulness that must be exposed. First of all forgetfulness ignores and passes over in silence the injustices and sufferings of the victims in the past. In doing so, forgetfulness implicitly sanctions the evil inflicted by perpetrators on the victims of history. In the end forgetfulness leaves the official historical-narrative intact and unquestioned. In effect forgetfulness changes nothing and promotes the status quo in favour of the victors of history and those in political power. The question must be asked: is it possible to forgive when there is no acknowledgement of injustices and sufferings in the past?

A further difficulty with these arguments in favour of forgetfulness is they assume an understanding of forgiveness and reconciliation which is quite different to that of reconciliation within Christianity. There is no such thing as easy forgiveness, no such thing as cheap grace, no such thing as a quick fix, within the Christian process of healing. The Christian language of reconciliation has been all too easily co-opted by the world of politics which has paid very little attention to the real demands of healing. Within the Gospel of Jesus Christ and throughout the Christian tradition there is a strong emphasis on the need for conversion, a *metanoia*, literally meaning an interior change of heart, as the key to forgiveness. Without conversion there is no true reconciliation. When politicians talk about reconciliation they mean something quite different and this can be seen in their rhetoric of reconciliation, which all too frequently talks about external compromise, accommodation and negotiation.

---

[26] Some of these arguments are constructively discussed and critiqued by Stanley Hauerwas in his pamphlet *A Time to Heal*, Belfast: ECONI, 1999, pp. 18–21.

In contrasting memory and forgetfulness with each other we should not, however, separate them. Memory arises as a reaction and a protest against the constant human temptation to forget. The temptation to forget, whether it is proposed by politicians or simply the outcome of human frailty, alerts us to the need for an active and vigilant memory, especially in regard to the forgotten ones of history.

Furthermore, in contrasting memory and forgetfulness we must be able to articulate what memory seeks to achieve. This can be summed up in terms of a threefold objective attaching to every act of remembering in relation to the sufferings and injustices of the past. In the first instance the work of memory is a step on the road to reconciliation and therefore is not an end in itself. Memory is not reconciliation but it can lead to reconciliation. Memory is about reopening what appears to be closed and in doing this it can initiate a process that leads ultimately to reconciliation. Secondly, the work of memory seeks justice for the victims of history as well as trying to change the ways of the perpetrators of the injustice. Memory seeks to redress and repair the injustices of history. Thirdly, by narrating the memory of injustices in the past there is the specific and declared hope that such injustice will not be repeated in the present or the future.

5. Memory and Reconciliation

There is a growing awareness within society, Church and theology that a very complex relationship exists between memory and reconciliation. A number of important issues arise in mapping out this relationship between memory and reconciliation. The invocation of memory is rarely an end in itself and nearly always a means to bringing about justice and leading ultimately to reconciliation. It is increasingly clear that there can be no authentic Christian reconciliation without prior attention to the demands of justice. This principle was brought to public attention in the now famous 1986 *Kairos Document*, which is worth quoting here in full here:

> ... there can be no reconciliation and no genuine peace without justice. Any form of peace and reconciliation that allows a sin of injustice and oppression to continue is a false peace and a counterfeit reconciliation.[27]

---

[27] *The Kairos Document,* London: CIIR and BCC, 1986: 9. The same point is made with equal force in the more recent *1998 European Kairos Document: For a Socially Just and Life Sustaining and Democratic Europe* published by Sarum College Press, Salisbury, in Association with the Churches' Commission on Mission, Inter-church House, 35–41 Lower March, London, SE1 TRL.

This foundational principle has now been the subject of considerable commentary by the theological community.[28] There are two extremes to be avoided in describing the relationship between memory and reconciliation. On the one hand there are those who once the injustices of history have been exposed by the power of memory rush in with calls for forgiveness and reconciliation. As already emphasized there is no such thing as cheap grace: facile calls for reconciliation without addressing the prior demands of justice can be counterproductive. Premature pleas for reconciliation can inhibit the emergence of the truth and all too easily gloss over the hard questions about justice. This tendency to rush towards reconciliation is found sometimes within the official theologies of the different Christian Churches.

At the other extreme there can be such a preoccupation with the demands of justice that the possibility of reconciliation is lost sight of and disappears from the agenda. By focusing solely on justice, especially just equivalencies or retributive justice, there is the risk of allowing the victim to remain an injured party and leaving the perpetrator unchanged. In contrast to these two extremes memory has the capacity to initiate a process, albeit a long and painful process, that can lead to forgiveness and reconciliation. When this happens the meaning of the past and the present can be changed in the service of a new future. As Ricoeur points out 'Forgiveness gives memory a future'.[29] The bridge between memory, reconciliation and the future is the performance of justice and the offer forgiveness.

An important stimulus in crossing this bridge is the necessary awareness that every human being has been created for community, that all human beings belong to each other, and that no one individual can exist alone. However, within the contemporary culture of individualism and a free floating self-centredness it is all the more difficult to cross this bridge from individualism to becoming a being-present-in-community. Without this awareness of the intrinsically social character of human existence forgiveness and reconciliation are all the more difficult to realize.

The injustices of the past must be redressed in the present through the prophetic power of memory-narratives. If, however, the wounds of history are allowed to fester, they can turn into 'a hereditary disease'[30]

---

[28] See in particular the important and nuanced article by Gerry O'Hanlon, 'Justice and Reconciliation', Michael Hurley (ed.), *Reconciliation in Religion and Society,* Ulster: The Queens University of Belfast in association with the University of Ulster, 1994, pp. 48–67.
[29] Paul Ricoeur, 'Memory-Forgetfulness-History', *ZIF: Mitteilungen,* 2/95: 3–12 and 12.
[30] The image of 'a hereditary disease' is taken from Stanley Hauerwas, *A Time to Heal.* 10, who is quoting Wendel Berry in reference to the influence of slavery within US history.

which can further perpetrate recrimination and retribution. Only when the injustices of history have been recognized and named can a movement begin towards the possibility of forgiveness, conversion and ultimately reconciliation. There are no short cuts to reconciliation and it must be recognized that different people will be at different places within the journey towards reconciliation. Indeed it must be acknowledged that the reality of reconciliation is never fully realized in this life and that there will always remain an unfinished or better an eschatological aspect to reconciliation that only God can effect in this life and in eternity as pure gift.

What this means in reality is this. If the victims of injustice never get beyond the demands of strict justice to the possibility of healing, then there is the distinct danger that the cycle of violence will continue, that at worst the victims will become vengeful and possibly create new victims. The cycle of violence in history can only be broken by the gift of reconciliation offered by God in his Son Jesus Christ. Without reference to God's offer of reconciliation in Christ, especially the reconciliation that took place in Christ on the Cross, then it does become difficult to break the cycle of violence and talk about the gift of reconciliation in this life. Such reconciliation, however, is made possible through the memory of the action of God in Christ crucified. What begins with memory, namely the memory of injustice in history, ends by references to the memory of God's action of reconciliation in Christ as gift and offer to all. Something similar should apply to the perpetrators of injustice who can also be transformed by the offer of forgiveness from the victim. If this does not happen then the injustices performed by the perpetrators are likely to continue within history.[31]

The criterion that must be applied in the movement from the memory of injustice to the reality of reconciliation is whether that movement effects not only personal conversion but also whether it brings about social and/or political and structural change. The question must be asked: does reconciliation change the system supporting violence and injustice, or does it leave social structures of injustice intact? Unless this kind of change, individual and social change, takes place in history, it becomes increasingly problematic for Christian faith to talk credibly about reconciliation in this life. In the end it is creative power of memory, both human and divine memory, that can effect these individual and social changes as intrinsic to the gift of reconciliation.

---

[31] The journey from Memory to Reconciliation is uneven, unpredictable and not easily mapped. Nonetheless this movement could be said to include the following steps which should be understood as taking place more in a cyclical movement rather than a straight line: Memory-Narratives→to Historical-narrative→Persistent Memory (memory-repetition)→the Work of Recollection→the Question of Justice→Forgiveness and Conversion (personal and social)→Reconciliation→Hope for a new future.

The shocking death of Oscar Romero in 1980, the extraordinary murder of Bishop Juan Gerardi in 1998, and the disturbing death or disappearance of 200,000 people in Guatemala are deep wounds in the history of Central America in the twentieth century. Each of these realities calls for the transformation of the official historical-narrative, each cries out for the performance of justice, each demands some form of forgiveness and conversion, and ultimately each seeks a process of reconciliation. The work of recollection through the power of memory can help in the journey towards the realisation of these objectives. Hearing the moving memories of those who have lived through these atrocities, is surely an important step forward in healing the painful wounds of history.[32]

---

[32] I am indebted to Paul Couture Terrence Tilley and Peter Junker-Kenny who offered constructive comments on an earlier draft of this chapter.

'He is not here':
Disappearance, Death and Denial

DAVID TOMBS

> ... today [1980] we see new and more refined ways of despoiling the poor being practised by imperialism and its allies within our own countries ... to repress them brutally by instilling fear and sowing death.
>
> Gustavo Gutiérrez[1]

1. The Threat of Disappearance

One of the most distinctive new ways to instil fear and sow death in Latin America in recent decades has been the use of 'disappearances' as a tool of state terror.[2] The military coup in Brazil in 1964 laid the foundation for a new era of civil repression perpetrated by military

---

[1] G. Gutiérrez, 'The Poor and the Christian Communities' in S. Torres and J. Eagleson (eds.), *The Challenge of Basic Christian Communities,* EATWOT International Ecumenical Congress of Theology, São Paulo, Brazil, 20 February–2 March, 1980, Maryknoll, NY, Orbis Books, 1981, pp. 107–23 (109). For a helpful collection on the politics and cultural psychology of state terror in Latin America during recent decades, see J.E. Corradi, *et al.* (eds.), *Fear at the Edge: State Terror and Resistance in Latin America*, Berkeley and Los Angeles, CA, University of California Press, 1992.

[2] Given the denials that invariably accompany disappearances it is fitting that the English grammar checker on my word-processor refuses to accept the term 'being disappeared' and insists that it is a 'verbal confusion'. The Spanish word *desaparecido* 'disappeared' has come to be used as a noun as well as a transitive or intransitive verb referring to a forced disappearance. Patricia Marchak points out: 'one speaks of "the disappeared" and says, "The army disappeared him" as well as "She disappeared" ... though the English language (reflecting a very different experience) is less flexible with that verb', *God's Assassins: State Terrorism in Argentina in the 1970s*, Montreal and London, McGill-Queen's University Press, 1999, p. 16. The term acquired this grammatical versatility in Guatemala in the repression beginning in 1966, almost a decade before the term was exported to Argentina or Chile. For general overviews of disappearances and their role in state terror, see: Amnesty International, *Disappearances: A Workbook*, New York, Amnesty International USA, 1981; Independent Commission on International Humanitarian Issues, *Disappeared: Technique of Terror*, London, Zed Books, 1981.

regimes.[3] Brazil's Institutional Act V in 1968 marked a sharp rise in political arrests and torture.[4] The Brazilian military were eager to promote the ideology of the National Security State in neighbouring countries throughout Latin America's Southern Cone.[5] Further military coups installed hard-line military regimes in Chile (1973–89), Uruguay (1973–85) and Argentina (1976–83).[6] Off-duty soldiers and paramilitaries in Guatemala in the late 1960s pioneered disappearances and secret executions as a form of repressive terror.[7] In the early 1970s, right-wing death squads in Argentina – under names like 'The Hand' and the 'Argentine Anti-Communist Alliance' (or 'Triple A') – started to kidnap their opponents (workers, students, union organizers, Peronists and leftists) and make them vanish without trace.[8] After the

[3] This chapter is primarily concerned with the disappearances that were part of deliberate state-terror campaigns conducted by security forces and related para-militaries. The victims were often entirely innocent, but in the Cold War context of the 1970s and 1980s they were seen by the military as potential subversives. There are, however, other types of disappearance that are part of what has been called the 'everyday violence' of countries like Brazil, El Salvador and Guatemala today. Street children and others perceived as 'socially undesirable' continue to suffer disappearance and deaths at the hands of vigilantes, the police and other right-wing groups. See, for example, M. McCaughan, 'The Police on Permanent Death Duty', *The Guardian*, 15 February 1999, p. 9; N. Scheper-Hughes, *Death Without Weeping: The Violence of Everyday Life in Brazil*, Berkeley, University of California Press, 1992, pp. 216–267.

[4] On torture under the Brazilian military regime (1964–85), see Archdiocese of São Paulo, *Torture in Brazil: A Report by the Archdiocese of São Paulo*, trans. J. Wright; ed. J. Dassin; New York, Vintage Books, 1986 [1985].

[5] On National Security State Doctrines, see J. Comblin, *The Church and the National Security State*, Maryknoll, NY, Orbis Books, 1979.

[6] Other countries already under military rule also showed a marked shift to more hard-line regimes. These included, Bolivia under Hugo Banzer Suarez (1971–1978) and Peru in the period 1975–1980. For an overview of human rights abuses by the regimes with particular attention to the response of the church, see P. Lernoux, *Cry of the People: The Struggle for Human Rights in Latin America – The Catholic Church in Conflict with US Policy*, New York, Penguin Books, rev. edn, 1982 [1980]; J. Klaiber, *The Church, Dictatorships and Democracy in Latin America*, Maryknoll, NY, Orbis Books, 1998.

[7] See Amnesty International, *Disappearances*, pp. 17–30. On political repression in Guatemala after 1966, see E. Galeano, *Guatemala: Occupied Country*, trans. C. Belfrange, New York and London, Monthly Review Press, 1969 and T and M. Melville, *Guatemala: Another Vietnam?* Harmondsworth, Penguin Books, 1971.

[8] Rita Arditti estimates that by 1971 one such disappearance was happening every eighteen days in Argentina, (R. Arditti, *Searching for Life: The Grandmothers of the Plaza de Mayo and the Disappeared Children of Argentina* [Berkeley and London: University of California Press, 1999], p.10). On events leading up to the coup and a brief overview of the social turbulence in Argentina in the early 1970s, see D. Rock, *Argentina 1516–1987: From Spanish Colonization to Alfonsín*, Berkeley, University of California, rev. edn. 1987 [1985], pp. 351–366. It should be noted that any danger to the state from leftist guerrillas – which was the notional excuse for the coup – had already been eliminated by the military's brutal campaign of repression after 'state of siege' declarations by Isabel Perón (1974–76).

military coup of March 1976 the Argentine military refined this practice into an official strategy of state terror targeted selectively against particular victims but also designed to intimidate the population as a whole.[9]

The Brazilian experience and the early years of the Pinochet regime – where the frequent torture of the arrested had prompted protests against the regime – showed the advantages of clandestine disappearances instead of formal arrests.[10] In Argentina's 'Dirty War', clandestine disappearances and official denials were a very effective way to eradicate potential opposition whilst disguising the military's responsibility for torture and executions.[11] Disappearances had the added benefit of creating uncertainty and anxiety in the rest of society that encouraged a complicit silence and culture of denial and passivity

---

[9] On the use of disappearances in the Argentine 'Dirty War', see: National Commission on Disappeared People, *Nunca Más: A Report by Argentina's National Commission on Disappeared People*, trans. Writers and Scholars International; Boston and London, Faber & Faber, 1986 [1984], pp. 9–20. The report documents nearly 9000 disappearances and suggests that the total number may have been significantly more (p. 10). See also, J. Simpson and J. Bennett, *The Disappeared and the Mothers of the Plaza*, New York, St Martin's Press, 1985; I. Guest, *Behind the Disappearances: Argentina's Dirty War Against Human Rights and the United Nations*, Philadelphia, University of Pennsylvania Press, 1990.

[10] After the success of the 1973 coup in Chile, General Pinochet initially did little to hide the arrests, torture and mass disappearances of political opponents. In 1976, in the face of international criticism of the regime he switched to more selective – and clandestine – repression. The newly established DINA carried out disappearances and torture interrogations similar to their Argentine colleagues. The Chilean National Commission on Truth and Reconciliation – sometimes known after its chairman as the 'Rettig Report' – documented nearly 1000 disappearances and over 1000 deaths caused by security forces during Pinochet's regime (1973–1990), see *Report of the Chilean National Commission on Truth and Reconciliation*, trans. P. Berryman, 2 vols; Notre Dame, IN: Centre for Civil and Human Rights, Notre Dame Law School, 1993 [1991], pp. 889–90. These deaths and disappearances were at the heart of the case that the Spanish magistrate Baltasar Garzón tried to bring against Pinochet, which led to his sixteen-month arrest in London on 16 October 1998 pending a decision over extradition. Pinochet was finally released on medical grounds on 2 March 2000 and immediately flew back to Chile where he has faced further legal proceedings on the fate of prisoners disappeared in the early weeks of the regime whose fate has never been determined. Whatever the outcome of current law proceedings in Chile, the ruling by the British Law Lords that he was internationally liable for prosecution has been described as one of the most important new developments in International Human Rights Law since the Nuremberg trials. For a brief overview of Pinochet's regime and Garzón's attempt to extradite him to Spain, see H. O'Shaugnessy, *Pinochet: The Politics of Torture*, London, Latin America Bureau, 2000.

[11] The Argentine military consciously modelled their approach on Hitler's 'Night and Fog' decree which ordered the death penalties for prisoners opposed to the Nazi regime to be carried out without trial and without trace, see F. Graziano, *Divine Violence: Spectacle, Psychosexuality, and Radical Christianity in the Argentine 'Dirty War'*, Boulder, CO and Oxford, Westview Press, 1992, pp. 15–16.

in society as a whole. The Argentine example was readily imitated by others and a system of close co-operation known as the Condor plan soon developed between Argentina and neighbouring military regimes.[12] After the successful Sandinista revolution in Nicaragua in 1979, the Salvadoran and Guatemalan militaries increased their own campaigns of repression and the Argentinean military helped them to adapt techniques pioneered in the Dirty War.[13] Disappearances became commonplace as the two countries emerged as centres of some of the worst abuses on the continent.[14] During the years of repression that followed it is estimated that 7,000 or more disappeared in El Salvador and up to 50,000 in Guatemala.[15]

[12] Under the Condor plan, security forces co-operated together to track down political exiles and refugees. The Argentinean, Brazilian, Bolivian, Chilean and Uruguayan militaries developed co-operative arrangements known as the Condor plan to assist each other in arrests and disappearances throughout the region. This international dimension to disappearances provided the Spanish magistrate Baltasar Garzón with the initial impetus to investigate disappearances under the Condor plan in terms of international law, first with reference to Argentina and then including Chile.

[13] See A.C. Armony, *Argentina, the United States and the Anti-Communist Crusade in Central America 1977–1984*, Athens, OH, Ohio University Press, 1997, pp. 83–93. On US involvement, see: M. McClintock, *The American Connection: State Terror and Popular Resistance in El Salvador*, London, Zed Books, 1985; M. McClintock, *The American Connection: State Terror and Popular Resistance in Guatemala*, London, Zed Books, 1985.

[14] For authoritative accounts of these human rights abuses see especially, United Nations Truth Commission, *From Madness to Hope: The 12-Year War in El Salvador*, New York, United Nations, 1993; Recovery of Historical Memory Project [REMHI], *Guatemala: Never Again!* (The Official Report of the Human Rights Office, Archdiocese of Guatemala [ODHAG]); trans. G. Tovar Siebentritt, Maryknoll, NY, Orbis Books, London, Catholic Institute for International Relations and Latin America Bureau, 1999 [1998]; United Nations Commission for Historical Memory, *Memory of Silence*, Guatemala, United Nations, 1999.

[15] The nature of the oppression and the difficulty in keeping clear records make these numbers tentative best estimates. For additional information on the role of death squads and disappearances in the conflict in El Salvador, see: Americas Watch and American Civil Liberties Union, *Report on Human Rights in El Salvador*, New York, Vintage Press, 1982; Lawyer's Committee for Human Rights, *El Salvador: Human Rights Dismissed: A Report on Sixteen Unresolved Cases*, New York, Lawyers' Committee for Human Rights and Americas Watch, 1986; Amnesty International Report, *El Salvador Death Squads: A Government Strategy*, London, Amnesty International, 1988; Americas Watch, *Carnage Again: Preliminary Report on Violations of the Laws of War by Both Sides in the November 1989 Offensive in El Salvador*, Washington, DC, Americas Watch, 1989; Ecumenical Programme on Central America and the Caribbean, *Condoning the Killing: Ten Years of Massacres in El Salvador*, Washington DC, Ecumenical Programme on Central America and the Caribbean, 1990; Americas Watch, *El Salvador's Decade of Terror: Human Rights Since the Assassination of Romero*, New Haven and London, Yale University Press, 1991. On massacres and disappearances in Guatemala, see especially: Americas Watch, *Human Rights in Guatemala: No Neutrals Allowed*, New York and Washington DC, Americas Watch Committee, 1982; Amnesty

Plain-clothes soldiers and secret police usually dragged their victims away from family and friends in the middle of the night. After kidnap, the victims were taken to secret interrogation and torture centres.[16] Sometimes they would be released so that their treatment would serve as a warning to others. Others were killed and their bodies dumped by the roadside. Many victims of abduction were simply 'disappeared' without trace.[17] In Guatemala and El Salvador, the disappeared were usually buried in secret in unmarked mass graves.[18] Official silence and denials greeted relatives who tried to find out what had happened to them. As anxious enquiries were made with the different authorities, the official answer was invariably the same: 'He/She is not here' ('*No esta aquí*').

The Archdiocese of Guatemala's Recovery of Historical Memory Project (REMHI) offers a typical example of what it describes as 'a systematic practice' of 'numerous disappearances'.[19] The victim

---

International, *Guatemala: A Government Programme of Political Murder*, London, Amnesty International, 1982; R. Falla, *Massacres in the Jungle* Boulder and Oxford, Westview Press, 1995; EPICA and Committee on Human Rights in Latin America, *Unearthing the Truth: Exhuming a Decade of Terror in Guatemala*, Washington, DC, EPICA, 1996; on Guatemalan death squads, see B.D. Paul and W.J. Demarest, 'The Operation of a Death Squad in San Pedro la Laguna' in R.M. Carmack (ed.), *Harvest of Violence: The Maya Indians and the Guatemala Crisis*, Norman OK and London, University of Oklahoma Press, 1988, pp. 119–154.

[16] The UN Truth Commission report on El Salvador documents three representative cases to show how disappearances were conducted and then covered up in El Salvador, *From Madness to Hope*, pp. 101–113. On abduction procedures adopted by Guatemalan Intelligence operatives (known as G2) based on interviews with military personnel, see J. Schirmer, *The Guatemalan Military Projects: A Violence Called Democracy*, Philadelphia: University of Pennsylvania Press, 1998, p. 155.

[17] The REMHI report states that only fourteen percent of those abducted reappeared alive, about thirty-three percent reappeared dead and most did not reappear at all (*Guatemala: Never Again!*, p. 156). In exceptional cases – most usually involving capture of guerrilla combatants – the military publicly faked deaths and secretly kept the victims alive. They hoped to pressure these captives into becoming informants due to their fear of what might happen to family members. In these unusual circumstances, the disappeared were declared dead even though they were still alive. For a personal account of the search for one such 'disappeared', see J. Harbury, *Searching for Everardo*, London, Macmillan, 1997.

[18] In recent years some bodies have been unearthed and recovered but it is impossible to trace or exhume all the victims. In Argentina, it was common for victims to be drugged, flown in planes far out to sea and then thrown alive to disappear into the waters below.

[19] REMHI, *Guatemala: Never Again!*, pp. 19–22 (19). Testimonies to REMHI confirmed nearly 4000 disappearances, which account for one out of every five cases of human rights abuse reported to REMHI (*Guatemala: Never Again!*, pp. 159–161 and 294). Some estimates suggest the figure for disappearances in Guatemala is as high as 50,000-plus, see F.M. Afflitto, 'The Homogenizing Effects of State-Sponsored Terrorism: The Case of Guatemala' in J.A. Sluka (ed.), *Death Squad: The Anthropology of State Terror*, Philadelphia, University of Pennsylvania Press, 2000, pp. 114–26 (122).

Marco Antonio Molina Theissen was fourteen-years-old.

> They put a sack over his head, threw him into the back of the pickup truck, and took him away, ignoring his mother's pleas. We never found out anything about what happened to him.[20]

The REMHI report also describes the impact of disappearances on the family left behind:

> The pain was so strong that I think we didn't even know what we were doing; the only thing was to rescue our loved one. Our only thought was for the other person, whom we believed was being tortured. We had to do everything possible to rescue him.[21]

Some of the most poignant accounts of disappearances and their impact on those left behind are offered in Latin American fiction and poetry. For example, in her first novel *Of Love and Shadows*, Isabel Allende (Chile) suggests the type of advice that those with more experience give to new enquirers:

> 'Don't look any longer. I'm sure someone's hand slipped, and they were rougher on her than they intended.'
> 'Go to the Ministry of Defence, there are new lists there.'
> 'Come back next week at this same time.'
> 'The guard changes at five – ask for Antonio, he's a nice man and can give you information.'
> 'It's best to begin at the Morgue. That way you don't waste time.'[22]

Likewise, the poem 'Red Tape' by Ariel Dorfman – born in Argentina and later a political refugee from Pinochet's Chile – records the bureaucratic marathon of petitions, office visits and knocking on doors that needs to be undertaken in the quest for a disappeared son.[23]

Disappearances created an on-going trauma of disruption amongst

---

[20] REMHI, *Guatemala: Never Again!*, p. 20.
[21] Interview 015 cited in REMHI, *Guatemala: Never Again!*, p. 83. The REMHI report continues: 'The search became the only means of standing up to the army and defying the terror behind the disappearances' (*Guatemala: Never Again!*, p. 83).
[22] I. Allende, *Of Love and Shadows*, trans. M. Sayers Peden, London, Jonathan Cape, 1987.
[23] A. Dorfman, 'Red Tape' in *idem*, *Widows and Last Waltz in Santiago*, trans. E. Grossman and A. Dorfman, London, Nick Hern, 2nd edn, 1991 (ET *Last Waltz in Santiago*, 1988) p. 183. On Dorfman's eventful political life, see A. Dorfman, *Heading South, Looking North: A Bilingual Journey*, London, Hodder and Stoughton, 1998.

friends and relatives. Uncertain whether the disappeared are dead or alive the surviving relatives are left in an indefinite limbo, a slow and destructive mental torture.[24] This can be much more socially disruptive than a simple killing.[25] Family members are tormented by thoughts of how the victim may be suffering. In the REMHI report a family member describes the difficulty in holding a wake and bringing the grieving process to a close: 'For three days I cried, crying that I wanted to see him.... Just a little bit of earth to be able to say there he is.... There isn't any place. I feel so much pain.... Where can we go?'[26]

In the novel *One Day of Life*, the Salvadoran writer Manlio Argueta refers to the paralysis that could be created by this anguish of uncertainty. The novel tells the story of a tragic day in the life of the Salvadoran *campesina* woman 'Lupe' (Guadalupe Fuentes). Flashbacks recall the murder of her son Justino and the disappearance of her son-in-law Helios. Lupe starkly describes the dislocation caused by Helios' disappearance:

> They won't give the poor man up, they won't even say a word about him; at least we could see Justino's body, we know he is dead. It's worse, the anguish for a disappeared person; at least consolation comes with death. With a disappeared person they kill two birds with one stone: all of the living who revolve around the disappeared are chained to anguish. Anguish is a slow form of death.[27]

In its denial of life disappearance could make the past vanish along with the present. Victims not only ceased to be, it was as if they had never

---

[24] However, due to a further political twist, it may be the open-ended nature of disappearances that provides the strongest basis for the prosecution of Pinochet in Chile. On 23 May 2000 a twenty-two member Chilean court voted (by majority of thirteen versus nine) that Pinochet should be stripped of his Senatorial immunity so that he could be prosecuted on approximately 1000 disappearances where no body has been found. These cases were still open and therefore not covered by the amnesty law of April 1978 that Pinochet had passed to pardon any crimes committed during the state of siege (11 September 1973–10 March 1978).

[25] The REMHI commission reports (*Guatemala: Never Again!*, p. 19): 'Living with this type of loss is much more difficult, even in cases where it is clear that the victim was ultimately killed. Disappearances create a sense of ambiguity and heightened distress and anxiety over what actually happened and the whereabouts of the body.' A family member cited by the Rettig Report says: 'If they had killed him outright it wouldn't be so hard. But since you know they tortured him and don't know what they did to him, your imagination torments you more that the death itself' (Chilean National Commission on Truth and Reconciliation, *Report of the Chilean National Commission on Truth and Reconciliation*, II, p. 782).

[26] Case 8673, Sibinal, San Marcos, 1982, cited in REMHI, *Guatemala: Never Again!*, p. 20.

[27] M. Argueta, *One Day of Life*, trans. W. Brow, London, Chatto and Windus, 1984 [1980], p. 178.

been. In the eyes of officialdom it was as if the disappeared person had never even really existed. For example, in Marta Traba's novel *Mothers and Shadows* (set in Montevideo and Buenos Aires) the character Irene describes how her friend Elena searched for her daughter Victoria who had been disappeared.

> It dawned on me that they'd dealt her [Elena] the killing blow ... not when they took her [Victoria] away but later on, when no one, anywhere she went, in any office, would admit to having seen her or known her or filed her name or imprisoned her or interrogated her; no one had ever set eyes on her, she never went down any corridor, they never kept her standing for hours on end in front of anyone, they never moved her from place to place, they never bundled her into any car without a number plate, they never threw her into any cell, they never entered her name on any list. Never heard of the girl. Some of them, Elena said, flatly refused to look at the photograph. Sinister figures would shake their heads, scratch them, make clucking noises or, worst of all, smile blankly. She probably never existed. But what about her identity card, her passport, the marriage certificate of such eminent parents, the photographs? None of that means a thing, especially nowadays.[28]

Relatives who refused to give up hope found it hard to adjust to their new situation in which their loved ones were neither alive nor dead. Following a similar pattern in Chile, Argentina, El Salvador and Guatemala, relatives of the disappeared – very often women – went from prison to morgue to body-dumps to police stations asking for their husbands or children.[29] Invariably they were greeted with the same stonewalling reply: '*No está aquí*'. The authorities denied any responsibility for the disappeared and often tried to blame and shame the relatives instead. Security forces would tell a woman who was seeking her husband that he must have run away with another woman or joined a subversive group.

The REMHI report describes the heartbreak this causes:

---

[28] M. Traba, *Mothers and Shadows* trans. J. Labanyi, New York and London, Reader's International, 1986 [1981], p. 74.

[29] On these women's movements in El Salvador and Guatemala, see J. Schirmer, 'The Seeking of Truth and the Gendering of Consciousness: The Comadres of El Salvador and the Conavigua Widows of Guatemala' in *'Viva': Women and Popular Protest in Latin America*, London, Routledge, 1993, pp. 30–64. Schirmer (p. 56) reports that Oscar Romero compared the Comadres with Mary: 'Ah, women, you are the Marys of today. Mary spent a long time searching for her son, and you mothers are also walking along the same path that Mary walked. All of you are suffering the same loss, the same pain.'

> The search for relatives who have been disappeared has been one of the most anguishing struggles arising from political repression, and the one that has been spearheaded by women. Perpetual uncertainty about what happened, where they are, if they are alive or dead, and if they can be found, are some of the innumerable questions asked by those who day after day have travelled every road, have looked everywhere, in the hope of discovering their loved ones.[30]

In some cases, relatives had to decide for themselves that the disappeared were dead and never to be seen again. Assuming this responsibility could add a new layer of heartbreak to the families caught in an impossible situation in which they had to struggle on in uncertainty or finally decide to designate a relative as dead.[31]

2. The Garden of Gethsemane

The fear of disappearance that permeated Latin American societies during the years of repression is also a surprisingly striking motif in the story of Jesus' passion. In the Gospel stories of Matthew, Mark and Luke the threat of disappearance looms particularly large at the arrest in Gethsemane and tomb-side in the Garden and the modern politics of memory and disappearance shed light on the traumatic events told in the Easter story. The threat of dis*appearance* in the 'arrest' of Jesus is a dramatic backdrop to the Easter 'release' of Jesus seen in his post-resurrection *appearance*. In recent years the words 'He is not here' have been used to deny truth and mask death. Re-reading the Easter story in the light of Latin American disappearances suggests that what Peter feared on the night of Jesus' arrest – and the women feared when they discovered the empty tomb on the Sunday morning – was officially sanctioned disappearance and denial.[32] In this context it is not surprising the women heard the tomb-side proclamation 'He is not here' (Mark 16.6; Matt. 28.6; Luke 24.5) with fear and alarm.

The Gospels do not use the term 'disappearance' to describe Jesus'

---

[30] REMHI, *Guatemala: Never Again!*, p. 83.
[31] For a detailed anthropological study of Guatemalan widows, see J. Zur, *Violent Memories: Quiché War Widows in Northwest Highland Guatemala*, Unpublished PhD thesis, University of London, 1993. Zur notes, that by the mid 1980s, it was estimated that the violence in Guatemala had created over 130,000 widows and 40,000 widowers (p. 18).
[32] John – who reports that Jesus himself appeared to Mary Magdalene outside the tomb, Jn 20. 11–18 – is the only Gospel not to include the proclamation 'He is not here' and John's account of the arrest and trial has a far less menacing tone when compared with the synoptics.

detention but the events they describe have parallels with practices of detention and disappearance in Latin America. Security forces apprehended Jesus of Nazareth on the eve of the Passover festival. Under the cover of night, an informer identified him and armed men arrested him and hustled him away. The reaction of Jesus' followers when they witnessed the abduction of their leader is readily understandable. In view of Latin American disappearances, it is hardly surprising that at first they were afraid and ran away when confronted by the sudden arrival of a snatch-squad.[33] This style of arrest was intended to confuse and terrorize. The strong show of force was to scare the followers as well as to subdue the target. It would be easy to blame the disciples for not showing more bravery or loyalty as they panicked and ran into the night but they should not be judged too harshly. The clandestine seizure of Jesus showed that none of the disciples were safe. It is not surprising that almost all of them turned and ran. The surprise is not that so many of them ran but that at least one of them did not. Simon – known by the nickname 'the Rock' (Peter) – dared to follow the arrest party at a distance (Mark 14.54; Matt. 26.58; Luke 22.54–55).[34] Despite the fears Peter may have had, he followed Jesus to the High Priest's house and waited in the courtyard to observe what was happening.

It is easy to miss the significance of this part of the narrative. The way the Gospel accounts are written encourages the reader to see Peter in the same way as the other disciples by focussing on Peter's denial of Jesus. The Gospels want to show that the disciples abandoned Jesus when they ran away and they also show that Peter abandoned Jesus when he denied him in the High Priest's courtyard. Thus, at this climax to his life, Jesus is presented as alone and betrayed by even his closest followers. The contrast between the behaviour of Jesus and his disciples enhances Jesus' moral status and dramatises the tension of the passion stories. This is quite probably how it looked, in retrospect, to the Gospel writers. However, the stories of disappearances from Latin America may help us to recognize deeper political and emotional undercurrents in what was happening.

The records of disappearances in Latin America both illuminate the risk that Peter took in following Jesus and help to explain why he did so. In Latin America, failure to locate the victim of a disappearance

---

[33] Lk. 22.52 suggests a crowd that included the Temple police, the chief priests and elders; Jn. 18.3 mentions a detachment of Roman soldiers alongside Temple police from the chief priests and Pharisees; Mk. 14.43 and Mt. 26.47 simply refer to a crowd from the chief priests and elders.

[34] Jn. 18.12–17 suggests that both Peter and 'another disciple' followed Jesus and that the other disciple was an acquaintance of the High Priest. In this version, the other disciple accompanied Jesus into the High Priest's courtyard whilst Simon Peter waited outside. The other disciple then returned and led Peter inside as well.

increased the chances of torture and death for the victim and ensured long-standing uncertainty for survivors. By contrast, early location of where a prisoner was held might improve their chances of being acknowledged as alive and perhaps treated more humanely. Most importantly, it removed the paralysing uncertainty that often went with not knowing the whereabouts of a loved one.

If Peter feared that Jesus might never be seen again, it was a remarkable act of personal courage for him to follow him and keep quiet vigil amongst the guards who had arrested Jesus. Because Peter stayed in the courtyard until the cock crowed, he could at least try to bear witness to the events (Mark 14.72; Matt. 26.74; Luke 22.60; John 18.27).[35] This can be the most effective deterrence to disappearance.[36] At the very least, Peter's presence ensured that if Jesus did not reappear for a trial there was a witness to the truth who could preserve the memory of his last hours. If Jesus had been transferred to Roman custody during the night, Peter would have been able to observe this.[37] If the Romans later denied having anything to do with him, Peter would have known the last place that Jesus had been seen alive was in their hands. This would have been vital information if they were greeted with the reply 'He is not here' from Pilate and his men. Despite the horrors of what was to follow, the importance of Peter's vigil during the night of Jesus' arrest deserves to be remembered and admired. If we only remember Peter's verbal denials of Jesus under pressure from suspicious bystanders we can miss the courage of his non-verbal actions. His physical presence was a courageous act of solidarity that he shares with many relatives of the disappeared.

If Peter's presence in the courtyard was an act of extraordinary bravery, it does not fit the profile of someone who a few hours later

---

[35] Only Mark says that this was the *second* time that a cock crowed (Mk. 14.72). It is noteworthy that John mentions the cockcrow even though he does not mention Jesus' prophesy of denial related to it or that Peter wept because of it.

[36] In Guatemala and El Salvador the physical presence of witnesses was adopted by the organization Peace Brigades for the unarmed accompaniment of people and communities at risk. On the work of Peace Brigades in support of Human Rights in Guatemala, El Salvador and elsewhere, see L. Mahony and L. Enrique Eguren, *Unarmed Bodyguards: International Accompaniment for the Protection of Human Rights*, West Hartford, CT, Kumarian Press, 1997.

[37] Even if the High Priest's house had some official status as a judicial venue this was no guarantee that prisoners who were taken from it might not disappear without trace. The Salvadoran Truth Commission documents the case of two students protesters – José Humberto Mejía and Francisco Arnulfo Ventura – who were disappeared from the US Embassy car park on 22 January 1980. The National Guardsmen who had arrested them at the Embassy entrance handed them over to unidentified men in plain clothes who took them away in the boot of the car and they were never seen again. In the absence of a political will to denounce disappearances the public status of a location is not in itself enough to prevent abuses from happening.

simply denied any knowledge of Jesus to save his own skin. Perhaps the oppressive atmosphere became too much for him and Peter's nerve finally failed him. Perhaps he heard or saw things that brought home the risk he was running. Alternatively, perhaps commentators have moved too quickly to assume that he would so readily betray Jesus out of cowardice. Some of the literature on disappearances in Latin America might suggest that Peter's denial of Jesus – assuming that it is historical – might be viewed in a very different way.

For example, Manlio Argueta's *One Day of Life* climaxes when National Guard soldiers confront Lupe with the body of a severely injured man that she recognizes as her husband José. Argueta describes how Lupe's body turns to ice when she recognizes José but she remembers her husband's warning 'If at any time you detect danger to yourself or to our family, don't hesitate about denying me.... Leave it to me to save myself, if you see that there's no other way'.[38] To protect herself, her children and her granddaughter Lupé forces herself to deny knowing her own husband. Argueta poignantly captures the conflict between her calm spoken words and her quavering inner emotions. Rather than an act of cowardice, her denial showed a remarkable strength. She denies her own emotion, to be faithful to her husband.[39]

Perhaps Peter felt he was in a similar situation. There was little he could do to help Jesus other than to preserve the truth and memory of his arrest. When asked whether he knew Jesus he first tried to evade the questions put to him.[40] When pressed further he felt forced to lie and deny that he knew Jesus. If Jesus had told him that this would happen (Mark 14.72; Matt. 26.75; Luke 22.61) then perhaps he now understood why. It may indeed have been a heart-breaking moment that quickly reduced him to private tears, but nonetheless it might have been

---

[38] Argueta, *One Day of Life*, p. 192.
[39] In Argueta's other famous novel on El Salvador *Cuzcatlan* the character Beatriz also describes how personal feelings must sometimes be hidden: 'The key is to learn to hide your emotions. That's very characteristic of this war. We're not even allowed to cry'. M. Argueta, *Cuzcatlán*, trans. C. Hansen, London, Chatto and Windus, 1987 [1986], p. 9.
[40] Mark and Matthew suggest a clear progression in the three denials from claiming not to understand the question (Mk 14.67–68; Mt. 26.69–70), to a general denial (Mk 14.69–70a; Mt. 26.71–72) and finally a more emphatic denial and curses (Mk 14.70b–71; Mt. 26.73–74). Luke 22.56–60 suggests a slightly different order by putting the general denial first (vv. 56–57), then an emphatic denial (v. 58) and then the claim not to understand at the end (vv. 59–60). In John 18.17–27, Peter's first denial (vv. 17–18) is separated from the second (v. 25) and third (vv. 26–27) by Annas questioning Jesus (vv. 19–24). There is less sense of a building climax and Peter simply replies 'I am not' to the first two suggestions that he is a disciple (vv. 17 and 25) and denies it again a third time (v. 27).

an act of discipleship rather than betrayal.[41] Peter's denials may have allowed him to continue as a crucial witness to where Jesus was being held. Peter has often been criticized because he chose to 'disappear' his discipleship and deny his real identity, but his actions meant that at least somebody would have known if Jesus had been disappeared on the Thursday night/Friday morning of his arrest.

3. The Empty Tomb

As it turned out, Jesus did not disappear in the night. He re-emerged on Friday morning and was handed over to the Romans (Mark 15.1; Matt. 27.1-2; Luke 23.1).[42] It was the Romans who then condemned him to death and crucified him.[43] After crucifixion, the Gospels describe how Jesus was taken down from the cross and was buried hurriedly inside a rock tomb (Mark 15.46; Matt. 27.59-61; Luke 23.53-56; John 19.38-42). As soon as the sun rose on Sunday morning some of the women followers who had witnessed the burial hurried to the tomb.[44] However, when they arrived they found an open tomb and

---

[41] There has been considerable debate amongst New Testament scholars about whether Jesus anticipated his arrest and death. If he did so at all, there are further questions about the point in his life when he first foresaw it, what he expected to happen and what he told the disciples. Although some expectation of his violent death is historically quite plausible, Jesus' clear warnings to the disciples and his prediction of Peter's denial cannot be assumed as historical 'givens' in reconstructing the events behind the Easter story. The point at issue here, however, is that even if Jesus did predict his own death and Peter's denial, no reason is given for Peter's denial and it is was not necessarily an act of cowardice or betrayal. For an excellent discussion and bibliography on how the Gospels present Peter's presence in the courtyard – including an assessment of the historicity of the denials – see R. E. Brown, *The Death of the Messiah: From Gethsemane to the Grave*, Anchor Bible Reference Library, 2 vols, New York, Bantam Doubleday Dell, 1994, pp. 587-626.

[42] John suggests that before this Jesus was sent to Caiaphas' house for further questioning (18.24) and then on to Pilate in the morning (18.28).

[43] I have suggested elsewhere that tales of terror and torture from Latin America can illuminate the political framework of the crucifixion in terms of state terror and the dehumanizing sexual abuse commonly used in torture, see D. Tombs, 'Crucifixion, State Terror and Sexual Abuse', *Union Seminary Quarterly Review*, 53 (Autumn 1999) 89-108. The REMHI report provides further evidence for the central thesis on a number of points. See especially the horrifying accounts of contemporary crucifixions as torture of indigenous women: for example, 'Before murdering her, they nailed her to the cross they had made. They stuck huge nails into her hands and chest... (Case 1319, Parraxtut, Sacapulas, Quiché, *Guatemala: Never Again!* p. 79). For further analysis of the REMHI's documentation on sexual violence see, D.Tombs, 'Honour, Shame and Conquest: Male Identity, Sexual Violence and the Body Politic' paper presented to *Religion in Latin America and the Caribbean Group*, American Academy of Religion Annual Meeting, Nashville, 19 November 2000.

[44] The Gospels vary slightly at this point. Mark says that Mary Magdalene and Mary the

no sign of the corpse. The women's reaction of immediate alarm is not surprising. It would have seemed a particularly bitter final twist to events. Jesus had been disappeared after all.

An awareness of the powerful symbolism that can surround corpses helps to explain why the women would naturally jump to such a conclusion. Corpses can be as subversive as living human beings, sometimes even more so. Removing Jesus' body would have allowed the authorities to say 'He is not here' to those who might look for the tomb in order to pay reverence to him.

The power of the corpse to become a political focus has been frequently demonstrated in modern politics. In Moscow, Lenin's tomb became the pre-eminent shrine of the revolution. In Chile, Salvador Allende – the democratically elected Socialist President that Pinochet overthrew in the 1973 coup – refused to leave La Moneda (the Chilean equivalent of the White House) or surrender to the coup leaders. He eventually died along with his bodyguards in the attack on La Moneda. To prevent the funeral and grave from becoming a focal point of resistance, General Pinochet refused to allow him to be buried in Chile. His remains were eventually given a state funeral on 4 September 1990, six months after the transition to President Patricio Aylwin's civilian government. Likewise, the Bolivian army was so determined to prevent anyone from laying claim to the body of Ernesto 'Che' Guevara that he was photographed to prove he was dead and then immediately buried in a communal grave at an undisclosed spot.[45] The authorities feared that if his whereabouts were

---

mother of Joses (previously identified as also the mother of James the younger in Mk 15.40) witnessed where the body was laid (Mk. 15.47). According to Mark they waited until the Sabbath was over before they and Salome bought spices and then went to the tomb early Sunday morning (Mk. 16.1-2). Luke is less specific on names and simply says that the women who had followed Jesus from Galilee witnessed the burial, then prepared spices and ointments immediately afterwards, before resting on the Sabbath and visiting the tomb on Sunday morning (Lk. 23.55–24.1). Shortly after this it is implied that the women included Mary Magdalene, Joanna and Mary the mother of James, but these names may be a later interpolation (Lk. 24.10). Matthew says that Mary Magdalene and 'the other Mary' witnessed where Jesus was buried (Mt. 27.61) and went to visit him on the Sunday morning (28.1). However, there is no reference to preparing or taking spices or ointments and Matthew does not give a specific reason for the visit other than to see the tomb. Matthew's account is also the only one that mentions a guard of soldiers at the tomb (27.66). John (20.1-4) offers some significant variations. He does not mention any women witnessing the burial and reports that Mary Magdalene came to the tomb whilst it was still dark on the Sunday morning (v. 1). When she saw the stone had been rolled away she ran back to tell Peter and another disciple (vv. 2–4).

[45] The photo was by Freddy Alborta Trigo on 9 October 1967, shortly after Guevara's execution at Vallegrande, Bolivia, where he had been tracked down and ambushed by the Bolivian army whilst trying to precipitate a popular uprising. The photograph shows him on a rough stretcher laid out across a concrete washbasin with his head

known his body would be a subversive force and his corpse was not returned to Cuba for a state burial until July 1997. Even more elaborately, Eva Peron's death in 1952 sparked a particularly bizarre chain of events during which her body was stolen and then secretly dispatched to Italy. Her remains were finally returned to her husband – former President Juan Peron – in exile in Spain in 1971. Peron drew heavily on Evita's legacy in his successful Presidential bid of 1973. When he died soon afterwards his third wife Isabelita – who succeeded him in the Presidency – in a bid to win popular favour finally brought Eva's body back to Argentina in November 1974 and installed it in the crypt of the presidential palace next to her husband. When the anti-Peronist military junta took power in 1976 they insisted on Eva's removal to her family cemetery.[46]

The novel *Widows* by Ariel Dorfman tells the story of a community in which almost all the local women have become widows to disappearances. The story is set during the military dictatorship in Greece but is clearly intended to apply to Latin America as well. It focuses on the struggle of one woman to claim the bodies of her father, husband and son and give them an honourable burial. When an unrecognizable body is washed up on the river-bank, she claims it and demands permission to bury it. When the military rejects her claim she is joined by the other widows in the village who each claim that the body is one of their family and should be returned for burial. As the confrontation unfolds, it is clear that the symbolic after-life of a corpse can be a potent force for popular organization. In addition, *Widows* suggests how an improper burial might also have served to discredit a victim in the eyes of respectable society. In a culture marked by honour and shame values, the treatment of the dead was as important as the treatment of the living. Disappearing the body and preventing burial inflicted new humiliation on the victim and the victim's family.

On this basis, the political authorities might well have wished to disappear Jesus' body to avoid such difficulties. It is at this point of

---

raised and his eyes open. The Bolivian army did not count on the fact that the hastily taken photograph would itself become the focus for remembering Guevara. Ironically, washing Guevara's limbs and combing his hair for the photograph gave the barefoot and shirt-less Guevara a numinous and almost Christ-like appearance. Inevitably, this gave the photo a significance and symbolic power for commemorations of Guevara, which was completely contrary to its original purpose.

[46] A recent novel takes these bizarre events as its inspiration to tell how the body was hidden, hijacked, replicated, smuggled abroad, buried, resurrected and eventually repatriated, see T. Eloy Martínez, *Santa Evita*, trans. H. Lane, London, Anchor, 1997 [1996]. On the significance of Evita's body and burial, see also D. Taylor, *Disappearing Acts: Spectacles of Gender and Nationalism in Argentina's 'Dirty War'*, Durham and London, Duke University Press, 1997, pp. 48–51.

Jesus', story that there is a dramatic reversal of the expected. It was not the authorities that said 'He is not here'. Instead it was the angelic figure(s) who addressed them this way (Mark 16.6; Matt. 28.6; Luke 24.5).[47] For the women this would have been an extraordinary inversion of the expected. 'He is not here' was not the lie of the tight-lipped authorities they feared. It was not the expected cloak for suffering, death and disappearance. Instead it was God's announcement that death itself had been defeated. In the mystery of resurrection, the disappearance of the body was a disappearance to be welcomed as a sign of new life and a pointer to Jesus' subsequent reappearance.[48]

4. Conclusion

Testimonies of the repression in El Salvador and Guatemala can illuminate the drama of the Gospel's words 'He is not here' at the empty tomb. The dramatic announcement 'He is not here' confronts head on the menace of disappearance, death and denial that looms over the passion narrative from the arrest at Gethsemane, through the vigil in the courtyard, to the arrival at the tomb. Against this sinister backdrop the empty tomb proclaims a message of hope and new life for the victims. The narrative's painful progress from freedom to death and despair is finally reversed and shown to be a movement from death to freedom and from despair to hope.

In 1980 Gustavo Gutiérrez, the Peruvian priest and renowned liberation theologian cited at the start of this chapter, referred to the new ways of repression being used to instil fear and sow death in Latin America.[49] Since then it is estimated that a further 200,000–300,000 people have 'disappeared' worldwide.[50] At the same time that he denounced the horror, Gutiérrez also indicated that these deaths could be as subversive a protest against injustice as the death of Christ:

---

[47] Mark refers to a young man in a white robe (Mk. 16.5), Matthew refers to an angel (Mt. 28.2) and Luke speaks of two men in dazzling clothes (Lk. 24.4).

[48] For more on resurrection in the light of the Salvadoran experience, see D. Tombs, 'Oscar Romero and Resurrection Hope' in S.E. Porter, M.A. Hayes and D. Tombs (eds.), *Resurrection*, Sheffield, Sheffield Academic Press, 1999, pp. 218-248. See also, J. Schirmer, 'Those Who Die for Life Cannot be Called Dead: Women and Human Rights Protest in Latin America', *Harvard Human Rights Yearbook* 1 (Spring 1988), pp. 41-76.

[49] In the 1980s, disappearances came to the fore in Peru's own 'dirty war' against Sendero Luminoso, see: Amnesty International, *Peru: Violations of Human Rights in the Emergency Zones*, New York, Amnesty International, 1988; Americas Watch, *Peru Under Fire: Human Rights Since the Return to Democracy*, New Haven, Yale University Press, 1992.

> ... so many of our companions are being subjected to prison, exile, torture, and death... These brothers and sisters, these martyrs, bear witness to the fact that the poor die before their time, victims of hunger and bullets. That is why their very corpses are subversive, why so often on this continent the repressive authorities do not hand them over and lie about the exact circumstances of their death. Those exercising domination fail to realize that it was the experience and crisis of the 'empty tomb' that enabled the friends of Jesus long ago, as it does his followers today, to comprehend the fullness of life of the risen one that conquers death completely.[51]

For Christians, Gutiérrez's words suggest how the many deaths and disappearances in El Salvador, Guatemala and elsewhere can be like Christ's as living memorials against the inhuman treatment of the world's oppressed and ongoing challenges for Christian faith and the struggle for justice.

---

[50] Idem: 'Introduction: State Terror and Anthropology', J.A. Sluka (ed.), *Death Squad*, pp. 1–45 (4).
[51] Gutiérrez, 'The Poor and the Christian Communities', p. 112.

Part 4:

Theology and the Quest for Liberation

The Liberating Vision of Medellín in Feminist Theology*

MARÍA PILAR AQUINO

When the event at Medellín[1] took place in the sixties, current feminist theology of liberation was still in its infancy. This theology emerged from the lowest level of the pyramidal churches as a reflective religious language articulating critically women and men's experiences of God in our struggles for true justice, according to the liberating vision of the Christian message. From the beginning, Medellín recognizes that the churches and societies have not made sufficient efforts towards 'assuring that justice be honoured and realised in every sector of the respective national communities', and adds that the 'almost universal frustration of legitimate aspirations which creates the climate of collective anguish in which we are already living' (Justice 1) cannot be ignored. The reality of widespread inequality and the collective dispossession of fundamental rights experienced by women are injustices that cry to heaven. For feminist theology, the liberating vision of the Christian message leads us to confront these realities and demand a collective commitment towards the elimination of systematic injustice, sexist exclusion and kyriarchal domination. There can be no true liberation of society as a whole without addressing the problem of the injustice and oppression suffered by women. Supported by the contemporary feminist theory that emerged in the 1950s, the Second Vatican Council's vision of change, and the Medellín impetus towards social

---

* An earlier and briefer version of this chapter was published under the same title used here, in *Revista Latinoamericana de Teología* 45/XV (1998): 269–275. This is the first time it has appeared in English (translation by John McCarthy in consultation with Jorge Díaz-Cintas).

[1] Second General Conference of Latin American Bishops, *The Church in the Present-Day Transformation on Latin America in the Light of the Council. Conclusions*, Second edition, United States Catholic Conference Division for Latin America, Washington, DC, 1973.

justice, feminist theology as a formal systematic discourse begins, in the Western European and North American context, in the 1960s.

In the global context, in fact, the whole of this decade is characterized by the irruption of large popular, political, social and intellectual movements struggling to establish the socio-political agency and full rights due to every person, and to eliminate the systematic injustice present in practically all corners of the world. Formally and systematically, what we know today as feminist theories and theologies began life linked to these movements, even if historically they show different conceptual and political developments. My reflection focuses on the contribution the liberating vision of Medellín has upon the development of critical feminist theology.[2] To address this topic, I will first examine some historical processes that have influenced the development of feminist theology in our region. The second part explores the legacy Medellín has given to the feminist theological process, and I conclude by underlining the demands Medellín continues to make of theology and the churches, now and in respect of the future. With this article I wish to honour the work of Amerindia[3] in its more than twenty years of firm commitment to directing the socio-political power of the churches and theology towards the objectives of the Christian faith summarized in our vision of true liberation.

I want to open my reflection by pointing out that the formal articulation of feminist theory in the mid-twentieth century is not limited to the richest countries of the North. There is substantial and growing documentation of the historical development of Latin American feminism.[4] The prominent Peruvian feminist sociologist, Virginia Vargas,

---

[2] I must express my gratitude to Jon Sobrino for inviting me to make these reflections for the earlier version of this chapter in *Revista Latinoamericana de Teología*.

[3] Amerindia is simply the name we use as a group of bishops, theologians (male and female, clerical and lay), and pastors in reference to a gathering space where experiences are exchanged in order to help us strengthen our work towards a liberating church. Its founder, the theologian Sergio Torres, has supported our activities for the building of a community of faith in keeping with the vision and spirit of Medellín.

[4] Regarding reading resources for the grassroot communities, one of the most notable efforts in this area comes from Equipo de Mujeres en Acción Solidaria (EMAS), and the 'Vasco de Quiroga' Michoacano Centre for Research and Education (CEMIF), both in Mexico. With the guidance of Maruja González Butrón, EMAS-CEMIF a significant number of short books (Cuadernos) in which prominent feminists use simple formats and accessible language to trace the history of Latin American feminism. See *Cuadernos para la mujer*, Pensamiento y Luchas series, EMAS-CEMIF, Morelia, Mexico. As for academic studies, see Jean Baelen, *Flora Tristán: Feminismo y socialismo en el siglo XIX*, Taurus, Madrid, 1973; Adelaida R. Del Castillo, (ed.), *Between Borders. Essays on Mexican/Chicana History*, Floricanto Press, Encino, CA 1990; María Candelaria Navas Turcios, (ed.), *Jornadas Feministas. Feminismo y sectores populares en América Latina*, Emas-Cidhal-Gem-Mas-Cem-Covag-Apis, Mexico, 1987; and the excellent recent book edited by Ana María Portugal and Carmen Torres, *El Siglo de las Mujeres*, Isis Internacional, Santiago, Chile, 1999. As

has remarked that,

> the participation of women in the Latin American political scene is a visible and growing phenomenon in recent years in all countries within our region. Numerous studies have been written about this presence, paying attention to the concrete analyses in specific historical contexts as well as their theoretical-political significance. Most of these studies place this increasing participation of women within the context of what has been called the new social movements.[5]

For me, as a Mexican woman of *Mestiza* condition and grassroot origin, knowledge of the historical background of this theory in Mexico makes me feel energized and hopeful because it validates my theological activity as an integral part of a *dynamic tradition in the process* of being constructed. The Mexican feminist sociologist E. Tuñón Pablos has thoroughly researched and documented this tradition, and her efforts have highlighted the historical importance of three events that have been marginalized by conventional history: the First Feminist Congress, which took place in Tabasco, Mexico in 1915; the Yucatán (Mexico) Feminist Congress, held in 1916; and the 1923 Feminist Congress in Mexico City.[6] In a similar way, studies in the USA Chicana/Latina feminist theory have established feminist hereditary lines which not only connect with the Mexican-USA contribution of the

---

for journals, certainly the Mexican FEM, founded in 1976, occupies a prominent position for being the first journal of feminist analysis in Latin America. But also worthy of note are Isis Internacional and FEMPRESS (Chile), 'La Boletina' Puntos de Encuentro (Nicaragua), Ediciones Populares Feministas (República Dominicana), Cotidiano Mujer: Revista Feminista (Uruguay); Debate Feminista, La Correa Feminista, Cuadernos Feministas (Mexico), Mandrágora (Brazil), and Revista Chacarera (Peru). For feminist information, communication and documentation on the Internet, note the following: FEMPRESS, Red de Comunicación Alternativa de la Mujer (Women's Alternative Communication Network) http://www.fempress.cl/index.html; ISIS Internacional http://www.isis.cl/; Centro Florista Tristán http://ekeko.rcp.net.pe/FLORA/; Comunicación, Intercambio y Desarrollo Humano en América Latina CIDHAL (Communication, Exchange and Human Development in Latin America) http://www.laneta.apc.org/cidhal/cidhal1.htm; and Making Face, Making a Soul – A Chicana Feminist Homepage <http://www.chicanas.com/>.

[5] Virginia Vargas Valente, *EL Aporte de la Rebeldía de las Mujeres*, Ediciones Flora Tristán, Lima, Peru, 1989, p. 117.

[6] Esperanza Tuñón Pablos, 'Del porfiriato a la etapa de la luch armada: Los años veintes y primera mitad de los treintas', in María Arcelia González Butrón, (ed.), *También somos protagonistas de la historia de México*, Equipo de Mujeres en Acción Solidaria EMAS (Women's Solidarity Action Group), Mexico, DF, 1999, 7–25; Shirlene Soto, 'The Women's Movement in Mexico: The First and Second Feminist Congresses in Yucatán, 1916', in *Between Borders: Essays on Mexicana/Chicana History*, pp. 483–491 (quoted in note 4).

beginning of the twentieth century, but also, in the vast contribution of Sor Juana Inés de la Cruz (1651-1695), with the feminist legacy of the seventeenth century and even with the feminist memory that has its roots in the emancipatory struggles of women in the fifteenth and sixteenth centuries.[7] I make this brief illustration only to note that feminist research has brought to light the central landmarks in which lies the subsequent construction process of the feminist movement, its theory and vision, within our context. I could mention many names as precursors of contemporary feminism within our region, but here I wish only to honour the memory of Guatemalan feminist pioneer Alaíde Foppa, who was the impulse behind Central American and Mexican critical feminism. Alaíde was kidnapped and 'disappeared' in Guatemala by the military intelligence forces in 1980.[8] Her body has never been found, but her creativity, rebellious imagination and vision of justice continue to open new roads in the process of critical feminism in the Americas.

The Feminist Processes: A Brief Approach

From the 1960s, feminism already gave a hint of its critical, transforming and subversive profile in respect of the kyriarchal paradigm in which humanity had lived for millennia. The asymmetric order of contemporary societies, cultures and religions, certainly makes clear that this paradigm continues to impose it hegemonic power around the world. The *kyriarchal* nature of this order lies in the fact that, by its own dominant force, it constitutes the whole of historical reality in E. Schüssler Fiorenza's words, as 'a complex social pyramid of graduated dominations and subordinations'.[9] With the kyriarchal analytical category, the author wants to point out that in the kyriarchal social order, 'not all men dominate and exploit all women without difference and that elite Western educated propertied Euro-American men have articulated and benefitted from women's and other "nonpersons" exploitation'.[10] Consequently, as E. Schüssler Fiorenza shrewdly notes, a systematic analysis of powers and social relations cannot be reduced

---

[7] Anna Nieto Gómez, 'Chicana Feminism', in Alma M. García, (ed.), *Chicana Feminist Thought. The Basic Historical Writings*, Routledge, New York, 1997, 52-57; Martha P. Cotera, *The Chicana Feminist*, Information Systems Development, Austin, TX 1977, 1-12.
[8] Equipo de Dirección Colectiva, 'Los cinco años de Fem', *FEM Publicación Feminista* V/20 (1981-1982): 3.
[9] Elisabeth Schüssler Fiorenza, *Jesus Miriam's Child, Sophia's Prophet, Critical Issues in Feminist Christology*, Continuum, New York, 1994, p. 14.
[10] Ibid.

to the inequalities and marginations of gender,[11] there must also be a tackling of:

> the complex multiplicative interstructuring of gender, race, class, and colonial dominations and their imbrication with each other. It seeks to expose the embeddedness of wo/men's oppression in the entire domain of western society, culture, and religion and thereby to reveal that the subordination and exploitation of wo/men is crucial to the maintenance of kyriarchal cultures and religions. Hence any adequate theory or praxis of emancipation and liberation must explicitly take into account the multiplicative interlocking structures ... of domination and marginalization.[12]

Kyriarchal societies, cultures and religions erect a historical order, which, because of the hegemonic force of the elites in power, forcefully divests those social groups situated at the bottom of the social pyramid. In her excellent book *Muera la Gobierna!*, which offers an analysis of the historical dynamics of colonization, Dora María Téllez the legendary Nicaraguan 'Comandante' and today's president of the Sandinista Renewal Movement (MRS) – states that in any social order *hegemony* is determined by the control of political power, but also recognizes that such hegemony includes the control of the complex system of power relations within the whole social setting. The 'hegemonic groups'[13] legally and institutionally validate the power they hold, and found the legitimacy of this power in the prerogatives of property that they derive 'by right of birth, ethnic origin, and inheritance'.[14] This validation places these elites of property owning men at the top of the social pyramid, from which they not only impose their interests under the guise of them being those of the grassroot population, but also decisively influence the direction of the economy and society as a whole. As an analytical category, the idea put forward by Téllez concerning the hegemonic groups allows for an understanding of these groups as the kyriarchal elites that not only control political power, the instruments of the State apparatus, the property of the land and of people, the financial and commercial systems, legal and symbolic codes, and the systems necessary for the construction of ideology and

---

[11] Elisabeth Schüssler Fiorenza, *But She Said. Feminist Practices of Biblical Interpretation*, Beacon Press, Boston MA, 1992, p. 8.

[12] Elisabeth Schüssler Fiorenza, *Rhetoric and Ethic, The Politics of Biblical Studies*, Fortress Press, Minneapolis MN, 1999, pp. 5–6.

[13] Dora María Téllez, *Muera la Gobierna! Colonización de Matagalpa y Jinotega (1820–1890)*, Universidad de las Regiones Autónomos de la Costa Caribe Nicaragüense, Managua 1999, p. 19 and p. 303.

[14] Ibid., p. 298.

knowledge, but also profoundly affect the identifying frameworks of religions, churches and theologies. The kyriarchal elites exercise their power to establish the hegemony of their values, interests and ideas, the effect of which is to mark and establish the direction of societies, cultures, religions and socio-cultural identities. However, the global consequences of the present kyriarchal paradigm clearly show how the hegemonic project of these elites consistently inhibits the protection and support of the lives of all people, all social groups, and everything around them. It is in this context we can best understand why feminism, in its struggle against kyriarchal hegemony, emerges as a socio-historical force with a profile unambiguously critical, transforming and subversive.

Along with other social movements that began to erode kyriarchal hegemony during the sixties, Vargas states that the significance of feminism lies in the fact that:

> its mere existence profoundly questions the logic with which society is articulated. These movements are justly showing the presence and demands of large social sectors and categories that have traditionally been excluded from institutional politics and discourse.[15]

Society, along with the world's cultures and religions, were seen as historical constructs that, through conscious and deliberate human action, could unleash their *open possibilities* for change and move towards the direction of more just, democratic, participatory and humane models of life. The involvement of many Christian women in the feminist process found validation in the liberating power of the Gospel that sustains the Christian faith. For these women, the kyriarchal order simply does not correspond with the vision of wholeness desired by God for the whole of creation.

In keeping with the social movements seeking a profound transformation of the present order, feminism strengthened a process of criticism and reformulation of modes of understanding and exercising power, religious convictions and worldviews, the creation and expression of knowledge, spaces and contents of political and social activity, and of ways of understanding and conducting human relations.[16] From its beginnings, feminism adopted as a central objective the transformation of the pyramidal, hierarchic, authoritarian and imposing logic of existing societies, cultures and religions. In our region, this is the logic

---

[15] Vargas Valente, *El Aporte de la Rebeldía*, p. 117.

[16] For a brief decription of the processes that influenced the development of feminism, see Natacha Molina, 'Las mujeres en la construcción de la igualdad y la ciudadanía en América Latina', La Ventana, Centro de estudios de género (Centre for Gender Studies), http://www.udg.mx/laventana/libr5/mujeres.html.

that has run through the various contemporary social models, from the military dictatorships and restricted democracies, to the current global neoliberal capitalism; that is why these models can be seen as mobile historical adaptations of the constant kyriarchal domination. The Mexican researchers Gisela Espinosa Damián and Alma Rosa Sánchez Olvera point out that the development of feminism during the sixties – known then also as 'neofeminism', in order to differentiate it from the feminism emerging at the end of the nineteenth century – was influenced by various socio-political processes, such as:

> The 1968 student uprising in Paris, the 'Prague Spring', the triumph of the Cuban Revolution and the national liberation movements in 'peripheral' countries. Out of the climate of questioning and mobilisation engendered by these processes, the so-called counter-cultural movements grew and severely criticized all types of alienation, oppression and authoritarianism and put to the test those theses that saw the only agents of social change as the proletariat and peasantry, organized along class party lines. Other movements comprized of and representing racial minorities, pacifists and ecologists, homosexuals, students, hippies and the feminist movement expressed new forms of social movement .... With neo-feminism a new way of interpreting reality came about, which expressed itself in personal changes and an emancipatory attitude on the part of women in the face of their oppression; this brought along with it a revolution in daily life, because its ideas question the gender relations in all areas of social life and lead to a struggle against 'paternal attitudes', patriarchal ideology, machismo, sexism, and phallocracy.[17]

Among the liberating movements, feminist theology arises in this decade as a language grounded in faith that gathers the critical reflection of that part of the Christian community that understood its identity and mission in terms of participation in the socio-ecclesiastical forces committed to the cause of justice. Feminist theological activity emerges bound to the activities of oppressed groups in favour of global transformation in order to build new social relations within societies and churches, but maintains that this construction involves the elimination of kyriarchal domination. The accepted premise of this assertion is that the elimination of socio-economic poverty does not automatically result in the elimination of the sexist exclusion of women.[18] More clearly

---

[17] Gisela Espinosa Damián and Alma Rosa Sánchez Olvera, 'Feminismo y Movimiento de Mujeres en México: 1970–1990', in María Arcelia González Butrón, (ed.), *También Somos Protagonistas de la Historia de México*, Equipo de Mujeres en Acción Solidaria EMAS, México DF, 1999, p. 58.

[18] From my contact with the Central American revolutionary processes in the late

stated, in order for the liberation of the poor to be real and true, it is imperative that those at the bottom of the social and ecclesiastical pyramid – women – are really and truly liberated.

Thus, the emergent feminist theology is constituted by four interrelated dimensions. First, it is the cognitive language of the experience of faith that exposes the dissatisfaction and indignation of God's people before the present reality that accepts the oppression, violence and sexism practised against women. Second, it is a socio-religious and political movement that takes God's revelation and responds to it through a deliberate commitment to new realities more compatible with the liberating vision of the Christian faith. Third, it is a plural body of religious, symbolic and cultural knowledge which proposes a global transformation for the benefit of the social whole. Fourth, it is a current of thought that generates new forms of social relations based upon democratic principles, such as the dignity of persons, the anthropological and political equality of women and men, social justice, and the freedom to manage one's own life.

In its criticism of the systematic oppression of kyriarchal hegemony in societies and churches, and its deliberate incorporation of the salvation and sin experienced by the Christian community within them, feminist theology emerges as a creative, original and necessary activity for showing historically the truth of revelation for Christian salvation. As such, along with the liberating vision articulated by Medellín in 1968, and with the transforming direction of the also emergent liberation theology, feminist theology comes along to show the complexity of the social fabric within which God's revelation, the experience of faith and the church's mission take place. However, at this point I wish to note that while liberation theology – initially articulated almost exclusively by men – was, thanks to the support of Medellín, quickly taken up and spread throughout the continent and Caribbean, this was not remotely the case with the fledgling feminist theology. Many bishops, priests, pastors, lay and clerical theologians, and the base ecclesial communities

---

seventies, I dared to point out that 'some theorists (Christian and non Christian marxists) have called women's oppression "secondary oppression" within the "fundamental contradiction". We differ radically with this view and its subsequent [practices]. Surely it is not "secondary" but simultaneous. We recall the Cuban historical experience; capitalism can be overcome, but not machismo. The domination of women has lasted all the societal models history has brought and might remain [as] an axis in the future. The religious standard demands coherence in all registers, both the subjective and the politically objective', María Pilar Aquino, 'El culto a María y María en el culto', *Fem Publicación feminista* V/20 (1981–1982): 46. The position I took here was certainly not seen in those days as theologically or politically 'correct'. The struggles for women's rights were seen by the leaders of the revolutionary movements as a 'deviation from the main struggle', and criticism of its vigorous sexism was not tolerated.

jointly pushed forward the views of liberation theology. But at the same time, during this period the majority of these ecclesial groups were opposed to feminist theological perspectives, mistakenly considering them foreign and irrelevant. Many theologians even claimed that the introduction of the 'women issue' only distracted from the 'central issue' of the poor, and that taking the cause in the direction of 'the women's struggle' only fragmented the 'main struggle' between rich and poor, oppressors and oppressed. The oppression of women was seen and described as at best a 'secondary conflict', a 'super-structural antagonism', or finally as something 'imported by white women from the developed world' with the aim of bringing about a cultural and ideological neo colonisation. In most cases, theologians considered that feminist theological views distorted and diverted the core of liberation theology.[19] It is therefore hardly surprising that today some people from these ecclesial groups persist with the same mistaken conceptions about feminism they learned back then. In my opinion, in this sense early feminist theology began in an exceptionally disadvantaged position from which to push for the dismantling of kyriarchal domination. Even so, although in this decade there are still no formal platforms for dialogue between feminist theology and the body of churches in Latin America, this theology progressively occupies an important place in the theological concerns of Latin American women.

During the 1970s, these concerns become even deeper with the awakening consciousness – in women more than men – of the necessity of tackling theologically the obvious structural sexism embedded in Latin American cultures. This awakening of consciousness led to an identifying of the multiple forms of oppression that affect women, and exposed the subordinate position of women within the Church, theology and the Christian tradition. But more importantly still, it led a large section of the Christian community to question itself about its responsibility for preserving or transforming these realities.

The theological sensibility of Christian women concerning these realities was fuelled by the significant diffusion of the analyses of the problems affecting women, especially of the alliance between capitalism and patriarchy, the role of ideologies and religions in the conformation of sexist cultures, the social and ecclesial mechanisms used to control the body and basic choices of women, and the institutions and theories of power that place women at a structural disadvantage. These analyses did not come from the academic establishment, the hegemonic political parties, or the revolutionary fronts of the time; nor did they come from the recognized liberation theologies

---

[19] To look at this in greater depth, see María Pilar Aquino, 'Teología feminista en América Latina. Evaluación y desafíos', *Tópicos 90*, no. 7 (1995): 107–122.

of the day, but from the popular and academic organizations that made up the growing feminist movement of the seventies. As Teresita de Barbieri and Orlandina de Oliveira point out, the whole of this decade 'is characterized by the appearance of women on the Latin American political scene'.[20]

Several events come together in this decade to give an impulse to the course of the feminist movement, and especially to create a space where feminist theology can grow. Of these events I must note the following, though I do not give precedence to one over any of the others. *First*, the impact in the churches of the International Year of the Woman, sponsored by the United Nations and held in Mexico City in 1975. With its focus on the agenda for 'equality, development and peace' this event encouraged the socio-political agency of women and for the first time allowed the protests of indigenous women, symbolized in the 'if you'll allow me to speak' of Domitilia Chungara, to be heard. *Secondly*, the implementation of the 'Decade of the Woman' programme on a global level, promoted by the United Nations between 1975 and 1985, which provided an important space for deepening the feminist consciousness of women's movements. *Thirdly*, the implementation on a global level of the 'Community of Women and Men within the Church' programme, initiated in 1978 by the Commission of Faith and Order of the World Council of Churches, which allowed for an examination of the ramifications of the exclusion of women from the churches and theology as well as for the implementation of an agenda to overcome such an exclusion. *Fourthly*, the increasing incorporation within the feminist movement of Catholic and Protestant Christian women (clerical and lay), who undertook important consciousness raising work in the marginal rural and urban areas. *Fifthly*, the deepening of critical awareness within the churches about the existing inequalities between women and men spurred by the worldwide distribution of UN annual publications in whch the marginal position of women around the globe is exposed in data and statistics. These publications continued to appear in the following decades, demanding of all societies an express effort to promote and protect the women's human rights. *Sixthly*, the impact of the Christian feminist women in the conclusions of the Third General Latin American Episcopate Conference, which took place in 1979 in the city of Puebla, Mexico.[21] In these Conclusions, for the first time in the history of the Latin American Church the Roman Catholic bishops note the seriousness of

---

[20] Teresita de Barbieri and Orlandina de Oliveira, *Mujeres en América Latina. Análisis de una década en crisis*, IEPALA Editorial, Madrid, 1989, p. 37.
[21] Third General Conference of Latin American Bishops, *Puebla. Evangelization at Present and in the Future of Latin America*, National Conference of Catholic Bishops, Washington DC, 1979.

the marginalization and poverty affecting women (Puebla, 834, 1135); the necessity for better organization from women in demanding their rights (Puebla, 836, 840); the exploitation and ill treatment suffered by many women (Puebla, 835, 838); and they call for the whole Church to make a preferential option for the impoverished majorities and declare their solidarity with them (Puebla, 1134), but note that *within these majorities*, the condition of poverty and misery is aggravated for women on account of 'their condition of being doubly oppressed and marginalized' (Puebla, 1135). *Seventhly*, the First Latin American Encounter of Christian women, which took place in Mexico City in 1979, to examine the activities and efforts of the churches and theology concerning women's liberation; to explore the feminist contribution to theological activity; and to encourage the involvement of women in this activity.[22] Because this event took place in the vicinity of Tepeyac, the beginning of feminist theological activity holds a strong symbolic value for me. I believe the founding event of this activity is *Guadalupana* faith, and that its daily growth is nourished and sustained by the Brown Virgin of Tepeyac, Our Lady of Guadeloupe. Along with countless women throughout the Americas, particularly the indigenous women of my land, I look to her to continue cultivating the flowers of truth and hope. This first meeting, in which I had the opportunity of participating, had a decisive influence on the orientation of my vocation as feminist theologian.

With this brief overview I merely wish to remark on the dynamism of a movement that leads to an examination of the situations of injustice in which the majority of poor and marginalized women live, pledges to eliminate injustice within the churches and societies, and contributes to the clarification of the Christian commitment to the full human dignity and rights of these majorities.

In the early eighties, feminist theology acquired a formal and visible identity within the Ecumenical Association of Third World Theologians (EATWOT) when, in 1983, the Association's executive committee approved the creation of the 'Commission on Theology from the Third World Women's Perspective'.[23] This commission adopted as its main objective 'to promote a theology of liberation from the perspective of women in the Third World, a theology that springs from a critical awareness of women's subjugated position and a commitment to change it'.[24] The immediate context of this event is the Sixth EATWOT

---

[22] Mujeres Para el Diálogo (eds.), *Mujer Latinoamericana. Iglesia y Teología*, Mujeres Para el Diálogo, México DF, 1981.

[23] Virginia Fabella, M.M., *Beyond Bonding. A Third World Women's Theological Journey*, Ecumenical Association of Third World Theologians and The Institute of Women's Studies, Manila, 1993, p. 36.

[24] Ibid.

conference, which took place the same year in Geneva, with the aim of reflecting, within the framework of a dialogue with male and female theologians from the developed world, upon the meaning of Christian faith in a divided world.[25] In the conference's final document, the participants recognize that 'liberation is never solely a question of political and economic transformation. It is also a question of profound cultural and religious renovation. The aspirations of the oppressed everywhere for dignity and a new life demand that we examine more closely the values and visions out of which new societies are created'.[26] According to the document, this examination will be more realistic and comprehensive the more it incorporates, seriously and rigorously, both the critical analysis of sexism and racism as structural components of marginalization in the global system of socio-economic domination, and the role of theology and the churches in the perpetuation of the patriarchal system (today re-conceptualized as kyriarchal).[27]

For the developing process of feminist theology, this conference represents a significant step in several senses. *First*, it recognizes that in the theological activity of men and women feminist analysis is essential for establishing both the complexity of the global system of oppression and the alternatives of transformation. *Secondly*, it makes clear that the struggle against sexism and the patriarchal structures is not only relevant to women, but demands too the commitment of men in effecting a transformation because it encompasses the basic fabric of human relationships in society. *Thirdly*, it affirms that Christian theology has an obligation to transform the structures and cultures that result in realities such as poverty, racism, sexism, and neo colonialism which are incompatible with the Gospel's message. *Fourthly*, it establishes that theologies claiming to be liberating have the particular responsibility of rectifying the churchs' and kyriarchal theologies' sanctification of sexism. *Fifthly*, it exposes the disinclination and lack of will on the part of male theologians to incorporate critical feminist frameworks, as well as the sexist ideas and behaviour of Third World male theologians – especially that of the EATWOT participants. *Sixthly*, it criticised the false belief, shared at the time by many men and women at EATWOT, that kyriarchal social relations and sexism can be challenged through the division of theological work in which women articulate a 'theology from the woman's perspective', while EATWOT has never either advanced or recognized the idea that there exists a 'theology from the perspective of men'. This theological dualism should disappear through

---

[25] Final Document, 'Doing Theology in a Divided World: Final Statement of the Sixth EATWOT Conference', in Virginia Fabella and Sergio Torres, (eds.), *Doing Theology in a Divided World*, Orbis Books, Maryknoll NY, 1985, p. 179.
[26] Ibid., p. 184.
[27] Ibid., p. 182, pp. 186–187.

the appropriation of a comprehensive analysis of the global system of domination by male and female theologians equally.

Consequently, this conference not only opens a formal space for the subsequent development of feminist liberation theology, but also gives formal recognition to the work begun by the women theologians at EATWOT in 1981. In that year the Fifth EATWOT Congress at New Delhi, India, took place.[28] The final document of that congress calls for the theological community to recognize women's struggles for liberation as a true source of doing theology, and further emphasizes that 'there can be no truly relevant theology, no genuine social transformation, no holistic human liberation'[29] unless injustice against women is eliminated. This aspect, however, has barely been worked on by male Third World liberation theologians. Nevertheless, EATWOT pledges in New Delhi to support 'women's struggle for equality in and through theology',[30] although it is not until 1983 that EATWOT sanctions the existence of the Woman's Commission.

Without the committed work of that commission, the articulation of feminist theology from the Third World would, in my opinion, have certainly had to face greater obstacles. Despite the lack of majority support from the ecclesiastical establishment, the theology departments of universities, and the majority of Third World [male] theologians, the activity of critical feminist theology has continued its process of expansion throughout the eighties and nineties. Feminist theology today has a profile which is plural in its expressions, emphases and disciplines; it is constructed by women and men of diverse cultural, racial and religious traditions, in the North and South; it has given new profiles to the intelligence of faith, both in method and theological content, and has constituted an essential space for establishing a creative dialogue between the movements for social change, racial and intercultural studies, critical feminist theories, and the collective forces of historical reality that bring divine revelation.

In the 1990s, there is no academic discipline or social, political, cultural or religious sphere untouched by the influence of the feminist vision in the Americas. Feminism shows that the relentless increase and deepening of poverty, and the denial to most people of those human rights essential for a dignified life has been particularly aggressive

---

[28] The papers from this conference were published in, *Irruption of the Third World. Challenge to Theology*, Virginia Fabella and Sergio Torres, (eds.), Orbis Books, Maryknoll NY, 1983.

[29] Final Statement, 'The Irruption of the third World: Challenge to Theology. Final Statement of the Fifth EATWOT Conference, New Delhi, August 17-29, 1981', in *Irruption of the Third World. Challenge to Theology*, Virginia Fabella and Sergio Torres, (eds.), Orbis Books, Maryknoll NY, 1983, 200.

[30] Ibid, p. 205.

towards women and their dependants. The vertiginous growth of feminism during these years is, in my opinion, a result of the active reception and enrichment of feminist objectives on the part of various collectives that deliberately sought channels for confronting this situation. The feminist agenda for global change of the whole of society, and its mobile proposals for action appropriate to the contextual demands and possibilities,[31] allowed for a spreading of the virtualities of this vision and these objectives, with the goal of effecting social change. The strength and vitality of the feminist process in the Americas is marked by the experiences and wisdom of black, indigenous, mestizas and white women who engender many and diverse struggles for our fundamental democratic rights, against inequality, injustice, and systematic exclusion within the present global configuration of kyriarchal neoliberal capitalism. V. Vargas points out that today we talk about 'feminisms' in the plural, because this process is expressed

> in multiple forms and in multiple spheres. The forms it assumes are diverse: as current of thought, as feminist institutions, as pressure groups, as artistic expression, as politico-cultural proposals. It is present in varying degrees of intensity, in the universities, in some mass media, in art and literature, the cinema, politics, even in the State, and it has spread to local, national, regional and global spheres. That is to say, the spheres and forms of questioning of the inequalities and marginalisations of the sexes and gender conflicts are multiple, and there are many ways in which they are making themselves known and attempting to transform the power structures in personal, sexual and social relationships.[32]

Since the 1990s, neither the hegemonic kyriarchal groups nor the various social movements are unfamiliar with the political strength of the global feminist movements. From today's perspective, this plural body of transforming political practices, politically and symbolically subversive knowledges, critical theoretical constructions, and rebellious philosophical-cultural convictions appear to be in a state of constant development and to be of a plural, multidimensional, interdisciplinary, inter-racial and inter-cultural character. For Sylvia Marcos, the

---

[31] Colectivo Feminista, 'Quinto Encuentro Feminista Latinoamericano y del Caribe. El feminismo de los 90: Desafíos y Propuestas'. Document presented at the conclusion of Fifth Latin American and Caribbean Feminist Conference held in San Bernardo, Argentina, in November 1990.

[32] Virginia Vargas Valente, 'De multiples formas y en multiples espacios', Red de Comunicación Alternativa de la Mujer FEMPRESS, http://www.fempress.cl/base/fem/vargas.html.

twentieth century closed with an explosion of feminist peculiarities 'laid out and forged ... not only by their historical, cultural, social and economic peculiarities, but also by their "cosmologies" ... in a social movement wishing to grow and stay alive. A movement attempting to offer answers to contemporary dilemmas'.[33] This movement, however, maintains a shared vision of women as democratic subjects, the attainment of full citizenship for women as constant horizon, and a commitment to a transformation of domination and exploitation in kyriarchal societies, cultures and religions as an unwavering matrix. According to various women scholars, with its growing base among excluded groups and its ramifications in popular women's movements, 'Latin American feminism is clearly a powerful, vibrant, energetic, creative and exuberant political force, although racked with tensions'.[34]

The present Latin American feminist process continues to strengthen the political identity of women through its sustained building of democratic vision and action. Feminist struggles for democracy, for the re-conceptualization of human rights, and for respect for women's rights, seem to have inserted themselves into all familiar and even unfamiliar spheres. I talk about familiar spheres, such as one's own body, the home, the neighbourhood, the city, the rural areas, the mountainside, the factory, the office, the university, the classroom, the State, the churches, the political parties, popular organizations, and other entities. I also refer to unfamiliar spheres because we do not yet know all the possibilities historical reality might contain for us, the whole humanity in the world. Not all the walls have fallen yet, we haven't fought from all the mountains, and we haven't yet opened all the gates. Today, it is no longer enough to talk about the 'necessities' of women; we have to engender knowledge and practices conducive to the access to and respect of women's rights. The feminist vision of democracy and equality in a justice based order truly opens new seams for social change and for the actualization of a new paradigm for social living. In this sense, the absence of a critical feminist analysis in the construction of societies and cultures has constituted a serious impediment in the bringing about of an historical enactment of justice, as Mirta Rodríguez Calderón from Cuba so aptly notes, when she says that the notion of 'feminism' is just beginning to be 'dusted off' or 'declassified' in the Cuban context,

[33] Sylvia Marcos, 'Feminismos al ritmo del merengue', [Eighth Latin American and Caribbean Feminist Conference, Santo Domingo, República Dominicana 1999], *Cuadernos Feministas* 3/10 (1999): 16–18.

[34] Nancy Saporta Sternbach, Marysa Navarro-Aranguren, Patricia Chuchryk, and Sonia E. Alvarez, 'Feminisms in Latin America: From Bogotá to San Bernardo', in *The Making of Social Movements in Latin America. Identity, Strategy, and Democracy*, Arturo Escobar and Sonia E. Alvarez, (eds.), Westview Press, Boulder CO, 1992, 235.

although it still hasn't reached the women's groups that could use it as an instrument for the clarification of their ideas, as a means of demanding a share of state as well as party power ...; in order to denounce the domestic violence that is kept secret ...; and, among many other things, as a way of understanding and grasping this system of ideas that has made so many contributions to this century's history, in particular for the recognition and self-recognition of women ... The major failure – she states – must be attributed to the Federation of Cuban Women and its [female] directors who did not sufficiently discourage, debate, or challenge machismo from the power base itself, to which they at least had access, even if they were not always present ... The absence of an arsenal of feminist and gender ideology as a category of analysis has resulted in many disadvantages for Cuban women ... As a Cuban woman I lament the fact that the theoretical arsenal and the practices of autonomy and empowerment with which feminism arms us have been absent from my sisters' reality.[35]

Calderón's opinion is not isolated, nor is it applicable only to her local context. The truth is that she summarizes the experience of many of us in the spheres in which we live and act. To expand a little further on this critical evaluation, the problem of disadvantage for many women today does not, in my opinion, stem from the simple absence of a critical feminist arsenal in our environments, but rather from the hegemonic political, socio-religious and cultural forces hostile to it. The critical feminist instrumental has been there in the movements that have formally carried and developed it throughout the second half of the twentieth century. However, the leaders of the popular movements and revolutionary organizations, heads of the church, the 'liberation' [male] theorists and theologians have shown their lack of will to incorporate this instrumental key, and have even been hostile to it. That is why such groups, whether or not they realize it, form a part of the hegemonic kyriarchal groups. Here I must note the possible lack of basic honesty these groups have shown before the open processes of historical reality, because they have had both the possibility and opportunity of referring to systematic feminist analysis. In recent years, these forces of the kyriarchal hegemony have advanced proposals whose intent is to curb the strength of critical feminism and alter the path of its objectives. To this end they have, among other methods, inserted a 'gender' language into the examination of women's subordination, the purpose of which is to weaken feminist political identity and the removal of the political character of feminism. Paradoxically, many women in theology have accepted this

[35] Mirta Rodríguez Calderón, 'Cuba: Desclasificar la palabra feminismo', *Cuadernos Feministas* 2/9 (1999): 24–31.

method, as though the 'gender' language established feasible routes for the transformation of kyriarchal societies, cultures and religions. The truth is that the only thing the 'genders' route makes possible is the hegemonic groups' sustaining of power, but now this power acquires a more 'humane' profile for taking into account the supposed 'masculinity' and 'femininity' of social subjects.

It is worth noting that while some of us in the ecclesial and theological field have made a deliberate choice to incorporate the analytical frameworks of critical feminism, other [female] theologians have chosen to articulate their theological activity in correspondence with the gender theories that mask and eliminate the naming of both the terms 'feminists' and kyriarchal domination. Recently, two Latin American [female] theologians – one in Brazil and the other in Costa Rica – vehemently told me that feminism is already something 'of the past', that today the 'widest' and 'most accepted' term is 'gender', and that 'gender' theology is more inclusive; one of them even suggested that the central themes most worth investigating are 'men's liberation' and 'masculinity'. Another prominent female theologian who took part in the conversation wittily observed that this proposed path was the equivalent to black theologians putting forward a theological project centring on the 'liberation of the white race', or indigenous theologians working on the 'liberation of the colonisers'. Neither of my two Latin American colleagues accepted that their deliberate rejection of the critical feminist instrumental resulted not only in a great disadvantage for them themselves, but also for those reading their writings and especially the poor excluded women listening to their advice.

Certainly, as Lucila Diaz Rönner clearly points out, the gender category was 'initially developed by Anglo Saxon feminism in the 70s and ... provides a fundamental base for questioning the biological determinism that distinguishes between the anatomy of bodies and the roles socially constructed for them.'[36] However, as E. Schüssler Fiorenza says, contemporary gender theories have their theoretical roots in functionalist sociology, and have the effect of leading towards a socio-religious and cultural recuperation and re-inscription of the supposed characteristics of gender in binary terms.[37] This focus of

[36] Lucila Diaz Rönner, 'Feminismo, Género y Política', Red de Comunicación Alternativa de la Mujer FEMPRESS, in http://www.fempress.cl/base/1995fp166reflexione.htm.

[37] Gender and critical feminist theories were fully expressed and discussed at the panel called 'Feminist theology and hermeneutics', organized by the Núcleo de Estudos Teológicos da Mulher na América Latina (NETMAL), at the Methodist University in São Paulo, Brazil, 19 June 2000. The prominent Professor Maria José Rosado Nunes was in charge of the panel's co-ordination, to which I had the honour of being invited, along with the well known Professor E. Schüssler Fiorenza. I refer here to the paper given by E. Schüssler Fiorenza, entitled 'A critical feminist hermeneutic of the liberation: 10 theses'.

gender theories not only feeds 'the compulsion [of men and women] to negotiate identity in essentially gender terms',[38] but also hinders the exposure of gender as an intrinsic part of the inter-structuring of the dominant relationships in present kyriarchal societies, cultures and religions. Due to the fact that 'gender' theories avoid rigorous analysis of the systemic character of the domination and exclusion of women, these theories have become very attractive for a prominent group of male and female theologians with crucial influence in the developments of theology in the Americas. In their theological activity, this group cheerfully explores the cultural and psychological 'dimensions of gender', but avoids honest criticism of the systemic exclusion of women in kyriarchal Christianity, particularly in Roman Catholicism.

The theological approach based on the functionalist theories of gender has various effects, among which are:

a) it attempts to halt feminist criticism's incisive politics;
b) it negotiates socio-cultural values and behaviours that supposedly validate an 'acceptable' identity for women and men, but does not address the causes that support the domination of women;
c) it prevents the exposing and naming of hegemonic groups that continue to benefit from the exploitation of women in societies and churches;
d) it generates a depoliticized theological language that hinders the critical analysis of the socio-political realities of profound sexual inequality in which we live, obstructing the search for transforming routes.

What I mean to say by this, is that in theological activity the mere fact of being a woman is no guarantee for the modelling of a critical consciousness regarding the systemic relationships of domination; neither should it be assumed that we women theologians have the same understanding of the socio-political implications of our theological activity. There are some [women] theologians who, not infrequently, prefer to maintain those gender based theological approaches that are so attractive and acceptable to their male colleagues, who (especially when they are clerics) oppose feminism, whether it is with their words or their silences.

Despite this atmosphere, and against the will of various male and female 'liberation' theologians, feminist theology is gaining influence and continues its process of development in our countries. A new interracial generation of Latin American theologians, supported by some of we theologians who started our work in the 1970s, is opening up new

---

[38] Schüssler Fiorenza, *Rhetoric and Ethic*, p. 5.

perspectives as feminist liberation theologians through its sustained conversation with the well established critical feminisms of the Americas. In the nineteen-nineties, therefore, there is a clear demarcation in the theological activity of Latin American women (and US Latinas), which is marked by the adoption or not of the critical feminist instrumental for a systemic analysis of kyriarchal domination.

To sum up, the feminist experience of this decade continues to be fraught with tensions but there is, too, great hope. In the midst of an adverse cultural, religious and political social context, the feminist movements have not only brought to the fore critical dialogue concerning the implications of the relationship between feminism and democracy, but have also continued to work along constant axes, such as: the eradication of poverty and illiteracy, the elimination of violence against women, equality in public and domestic work, access to formal higher education, affirmation of sexual self-determination, recognition of women's reproductive rights, political representation, and the empowerment of grassroot women. The theological work of various feminist theologians reflects their involvement in these explorations and activities. All in all, the feminist process is showing in its concrete results its ability to transform the kyriarchal relationships of power in the personal, sexual and social spheres. Because of the plurality of both the people and the specific struggles involved in it, we cannot understand feminism as something static, one-dimensional, or closed. The dynamics of the feminist movement's experiences reflect the tensions and changes that have affected humanity in the past few decades, and because of this bring unexplored possibilities for a new socio-cultural paradigm that supports the integrity of life for every creature.

For now, in the words of V. Vargas:

> democracy in the country and the home is the slogan that the Latin American region offers the world, showing not only the political nature of the private but also a different and radical way of understanding democracy. With this slogan we articulate ourselves with the whole of society in its struggles against all types of authoritarianism. It is the slogan of this century that will continue to have meaning in the new millennium.[39]

On the verge of the new millennium, it no longer falls to the kyriarchal religions and churches, or the theorists and theologians supporting the hegemonic groups, to determine the validity of the feminist experience. The feminisms are outside their control now, but inevitably women will continue to abandon the kyriarchal churches if they do not

---

[39] Vargas Valente, 'De múltiples formas'.

change in the near future. Bishops, theologians and priests, especially those who subscribe to the language of 'liberation', can choose to go along with contemporary feminisms, or opt to remain behind the times. But those of us who understand that the Christian faith exists to make a reality of God's purpose of salvation, and that this purpose has socio-political implications, can and surely ought to take a clear decision to place ourselves in the critical feminist sphere. We can and must accompany this global social movement, using religion's enormous resources to promote the correcting of injustices generated by the kyriarchal powers. We can and must participate, with the socio-political force of our religious language, in the search for open historical possibilities for the realization of liberation, whose primary objective, in the words of I. Ellacuría, is justice.[40]

In my opinion, as I later explain, the combination of these historical and theological processes allow us to locate Medellín in the group of socio-political and ecclesial forces that, in the second half of the twentieth century, sought to contribute to the establishment of greater justice for the women and men of our lands. Further still, with this brief historical overview, I would like to suggest avenues that will allow for a better understanding of the impact Medellín has had upon subsequent feminist theological developments, focusing on the transformation of kyriarchal societies, cultures and churches for an authentic liberation.

Medellín's Legacy to Feminist Theological Processes

This brief historical overview is of primary importance, especially in making an honest and fair evaluation of the ecclesial and theological legacy Medellín has brought to feminist theology. It also serves to underline what of Medellín we need to maintain in today's church and theology, and what Medellín continues to demand from them. Without this context, any retrospective look from the present development of critical feminist theology could easily fall into interpretative simplifications. For example, a simplistic reading of the Medellín documents could lead to a rejection of its liberating vision and spirit of transformation because of the following: the sexist character of the theological religious discourse used in all the documents; the reductive character of the analysis Medellín makes of Latin American historical reality when it fails to tackle the dominant kyriarchal structures; the absence of a critique of the kyriarchal hegemony that sustains cultures of exclusion; Medellín's complicit silence regarding the exclusion and

---

[40] Ignacio Ellacuría, 'Liberación', in Casiano Floristán and Juan José Tamayo, (eds.), *Conceptos Fundamentales del Cristianismo*, Trotta, Madrid, 1993, p. 702.

exploitation of women in the Catholic Church; the semidarkness to which Medellín condemns women's contributions to the life of the Latin American Church, from its beginnings right up to the important socio-ecclesiastical movements of the sixties. In the absence of this brief historical overview, feminist theology would, in my opinion, lack intellectual honesty in failing to recognise that in the sixties, the analytical frameworks of contemporary critical feminism were only at the initial stage of development. Consequently, the analytical categories of feminism – such as patriarchy, androcentrism, sexism, homophobia, or the more recent comprehensive category of *kyriarchy* had not yet been incorporated in a conscious, critical and systematic form either in theological discourse or the 'liberating' political theories of the sixties, or, indeed, general intellectual life. That is why I suggest that only by taking into account this context, are we able to appreciate the magnitude of the impact Medellín has had on the development of critical feminist theologies in our times.

I find in my appreciation of Medellín, that this event and its conclusions lent validity to the socio-political and ecclesial forces that were searching for ways of making new cultures and paradigms of social living free of exclusion and kyriarchal violence. Medellín does nothing to stifle these forces, but rather opens the doors of the Church and theology to all efforts that contribute to the establishment of a greater social justice, which is 'understood as a whole of life and as an impulse toward the integral growth of our countries' (Justice 5). For Medellín, the Christian vision of justice means: to respond and participate as a Christian community in the struggles for greater equality between women and men (Justice 1); a greater consciousness about the contribution of Catholic religious instruction, moving from the traditional patriarchal family towards new and more advanced family models that promote a fairer distribution of responsibilities and chores between women and men (Catechesis 8, Family 2); efforts to transform people's daily living conditions in the interests of greater humanization, solidarity and respect for human dignity (Justice 9, Laity 9); work dynamically to organize and raise awareness in order to tackle injustices (Peace 18, Justice 23); the Catholic Church's firm and deliberate commitment to a new social order, based on the principles of justice, peace, participation and solidarity (Peace 20, Justice 7); the building of a church free of temporal ties, connivance and dubious renown, breaking the ties of the selfish ownership of assets, encouraging people to run the economy organically, and exercising its power for the well-being of the community (Poverty of the Church 7, 18). Taking these aspects into account, today I still think Medellín not only lent religious validity to historical liberating forces, but also made possible the emergence of a liberating feminist vision that is today part of many Christian communities throughout the continent and the Caribbean. As I have suggested elsewhere:

> in Medellín the seeds of the axes that were later to be specified and taken up by the theological and pastoral reflection of Christian women in Latin America can be found. These axes, rather than holding back the process of women's liberation, will strengthen it to the extent that they favour the acquisition of a clear and profound consciousness concerning the mission and identity of women as co-participant Subjects in the construction of the Church's history and renewal.[41]

Without the Medellín event, its commitment to global change, its classical options for the poor and for the liberation of oppressed people, we Latin American women would probably still be in that darkness where the kyriarchal hegemony wanted us. The Medellín vision, on the other hand, allowed us to comprehend and cultivate the liberating force of the Christian faith in everything that constitutes our daily lives. Furthermore, I am convinced that the Medellín vision *continues to be necessary in the current Church and theology*. I will now mention some of the most important aspects that lead me to believe this. From my point of view, the significance of Medellín for the life of the Church and the feminist theological activity of women and men is manifold.

First, Medellín continues to be the most important historical event in the Latin American Church in the second half of the twentieth century. Its importance stems from the critical reinterpretation it makes of the teachings of the Second Vatican Council from the reality of Latin American history, and the interpretation it makes of this reality as a collective and structural situation of injustice and misery, demanding of the Church a transforming commitment towards greater justice and a defence of human dignity. According to Medellín, 'Such a situation demands urgent, courageous and profoundly renovating global changes' (Peace 16). For José Oscar Beozzo, after Medellín, the Latin American Church has its own identity.[42]

Secondly, Medellín is still the ecclesial event of greatest relevance, due to its vision of a new Church model, embodying the transforming dimension of the Gospel, which recognises the ethical and socio-political dimensions of the evangelizing mission, and affirms the salvation dimension of the Christian faith, understood as a historical praxis of liberation. For Clodovis Boff, Medellín establishes the three principal

---

[41] María Pilar Aquino, *La teología, la Iglesia y la mujer en América Latina*, Indo-American Press, Bogotá, 1994, p. 79.

[42] José Oscar Beozzo, 'Medellín: inspiração e raízes', *Revista Latinoamericana de teología RELaT*, http://www.uca.edu.ni/koinonia/relat/202.htm.

features of the Latin American Church: option for the poor, liberation theology, and grassroot ecclesial communities.[43]

Thirdly, Medellín constitutes a theological event of great importance because it affirms that true knowledge of faith occurs in a priviledged way from active solidarity with the world of the poor and oppressed, and with this confirms a new way of doing theology. Jon Sobrino emphasizes that 'Medellín showed the location to do theology from so that theology can be both evangelical and Latin American, truly Christian and relevant'.[44] Medellín's impact on our ways of living and understanding the identity of the Church and the nature of theological activity in the contemporary world, make it an event of universal magnitude. This is because it understands that the universality of Christian salvation is primarily realized through the socio-ecclesial forces that seek to humanize and liberate the excluded groups from all oppressive situations. Since Medellín, the Church and theology exist to empower those forces of salvation that take place in daily historic reality. The Church and theology have a duty to be a staunch part of the faith lived, thought and celebrated by our communities in their daily journey towards a better quality of life, and in this way re-define both the foundations and purpose of their existence.

In this sense, the present Church and theology have still much to learn from Medellín. Today, it is no longer enough to say that the Church and theology 'form a staunch part' of the people's faith, if there does not exist in them a welcoming attitude and an explicit openness towards the socio-ecclesial forces proposing an end to the suffering caused by the kyriarchal domination and violence beleaguering the daily lives of women and their dependants. Today's Church and theology can only make Medellín their historical, ecclesial and theological legacy in as far as they clearly incorporate the vision and purpose of critical feminist theology, which today forms part of the faith lived by countless Christian communities. There will be no shortage of those who will argue that Medellín fails to adopt critical feminist concepts, and thus attempt to justify their lack of commitment to feminist theological activity. My answer to this argument is that it was due to historical circumstances that Medellín did not do this, not because of any negligence or lack of will.

Considering the undoubted reception Medellín gave to modern critical-liberating rationality and the latest analytical and theological frameworks of the time, I believe it would equally have incorporated the

---

[43] Clodovis M. Boff, 'A Originalidade histórica de Medellín', *Revista Latinoamerican de teología RELaT*, http://www.uca.edu.ni/koinonia/relat/203.htm.

[44] Jon Sobrino, 'Teología en Latinoamérica', in Bernard Lauret and François Refoulé, (eds.), *Iniciación a la práctica de la teología*, vol.1, Cristianidad, Madrid, 1984, p. 368.

critical feminist contribution, had it been available then. Asking Medellín for a rigorous analysis of serious Latin American cultural sexism, comprehensive analysis of kyriarchal neo capitalism, or a denunciation of the pernicious hegemony of kyriarchal theologies, constitutes a historical and epistemological anachronism. It was only in the decades after Medellín that current critical-feminist rationality acquired a solid profile. This type of rationality occupies *today* a prominent place in any kind of approach to the cultural, social and theological dynamics that attempt to establish new ways of life and thinking; that is, new ways of coexistence that uphold the integrity of people, races, ethnic groups, and eco-biotic systems. Medellín is in tune with the intellectual movements of its time, but so today are the Church and theology when we incorporate critical-feminist rationality. Consequently, we cannot accuse Medellín either of negligence or bad will in respect of the developments of critical-feminist theology, although we cannot say the same in respect of the Church and the theological activity being undertaken by female and male theologians who continue to ignore the aforementioned theology at the dawn of the third millennium. Today we have need of the spiritual sensitivity, intellectual creativity, solidary intuition, and wholly liberating vision of Medellín.

Medellín's Demands on the Current Church and Theologies

In the light of the paths mapped out by Medellín, I wish to conclude these reflections by suggesting some aspects of the demands Medellín continues to make of the Church and current theologies for a future free of kyriarchal domination.

The prophetic nature of Medellín stems from its announcement and experience of the Gospel in its transforming radicalness within realities framed by conflict, injustice, and institutionalized violence (Peace 16). Through its clear position of support for excluded groups, Medellín nourishes the hopes of these groups, defends their interests against the dominant powers, denounces the roots of oppression, sin and violence, gives them the religious reasons that inspire their struggles for global change, and marks their pathway for active participation in the historical realisation of God's saving purpose. Medellín's radical prophecy continues to demand of the Church and theology an attitude of greater honesty and courage to confront the circumstances of sin and misery that still beleaguer our peoples. Since the Medellín vision, the plundering of our fundamental rights that we women experience can no longer be hidden, silenced, and much less permitted. In the light of this, I would like to underline just five of the demands that Medellín continues to make.

Tell the truth about reality. In the present situation, the Church and theology must confront more critically and with greater courage the economic and socio-political processes produced by the globalization of kyriarchal neoliberalism, which incessantly diminish our peoples' quality of life. For this reason, we have to strengthen the global forces that are deep-rooted in communities, cultures, and socio-ecclesial movements struggling for an alternative civilization, with greater humanization and the elimination of kyriarchal violence. Based on the Christian vision of justice, human dignity and common good, the Church and theology must incorporate the critical theories of systemic analysis, critical feminist theories and the recent intercultural and interracial studies that help us examine the liberating identity of Christianity.

Confront the sin of systemic kyriarchy and sexism. For Medellín, the structural sin is the systematic negation of salvation (Justice 3, Peace 1). This central idea refers to the organisation of everything social in structures that create and reproduce unjust relationships in people's public and private life. Moreover, with this idea Medellín means to expose the moral and religious responsibility of persons and social groups in relation to the structures, institutions and ideologies created by human action that violate people's dignity and prohibit the integrity of creation. In this sense, structural injustice, generated by the kyriarchal organization of the Church and society, must be confronted by the current Church and theology, because the kyriarchal order constitutes a permanent base of structural sin. The time has come for Latin American liberation theology to name and confront the sin of sexism.

Violence against women and the social teachings of the ecclesiastical hierarchy. Medellín understands that 'the sense of service and realism demands of today's hierarchy a greater social sensitivity and objectivity. In that regard there is a need for direct contact with the different social-professional groups ... to articulate social doctrine applying to our problems' (Justice 18). The purpose of the ecclesiastical hierarchy's social teaching is 'restoring justice in human relations' (Justice 22). In this light, Medellín continues to challenge the ability of the ecclesiastical hierarchy, theology and the Church as a whole, to approach with greater sensitivity the serious problem of social, family and domestic violence that affects the vast majority of Latin American women. In addition to the social violence continually experienced by indigenous and black women, domestic, sexual and racial violence is an everyday part of such women's existence and has a very damaging effect on their lives. Medellín demands that theologians, bishops and priests have direct contact with the victims of this violence and direct dialogue with feminist and women's movements, in order to establish effective platforms of joint work to confront the serious problem of injustice within our midst.

The feminist option for the poor. As I have said elsewhere[45] for modern theoretical reason the option for the poor is a scandal, and madness for postmodern neoliberal thinking. But for a *Mestiza woman* like me, daughter of a grassroot rural family, still struggling with anguish and uncertainty (Poverty 3), the option for the poor and oppressed is a source of strength and wisdom. This option is not for abstract faces and bodies, but for those who survive, resist and struggle from the bottom of the kyriarchal pyramid: marginalized women and their dependants. As a Christian and Catholic theologian, Medellín continues to demand I work for the destiny of my people and stand by their side. As a woman, Christian and theologian, Medellín inspires my commitment to live my feminist theological vocation in active involvement for advancing toward new cultures, new ways of humanizing relationship, and a new Church free from all kinds of kyriarchal domination. In the present reality, however, Medellín demands of the Church and of all theologians, a conscious and deliberate choice to promote greater justice and respect for the rights of women that are still dictated to us by the kyriarchal hegemony, and a deliberate commitment to incorporate grassroot women in critical theological activity.

Commitment to new Church structures. Taking into account the nature of the Church, Medellín planted the seed to begin the serious revision of ecclesial structures 'in order to satisfy the requirements of concrete historical situations', but in observance of the communion and catholicity (Pastoral de Conjunto 5). Medellín's vision of the identity and mission of the Church includes the search for new models, free of clericalism and kyriarchal domination. The principles Medellín considers the Church should articulate are solidarity, collegiality and communion. (Pastoral de Conjunto 7, 9). This vision of the Church, because it is supported by the intrinsic baptismal and anthropological dignity of every believer, accepts the revision of ecclesial structures with the aim of eliminating the exclusion of women. A new Church model, which responds to the challenges of the historical situations in the third millennium, must eliminate such judicial, sacramental and theological exclusion. In fact – and I believe there is little argument against this – the judicial exclusion of women from the presidency of sacraments, is only resulting in the utter abandonment of countless poor communities of God's People. In my view, it is not the faith of the people that 'needs' someone to lead it, but rather the institutional Church that needs the faith of the poor in order to learn what is meant by communion, solidarity and catholicity. Because of their immense

---

[45] María Pilar Aquino, 'Theological Method in U.S. Latino/a Theology: Toward an Intercultural Theology for the Third Millennium', in *From the Heart of our people: Latino/a Explorations in Catholic Systematic Theology*, Orlando O. Espín and Miguel H. Díaz, (eds.), Orbis Books, Maryknoll NY, 1999, 29-32, 41.

generosity and deep nobility, our peoples living in isolated geographical areas would certainly welcome someone from *their own midst* to formerly preside over their sacraments, ceremonies and rituals. When the lives of the People of God are at stake, whether one is a woman or a man should be of secondary importance. In addition, the silence of male and female Latin American theologians over the exclusion of women in Roman Catholicism is only helping to maintain kyriarchal hegemony within the Church. Our silence has not resulted in an improvement of either the situation or the position of Catholic women in the Church. That is why I believe there will be no new civilization unless we join forces to rectify what I. Ellacuría calls 'the mistaken paths'[46] of societies and the Church. Medellín asks us to discard the old structures and calls upon us to don the warm robes of true communion, solidarity, collegiality, and catholicity. We envisage here a Church that seeks to bring together all the global forces to establish universal justice in a world where there is room for every one.

---

[46] Ignacio Ellacuría, *Conversión de la Iglesia al Reino de Dios. Para Anunciarlo y Realizarlo en la Historia*, Sal Terrae, Santander 1984, p. 122.

Truth, Memory and 'New World' Theology: In Search of Interpretative Tools

JASON GORDON

May my blood be the seed of liberty, and a sign of hope that will soon become a reality.

(Oscar Romero)

The memories of Archbishop Oscar Romero and Bishop Juan Gerardi, are mediated through our interpretative framework. It is this framework, which we seldom investigate, that grounds our memory in truth or fiction, or constructed realities. This chapter is an attempt to reflect critically upon the interpretative framework of theology that has emerged in the 'New World' in the post 1968 era. The first part of the chapter will trace the early development of this theology with its fragmentation into multiple interpretative frameworks. In the second part, the chapter will delve into the act of interpretation in an attempt to ground the truth claims of this theology. And in the third part, it will explore a historiography that pushes theology beyond the fragmentation of our interpretative tools. The conclusion of the work uses this new reading to shed light upon the history explored through a reading of the facts from a different perspective. The thesis of this chapter is that theology starting with a commitment to liberative praxis, is in the service of truth and memory.

The Emergence of 'New World' Theology 1960–70

The five hundred year history of theology grounding itself in the life options of 'New World' peoples has had many departures. In recent memory, the most significant for Catholics, was the council of Vatican II, followed by the meeting of Latin American Bishops in Medellín. The paradigmatic shift of theology in the 'New World', towards liberation has its genesis here. In the late fifties and early sixties there was a growing student movement in Latin America experimenting with sociology as a way of gaining access to the truth of society. This ferment within the universities spread through the continent raising new issues, calling for a new way of being authentic.[1] This new awareness, together with the new tools available to analyse the social context, led to the radicalization of those committed to the cause of the poor. This mobilization gradually led to a critical dissatisfaction with the current theological paradigm – theology of development. The latter was dualistic and blind to the issue of injustice as the root cause of poverty.[2] About this period Peruvian theologian Gustavo Gutierrez says:

> The political radicalization of the continent led growing numbers of Christian groups to a revolutionary stance. At first, faith appeared as the motivation and justification for a revolutionary commitment, stripping it of every ideological element, which falsifies a cruel and conflictual social reality; the gospel for these Christians was not at variance with but demanded revolution. In this perspective the revolution is more radical and challenging of the whole established order, and the political analysis is more penetrating than in its earlier position.[3]

In the attempt to reflect theologically upon the events of the continent a new way of theologizing was being born. This new theology, by taking its point of departure from the empirical world, sought to be in the service of truth. But, also by becoming more conscious of history and social reality, it uncovered the selective memory of the Christendom model of Christianity. This new commitment to truth and memory facilitated theology's move away from the classical centres of production – the university – so that it could more adequately grapple with the life situations of the majority of the people. The change in theological locus precipitated a further shift – from a speculative interpretation of ontology, to the commitment of transforming social reality in the light of the Gospel. The concreteness of this task forced theology to leave behind its traditional dialogue partner (philosophy) and engage in dialogue with the social sciences. Theology left the Ghetto of the Christendom model in which it was confined to an intra-ecclesial dialogue. Having thus left, it took residence within the secular city; its

---

[1] Robert Oliveros Maqueo, 'Meeting of Theologians at Petropolis' (March 1964), in Hennelly Alfred T. (ed.), *Liberation Theology: A Documentary History*, New York, Orbis, 1990, pp. 43–47.

[2] See Monika Hellwig, 'Liberation Theology: An Emerging School', *Scottish Journal of Theology*, 30(1977) 137–151.

[3] Gustavo Gutierrez, 'Faith As Freedom: Solidarity with The Alienated and Confidence in the Future', *Horizons*, 2 (Spring 1975) 25–60.

new function was to be midwife of a more humane world. The conceptual grammar of the former dialogue revolved around a sin-redemption paradigm. The new grammar that emerged was liberation, creation, and life. The former paradigm was confined to the realm of religion; the new paradigm opened religion to the experience of ordinary people in their search for a meaningful life.

By July 1968 Gustavo Gutierrez, in a keynote address at Chimbote, Peru, coined the term 'Liberation Theology.'[4] In essence it was asking a new question – How could we speak an honest word about the God of love to a people who only experienced oppression? This new word about God (theo-logos) demands a dismantling of the structures of oppression through a commitment to truth. This was not a new theology – as Juan Louis Segundo points out – it was a new way of doing theology.[5] The theologian could not stay in the ivory tower; s/he had to descend to the reality of the social context. As such, it was not about a theology of liberation, as much as it was about the liberation of theology.[6] And, thus, represents an epistemological rupture with classical theology. Making deliberate choice on the level of ontology and ideology. Its evaluative – or rather, epistemological principle – is the preferential option for the poor.[7] This theology, thus, uses an anthropological base to make options on the level of ideology (historical projects) and ontology (the level of meaning). Thus, what is observable – the anthropological – becomes criterion for evaluating what is more intangible. Any theology seeking relevance in the post-1968 era must rigorously scrutinize these four categories – ideology, ontology, epistemology and anthropology. Scrutiny on this level is the only real assurance that theology can have of being liberative.

[4] This talk was first published in Lima, then in Montevideo, Gustavo Gutierrez, 'Hacia una teologia de la liberacion', MIEC-JECI (first series, 16), Montevideo, 1969. Later it was published in English as 'Towards a Theology of Liberation', *Theological Studies*, 31(1970) 243–261. It finally became the most influential text of the movement; Gustavo Gutierrez, *A Theology of Liberation* (1971), New York, Orbis, 1973; London, SCM, 1974.

[5] See: Theo Witvliet, *A Place in the Sun: An Introduction to Liberation Theology In the Third World*. London: SCM, 1985; Rosino Gibellini,. *The Liberation Theology Debate*, London, SCM, 1987. These two give a good overview. For the methodology of Liberation Theology; Leonardo and Clodovis Boff, *Introducing Liberation Theology*, New York, Orbis, 1986.

[6] Juan Louis Segundo coined this tern in the title of his book; Juan Louis Segundo, *The Liberation of Theology*, New York, Orbis, 1976. This book demonstrates that theology itself has been used as one of the weapons of oppression in understanding the discussion on epistemology it is an important work.

[7] For an understanding of this concept See, Frostin, P. 'The Hermeneutics of the Poor – The epistemological "Break" in Third World Theologies'. In *Studia Theologica* 39(1985) 127–250; T. Witvliet, op. cit. R. Gibellini, op. cit. Cormie Lee, 'The Hermeneutical Privilege of the Oppressed' *CTSA* 33 (1978) 155–181.

The Medellín Conference of Latin American Bishops (1968) gave strong ecclesiastic support to this new direction of theology. But Gutierrez was not the only theologian pushing forward the theological frontiers. In Latin America Juan Louis Segundo had already published his, *Función de la Iglesia en la Realidad Rioplatense* (1962), and 'The Future of Christianity in Latin America' (1963).[8] Hugo Assman published *Opresion-Liberacion. Desafio a los Cristianos* in 1971,[9] and the Brazilian theologian Leonardo Boff published his *Jesus Christ Liberator* in 1972.[10] The theological ferment in the 'New World' was toppling the old paradigms.

Independently of Gutierrez and Latin America, Mary Daly in North America published her *The Church and The Second Sex*,[11] thus ushering in the Feminist theological tradition. Also in North America, James Cone came to the notion of liberation through his reflections on Martin Luther King, Malcolm X, and the Civil Rights movement. In 1969 Cone published *Black Theology and Black Power*.[12] At the same time in Europe Johann Baptist Metz[13] and Jürgen Moltmann[14] were working out their political theologies and theologies of hope, both of these reflecting upon the situation of oppressed peoples. In the English-speaking Caribbean the 1971 publications in preparation for the Caribbean Ecumenical consultation for development ruptured the five hundred year tradition of colonial missiology.[15] This was taken further with the 1973 publication of the papers for the Christology conference, *Troubling of the Waters*.[16]

The lecture by Gutierrez, the Medellín conference, and the publica-

---

[8] Juan Luis Segundo, *Función de la Iglesia en la Realidad Rioplatense*, Montevideo: Barreiro y Ramos 1962; Juan Luis Segundo, 'The Future of Christianity in Latin America', in *Cross Currents*, 13 (summer 1963) 273–281.

[9] This was taken up and reworked into; Hugo Assman, *Theology for a Nomad Church* (1973), New York, Orbis, 1976.

[10] Leonardo Boff, *Jesus Christ Liberator*, New York, Orbis, 1978 [1972].

[11] Mary Daly, *The Church and The Second Sex*, London, G. Chapman, 1968.

[12] James Cone, *Black Theology and Black Power*, New York, Seabury, 1969.

[13] Johann Baptist Metz, *Theology of the World*, New York, Herder & Herder,1967.

[14] Jürgen Moltmann, *Theology of Hope: On the Ground and the Implications for a Christian Eschatology*, London, SCM, 1967.

[15] Idris Hamid, *In Search of New Perspectives*, Bridgetown, Barbados, Caribbean Ecumenical Consultation for development, 1971; Seon Goodridge, *Politics and The Caribbean Church: A Confession of Guilt*, Study Paper 2, Bridgetown, Barbados, 1971; Caribbean Ecumenical for development; P.A. Edwards, *Education for Development In the Caribbean*, Study Paper 3, Bridgetown, Barbados; Caribbean Ecumenical for development, 1971; William Demas, *The Political Economy of the English Speaking Caribbean: A Summary View*, Study Paper 4, Bridgetown, Barbados; Caribbean Ecumenical for development, 1971; Michael McCormack, *Liberation or Development: The Role of the Church in the New Caribbean*, Study Paper 5, Bridgetown, Barbados; Caribbean Ecumenical for development, 1971.

[16] Idris Hamid (ed.), *Troubling of the Waters*, Trinidad, Published by author, 1973.

tion of *A Theology of Liberation* were just the opening of the flood gates; by 1975 there appeared numerous publications in leading journals, and books and several conferences which fostered further reflection on the movement. From then on, however, liberation theology has been under suspicion and attack from the official Church.[17] It still flourishes in grass root communities. Other 'Third World' countries quickly caught on, each new context using the shift in theological paradigm and the method of socio-analytical mediation, hermeneutical mediation and practical mediation, to find the truth of their society by honouring the memory of the oppressed.

Liberation and Methodology

Theology in this context saw commitment to the praxis of liberation as the first step. The second step involved the word of God and the tradition of the Church shedding light on the truth of sin, dehumanisation and oppression. By shining this light, theology points to a new and more authentic way of being Christian within this specific context.[18] The first definition of theology that comes from Gutierrez in 1968 describes theology as 'a critical function of the pastoral action of the church'.[19] By 1973 in *A Theology of Liberation*, the definition had changed significantly to: 'Theology as a critical reflection on Christian

---

[17] The first attack was directed at Gutierrez, see: Sacred Congregation For Doctrine Of The Faith, (1983), 'Ten Observations on the Theology of Gustavo Gutierrz', in Hennelly Alfred T. (ed.), *Liberation Theology: A Documentary History*, New York, Orbis, 1990. The second was more general, see: Sacred Congregation For Doctrine Of The Faith, *Instruction on certain aspects of the 'Theology of Liberation'*, Vatican City, Vatican Polyglot Press, 1984. This document was a full-scale attack on liberation theology. It never really dealt with the real issues, as it was a parody of the position of the theologians. For a good critique of it, see: Juan Louis Segundo, *Theology and the Church: A Response to Cardinal Ratzinger and a Warning to The Whole Church*, London, Geoffrey Chapman, 1985. The third significant attack was of Leonardo Boff, see: Sacred Congregation For Doctrine Of The Faith, 1985, 'Notification Sent to Fr. Leonardo Boff regarding Errors in His Book, Church Charism and Power', in Hennelly Alfred T. (ed.), *Liberation Theology: A documentary History*, New York, Orbis, 1990, pp. 425–430. For Boff's response to the charges see: Leonardo Boff, 1984, 'Defence of his Book, Chruch Charism and Power', in Hennelly Alfred T. (ed.), *Liberation Theology: A documentary History*, New York, Orbis, 1990, pp. 431–435. The next document, a second general instruction, was much better in tone and content. It opened with an appreciation for the notion of liberation as a Paradigm in Christian theology; Sacred Congregation For Doctrine Of The Faith, *Instruction on Christian Freedom and Liberation*, London, Catholic Media Office, 1986.

[18] See, Boff, op. cit. chapter 3.

[19] Gustavo Gutierrez, *La pastoral de la Iglesia en America Latina*, MIEC-JECI, Montevideo, 1968.

praxis in the light of the Word.'[20] This definition further changed by 1983 with the publication of *The Power of The Poor In History*. Here speaking about Latin America Gutierrez says:

> Theology in this context will be a critical reflection both from within, and upon, historical praxis, in confrontation with the word of the Lord as lived and accepted in faith ... a faith that comes down to us through manifold and sometimes ambiguous historical mediations.[21]

In all of these definitions there is one common link: theology is always a second act in a process of action faith and reflection. Theology is neither the beginning of the process nor is it an end in itself, it is in the service of pastoral action (1968), historical praxis (1971–83) or Christian praxis (1973). Theology presupposes a first act to reflect upon; it presupposes faith born out of love and hope as an adequate response to a specific socio-cultural context; it presupposes a spirituality. Each new context raised new challenges and broadened the scope of the method and content of this theology. It is now generally recognized that we are dealing with Liberation Theologies. This plurality witnesses to the richness and the fertility of the theological exercise.[22] Within this plurality, theology seeking to be liberative must employ tools of analysis that expose and overcome oppression, both at the level of concrete economic and political oppression, and also at the level of

---

[20] Gustavo Gutierrez, *A Theology Of Liberation*, p. 13. In fact this represents more than one shift, since the definition of the 1971 original Peruvian edition, *Teologia de la liberacion*, CEP, Lima 1971, 31, translates 'Theology as critical reflection from historical praxis in the light of faith'.

[21] Gustavo Gutierrez, *The Power Of The Poor In History*, London, SCM, 1983, p. 60. Further on in the passage Gutierrez expands his definition – he says: 'Hence theology in Latin America today will be a reflection in, and on, faith as liberation praxis. It will be an understanding of the faith from a point of departure in real, effective solidarity with the exploited classes, oppressed ethnic groups, and despised cultures of Latin America, and from within their world. It will be a reflection that starts out from a commitment to create a just society, a community of sisters and brothers, and that ought to see that this commitment grows more radical and complete.' The addition of the cultural elements into this definition and even in the one in the text had caused Juan Louis Segundo to speak about two theologies of liberation, see: Juan Louis Segundo, 'Two theologies of Liberation', in *The Month* (October 1984) 321–27.

[22] See: D.W. Ferm, *Third World Liberation Theologies*, NY, Orbis, 1985; T. Witvliet, op. cit. This theological method has now given expression to the religious aspirations of disenfranchised people around the globe. The Black in America, the Palestinians in the Middle East, Christians who are minority religion in Asia, Africa and its search to root Christianity within an ancestral pass. Women in the 'First and Third Worlds' have all used some variation of this theology to articulate their Christian hope for liberation from concrete oppression. We in the Caribbean are no exception.

the project of theology itself.[23] Liberation must be at once theological and soteriological. But we must remember that methodological adequacy hinges upon liberating praxis.

The Problems of Methodology

From this early stage the new theology responding to the context of the Americas was split along different axes. Latin America, responding to the crisis of poverty and distribution of wealth, promoted class analysis and Marx's historical dialectics as a tool for reading the social reality. North America, responding to oppression of women and blacks, went in very different directions. For the oppression of women, patriarchy as a hermeneutic of suspicion was employed to interpret the latent structures of the social reality. The black community, on the other hand, employed race analysis as a hermeneutic of suspicion thus unmasking structural racism. In the Caribbean, race was subsumed into the general sphere of culture. Theology emerging in the Caribbean employed two different tools of cultural analysis – cultural anthropology and literary analysis.

These strands of 'New World' theology emerged in the same period and have similar histories. Linda Moody, in her book *Women Encounter God: Theology across the Boundaries of Difference*, documents the emergence of cultural reading within the gendered discourse of North America.[24] As early as 1970 black women had started to critique black theology and its blindness to the issue of gender.[25] This was not unique to feminism. In 1975, with the Detroit conference 'Theology in the Americas',[26] it became evident that white middle class North Americans could not speak for all groups on the continent. Gregory Baum recognized that race, and thus culture, was splitting the theological discourse of liberation. The Catholicity of Hispanic and African-Americans was held in suspicion by the white North Americans. Within this conference European theological tradition remained the governing norm and this was imposed upon all other cultural groupings.[27] The split in the discourse along the lines of race and culture led to the growing consciousness of black and Hispanic American women. As they had

[23] For an exploration of the claims of rupture see, Juan Louis Segundo, *The Liberation of Theology*, NY, Orbis Books, 1985.
[24] Linda Moody, *Women Encounter God: Theology across the Boundaries of Difference*, NY. Orbis, 1996.
[25] See Toni Cade (ed.), *The Black Woman: An Anthology*, New York, New American Library, 1970 (pp. 383ff).
[26] Sergio Torres and John Eagleson, *Theology in the Americas*, NY, Orbis, 1976.
[27] Gregory Baum, 'The Christian Left at Detroit', in Sergio Torres and John Eagleson, *Theology in the Americas*, NY, Orbis, (1976)411–4, 412.

introduced a gendered reading into black theology and Latin American liberation theology, they soon pushed for their own voice renaming their projects in North America, womanist and Mujerista theologies, respectively.[28] The ethic of sisterhood and solidarity within feminist discourse came under the cold light of cultural reading and was found wanting. It is apparent that no single tool, whether Marx's historical dialectics, cultural analysis or the critique of patriarchy, is sufficient to mediate the structures of oppression of the 'New World'. Each of these tools contribute a significant reading. But each leaves out important data thus making its commitment to truth and memory tenuous at best.

During 20–23 September 1996, The Centre of Liberation Theology of the University of Leuven hosted an international symposium titled: 'The Paradigm Shift in Third World Theologies of Liberation: From socio-economic Analysis To Cultural Analysis: Assessment and Status of the Question.' The discussions of the symposium were based upon a document prepared specially for the occasion by Professor George De Schrijver, chairperson of the centre. The text of De Schrijver presents a serious challenge to all Third World theology.[29] In reflecting on the continuing commitment of theology to the project of concrete liberation, De Schrijver makes the connection between modernity, capitalism and the dependency of the 'Third World'. Thus, the emergence of liberation theology is cast within the broader interpretative framework of European economic and cultural transformation. It was the ideological framework of modernity and capitalism that kept the 'Third World' underdeveloped. The emergence of Liberation theology is a challenge to modernity and its imperialist ideology. In its genesis, Latin American liberation theology used Marxist analysis to mediate the social reality. This analysis says De Schrijver, '... wagers on the power of the exploited class to debunk the mystification's of those ideologies that call for conformity'.[30] Built into the analysis was the gathering of the exploited into one group – a social class – who resisted and overthrew the dominant class and their ideology. The mass mobilisation of the exploited is seen as the key to social change.

De Schrijver notes that the fragmentation of the oppressed into several interest groups negates the potential of mass mobilisation. He says:

[28] See, Delores S. Williams, 'Women's oppression and lifeline politics in black women's religious narratives,' *Journal of Feminist Studies in Religion*, 2 (Fall 1985) 59–71; Katie Geneva Cannon, *Black Womanist Ethics*, Atlanta, GA, Scolars Press, 1988; Ada María Isasi-Díaz, *Hispanic Women: Prophetic Voice in the Church*, San Francisco: Harper and Row, 1988.

[29] George De Schrijver, *The Paradigm Shift in Third World Theologies of liberation: From Socio-Economic Analysis to Cultural Analysis. Assessment and Status of The Question*, Leuven, Preprint, Bibliotheek van De Faculteit Godgeleerdheid, 1996.

[30] De Schrijver, p. 25.

What is mainly striking is not only the fragmented panorama of the fields of action but also the determination to uncouple those fields from any unifying centre that might command the march for revolutionary change.[31]

The shift from a unity of the oppressed in one social class to a multiplication of groups each searching for their cultural identity has serious implications for the liberation of the oppressed. Thus, in De Schrijver's evaluation, the challenge of the three readings has weakened the theology by fragmenting the oppressed. This Marxist reading does not take seriously the cultural challenge. Nor does it take seriously the plurality of the 'New World' context.

The potency of Marx as a tool of analysis is its ability to read the reality collecting the disenfranchised into one group – the proletariat. The emergence of race and gender as other modes of social discourse has challenged, not only the methodological base of Marx's analysis, but also its practical efficacy. What is clear is that any reading of the social reality demands the three-fold reading of class, race and gender. The point being that the dominant hermeneutics of the sixties and early seventies could not adequately read the subtleties of the complex reality, which were socio-political, cultural and gendered.

The methodological shift to incorporate gender and race over the last three decades has been read by De Schrijver as a degenerative process. But here it must be asked whether De Schrijver's commitment to a homogeneous movement that fits the reading and social project of Marx, is not in itself an ideological imposition. I agree here with Kathleen Drayton who claims that: 'The monster we fight has three heads (class, race and gender exploitation), each with its contradictions and strategies of control, and to aim the axe at one head will not destroy it.'[32] Rather than essentializing any of the three constituents (race, class or gender) in the reading of reality, the task is rather to narrate the interaction of the three social forces in the mediation of human action so as to better evaluate their effect upon the pastoral action of the community of faith.

The way forward is to shift focus from the competition between the three, to seeing each of these as a part of the whole complex manipulation of the social reality in the service of sustaining power. The issue at hand is one of mediation of social reality. Theologies that claim to be liberative stand or fall by their in/ability to perform this task. To

---

[31] De Schrijver, pp. 30–31.

[32] Kathleen Drayton, 'White Man's Knowledge: Sex, Race and Class in Caribbean English Language Textbooks', in Elsa Leo-Rhynie, Barbara Bailey and Christine Barrow (eds.), *Gender – A Caribbean Multi-Disciplinary Perspective*, Kingston, Ian Randle Publishers, 1997, p. 159.

move the project of theology forward we must explore again the art of mediation – hermeneutics.

Once theology begins with a critical reflection upon human action (praxis) rather than a reflection upon transcendental data, the terms of the enterprise have dramatically shifted. This shift has raised a methodological problem with two parts. (1) Finding an adequate tool to mediate the historical praxis (human action) of the community of faith so that (2) race class and gender are read as integral and organic aspects of the social reality. The first part of the problematic revolves around a hermeneutic that can read and re-interpret human action. It assures that theology is connected to truth. The second part necessitates that this tool reads social reality as an integral whole. This assures that theology does not suffer from promoting partial memory. Put differently, we could ask the question: How do we mediate the historical praxis of a community of faith, so as to challenge and expose the sedimentary paradigms of its civilization, that the act of re-presenting may challenge the historical engagement of the community opening it to new and more fruitful possibilities for discipleship? For the hermeneutics of human action we will look to Paul Ricoeur. For the overcoming of the false divisions in the social reality we will follow the historiography of Fernand Braudel.

Paul Ricoeur: Hermeneutics of Action

Theology here is a second act in a process of action, faith and reflection. Theology is neither the beginning of the process, nor is it an end in itself; it is dependent upon a mediation of historical praxis with the aim of renewing the community. To explore the concept of mediation we will follow Paul Ricoeur's work in *Time and Narrative*.[33] Mediation for Ricoeur is linked to the interplay of the Greek concepts of emplotment (the act of constructing a plot) and 'mimesis' (representation). Emplotment in Ricoeur is the active organization of the individual and dispirit elements into a systematic whole.[34] The emphasis here is on the active organization and active stresses selection, and thus motive and criterion. It is the composition or the creation of a plot. Mimesis, on the other hand, is imitation or representation, not in the platonic sense of copy of the pre-existent. It is creative imitation, that in itself opens a space for interpretation, or mediation. It opens a space between the object being represented and that which is received. It is this understanding of mimesis and emplotment that open to new interpretations.

---

[33] See Paul Ricoeur, *Time and Narrative*, Vol. 1, Chicago, University of Chicago Press, 1984.
[34] Ricoeur, *Time and Narrative* Ch. 2. The Greek word Ricoeur uses is *Muthos*; for simplicity I would use the English 'emplotment'.

In mediation there are three phases that must be held together. The first phase, which Ricoeur calls mimesis$_1$, is the precondition for all action. An act in a cultural vacuum would signify nothing. It is only because we share a cultural world of meaning and paradigms that govern the interpretation of this common world, that an act can convey meaning to another. Thus, the first phase of interpretation is beyond both the world of the interpreter and of the receiver. Here the precondition for act is identified through three features – the semantic, symbolic and the temporal. The semantic features of interpretation would be the rules governing the construction of the act. In this case, the aesthetic and technical rules of history. The symbolic would refer to shared meaning system to which we refer to as a cultural world. The temporal would refer to the different dimensions of time, for to speak of action is to speak of time and its passage.

It is the second phase – mimesis$_2$ or emplotment – where the signifiers are configured into a whole. The individual events of history, in itself, may mean different things depending upon how they are connected. Through emplotment, the elements of our shared culture are used, sometimes in new ways, with nuances that had not been there before. Emplotment is thus about composition. This connecting of dispirit elements, whether in history, literature, or art, reconfigures the common cultural elements opening them to new meaning. This middle phase (mimesis$_2$) is both inspiration and reflection through interpretation and reinterpretation.

The third phase (mimesis$_3$) is the reception of the work by its audience. In this phase the intersection of the world created by the piece of art – whether it be text or building – and the world of the receiver, restores the work or art to the time where action and transformation takes place. The transformative power of interpretation, although it takes place in this third phase, is only possible because of the integrity of the link between the three phases. The completion of the process of mediation, the process which allows mediation to be transformative within society, only occurs in the reception of the dispirit signifiers that the work configured into a whole.[35] Thus it is the act of reading that connects precondition for action (mimesis$_1$) to emplotment (mimesis$_2$), but it also connects the emplotment to the final stage in the hermeneutic circle – mimesis$_3$. Thus it is by connecting the three stages of mimesis that we 'institute the mediation between time and narrative'.[36] It is this mediation that leads to refiguration of the temporal experience. Thus, the act of reading is 'our connection to the capacity of a plot to model our experience'.[37] Further on he says:

[35] Ricoeur, *Time and Narrative*, p. 70.
[36] Ricoeur, *Time and Narrative*, p. 71.
[37] Ricoeur, *Time and Narrative*, p. 71.

It is the final indicator of the refiguring of the world of action under the sign of the plot.[38] It is this capacity of the plot to refigure the world of action that opens reading back to new dimensions in the exploration of truth, when it is used in conjunction with history.

The process of mediation involves taking all the dispirit parts of this complex web we call society, or religion, and re-presenting them in a way that ruptures our old paradigms, thus, re-presenting to the community new possibilities. Or as Ricoeur says:

> The task of hermeneutics is to charter the unexplored resources of the to-be-said on the basis of the already said. Imagination never resides in the unsaid.[39]

In Latin America, theology employed Marx's historical dialectics as a tool of mediation. Theological reflection here operates within the space and grounding of the lived reality. This, when brought to thematization is history – the historical unfolds our existence. But here again the problem at hand was hermeneutics. Thus, the search here was for a historical methodology to thematize (read configure) our lived experience in such a way that critical reflection upon it would allow us to recognise and locate ourselves within the complex web of social relationships. This recognition would allow a new way of interpreting our lived experience, leading to new ways of being faithful to the Gospel (read catharsis). Here hermeneutics begins in, and returns to, the world of action. Through an investigation of the notions of mimesis and emplotment, Ricoeur explored the task of hermeneutics at another level – not as a clarifier of ideas, but rather oriented to catharsis.

The process of themetizing – emplotment – becomes a pivotal stage in the process of representing reality. In this approach to the historical, the object is not to represent reality 'as it actually happened'; such a task of history has already been exposed as an illusion. The task, moreover, is to represent, or rather, to themetize our lived experience in such a way as to engender recognition and location of the individual and group within the complex web of the social reality. This recognition of the self or group, when combined with the reconfiguration of the reading of reality through challenging the sedimentary paradigms and proposing alternative ones, opens hermeneutics to the reconfiguration of the world of action – the lived reality of the community of faith: catharsis.

Within this schema Braudel, a French historian of the Anales

---

[38] Ricoeur, *Time and Narrative*, p. 77.
[39] R. Kearney, 1984, p. 25.

schools, gives a theory of history which allows praxis to be thematised as narrative history. In *Time and Narrative*, Paul Ricoeur argues convincingly for the theory of history of Fernand Braudel as a tool of mediation of action. This theory of history, Ricoeur shows, has a dual character. For it is at once governed by the covering law – it thus is rooted in truth and science. It is also governed by the laws of narrative – it mediates reality through the complex of emplotment and mimesis.

Overcoming the Divide: Braudelian Historiography

Fernand Braudel's (1902–1985) seminal thesis and classic study, *La Méditerranée et le Monde Méditerranéen à L'Epoque de Phillippe II* (*Mediterranean and the Mediterranean World in the Age of Philippe II*) was published in 1949 and revolutionized historical writing. The work focuses upon geographical space as the backdrop to a three-layered understanding of history which unfolds at three speeds or time spans: the deep currents of geo-history relating to the environment, the quicker currents of economic and socio-political history, and the immediate surface history of historical events. Events for Braudel were mirrors revealing underlying structures to which more attention should be paid. They had to be located and interpreted within the much deeper currents of history.

In writing about the Atlantic, Braudel says:

> ... the Mediterranean shaped the Atlantic and impressed its own image on the Spanish 'New World'.[40] His sensitivity to the 'New World' was cultivated during a teaching assignment in San Palo Brazil in the 1930s. Latin American scholars have been deeply influenced by his work.[41]

Braudel was a member of the Annales school founded in 1929 by Lucien Febvre and Mark Bloch with the creation of a new interdisciplinary and international journal: *Annales d'historie Economique et Sociale*.[42] The school was a reaction against an older historiographical approach. They reacted against historical discourse that was conducted in isolation from other related disciplines. A growing recognition emerged that their answers no longer fitted the new questions being

---

[40] Fernand Braudel, *The Mediterranean and the Mediterranean World in the Age of Philip II*, London, BCA, 1992 [1949] p. 165.

[41] Peter Burke, *The French Historical Revolution: The Annales School 1929–89*, Cambridge, Polity Press, 1990; Alan Knight, 'Latin America', in Michael Bentley (ed.), *Companion To Historiography*, London, Routledge, 1997, pp. 728–758.

posed by life, culture and the emerging social sciences. At the height of its glory, Ranke would speak of the 'the solid ground of history', believing that history related 'things just as they really happened'. But the ordinary people rarely figured, except as landscape against which the important could be cast. Braudel wrote:

> The problem of history is not to be found in the relationship between painter and painting, nor even, though some have thought such a suggestion excessively daring, in the relationship between the painting and the landscape. The problem is right in the landscape, in the heart of life itself.[43]

The new history aimed at 'history from below' or total history relating to the economic, the domestic, history of art, the image, the family and the many strands of life. It had to be in dialogue with social sciences: sociology, anthropology, geography, psychology, etc. The new history realized that it was life that caused the greatest challenge for history – its complexity, 'fast motion', 'fleeting spectacle', 'web of problems meshed inextricably together', the multiple and, yes, contradictory perspectives available. Braudel asks: 'How should one tackle such a complex, living entity and break it up so as to be able to lay hold of it, or at least of some part of it?'[44] The failures of those who have gone before are there as witness to the difficulties. Gone is the notion of an all-embracing dominant factor able to explain all – 'There is no unilateral history'. Gone, too, is the cult of heroes – there are no individuals entirely sealed off-from the deeper current flowing. Braudel says:

> ... all individual enterprise is rooted in a more complex reality, an 'intermeshed' reality, as sociology calls it. The question is not to deny the individual on the grounds that he is the prey of contingency, but somehow to transcend him, to distinguish him from the forces separate from him, to react against a history arbitrarily reduced to the role of quintessential heroes. We do not believe in this cult of demigods, or to put it even more simply, we are against Treitschke's proud and unilateral declaration: 'Men make history'. No, history also makes men and fashions their destiny – anonymous history, working in the depths and most often in silence, whose domain immense and uncertain as it is, we must now approach.[45]

This is Braudel's great insight. The complexity of life demands that the

---

[42] Burke, *The French Historical Revolution*.
[43] Fernand Braudel, *On History*, Chicago, University of Chicago Press, 1982, p. 9.
[44] Braudel, *On History*, p. 10.
[45] Braudel, *On History*, p. 10.

whole be investigated, not just the peaks (great events or heroic actions), but the valleys (the deeper currents into which the events and the heroes are enmeshed). Again Braudel says:

> Unless I am much mistaken, the fundamental movement of history today is not one of choosing between this or that path, or different point of view, but of accepting and absorbing all the successive definitions in which, one after another, there have been attempts to confine it. For all the different kinds of history belong to us.[46]

The Annales School is, by definition, interdisciplinary. Its new impetus has come from reworking the role of history in relation to the other social sciences. It has become known for its meeting of the different social sciences in a mutual exchange. Braudel says:

> From that time on, the historian has wanted to be, and has become, an economist, sociologist, anthropologist, demographer, psychologist, linguist. These new meetings of the mind were at the same time meetings of friends and of feelings.[47]

But within this interdisciplinary exchange what is history's role? History, like the other social sciences of the time, became imperialistic and sought to become a universal science of the human. After the Second World War, history was faced again with defining its role in this interdisciplinary exchange. Rising to the challenge Braudel gives his definition.

History is a dialectic of the time span; through it, and thanks to it history is a study of society, of the whole of society, and thus of the past, and thus equally of the present, past and present being inseparable. In a remark he repeated again and again during the last ten years of his life, Lucien Febver put it this way: 'History, science of the past, science of the present'.[48]

Two key characteristics of first and second stage Annales history are its problem-centred methodology and its foundation in geography. That history is constructed around a problematic may seem obvious today. In the early years of the Annales it was not so. Febvre in his *Biography on Luther* justifies the project because it is problem-oriented. He devoted himself to 'the problem of the relationship between the individual and the group, between personal initiative and social constraint'.[49]

[46] Braudel, *On History*, p. 66.
[47] Braudel, *On History*, p. 68.
[48] Braudel, *On History*, p. 69.
[49] Burke, *The French*, p. 20.

For Febvre and Braudel geographical space is the indispensable foundation of history.[50] Lucien Febvre insisted that:

> ... at the basis of every civilization are its vital, endlessly repeated links with the environment, links which it creates or rather has to recreate throughout its long destiny, all those elementary and seemingly primitive relationships with the soil, the vegetation, the animal population, endemic diseases.[51]

Or, as Braudel reminds us, all civilizations can be found on a map. Civilization and its particular characteristics are shaped by the interaction of the human with the constraints of geography. The deepest of Braudel's three timespans is the geo-history. For Braudel geography is the stage upon which the actors of history cross. The task of the historian is to narrate the interaction of the actors upon the stage. By shifting the foundation of history to geography, history is grounded in the immovable, the given rather than the construct – economy, class, race or gender. Our three actors, rather than being in competition for primacy, thus carving up the social reality, are simply actors interacting upon the geographical stage. The historian's task is the narration of these actors from three different perspectives of time. Whereas geography allows the grounding of history in reality, it is Braudel's problematic of the different rhythms of time that allows for a multi-layered reading, or what Braudel would call a total history.

History and Time Span

Central to Braudel's theory of history is the notion of timespan. It is through this notion that Braudel opens a new way for the historical endeavour. It is also the significant advancement that he brings to the Annales School. His new task is to move beyond the history of events to the *longue durée*. This necessitates a whole new way of doing history. Braudel says:

> It is precisely our task to get beyond this first stage of history. The social realities must be tackled in themselves and for themselves. By social realities I mean all the major forms of collective life, economics, institutions, social structures, in short and above all, civilizations – all aspects of reality which earlier historians have not exactly overlooked, but which with a few outstanding exceptions

[50] Burke, *The French*, pp. 13–15, 36–37; Fernand Braudel, *A History of Civilisations*, Middlesex, Penguin Books, 1993.
[51] Braudel, *On History*, p. 206.

they have all too often regarded as a backdrop, there only to explain or as if intended to explain the behaviour of the exceptional individuals on whom the historian so completely dwells.[52]

Rather than moving the historical plot along by configuring historical time according to the chronology of events or the great personages, Braudel sees history as a total view of every aspect of society. In this service historical time is divided into three rhythms – (1) the short time span of individuals and events (2) the middle time span related to economic and social history. '... there is an account of conjunctures which lays open large sections of the past, ten, twenty, fifty years at a stretch...'[53] (3) '... the history of the long, even of the very long time span, of the *longue durée*.' This history has a span of centuries, and is moved along by the slow and imperceptible changes at the very structure of society. In another place, Braudel says:

> History exists at different levels, I would even go so far as to say three levels but that would be only in a manner of speaking and simplifying things too much. There are ten, a hundred levels to be examined, ten, a hundred different time spans. On the surface the history of events works itself out in the short term: it is a sort of microhistory. Halfway down, a history of conjunctures follows a broader, slower rhythm. So far that has above all been studied in its developments on the material plane, in economic cycles and intercycles.... And over and above the 'recitatif' of the conjuncture, structural history, or the history of the *longue duree*, inquires into whole centuries at a time. It functions along the border between the moving and the immobile, and because of the long-standing stability of its values, it appears unchanging compared with all the histories which flow and work themselves out more swiftly, and which in the final analysis gravitate around it.[54]

a. The Short Time Span

The three timespans are important to understand Braudel's rupture with earlier historiography and, thus, his own unique approach. The *longue durée*, he continually says, is opposed to 'l'histoire evenementielle', the history of events which is sharp and short and explosive 'its delusive smoke fills the minds of its contemporaries, but it does not last, and its flame can scarcely ever be disregarded.[55] Braudel's contempt for the

---

[52] Braudel, *On History*, p. 11–12.
[53] Braudel, *On History*, p. 27.
[54] Braudel, *On History*, p. 74.
[55] Braudel, *On History*, p. 27.

short time span forms the most consistent perspective from which to understand his views of history.[56] Rather than speaking about history of events, which could be construed variously by philosophers, Braudel prefers to speak about the short time span, which is:

> proportionate to individuals, to daily life, to our illusions, to our hasty awareness – above all the time of the chronicle and the journalist.[57] Social science has almost what amounts to a horror of the event. And not without some justification, for the short time span is the most capricious and the most delusive of all.[58]

Thus the traditional history of the event is distrusted by the Annales School.

b. The Medium Time Span

Conjuncture and cycles: In the recent break within historiography the main shift has been in the changing notions of historical time. The time span has moved beyond the day or the year, which now seem inadequate to chart the deeper movements of economics. Braudel says:

> Time, after all, was made up of an accumulation of days. But a price curve, a demographic progression, the movement of wages, the variations in interests rates, the study ... of productivity, a rigorous analysis of money supply all demand much wider terms of reference.[59]

It is the field of economics which first pushed the time span beyond the short span of the event towards the longer span. Braudel says:

> A new kind of historical narrative has appeared, that of the conjuncture, of cycle, and even of the 'intercycle', covering a decade, a quarter of a century and, at the outside, the half century of Kondratiev's classic cycle.[60]

Braudel's point here is that economic analysis demands an exploration of cycles whose daily fluctuations are often misleading vis-à-vis their life span. It is only by thorough investigation of the cycle, whose span may be one or more decades, that analysis yields truth. Available to the

[56] Braudel, *On History*, p. 4ff., 35–38, 74–75.
[57] Braudel, *On History*, p. 28.
[58] Braudel, *On History*, p. 28.
[59] Braudel, *On History*, p. 29.
[60] Braudel, *On History*, p. 29.

historian now is a new notion of time, one that is 'raised to the level of explication, and that history can attempt to explain itself by dividing itself at new points of reference in response to these curves and to the very way they breathe'.[61]

The weight of history, the need for safety, the conservative pull, have all played their part in shifting the gaze of history back to the short time span, rather than lengthening it beyond the cycle and intercycle to the *longue durée*. Braudel says:

> In all logic, this orchestration of conjunctures, by transcending itself, should have led us straight to the *longue durée*. But for a thousand reasons this transcendence has not been the rule, and a return to the short term is being accomplished even now before our very eyes.[62]

Thus, at the moment when history was poised to move to the next stage of the *longue durée*, it turned back to deal with the 'more urgent' or 'pressing' tasks at hand.

c. The Long Time Span: The Longue Durée

In making the transition between conjunctures and the *longue durée* Braudel again takes his lead from economics. The first key they provide comes from the deliberation of economics about structural crises. Although this discussion was tentative and, thus, not held up for verification and scrutiny, it pushed the time frame beyond the quarter century. The second key came from the concept of structure. Braudel says:

> For good or for ill, this word dominates the problems of the *longue durée*. By structure, observers of social questions mean an organization, a coherent and fairly fixed series of relationships between realities and social masses. For us historians, a structure is of course a construct, an architecture, but over and above that it is a reality which time uses and abuses over long periods. Some structures, because of their long life, become stable elements for an infinite number of generations: they get in the way of history, hinder its flow, and in hindering it shape it. Others wear themselves out more quickly. But all of them provide both support and hindrance. As hindrance they stand as limits (envelopes, in the mathematical sense) beyond which man and his experience cannot go. Just think of the

---

[61] Braudel, *On History*, p. 30.
[62] Braudel, *On History*, p. 30.

difficulties of breaking out of certain geographical frameworks, certain biological realities, certain limits of productivity, even particular spiritual constraints: mental frameworks too can form prisons of the longue duree.[63]

Structure as a way of seeing reality is both help and hindrance. It makes reality interpretable, but it also conceals it. It is this dual notion of structure which allows greater understanding of the longue duree as a historical time-frame. The discernment of structure, its change or resistance to change, demands analysis over centuries. Decades, quarter centuries, or half centuries will not suffice. Braudel gives many examples of structures, which endured in geography, culture, science and art. From this time span history slows right down, in fact, Braudel claims it often seems motionless. He says:

> Among the different kinds of historical time, the *longue durée* often seems a troublesome character, full of complications, and all too frequently lacking in any sort of organization. To give it a place in the heart of our profession would entail more than a routine expansion of our studies and our curiosities. Nor would it be a question of making a simple choice in its favor. For the historian, accepting the *longue durée* entails a readiness to change his style, his attitudes, a whole reversal in his thinking, a whole new way of conceiving of social affairs. It means becoming used to a slower tempo, which sometimes almost borders on the motionless.... In any case, it is in relation to these expanses of slow-moving history that the whole of history is to be rethought, as if on the basis of an infrastructure. All the stages, all the thousands of stages, all the thousand explosions of historical time can be understood on the basis of these depths, this semistillness. Everything gravitates around it.[64]

What Braudel is proposing is a paradigmatic shift in our approach to history. A shift which demands that we slow right down to, broaden our gaze and lengthen our time frame. This double demand moves history beyond the parameters, which previously defined it. History, to gain perspective, must now dialogue with all of the social sciences, it must seek to access a total view of society.

A key benefit of this methodology is Braudel's understanding of his history as a 'total history' investigating both the infrastructure and superstructure of society. The second, is the fact that the method is phenomenological. This guarantees, as far as is humanly possible, that

---

[63] Braudel, *On History*, p. 31.
[64] Braudel, *On History*, p. 33.

a single interpretative structure is not imposed upon reality *a-priori*. Unlike other interpretative tools, Braudel's theory of history allows us to begin by observing as faithfully as possible, what is. Only after careful observations are made about the reality before us, can we start to speak about, and choose what theories would be helpful to illuminate the reality. The task of Braudel's history within this project is as a tool of mediation of the lived experience of 'New World' people. This mediation, or re-presentation of the total complex in all of its levels, is in the service of theology. As Ricoeur has helped us to overcome the problematic of adequate tools for mediation, Braudel has helped us overcome the false divisions imposed upon the social reality.

Conclusions

Truth and Memory are tied to methodology. In our approach, Ricoeur's hermeneutics guarantees the claims of truth grounding the process of interpretation in human action. On the other hand Braudel's historiography opens a new way of reconfiguring our collective memories. Not just the sequence of isolated events, but rather the subterranean structures that work tirelessly to defy memory by defying visibility. The truncating or fragmenting of reality is one way to ensure the erosion of memory, or rather to structure selective memory. This structuring, when it is an integral part of our theological methodology, pushes the enterprise of theology away from its claims to truth.

One key question in the reconfiguring of memory, is the incidences of hostility to liberation theology. Are these the prejudices of individual people, or part of a greater collective? It is my contention that liberation theology cannot be interpreted except within the wider ecclesial context. Here I would look at the Catholic context because of the hostile relationship between the Congregation for the Doctrine of the Faith (CDF) and the liberation theologians.

To select some Papal documents that highlight the relationship between the Church and the modern world shows the cyclical nature of this history. Conjunctures –

- 1864: Pius IX's *Quanta Cura* (Syllabus of Errors) – condemns modern critical tools
- 1891: Leo XIII's *Rerum Novarum* – opens to modern critical tools
- 1907: Pius X Condemnation of Modernism – Modern critical tools condemned
- 1950: Pius XII *Humani Generis* – A new Syllabus of Errors
- 1962: John XXIII Vatican II – Openness to modern critical tools
- 1968: Paul VI, *Humanae Vitae* – Modern critical tools?

- 1998: John Paul II's *Fides et Ratio* (Faith and Reason) – A Closure to modern critical tools

From these milestones we can see that the Church has had cycles of openness and closure to the modern project. The regression of the Church in our own time regarding social transformation and the issues of justice is not isolated or novel. During the last century there were several papal approaches to modernity, within this cyclical motion 1864 and 1998 as the bookends that signal a firm closure between the Church and the modern tools of criticism. To situate this ecclesial cycle, it is important to situate it within the world system and the economic cycles. Here, 1864 and 1998 are not significant in themselves. What is significant is their relationship to two other dates, 1848 and 1968.

1848 and 1968 were revolutions with far reaching effects for the Western world.[65] Commenting on 1848 historian Norman Davis says:

> In February 1848 the head of revolutionary steam was much stronger than in 1830, and the rash of explosions spread to all the major states except for Britain and Russia. In this case trouble was already afoot in Switzerland from 1845, in the Republic of Cracow from 1846, and in Sicily from 1847. The overthrow of Louis-Philippe sent the signal which set almost all the major cities of Germany, Italy, Austria, and Hungary ablaze.[66]

The formal closure of the Church to the modern world is related here to the revolution of 1848. Despite the revolution's failure to impose constitutional reform, no European nation that was touched escaped the constitution. In this revolution the high cost of monarchy became evident. As Davis says:

> The basic liberal principle of government by consent steadily gained widespread acceptance. One by one over the next two decades, the victors of 1848 abandoned their frozen postures. National and constitutional aspirations came again to the fore.[67]

The 1864 *Quanta Cura* of Pius IX was an attempt to establish in the Church, what every monarch had already resigned him/herself to. The reaction to the revolution nearly twenty years on, was really a reaction

---

[65] For a good assessment of the effects of these two cultural revolutions see: Giovanni Arrighi, Terence K. Hopkins and Immanuel Wallerstein, *Antisystemic Movements*, London, Verso, 1989.
[66] Norman Davies, *Europe: A History*, London, Pimlico, 1997, p. 804.
[67] Davies, *Europe*, p. 805.

to the growing democratization of Europe. From the perspective of the *longue durée*, this process has made steady progress despite the cyclical nature of the culture's reaction to democracy.

So what is 1998? Again to understand 1998 it is important to first see the cycle to which it is reacting. In the wake of Vatican II, as we said above, there was widespread optimism about reform within Catholicism. This optimism ended with great disillusionment in 1968 with the promulgation of *Humanae Vitae*. Many interpretations on the level of individual human motive have been explored. It is here that another reading is important. The cultural cycle had shifted dramatically in 1968. The Paris youth riots that challenged all authority, these together with the riots in Prague, USA, Mexico City, Tokyo and Italy challenged the power relations within these Nation States and within the whole world system. Just as *Humanae Vitae* typified the collision between liberal reformers and conservative forces in the Church in 1968, so to the assassination of Dr Martin Luther King Jr. typified the reaction of the system to the progress of civil rights. When one adds the protest against the Vietnam War, the sexual revolution with flower power and hippies, the picture of the 1968 cultural revolution becomes clearer. What is important here, is that it brought political structural change to the power relationships within the world.

> Inability of either East or West to police the South – Vietnam and Afghanistan.

> Change in power relations in status groups – Age, Gender and Ethnicities.

> Change in relation between Capital and Labor – International search for Safe labour.

> Autonomy of Civil Society – Bourgeois dictatorships have been displaced by democratic regimes.[68]

Like the 1848 revolution before it, 1968 was a failure, but this was not immediate. In 1848 the world recession and the revolution coincided. In 1968 the world recession (1973) followed the cultural revolution. This was the OPEC oil crisis. The recession further impacted upon the world structure:

> The benefits of 1968 were accrued to minorities within the different status groups – age, gender race.

[68] Arrighi et al, pp. 110ff.

Third World industrialization through migration of production from core caused stiffer competition, lower wages, greater impoverishment and underdevelopment.

Shift in status group lead to youth unemployment, more exploitation of women, and the worsening condition of minorities.

The gains of 1968 eroded by great inflation of late 1970s and unemployment of 1980s.[69]

That the central administration of the Church opposed liberation theology becomes more obvious from this perspective. By the early 1980s the notion of liberation was being opposed through the new styled politicians in the English-speaking powers – Margaret Thatcher and Ronald Reagan.

Now at the end of this long meandering path through methodology, we can see that the reaction against liberation theology in the 1980s was part of a global movement. It came in the wake of the infamous Santa Fe document prepared for President Reagan before he assumed office. In proposal 3 in the chapter significantly entitled *International Subversion*, it is stated: 'US foreign policy must begin to counter (not react against) liberation theology as it is utilized in Latin America by the "liberation theology clergy"'.[70] The hostility of the Church towards this theology has mirrored the hostility of the super power. Economic and theological orthodoxy, in the 1980s became connected at the hip.[71] The Church again, enmeshed within the cultural cycle, did not have the capacity to distance itself from the conservative push to the history of events. It, thus, mirrored the world system, rather than maintaining a creative and prophetic stanse.

In El Salvador, the 1970s were years of severe economic dislocation. It was a decade marked by economic contraction and, thus, brought great social transformation to the troubled nation. With the recession, the new elites joined with the old planters to secure their tenuous privilege. Here there was the collision of mentalities – the elites vs. the mass mentality shaped in the cauldron of 1968. The social forces within El Salvador were on collision for nearly five hundred years. The 1968 World Revolution gave impetus to the peasant communities towards mass

[69] Arrighi et al, pp. 104ff.
[70] The Committee of Santa Fe, *A New Inter-American Policy for the Eighties*, Santa Fe, NM, 1980.
[71] It is interesting here that in the 1990s as the Asian Tigers became the threat, the Church machinery to ensure theological orthodoxy turned its gaze to Asia excommunicating one theologian, question the Christology of another and pronouncing the writing of a spiritual writer heretical.

mobilization. The 1973 recession mobilized the elite towards preserving privilege. The point here is that the interpretation of the events that led up the assassination of Archbishop Romero cannot be confined to the Americas. El Salvador was enmeshed in the world system and its various cycles. Standing, as we do, in a cultural/social cycle against liberation, or rather I should say against life, should not lead us to despair. Rather, it should allow us to treasure the witness of our martyrs – Oscar Romero and Juan Gerardi – who gave their life when the tide of the world economic system flowed against 'action on behalf of justice'.

Towards a Theology of Solidarity

ANDREW BRADSTOCK

A particularly striking poster produced in Nicaragua in the 1980s depicts a mural from the Church of Santa Maria de Los Angeles in Managua above the simple inscription in Spanish, English and Italian, 'solidarity is tenderness of the people'. The central figure in the mural is a bowed and beaten *campesino*, weighed down by the burden of the cross he is carrying, and accompanied and aided on his painful journey by male and female *compañeros*. Among these are some 'mothers of the disappeared', and all are clearly sharing physically and spiritually in their comrade's sufferings. In a powerful and profound way this poster captures the essence of solidarity in the context of Latin America and other parts of the two-thirds world, since for the many 'crucified peoples' of those regions, solidarity is quite literally to carry each other's cross and share together, as a community, in each other's death and suffering. Solidarity *is* 'tenderness of the people'.

But what is the meaning of solidarity for us in the so-called developed world who also want to carry the crosses of our exploited and downtrodden sisters and brothers? I want to begin with this question before reflecting more specifically on what a 'theology of solidarity' might look like – a process which will bring us back to our image of the cross-bearing *campesino*. In other words, in fidelity to the liberation theology model, let us try to sort out our 'praxis' first and then do some theology in the light of that. So first of all, what is solidarity?

The dictionary talks of solidarity in terms of 'unity of interests', 'sympathies', and so on, especially as among a class; and this reminds us that the term has done sterling service over the years in the trade union and labour movement, including, in the 1980s, being adopted as the name of the organisation which united popular opposition in Poland to the then Communist administration. In the context of our relationship with the two-thirds world, however, the term will be more commonly understood and used in the sense of walking alongside, defending the rights of, and helping to empower, others, particularly those suffering injustice, exploitation and impoverishment.

We can help to clarify our thinking about solidarity by considering what it is not. Clearly it is not just giving – of money or even of time – though that will be a part of it. People often give money to causes with little or no awareness of why there is a need to do so, of the issues which have led to their support being solicited. Solidarity *will* involve generosity, but much more besides. Primarily it will involve a concern to understand the reasons *why* giving is necessary, working to see that those reasons are addressed, and, importantly, staying with those to whom support is offered long after everyone else has forgotten about them. So someone in solidarity with, for example, the people of Nicaragua and Honduras, will not just have given money or produce to help relieve the appalling effects of Hurricane Mitch in the autumn of 1998, nor have been content to have seen awareness of the issue raised briefly by the media before being dropped as the next 'big story' came along: solidarity, as opposed to charity, will have involved staying with the people when the spotlight moved away, working to maintain a high public profile for their situation, and campaigning for as long as it takes for structural and infra-structural changes to ensure that the effects of any future 'natural' disasters are infinitely less devastating.

The essence of solidarity surely must be this preparedness to stay with people when their situation is no longer trendy: for example, solidarity with South Africa now must mean continuing the struggle to build a civil society, working for reconciliation on the basis of justice and so on. This might seem to the casual observer or supporter a more mundane and less 'glamorous' crusade than the one waged earlier against the hated apartheid system, but to the committed it will be every bit as important as the former. And solidarity with Nicaragua must now mean accompanying the people through the massively depressing post-revolution phase, when the circle back to *somocismo* seems almost to have been completed and when the issues are not as clear-cut as they were at the time of the triumph in 1979 or the *contra* atrocities of the 1980s. It means continuing to try to interest our politicians and trade unionists in the issues, keeping alive town-twinning and sister-city links, offering ongoing support to community projects on the ground, helping the Nicaragua Solidarity Campaign (NSC) to maintain its base in Managua and so on. It can be a sad and frustrating business, as those of us in the NSC have to acknowledge: in the late 1980s we could fill Central Hall, Westminster, to capacity for a rally with Sandinista leaders Daniel Ortega and Miguel D'Escoto and writer and friend of progressive Latin American movements, Graham Greene; now, barely ten years later, we try to maintain our commitment to the Nicaraguan people and progressive forces in the country against the background of a deep rift in the Sandinista Front, a constitutional pact between the mainstream of the movement and the right-wing government, and a refusal by the Front to deal with allegations of sustained sexual abuse levelled at Ortega by his own step-daughter. How far have we come – or fallen – from the time when the Sandinistas' heroic campaign to defend their revolution from United States aggression captured the imagination of so many throughout the world. Yet real solidarity must mean staying with the people who continue to suffer when the issues become less sexy, when popular interest wanes, and when the media move on because nothing they deem newsworthy is happening in the region any more.

Solidarity is also not mission – at least, not in the traditional nineteenth-century sense of exporting a particular religious and cultural message. In fact it appears that much missionary activity today *is* becoming much more like solidarity, in the sense that many missionary organizations are becoming increasingly involved in development projects, and engaging in campaigning in the arenas of politics, world trade and so on; but in so far as mission implies attempting to bring people to embrace a different system of belief or values or life-style, it is a different thing from solidarity. This is in no way to knock mission *per se*, simply to recognize that it is not necessarily the same as solidarity. Solidarity is accompanying the people, but in the direction *they* not *we* want to go.

If solidarity is a ministry of accompaniment, there are two models of it: doing it with the people where they are, and doing it, as it were, from a distance. At first sight one seems more authentic than the other, and those of us who have not lived with people whose cause we try to champion often get asked why, if we are as bothered about them and their countries as we say we are, we have not sold up and gone off to live with them. But it is not quite as straightforward as that. Of course, working alongside those with whom one is in solidarity is presumably an intensely powerful experience: to be in a position to share the lives and dynamic of the people, give to and receive from them in person, and relay to the outside world up-to-date and first-hand news untainted by media interpretation and selection, is to be in a profoundly privileged place. But 'being there' can also open one's eyes to the stark reality of a situation, removing the rose-coloured spectacles which we at a greater distance sometimes find ourselves wanting to wear, and one also needs to be prepared for that. A volunteer who worked in El Salvador with the US solidarity movement CRISPAZ in the late 1990s, offers an example of one who went through 'a stage of tremendous disappointment' while working with the communities to which she was allocated. 'Like most fresh-off-the-boat volunteers', she writes,

I ... experienced a romantic phase at first, carried away by the stories from the war, stories about the unity, the dignity, the cause, the righteousness of the struggle. I felt with such passion that the Truth about the war needed to be disclosed to the entire world. It seemed so clear then. Of course I had set myself up. Viewing the campesinos as if they were somehow 'perfect' in a spiritual sense and projecting my desire to find meaning in life into the revolution and continued struggle was not the easiest perspective to maintain.[1]

She then describes how she went away from the community for a time only to find, on her return to work with them at a closer level than before, 'internal conflict, corruption, lack of commitment and apathy.... It seemed unfathomable how the people around me fought a revolution or created a refugee community together, side by side, for twelve years and could not even reach a consensus at a meeting on the same topic.'[2]

She goes on to explain how these internal conflicts are none too surprising given the people's experiences over recent years – something which we, viewing from afar, might not so easily understand or appreciate; and she also quotes some apposite words from Dean Brackley, which in a sense sum up what solidarity is about: 'It is not that the poor are all saints or cuddly. They can be just as petty and selfish as the rich. The point is that they are just like us and do not deserve to suffer this injustice.'[3] She also speaks of some of the other less glamorous aspects of this form of solidarity, including the difficulties of trying to stay 'neutral' in a situation of intense conflict, of the frustration she felt when this conflict prevented her programmes getting off the ground, of wanting to impose her own 'solutions' on to the crisis. But despite this, physically accompanying the people will always be an intensely valuable form of solidarity, and more often than not an irreplaceable one, bearing in mind the access which solidarity workers will usually enjoy to the outside world and the impact they will have in – and on – their own country and the world's media.

On this point, it is impossible to underestimate the impact that organisations such as 'Witness for Peace' (WFP) have had in Central America, maintaining a constant presence of United States citizens in regions targeted by their own government. (Perhaps their most well-known campaign was during the *contra* war in Nicaragua in the

---

[1] Crispaz, Salvanet, July–August 1999, p. 6.
[2] Ibid.
[3] Ibid, p. 7. Brackley himself provides a good model of what true solidarity might mean. After the murders of the six Jesuits at the Universidad Centroamericana in 1989 he moved from the US to El Salvador to teach theology and ethics at the University.

1980s).⁴ In part WFP worked on the 'protective shield' principle, which held that US-backed forces were less likely to attack communities where there was a risk that in so doing US citizens would be killed as well as indigenous people,⁵ but they also knew that, were they themselves to witness violence or even be killed – as indeed some were – the attention of the world's media, and therefore the raising of public consciousness in the States about what their government was doing in its so-called 'backyard', would be infinitely greater than if no US citizens were involved. As Mahony and Eguren have written in their study of international accompaniment in the protection of human rights, 'Although one of [WFP's] tools was protective accompaniment, its broader mission was to educate the American public and change US policy.'⁶ The British priest John Medcalf also made a significant contribution in this way through his presence in rural war zones in Nicaragua in the 1980s and in El Salvador in the 1990s, the steady stream of letters and articles he mailed back to the UK, describing the situations he was witnessing, being widely read in the Christian press.⁷

Yet it is also important to say that solidarity can be 'done' at a distance and with no less an impact. Perhaps I would argue this since this has been my main contribution, though I think we can move beyond the mere subjective. A key issue here, it seems to me, is *effectiveness*: as Camilo Torres used to say of charity, if it is not effective it is not anything at all, and so an important consideration is, in what way can we make the most difference through our solidarity? Much as we may like to go and work with a basic Christian community in Central America, would we be able to do there what we can do here – raise awareness locally and nationally via the media, put pressure on our politicians, business leaders and opinion formers, raise consciousness among our students, young people, and in our churches, and so

---

⁴ Witness for Peace is probably the best-known US solidarity movement committed actually to working in the Central American region but it is not the only one: others include the Nicaragua Network (formerly National Network in Solidarity with the Nicaraguan People, NNSNP), National Central America Health Rights Network (NCAHRN), and the Veterans' Peace Convoy.

⁵ Witness for Peace press release, 'US Christians Launch Witness for Peace in Nicaragua' November 1983, p.1.

⁶ Liam Mahony and Luis Enrique Eguren, *Unarmed Bodyguards: International Accompaniment for the Protection of Human Rights*, West Hartford, CN, Kumarian Press, 1997, p. 5.

⁷ Some of Father Medcalf's letters have been published in book form (and even performed on stage!) See John Medcalf, *Letters from Nicaragua*, London, CIIR, 1988. The significance of maintaining a close enough presence to those who are being persecuted in order to alert the outside world to their plight is highlighted by David Tombs in his contribution to this volume: see above where he discusses Peter's action of following Jesus in the aftermath of his arrest, calling it 'a courageous act of solidarity'.

on? Perhaps we do not speak Spanish very well, maybe we are not great at community-living (one of the single most difficult problems for solidarity workers), maybe we tend to see things rather too easily in black and white terms or according to our own 'Western' way of thinking, maybe we would be impatient for change and reform: would we make good accompaniers on the ground? And what would our motives be for going: to drop out of a society which is characterised by so many things of which we do not approve, a love of travel and adventure, the *romance* of it all...? But we can also be very positive about the contribution that we can make here, not least when we consider the achievements of, for example, the various solidarity groups based in the UK; the Jubilee 2000 Campaign; Amnesty International; and, specifically in the United States, the campaigns by grass-roots groups to persuade Congress to limit aid to the *contra*, particularly that which forced through the Boland Amendment of 1983. This is work that could only be done in the First World.

The campaign to ease the debt burdens of third-world countries, co-ordinated by the Jubilee 2000 coalition, is one 'solidarity' issue in which concerned people based in the northern hemisphere have a unique role to play, since it is *our* governments and financial institutions which have the power to decide whether these interest repayments should continue to be made or remitted; and not only can this struggle *only* be undertaken in the First World, it is one which people in the indebted countries are actually looking to us to engage in.[8] It is not the only way in which solidarity can be expressed from a distance, however: witness, for example, the work of organisations like the 'Labour Behind the Label Network', which in 1999 launched a campaign for a living wage in the global textile industry and highlighted the plight of workers in the export processing industry in Central America and Asia who are often not paid enough to cover their basic daily needs; or the 'Central American Women's Network', which also campaigns around the issue of (women) workers' rights and violence against women and girls. Both movements share at least one important aim, namely to raise awareness at the 'consumer' end of the equation about the inequities of the world trade system.

To emphasize the value of solidarity 'at a distance' is not, of course, to undermine the value of occasional visits to the country and people with whom one is in solidarity: such visits always give an enormous fillip to campaigning work at home, as well as offering moral, and, in the case of work brigades, practical support to the people and communities visited. But the point is that the solidarity expressed by those

---

[8] See, for example, Gustavo Gutiérrez, 'Liberation Theology and the Future of the Poor' in Joerg Rieger, (ed.), *Liberating the Future: God, Mammon and Theology*, Minneapolis, Fortress Press, 1998, p. 121.

unable even to contemplate an overseas trip is in no sense 'second best'. If anything it has become even more effective and influential with the advent of electronic communication, as a consequence of which messages and correspondence can reach much further and faster than before, even through barriers often not penetrated by more conventional forms of mail.

Where does all this leave us theologically: what inspiration, what models can we find for solidarity in Christian scripture and tradition? We could begin with the account in Acts 16.9 of St Paul's dream of a man from Macedonia pleading with him to go over to the region to help the believers there, to which he responds positively. In terms of actually getting alongside people (our first model of solidarity) perhaps the ultimate model is the Incarnation, particularly as expressed in the hymn in Philippians 2 with its depiction of Christ 'emptying himself' and being born in our likeness. Clearly we need to exercise caution when tempted to turn aspects of Jesus' ministry into examples to follow, though this *is* a suggestive one given that our concern in undertaking solidarity work, like that of Jesus himself as expressed at the outset of his ministry (Luke 4.18–19), is to bring good news to the poor, release to those in captivity, and freedom to the oppressed. Then there is the story of the Samaritan commended by Jesus, often known as the 'Good Samaritan', which, though it has been subjected to a wide range of political as well as theological interpretations, provides another example of solidarity – and not least in so far as it shows up the naivety of expecting help for the needy to come from the most 'likely' sources. The Samaritan's preparedness, having paid the innkeeper a sum of money to look after the man he has rescued, to return and settle up any further debts, also reminds us powerfully that a genuine, committed and practical standing with the wounded and exploited has to be ongoing.

Then there are two characters who appear very briefly on the gospel stage, both in the crucifixion narratives: Simon of Cyrene and Joseph of Arimathea. Though only accorded three, almost identical, verses in the synoptics, Simon – who probably in many respects shared a similar social position to Jesus – is called to suffer with Jesus in an intensely practical and painful way by relieving him, for a time, of the agony of carrying his cross. Admittedly he appears to have been press-ganged into this task, but it was a very powerful expression of solidarity – and one which clearly resonates deeply in the context of present-day Central America, as the mural from the church of Santa Maria, described at the beginning of this essay, underlines. Yet no less suggestive is the case of the man who comes out of the shadows following the death of Jesus to ask the authorities for permission to take away the body to bury in his own tomb. In the light of our consideration of the validity of solidarity 'from a distance' Joseph's position is instructive. First there seems little doubt that he is a follower of Jesus – both Matthew and John describe him as a disciple (Matt. 27.57; John 19.38) – though not one who identified openly with him during his public ministry: John in fact uses the adjective 'secret' of his discipleship. We also read that he enjoyed a position of some authority and power in the community, for although Matthew simply describes him as 'rich', Mark and Luke note that he was a member of the council which, according to the gospels, had an important role to play in the events leading up to the crucifixion. I believe it is possible to see Joseph working out quite a sophisticated ministry of solidarity, for perhaps it is precisely because he does not identify himself openly with Jesus that he is able to maintain his position on an influential and powerful body which he can then try to use in the interests of the cause. The Lucan account (23.51) is explicit in its claim that he was a dissenting voice in the council which condemned Jesus – part of the structures of oppression yet seeking from the inside to subvert their business – and all four Gospels attest to the ready and easy way in which he was able to make use of his privileged position both to gain access to Pilate, and, with no apparent trouble, get what he wanted. And who knows how significant his action in securing Jesus' body was for the rest of the passion narrative – including, of course the resurrection – considering that the alternative to burial in his tomb was presumably an unceremonious dumping in the public grave?

One final brief thought: considering both Jesus and Joseph as paradigms of solidarity suggests that it is not necessarily a one-way process but that both sides have much to give and take from each other. Here we are back to the idea that real solidarity is not and never has been 'charity' but rather, as Rueben and Sherman put it, 'a relationship based on mutual interests and respect'. Reflecting on a decade of US solidarity with Nicaragua at the end of the 1980s, these writers affirm that those North Americans involved in it learned a great deal from the people whose interests they were championing:

> The courage, optimism, and compassion displayed by Nicaraguans – from national leaders to rural farmers – has left a deep impression on all who have encountered it. If the people of the United States have in some small measure helped our Nicaraguan friends during the past decade, we have been repaid one hundredfold.[9]

There is also a sense in which, not only are we in solidarity with our brothers and sisters in the South, they and we are actually struggling

---

[9] Debra Rueben and Sylvia Sherman, 'Ten years of revolution, ten years of solidarity', *Barricada Internacional*, IX, 295/296 (8 July 1989) 41.

together against a common enemy. Campaigns like Jubilee 2000 may superficially give the impression that solidarity is essentially 'us' helping 'them', but at root, particularly in this post-Cold War world, it is about reversing some of the worst consequences of an economic system which marginalizes and impoverishes us all. As Joerg Rieger reminds us, 'Practical solidarity leads to new relationships.... The pressures of a global economy are bringing those who are left out closer together',[10] and a recent NACLA report defines solidarity today as 'the fellowship arising from shared struggle'.[11] For the simple truth is that this 'global economy', as it presently functions, diminishes us all as members of the human family, whereas solidarity, as Jon Sobrino has so movingly put it, is concerned above all to 'make us all human, more like brothers and sisters, more like sons and daughters of the same Father.'[12]

---

[10] Joerg Rieger, 'Developing a Common Interest Theology From the Underside' in Rieger, op. cit., p.140.
[11] Anon, 'Reinventing Solidarity', in NACLA, *Report on Solidarity*, 28.5, 1995, 15. This whole issue contains a number of essays reflecting on the nature of solidarity in the light of the changes that took place in Central America in the 1990s.
[12] Jon Sobrino, 'Preface' in Pamela Hussey, (ed.), *Freedom From Fear: Women in El Salvador's Church*, London, CIIR, 1989, p. ix.

Contributors

Professor María Pilar Aquino of Mexico is Professor of Religious Studies at the University of San Diego. She has written widely on feminist theology in Latin American and is author of *Our Cry for Life* (Orbis Books, 1992). She is a member of the Ecumenical Association of Third World Theologians and the Association of Catholic Hispanic Theologians in the US.

Dr Andrew Bradstock is currently the Secretary for Church and Society of the United Reformed Church and was formerly a lecturer in church history and political theology. He is author of *Faith in the Revolution* (SPCK, 1997) and *Saints and Sandinistas* (Epworth, 1987) and editor of the recently published *Winstanley and the Diggers 1649–1999* (Frank Cass, 2000).

Kevin Burke, SJ is assistant professor of systematic and historical theology at the Weston Jesuit School (Cambridge, Massachusetts) and is author of numerous articles and the book *The Ground Beneath the Cross* (Georgetown University Press, 2000) on the theology of Ignacio Ellacuría.

Michael Campbell-Johnston, SJ is a former provincial of the British Jesuits. His lengthy experience in Latin America includes service in Guyana and in El Salvador during the civil war. He is currently working in El Salvador at the retreat centre of *El Despertar* in northwest San Salvador where the priest Octavio Ortiz was killed during the time that Romero was Archbishop.

Judith Escribano is the communications officer for Central America at Christian Aid, the development agency of the Churches Together in Britain and Ireland, based in London.

Ruth Gidley lived in Guatemala for three and a half years working first in development and then as a journalist and editor (for the Central America Report). She has an MA in Latin American Studies and currently works for the Reuters Foundation. She co-authored *Guatemala: A Place for Memory* (1999) for the Guatemala Solidarity Network.

Fr. Jason Gordon is a Trinidadian priest who lectures in theology at the University of West Indies and has published on Caribbean theology and cultural interpretation.

Professor Mary Grey is currently professor of theology at Sarum College, Salisbury. She has published widely in contemporary theology and has particular interest in the theological significance of human rights and subversive memory. She has published widely on feminist theology, ecology and social justice, including: *Beyond the Dark Night: A Way forward for the Church* (Cassell, 1998), *Prophecy and Mysticism: The Heart of the Post-Modern Church* (T & T Clark, 1997), *Feminism, Redemption and the Christian Tradition* (Twenty-Third Publications, 1990).

Fr. Michael Hayes was formerly the Catholic Chaplain at University of Surrey Roehampton and is now Head of Department at St Mary's College Strawberry Hill London. His research is in psychology, counselling and theology and he is editor of various books including *Contemporary Catholic Theology* (Gracewing, 1988).

Dr. Dermot A. Lane is President of Mater Dei Institute of Education, a College of Dublin City University, and Parish Priest of Balally, Dublin. He is author of *Keeping Hope Alive: Stirrings in Christian Theology* (Dublin/New York, 1996) and editor of *New Century, New Society: Christian Perspectives* (Dublin, 1999).

Dr Marcela López Levy has studied psychology and anthropology and has worked on human rights campaigning and research for ten years. Specializing in Latin America, she is currently researcher and editor at the Latin America Bureau in London, a non-governmental agency which publishes on political, social and economic justice issues.

Martin Maier, SJ is the editor of *Stimmen der Zeit*, the monthly magazine of the German Jesuits, dealing with church, social and cultural issues. He is also a guest teacher at the Central American University (UCA) in San Salvador and was in El Salvador from 1989 until 1991 as successor to the UCA martyr Ignacio Martín-Baró as a pastor in a countryside parish. He is author of the book *Oscar Romero – Meister der Spiritualität* (Herder 2001).

Hannah Roberts has worked in Guatemala since 1993 on various development projects. She set up the truth monuments campaign and co-authored *Guatemala: A Place for Memory* (Guatemala Solidarity Network, 1999) and is currently working in mental health in the UK and as co-chair of the Guatemala Solidarity Network.

Jon Sobrino, SJ is a Professor in Theology at the Universidad Centroamericana Jose Simon Cañas, San Salvador. He has published widely on liberation theology and social justice issues including *Jesus the Liberator* (Orbis, 1992), *The Principle of Mercy* (1994) and co-edited the collection *Mysterium Liberationis* (Orbis, 1993) with Ignacio Ellacuría SJ.

David Tombs is Senior Lecturer in Theology in the School of Humanities and Cultural Studies at the University of Surrey Roehampton. His primary area of research is Christianity in Latin America.

Scott Wright worked for ten years as a Catholic lay missioner in El Salvador and is currently Director of the Ecumenical Program on Central America and the Caribbean (EPICA) in Washington DC. His publications include *Promised Land: Death and Life in El Salvador* (Orbis, 1994) and *Oscar Romero: Reflections on His Life and Writings* (Orbis, 2000) with Marie Dennis and Renny Golden.

Index

accountability, 154, 155–6
Afghanistan, 262
African-Americans: music, 138, 168–9; slaves, 138, 143, 164, 138, 168–9; women's consciousness, 166, 168, 237, 246–7
Aguilares, 15–18, 92
aid workers, 7, 267–9, 271, 272
AIDS, 169
Alexander VI, Pope, 144
Algeria, 138
Alianza Nueva Nación, 115
Allende, Isabel, 199
Allende, Salvador, President of Chile, 207
Amaya, Rufina, 12
Amerindia group, 214
amnesties: Argentina, 116; charges not covered by, 69, 112, 116, 120, 200n25; Chile, 200n25; El Salvador, 1–2; Guatemala, 69, 112; injustice of hasty, 137n5
Amnesty International, 270
Anamnesis, Eucharistic, 171–2
Anaya Sanabria, Herbert, 134
ANN (Alianza Nueva Nación), 115
Annales School of historiography, 251–60
anthropology, 144, 242, 246
apostolic visitors, 49
Ardón, Otto, 66, 71–2
ARENA, 50, 92
Arendt, Hanna, 147
Argentina: Condor plan for military assistance, 111, 197;

disappearances, 147, 195–6, 196–7, 198n18, 201, (National Commission on Disappeared People), 108–9, 196n9, (relatives' organizations), 112, 116; military regimes, 195; trial of former leaders, 116
Argentine Anti-Communist Alliance, 195
Argueta, Manlio, 200, 205
arms trade, 137n5, 151, 155
Arzú, Alvaro, President of Guatemala, 65, 80
Asian Tigers, 263n71
Assmann, Hugo, 151, 243
asylum seekers, 168
Atlacatl Batallion, 12–13, 113n17
Augustine of Hippo, St, 181
Auschwitz, 11, 12, 147
Aylwin, Patricio, President of Chile, 207

Baggio, Cardinal, 49
Balentine, Samuel, 170
Baloo (Fr Orantes' dog), 66–7, 76
banking system, 149
Barbieri, Tersita de, 222
Barcellona, Pietro, 154n35
Baum, Gregory, 246
Beatitudes, 40, 53
Benjamin, Walter, 163, 164, 177–8, 180, 187
Beozzo, José Oscar, 234
Berger, Oscar, 65
Beristain, Carlos, 131–2

Berlin Wall, 150
Bethlehem; Rachel's tomb, 161
Bilbao; Universidad de Deusto, 134–58
Bill of Rights (1689), 134n1
Bishops, Conference of Guatemalan (CEG), 60, 62, 65, 69
Bishops, Conference of Salvadoran, 49, 51, 49, 55, 92, 96
Bishops, Second Conference of Latin American (CELAM II, Medellín, 1968), 46; demands on current church and theologies, 214, 236–9; on family, 233; and feminist theology, 7, 6–7, 214, 220, 232–3, 233–9; and grassroot ecclesial communities, 234–5; and justice, 213, 233, 236, 237; and liberation theology, 61, 234–5, 240, 243; and preferential option for the poor, 3, 52–3, 91, 234–5, (feminist), 238; on property of church, 233; US reception, 47; and Vatican II, 46, 91
Bishops, Third Conference of Latin American (CELAM III, Puebla, 1979), 52–3, 222–3
black theology, and gender issue, 246
blaming of victims, 166
Bloch, Mark, 252
Boff, Clodovis M., 234–5
Boff, Leonardo, 243
Bolivia, 195n6, 197n12, 207–8
Bonillo, Mauricio López, 68
Brackley, Dean, 268
Braudel, Fernand, 251–60; on 'anonymous history', 253–4; and economic history, 252, 257–8; phenomenological approach, 259–60; structure, concept of, 258–9; and time span, 252, 254, 255–60
Brazil, 194–5, 196, 197n12
Brecht, Bertold, 165–6
Britain, 50, 119, 169, 269; Jubilee 2000, 270, 273; Pinochet case, 196n10; *see also* Westminster Abbey
Buber, Martin, 88–9
burial rites, 121–3, 125

Cabrera, Julio, Bishop of El Quiché, 22
Cabrera, Roberto, Director of REMHI, 11–12
Cafod, 169
Calderón, Alexis, 80
Calderón, Mirta Rodríguez, 227–8
Câmara, Archbishop Helder, of Brazil, 96
capitalism, 149, 151, 221, 247, 262; and MAI, 154–5; Romero on, 27–8
Caribbean, 243, 246; Christology conference (1973), 243; Ecumenical consultation for development (1971), 243
Casaldáliga, Pedro, 150n27
catechists, murder of, 20, 61, 106
catharsis of testifying, 35, 106, 121, 125, 251
Catholic Action, 18–19, 20
CDF, 244n17, 260
Cavanaugh, William, 171–2
CEG, *see* Bishops' Conference, Guatemalan
CEH (UN Historical Clarification Commission, Guatemala), 33, 43; anonymity, 105, 110; establishment, 69, 104–5; genocide charges, 69, 112, 120, 129; Gerardi's death as threat to, 71; limitations, 33, 112, 126; media coverage, 126–7; on number of victims and massacres, 13; recommendations, 43; and REMHI, 33, 104–5, 111–12; state response, 126; report at Washington Holocaust Museum, 11–12; strength of report, 42, 112, 126
CELAM, *see* Bishops, Second/Third Conference of Latin American
CELEP, 78
CEMIF, 214n4
Central American Women's Network, 270
Centre for Human Rights and Legal Action, Guatemala (CHRLA), 69n30, 71, 129
Chajul, 21
Chalatenango, 44, 100
Chanax, Ruben, 80
character assassination, 112
charismatic sects, fundamentalist, 47, 121

Chávez y González, Luis, Archbishop of San Salvador, 47, 48, 91
Chicana/Latina feminist theory, 215–16
Chichupac, 131
children: murder of, 107, 124, 195n3; resources consumed by, 149
Children of the Disappeared (HIJOS), 116
Chile, Allende's burial, 207; amnesty laws, 200n25; Condor plan, 197n12; disappearances, 195, 200n25, 201; legacy of violence, 116; military regimes (1973–89), 195; Pinochet regime, 109, 171, 195, 196n10, 200n25, 207; Rettig Report (National Commission on Truth And Reconciliation), 196n10, 200n26
Chimaltenango, 42
China, 46
Christendom model of Christianity, 241
Christian Aid, 169
Christian Union of Peasants and Agricultural Workers (FECCAS-UTC), 91–2
CHRLA, 69n30, 71, 129
chronos (chronological time), 188
Chungara, Domitilia, 222
Church in El Salvador, The (pamphlet), 46, 49
civil rights, 154, 243
Civilian Self-Defence Patrols, *see* PACs
class analysis, 246, 248
Codina, Victor, 93
Columbus, Christopher, 166
commemoration of dead: Gerardi, 42–3, 70; in Guatemala, 34–5, 105, 122, 126; martyrs, 100; reduces debt to dead, 184; Romero, 38, 41, 82, 96
communities: CELAM II and grassroot ecclesial, 234–5; destruction, 106; rebuilding, 34–5, 106, 113; solidarity, 265; and truth monuments, 5, 118, 125, 129–32, 132–3
'Community of Women and Men within the Church' programme, 222
compensation for victims, 111, 129
CONAVIGUA (National Coordination of Guatemalan Widows), 115n20

Condor plan for military cooperation, 197
Cone, James, 243
Congregation for the Doctrine of the Faith (CDF), 244n17, 260
conquistadors, 135, 142–6
consensus, ideology of, 151
conservatism in Church, 105; Romero, 47–8, 51, 92
consumption, US/Third World comparison, 149
Convergencia Guatemala, Nunca Más, 77, 78
conversion, 35, 165, 189, 192; *see also* poor (conversion to)
corpses, political power of, 207–8, 210
Costa Rica, 22, 44, 62
CRISPAZ (Christians for Peace), 267–8
Cristiani, Alfredo, President of El Salvador, 67
critical theorists of Frankfurt School of Philosophy, 177–8, 179
crucified peoples, 87, 89, 98, 134–58; community solidarity, 265; Ellacuría on, 82, 87, 88, 98; human rights, 136, 146–56; need to hear outcry of, 146–56; reality of, 148–50, 165; Romero on, 18, 98; use of term, 147–8
crucifixion, 170, 206n44
Crusades, 168
Cruz, Sor Juana Inés de la, 216
Cuba, 208, 219; women, 220n18, 227–8
cultural analysis, 246, 247
Czechoslovakia; Prague Spring, 219

Daly, Mary, 116, 243
D'Aubuisson, Major Roberto, 50, 92
Davis, Norman, 261
De Schrijver, Professor George, 247–8
debt, international, 148, 270, 273; of living to dead, 179–80, 184, 187
Declaration of the Rights of Man and the Citizen, French (1789, 1793), 134n1
Declercq, Fr Pedro, 51
democracy and feminism, 220, 227, 231
denial, official, of disappearance, 6, 119, 120, 198, 201, 202, 207,

209; of personal connection with victim, 6, 204–6, 272
Detroit; 'Theology in the Americas' conference (1975), 246
development, 55, 148, 241
Díaz Polanco, Judge Guillermo, 112n15
Diaz Rönner, Lucila, 229
dignity, 14, 35, 113, 123, 125–6
disappearance, 6, 194–210; Easter story interpreted in light of, 6, 202–9, (empty tomb), 6, 161–2, 173, 206–9, (Peter's denial of Christ), 6, 203–6, 269n7; as destruction of past, 200–1; impact on relatives and friends, 111, 117, 122, 170, 198–9, 199–202; international cooperation in, 197; legal need to establish death, 123; mass graves, 122, 123–5, 198; Mayan culture and, 122; ministry of lament, 170; monuments to, 131; numbers, 197, 198n18, 209; official denials, 'He is not here', 6, 198, 201, 202, 207, 209; Romero's support for families, 23, 25; torture, 198, 200n26; typical process, 198–9; use of term, 194n2; *see also under individual countries*
'Divinus Perfectionis Magister', 94
Dominican order, 143, 145
Dorfman, Ariel, 109, 199, 208
Drayton, Kathleen, 248
dreams, troubled, 120, 123
duress, acts committed under, 33, 106, 110, 128

East Timor, 138
EATWOT, 223–5
Echeverría, Roberto, 80
economic rights, 154–5
economy, world, 153, 247, 262–3, 273; Braudel's analysis, 252, 257–8; *see also* debt; wealth
Ecumenical Association of Third World Theologians, 223–5
education, 141; peace, 35
Eguren, Luis Enrique, 269
1848, revolutions of, 261–2
El Despertar, 100
El Mozote massacre, 12–13, 67
El Paisnal, 48

El Playon, 23
El Quiché, 18–22; Gerardi as bishop, 55, 61–2, (temporary closure of diocese), 21–2, 35, 61–2, 106; massacres, 42, 18–19, 20, 21, 22, 106, 131
El Salvador: amnesty law, 1–2; Argentines train military, 197; Bishops' Conference, 49, 51, 55, 92, 96; British support to Church, 50; Commission of Human Rights, 134; deaths and disappearances, 18, 91–2, 134, 197, 201, (El Mozote massacre), 12–13, 67, (number), 13, 18, 197, (priests), 29–30, 56, (*see also* Grande, Fr Rutilio; Jesuits; Romero y Galdames, Oscar Arnulfo); economic dislocation, 263–4; history of social movement and church, 91–2; John Paul II's visit, 55; land ownership, 17, 91–2; legacy of violence, 116; Papal Nuncio, 44; radio station, 50, 92; refugees, 23; and revolutions of 1968, 263–4; solidarity workers, 267–8, 269; structural injustice, 25, 27–8, 31, 91; UN Commission on the Truth, 1–2, 50; university sacked by army, 51; US support for regime, 12, 82n2; *see also* Romero y Galdames, Oscar Arnulfo
electronic communication, 271
Ellacuría, Fr Ignacio, SJ, 4, 81–9; assassination, 37, 81, 88, 135; on cloaking of First World intentions towards Third, 135, 146; and crucified people, 82, 87, 88, 98; definition of liberation theology, 84; on distorted account of European conquest of Americas, 145–6; on 18th-century human rights, 152n32; on justice, 232; on martyrdom, 4, 82, 84–8, 99; on 'mistaken paths' of societies and Church, 239; on right to biological life, 140; theology, 4, 81–9, (contextually embedded), 4, 84–6, (on doing of theology), 4, 84–6, 88–9
EMAS, 214n4
EMP (Guatemalan Presidential High

Command), 64, 72, 73-4, 75, 76, 110
emplotment (*Muthos*), 249-51, 252
Encounter of Christian Women, First Latin American, Mexico City (1979), 223
Enlightenment, 182
Episcopal Church, 121
epistemology, 135-46, 242
Equipo de Mujeres en Acción Solidaria, 214n4
Escobar, Major Juan, 73n40
Escoto, Miguel D', 266
Espinosa Damián, Gisela, 219
Espinoza, General Marco Tulio, 73
Esquivel, Julia, 173
Estrada Velásquez, Colonel Juan de Dios, 75
Ethiopia, 149
Eucharist, 171-2, 187
euphemism, 148
European Union, 64
Evangelii Nuntiandi, 20, 23-4
exhumations, 111, 118, 123-5, 129-31, 198n18
Exodus story, 135-6, 136-42, 186

family, models of, 233
Febvre, Lucien, 252, 254, 255
Federación Cristiana de Campesinos Salvadoreños-Unión de Trabajadores del Campo, 91-2
feminism, 6-7, 213-39; absence of critical feminist analysis in Latin America, 227-8, 232-3, 235-6; Chicana/Latina feminist theory, 215-16; Congresses, Latin American, 215; in Cuba, 220n18, 227-8; and democracy, 220, 227, 231; 15th-17th-century precursors of Latin American, 216; and human rights, 214, 227; as importation from developed world, 221; and issues other than gender, 216-17, 225-6; and kyriarchy, 216, 226-7, 233; in Latin America, 214-16, 227-8; option for poor, 231, 238; popular organizations, 222; as 'secondary conflict', 220n18, 221; sisterhood and solidarity ethic, 247; social transformation as aim, 218-19, 231; UN and awareness of, 222

feminist theology, 6-7, 213-39; and democracy, 220; and doing theology, 225; dynamism, 223; and EATWOT, 223-5; establishment, 213-14, 220, 233-6, 243; and gender theories, 228-30; and grassroot women, 238; historical influences on Latin American, 214, 216-32; and injustice, 213, 219, 232; and kyriarchy, 4, 7, 213, 218, 219, 220; liberation theologians and, 221, 224, 228-9; Medellín conference and, 7, 6-7, 214, 220, 232-3, 233-9; pluralism, 225, 226; and presidency of sacraments, 238-9; theologians opposed to, 224, 229, 230, 231, 236; US womanist theology, 247; Vatican II furthers, 213; widespread effect, 225-6
finance, 55, 137n5
Fiorenza, Elizabeth Schüssler, 164, 216-17, 229-30
Flores, Gerardo, Bishop of Alta and Baja Verepaz, 43, 77-8
FMLN guerrillas, 13
FNDG, 74, 115
Foppa, Alaíde, 216
forgetfulness: enforced systemic amnesia, 162, 166; and reconciliation, 188-90; right to forget, 114
forgivenness, 173, 184, 189, 191, 192n31
France; Annales School, 251-60; Declaration of the Rights of Man, 134n1
Frankfurt School of Philosophy, 177-8, 179
Frente Nacional Democrático de Guatemala, 74, 115
Frente Republicano de Guatemala, 74, 111
Freud, Sigmund, 183
FRG, 74, 111
Fukuyama, Francis, 150n28
fundamentalist churches, 47, 121
future and memory, 83-4, 180-1, 184, 185, 187, 191

Galeano, Eduardo, 149
Galindo, Celvin, 73, 74

García, General Romeo Lucas, President of Guatemala, 20, 61, 62, 69
García Villa, Marianella, 134
García Villatoro, Judge Flor de María, 75, 80
Garzón, Baltasar, 196n10, 197n12
Gaudium et spes, 100
gender issues, 228-30, 246, 248; *see also* feminism; women
Geneva; EATWOT Conference (1983), 223-4
genocide, *see under* indigenous peoples, Guatemalan
Gerardi Conedera, Juan, Auxiliary Bishop of Guatemala City, 18-22; and indigenous people, 32, 42, 60-1; and John Paul II, 62; legacy, 37, 42-3, 77-9, 193; and poor, 12, 14, 32, 55, 60-1, 63; Romero's situation compared, 31; resurrection in Guatemalan people, 78; sermons and writings, 19-20, 20-1, 31-7, ('The Response of the Catholic Church in Guatemala to the Processes of Social and Political Change)', 31-3; Suffering Servant image, 36-7; on truth, 69; unifying influence, 104; voice of the voiceless, 19, 65, 79
  BIOGRAPHY, 61-3; Bishop of Baja and Alta Verapaz, 55, 61; Bishop of Santa Cruz del Quiché, 55, 61; temporary withdrawal of clergy from diocese, 21-2, 35, 61-2, 106; exile, 22, 62; return, 22, 35, 62-3; Auxiliary Bishop of Guatemala City, head of Archdiocesan Human Rights Office (ODHAG), 22, 31, 62-3; and REMHI project, 35-7, 62-3, 77, 105, (possible connection with murder), 4, 42, 69, 71, 90-1, 104, (presents report), 34, 35-7, 59, 63, 69, 103
  MURDER, 2-3, 3-4, 55, 59-80; account of events, 63, burial, 77-8; commemoration, 42-3, 70; investigation, 3-4, 65, 67, 71-6, 80; public reaction, 90-1, 104, 111; significance of method, 37, 43, 79; timing and possible motives, 4, 34, 42, 67-71, 90-1, 103-4, 264; unintentional results, 77-9, 193
geschichte/historie distinction, 178
Gettysburg, Lincoln's address at, 176-7
Godoy, Coralia, 51
González Faus, J. I., 152
Good Friday liturgy, 170
Good News, 26-9, 30, 38, 151
Graham, Elaine, 167
Gran, Fr José Maria, 21
Grande, Fr Rutilio, 39, 92, 100; effect of death on Romero, 15-17, 48-50, 92, 99
Grandmothers of the Plaza del Mayo, 116
grassroots ecclesial communities, 234-5, 244
graves, mass, 122, 123-5, 131, 198
Great Lakes, 138
Greene, Graham, 266
grieving process, 5, 113, 123-6, 132-3, 200
groups, rights of social, 140-1
Group of Seven, 55
GSN (Guatemala Solidarity Network), 5, 118n
Guadeloupe, Our Lady of, 223
Guatemala, 5, 6, 103-17, 118-33; amnesty laws, 69, 112; Archdiocesan Office for Human Rights, *see* ODHAG; army, 13-14, 75, 109, 111, 197, (continuing power), 103-4, 112-13, 128, (creation of perpetrators), 33, 110, 128, (and Gerardi's death), 65, 69-71, 71-2; beliefs and practices concerning dead, 121-6; Bishops' Conference, 60, 62, 65, 69; Church's conversion to poor, 105; commemorative ceremonies, 122, 126; corruption, 68; disappearances, 61, 121-3, 193, 195, 201-2, 216, (effect on families), 117, 122, 198-9, 200, 201-2, (mass graves), 118, 122, 123-5, 198, (numbers), 197, 198n19, (typical process), 198-9; exhumations, 118, 123-5, 129-31; guerrillas, 13, 33, 61, 68, 105,

112, 115; healing, means of, 123–6; international support, 133; judicial system, 68, 79, 80, 109, 111, 120, 128, 129; lack of change, 103–4, 112–13, 120, 128 127; land ownership, 33, 68, 79, 111; legacy of violence, 116; massacres, 13, 61, 104, 106, 122, 129, 130–1, 131–2, 147; Mayans, *see* indigenous peoples, Guatemalan; media coverage of REMHI and CEH reports, 126–7; militarization, 106, 128; monuments, 5, 118, 119, 125, 126, 129–32, 132–3; number of victims, 12, 13, 104, 197, 198n19; Peace Accords (1996), 68, 69, 75, 77, 120; police, 13, 120; Public Ministry, 64, 66, 72, 73, 74; recovery and reconciliation, 119, 123, 132–3, (REMHI project and), 5, 34–5, 105, 106, 111, 113, 116–17, 125–6; regimes, 61, 62, 62n9; responses to reports, 126–8; silence, culture of, 5, 118, 119, 120; Spanish Embassy, 20; torture, 19, 69; UN Historical Clarification Commission, *see* CEH; and UN Human Rights Commission, 77; UN Verification Commission (MINUGUA), 77; US involvement, 82n2; wealth, disparity of, 19, 33, 68, 79; *see also* CEH; EMP; Gerardi Conedra, Juan; indigenous peoples, Guatemalan; ODHAG; PACs; REMHI

Guatemala City, cathdral of, 131
Guatemala Solidarity Network, 5, 118n
Guatemalan Alliance Against Impunity, 70
Guatemalan Republican Front (FRG), 74, 111
guerrillas: Argentinian, 195n8; Guatemalan, 13, 33, 61, 68, 105, 112, 115; Salvadoran, 13
Guevara, Ernesto 'Che', 207–8
Gutiérrez, Edgar, 37, 63, 70; on REMHI, 33–4, 35; and SAE, 75, 77
Gutiérrez, Gustavo, 89, 241; coins term Liberation Theology, 242, 243; 'The Poor and the Christian Communities', 194, 209–10; *The Power of the Poor in History*, 245; on Romero, 40, 41; *A Theology of Liberation*, 243–4, 244–5

Haiti, 147, 149
'Hand, The' (Argentinian death-squad), 195
'He is not here', 6, 198, 201, 202, 207, 209
healing, 35, 123–6, 188, 191
health problems caused by violence, 120
healthcare, lack of, 141
Hellenisation of Christianity, 182
heroes, cult of, 253
Hewitt, Marsha, 164n7
HIJOS (Children of the Disappeared), 116
Hispanic American women, 246–7
Hispaniola, 135, 142–6
historie/geschichte distinction, 178
history, 134–58, 176–85, 249–60; Benjamin on, 164, 177–8, 180; Braudel, *see separate entry*; end of, 150; Enlightenment and, 182; forgetfulness and reconciliation, 188–90; geo-history, 252, 254, 255; heroes, 253; materialism, 177–8; mediation of praxis, 249–52; New World theology and, 241; progressive view of, 188; and REMHI project, 5, 103–17; reality and perception, 178; and social sciences, 253, 254, 259; total, 255, 256, 259; underside of, 165–6, 187; US attitudes to, 176–7; *see also under* memory
Hitler, Adolf; 'Night and Fog' decree, 196n11
Holocaust, 11, 12, 147, 162–3, 175, 179
Honduras, 266
hope, 168–9; memory and, 11, 12, 14–15, 185, 190, 192n31
Horkheimer, Max, 177–8
housing, lack of adequate, 141
Huehuetenango, 42
human rights, 5, 134–58; abstraction, 135, 136; accountability for, 154–6; benefit to powerful, 135, 136, 139, 146, 152–3; of crucified peoples, 136, 146–56; 18th-

century notion, 134n1, 152n32; epistemology, 135–46; Exodus, 135–6, 137–42; failures in practice, 5, 134–6, 143, 145–6, 147, 156; feminist movement and, 214, 227; generations of, 134; hierarchy, 141, 146, 156; Hispaniola, 135, 142–6; the 'Humane' amongst crucified peoples, 147–50; 'It's not right' response, 136–7, 137–8, 142, 143–4, 147, 156–7; justification of infringement, 143, 144–5; language of, 148–50; life as basic right, 140, 141, 146, 148, 156, 157; mysticism of, 156–8; and neo-liberalism, 146; outcry of crucified peoples, 136, 146–56; outcry of victims, 135–6, 136–46; partiality, 5, 139, 153; of peoples and popular majorities, 140–2, 142–3, 146; primary experience, 135, 136–46; Salvadoran Commission on, 134; slumber to reality of, 5, 143–4, 150–2, 157; theory, 134–6, 143, 145–6, 147, 156; Universal Declaration of (1948), 134, 138, 147; universality, 5, 135, 138, 146, 152–3, 157; women and, 213, 214, 225–6, 227

Humanae Vitae, 260, 262
Hunger Cloths, 169
Hurricane Mitch, 266

Ibáñez, Fr, SJ, 48
identity and memory, 181
idols, modern, 3, 27–8, 54–5, 95–6, 151
imperialism, 247
impunity, 79, 109, 111, 128; *see also* amnesties
indigenous peoples, Guatemalan: centrality to national experience, 108; empowerment by REMHI, 117; genocide, 31, 42, 120, (legal charges), 69, 112, 120, 129; and Gerardi, 32, 42, 60–1; history of repression, 19, 20, 119–20; Indigenous Pastorate, 61; law, 128–9; Mayan language testimony to REMHI, 34, 108; Mayan spirituality, 5, 118, 120, 121–3, 130; unified by terror, 115

indigenous women, 222, 237
individualism, 187, 191, 253
industrialization, 263
information, privacy of, 156
injustice, 31, 57; decline in churches' denunciation, 151; feminist theology and, 213, 232; financial, 137n5; kyriarchy and, 232; martyrs of, 46; memory and redress of past, 14, 179, 180, 184, 185, 190; monuments to, 119; structural, 14, 31, 32–3, 46, 53, 216–17, 237; *see also* justice
intellectuals, oppression of, 141
intellectus fidei, intellectus amoris, 88
international support to oppressed, 119, 133
International Theology Commission, 175
International Year of the Woman (1975), 222
Iona community, 169n17
Irenaeus, St, 26
Israelites, 135–6, 136–42, 186
Italy; riots of 1968, 262
Ixcan, 13n14
Ixil, 61

Jansenism, 152
Japan, persecution of church in, 46
Jefferson, Thomas, US President, 176
Jeffery, Paul, 72
Jelín, Elizabeth, 113, 114
Jeremiah, Book of, 161
Jerez, Fr César, SJ, 48
Jesuits; martyrs of Central American University, 37, 39, 56, 81, 90, 113; chapel of, 40; Dean Brackley goes to teach in place of, 268n3; *see also* Ellacuría, Fr Ignacio
Jesus: Easter story compared with disappearance, 6, 202–9; living memory of, 186; paradigm of solidarity, 7, 271, 272
John, Gospel of, 105; Easter story, 161, 202n33, 203n34, 203n35, 204, 205n41, 206, 207n45, 272
John XXIII, Pope, 260
John Paul II, Pope, 55, 149, 175; 'Divinus Perfectionis Magister', 94; *Fides et Ratio*, 261; and Gerardi, 62, 64–5; 'Tertio

millennio adveniente', 56, 90; and Romero, 49–50, 92
Joseph of Arimathea, 7, 271–2
Joyabaj, 21
Jubilee, Vatican announcement of, 168
Jubilee 2000 Campaign, 270, 273
Judaism: memory, 6, 141–2, 182, 185–7; ministry of lament, 170; *see also* Exodus; Israelites
justice: demands for, 80, 116, 123, 128–9, 143; Mayan law, 128–9; Medellín conference and social, 46, 213, 233, 237; memory and, 11, 12, 14, 190; partiality, 139; and reconciliation, 188, 190–3; Spanish courts, 69n30, 129, 196n10, 197n12; *see also* injustice
Justice and Peace Conferences, 168

kairos (revelatory time), 188
Kairos Document (1986), 190
Kant, Immanuel, 144, 182
Keynes, John Maynard, 55
Kichí, 61
King, Dr Martin Luther, Jr, 14, 243, 262
Kirk-Duggan, Cheryl, 168–9
Krog, Antjie, 173–4
kyriarchy, 217–18; in church, 224, 231–2, 237, 238; feminism and, 216, 226–7, 233; feminist theology and, 7, 213, 219, 220, 231–2

La Libertad, 100
La Puerta, Quiché, 130
La Puerta del Diablo, 23
La Rue, Frank, 71, 75n46
Labour Behind the Label Network, 270
labour movement, 265
lament, ministry of, 169–70
land ownership: dominance of kyriarchal elites, 217; El Salvador, 17, 91–2; Guatemala, 33, 68, 79, 111; inheritance from disappeared, 123
language: euphemistic, 148; of gender, 228–9; of human rights, 148–50; postmodern positive, 150
Las Casas, Bartolomé de, 144–5, 148n20
Latin American Evangelical Centre for Pastoral Studies (CELEP), 78
law: dominance of kyriarchal elites, 217; inheritance, 123; Judaic, 139, 141–2; Mayan, 128–9; partiality, 139
Lawrence, Stephen, 119
Lazarus, parable of rich man and, 149
Lenhart, Christian, 178, 180
Lenin, V. I.; tomb in Moscow, 207
Lenten Veils, 169
Leo XIII, Pope; *Rerum Novarum* (1891), 260
liberalism, *see* neo-liberalism
liberation theology: class and cultural analysis, 246; and conflictual nature of reality, 95–6; and crucified people, 89; Ellacuría's definition, 84; emergence, 234–5, 240–4; and feminist theology, 221, 224, 228–9; in grassroots communities, 244; hostility to, 221, 224, 244, 260–4; and ideology of imperialism, 247; and martyrdom, 4–5, 89, 93–5; Medellín conference establishes, 234–5, 240, 243; methodology, 244–9; Papacy and, 260–1; plurality, 245; praxis, 89, 242, 244, 245, 249; and preferential option for the poor, 87; and race analysis, 175–93, 246; rapid spread, 220–1, 243–4; and truth, 242; US attitude to, 263
life, right to, 140, 141, 146, 148, 156, 157
Lima Estrada, Colonel Byron, 72, 73, 75, 80
Lima Oliva, Colonel Byron, 72, 73, 75, 80
Lincoln, Abraham, US President, 176–7
literary analysis, 246
longue durée, 255, 256, 258–60
López, Margarita (Gerardi's cook), 66, 76, 80
Louvain (Leuven), University of: Centre of Liberation Theology 1996 symposium, 'The Paradigm Shift in Third World Theologies of Liberation', 247; Romero's address, 'The Political Dimension of Faith', 25, 26–30; Sobrino's address, 38
Loyola, St Ignatius; *Spiritual Exercises*, No. 53, 87

Luke, Gospel of, 271; Easter story, 202, 203, 204, 205, 206, 207n45, 272
Lutheran Church, 121, 184n20

McDermott, Jeremy, 68
Madres of the Plaza del Mayo, 112
Magna Carta, 134n1
Mahony, Liam, 269
MAI (Multilateral Agreement on Investments), 154–5
majorities, rights of, 140–1, 146
Malcolm X, 243
Managua; Church of Santa Maria de Los Angeles, 265, 271
Marchak, Patricia, 194n2
Marcos, Sylvia, 226–7
Mark, Gospel of, 202, 203, 204, 205, 206, 206–7n45
market, 151
Martín-Baró, Fr I., SJ, 113
martyrdom, 4–5, 81–9, 90–100; collective, 98; and conflictual nature of reality, 95–6; expansion of classical concept, 4–5, 46, 93–5; in El Salvador, 91–2, (*see also* Grande, Fr Rutilio; Jesuits; Romero y Galdames, Oscar Arnulfo); in Guatemala, 104, (*see also* Gerardi Conedera, Juan); liberation theology and, 4–5, 89, 93–5; locally recognized, non-canonized, 5, 95; and memory, 4, 83–4, 88–9, 96; millennium martyrology, 56, 90; *odium fidei/iustitiae*, 46, 94, 96; as participation in death of Jesus, 97; and preferential option for poor, 96; Romero on, 29–30, 40–1, 44–6, 83, 95; resurrection of martyrs, 100; sacramental character, 4, 82, 83–4, 88–9; as sign of the times, 100; Tertullian on, 30, 56, 83; theology of, 4–5, 90–100, (Ellacuría's), 3, 4, 82, 84–8, 99; Westminster Abbey statues of, 44, 56, 57, 92
Marxist historical dialectic, 246, 247, 248, 251
Mary of Magdala, 6, 161–2, 173, 175
massacres, 12–13, 67, 98, 106, 122; see also under Guatemala
Matanza, 91

materialists, historical, 177–8
Matthew, Gospel of, 161; Easter story, 202, 203, 204, 205, 206, 207n45, 272
Mayans, *see* indigenous peoples, Guatemalan
Medcalf, Fr John, 269
Medellín Conference, *see* Bishops, Second Conference of Latin American
media, 50, 92, 126–7, 137n5, 149
Mejía, José Humberto, 204n38
Mejía Victores, General Oscar Humberto, President of Guatemala, 62n9, 69
memory: ambiguity, 6, 179; Benjamin on, 163, 164, 177–8; collective, 108, 114, 117, 133, 183, 260, (return to people), 35, 36, 111, 126; and debt of living to dead, 179–80, 184, 187; distortion, 127, 166; duty to remember the dead, 179–81, (benefits accruing from), 181–5; in early Church, 6, 186–7; Ellacuría and, 82; empathetic, 177; empowerment by, 114; ethical dimension, 80, 185; in Eucharist, 187; false, 166, 179; flight from, 182; forgetfulness as alternative, 114, 187–90; Freud on, 183; and future, 83–4, 180–1, 184, 185, 187, 191; and healing, 168, 179, 188; and history, 6, 176–85, 187, (appeal to memory), 179–85, (benefits of relationship), 182–5, (dangerous memory of), 165–6, (debates from recent centuries), 176–9, (memory- and historical-narratives), 183, 187–8, 191, 192n31; of Holocaust, 11, 12, 179, 182; and hope, 11, 12, 14–15, 185, 190, 192n31; and identity, 181; individual, 114, 183; in Judaism, 6, 182, 185–7; and justice, 11, 12, 14, 190, (*see also* redress *below*); liberating, 168, 179, 188; living, of Jesus as Christ, 186, 187; and martyrdom, 4, 83–4, 88–9, 96; and Mayan cosmovision, 121–3; and monuments, 133; 'mystic chords of', 177; in New World theology, 241; old people as repository, 108;

INDEX   287

of passion and resurrection of
    Christ, 163; past changed by, 11,
    12, 166, 178, 184, 185, 186, 187;
    problematic, 114; and promises,
    180, 182, 184–5; prophetic,
    187–8, 191; purifying, 168; and
    reason, 182; and reconciliation, 6,
    184, 188, 190–3; reconfiguring of,
    260; and redress of injustice, 179,
    180, 184, 185, 190; repetition-
    memory, 183, 192n31; restoration
    to people, 35, 36, 111, 126;
    selective, 241, 260; and social
    reconstruction, 105; trace of
    repressed, 167; Truth and
    Reconciliation Commissions and,
    179; work of recollection, 183–4,
    192n31; *see also* commemoration
    of dead; memory, dangerous;
    memory-narratives; *and under*
    REMHI; truth
memory, dangerous, 6, 161–74; and
    Eucharistic *Anamnesis*, 171–2; and
    ministry of lament, 169–70; origin
    and meaning, 162–4; poetics of,
    168–9; praxis of, 6, 167–74;
    REMHI and, 162, 164; and
    repentance, 166, 167, 173; and
    resistance, 168–9, 173; and
    Resurrection, 173; risk of
    remembering Romero, 96; silence
    broken by, 162, 166, 173;
    standpoint of those who remember,
    164–7; theology of, 6, 161–74;
    and truth, 11, 12, 162, 172, 175;
    of underside of history, 165–6
memory-narratives, 187–8, 191,
    192n31
Menchú, Rigoberta, 35, 69n30, 112,
    129
Menchú Foundation, 69n30
Mendoza, Rodolfo, 65
Menem, Saúl, President of Argentina,
    109, 116
mercy, principle of, 87, 88
Metz, Johann Baptist: 83–4, 150, 243;
    on memory, 83–4, 88–9, 96,
    163–4, 173, 179, 182
Mexico City, 215, 222, 223, 262
Micah, Book of, 170
militarization of communities, 106,
    120, 128, 129, 130
Millennium: debt relief campaign, 270,

273; Martyrology for, 56, 90
mimesis, 249–51, 252
MINUGUA (UN Verification
    Commission in Guatemala), 77
missionaries and politics, 267
Molina Theissen, Marco Antonio,
    198–9
Moltmann, Jürgen, 243
Monroy, Henry, 73–4
Montenegro, Nineth, 115n20
Montes, Fr Segundo, SJ, 134–5
Montesinos, Friar Antonio, 143, 144
monuments, 5, 118–33; and
    community, 5, 118, 125, 129–32,
    132–3; and grieving process, 5,
    132–3; in Guatemala, 5, 118, 119,
    125, 126, 129–32, 132–3;
    perpetrators and, 132; state-
    sponsored, 119
Moody, Linda, 246
Morales, Dario, 73–4
Morrison, Toni; *Beloved*, 166, 169
Moscow; tomb of Lenin, 207
mothers, Romero and, 23, 45
Mothers of the Disappeared,
    Argentina, 116
mourning process, 5, 113, 123–6,
    132–3, 200
MRS (Sandinista Renewal Movement),
    217
Mujerista theology, 247
Muthos (emplotment), 249–51
mysticism of human rights, 156–8

NACLA, 273
National Central America Health
    Rights Network (NCAHRN),
    269n4
National Coordination of Guatemalan
    Widows (CONAVIGUA), 115n20
National Network in Solidarity with the
    Nicaraguan People (NNSNP),
    269n4
national security, 28, 47, 54, 195
nationalism, 151
Navarro, Fr Alfonso, 17
NCAHRN, 269n4
neofeminism, 219
neo-liberalism, 55, 120, 146, 219
New Delhi, India; EATWOT Congress
    (1981), 225
New World theology, 7, 240–64;
    emergence, 240–4; fragmentation

of interpretative framework, 7, 246–9, 251; historical approach, 7, 241, 251–60; liberation and interpretative framework, 244–6; and Marxist historical dialectic, 246, 247, 248, 251; and memory, 241; methodology, 260; praxis as basis, 7, 240, 241, 249; Ricoeur's hermeneutics and, 249–52, 260; and social sciences, 241–2
New Yorker, 12–13
Nicaragua: mural from Managua, 265, 271; Sandinista revolution, 197, 217, 266, 267; solidarity work, 266–7, 268–9, 270, 272; post-revolution phase, 266–7; US involvement, 268–9, 270, 272
Nicaragua Network, 269n4
Nicaragua Solidarity Campaign (NSC), 266
'Night and Fog' decree, Hitler's, 196n11
1968, revolutions of, 219, 262–4
NNSNP, 269n4
Nobel Peace Prize for Rigoberta Menchú, 35
Noémi, Sister, 51–2
North American Congress on Latin America, 273
north/south polarization, 149–50
novus ordo saeclorum (motto), 176
NSC (Nicaragua Solidarity Campaign), 266
Nuncios, Papal, 44, 47
nuns, martyrdom of, 100

Obdulio Villanueva, José, 80
Ochaeta, Ronalth, 63, 70–1
ODHAG (Human Rights Office of the Archdiocese of Guatemala), 2, 60; Gerardi as head of, 22, 31, 62–3; and Gerardi's death, 70, 77; investigation, 65, 67, 70, 71–2, 80; REMHI project set up by, 31, 33, 105; *see also* REMHI project
odium fidei/iustitiae, 94, 96
OECD Multilateral Agreement on Investments, 154–5
O'Kane, Trish, 60
old people, violence against, 108
Oliviera, Orlandina de, 222
Orantes, Fr Mario, 63–4, 66, 73, 75–6, 80

orders, following of, as excuse, 110
Ortega, Daniel, 266, 267
Ortiz, Octavio, 100
Oslo Accord (1994), 2, 104–5

PACs (Civilian Self-Defence Patrols, Guatemalan), 106, 120, 128, 129, 130
Papacy: and modern critical tools, 260–1; *see also individual Popes*
Parecer de Yucay, 144n13
Paris; student uprising (1968), 219, 262
partiality in human rights, 5, 139, 153; *see also* poor (preferential option for)
Passover, 185
pastoral action, 125–6, 245
patriarchy, 221, 246, 247
Paul, Epistles of: Colossians, 99; I Corinthians, 138n6; Galatians, 138n6; Philippians, 271
Paul VI, Pope, 49, 61; *Evangelii Nuntiandi*, 20, 23–4; *Humanae Vitae*, 260, 262
Peace Brigades, 204n37
Pellecer Faena, Luis Eduardo, 110
Penados del Barrio, Archbishop Prospero, 72
Pentecost, 186
peoples, rights of, 140–2, 142–3, 146
perception and reality, 178
Perón, Eva, 208
Perón, Isabelita, President of Argentina, 195n8, 208
Perón, Juan, President of Argentina, 208
perpetrators: Argentinian, 108–9; effect of violence on, 5, 110–11, 132; and monuments, 132; need for conversion, 191, 192; REMHI's naming of, 5, 105, 110; still live locally, 120; systemic means of turning people into, 33, 110, 128, 162; testimony of, 5, 108–9
persecution of Church, for defending the poor, 30, 92, 96, 98; Romero on, 30, 54, 98; three models of, 3, 46–8
Peru, 195n6, 209n50
Peter, St, 6, 203–6, 269n7
Peukert, Helmut, 178
photography, political power of, 207–8n46

INDEX   289

Pinochet, General Augusto, President of Chile, 109, 171, 195, 196n10, 200n25, 207
Pius IX, Pope; *Quanta Cura* (1864), 260, 261-2
Pius X, Pope; Condemnation of Modernism (1907), 260
Pius XII, Pope; *Humani Generis* (1950), 260
Plan de Sánchez, Baja Verapaz, 130-1
poetics of resistance and memory, 168-9, 173
Pokonchí, 61
Poland, 265
police, 64, 65, 120, 195n3
political philosophy, 144
political rights, 154
political science and memory, 178
politics: corpse's subversive power, 207-8; and faith, 24, 25, 49, 51; hegemony of kyriarchal elites, 217; as idol, 54, 95; missionary involvement, 267; radicalization, 1960s, 241; of resistance, 173
poor, the: chronic poverty, 55; conversion to, (Guatemalan Church), 105, (Romero), 15-18, 26, 48-50, 92, 99; as crucified people, 87; feminist option for, 231, 238; head hierarchy of human rights, 156; and industrialization, 263; New World theology and, 241; partiality to, in Exodus, 139; as place of theologian, 86-7; preferential option for, 61, 96, 98, 242, (bishops' conferences and), 3, 46, 53, 223, 234-5, 238, (Romero and), 27, 28, 52-4, 57; as teachers, (of Church), 238, (of Romero), 3, 25, 26, 29, 39, 50-1; women suffer particularly, 219-20, 225-6; *see also under* Gerardi Conedera, Juan; Romero y Galdanes, Oscar Arnulfo
popular organizations, 23-4, 91-2, 222
Portillo, Alfonso, President of Guatemala, 64n14, 74-5
Portugal, 142-6
postmodernism, 150, 187
power: forgiveness promotes status quo, 189; as idol, 54, 95, 151; memory as conferring, 114; revolutions and, 262; REMHI and change in relations, 116-17; universal human rights as threat to, 153
Pozuelos, Colonel Rudy, 73n40
Prague Spring (rising, 1968), 219, 262
praxis: Braudel and, 252; memory influences present, 6, 185, 186; of solidarity, 265-71; and theory of human rights, 141; *see also* theology (doing of)
Prensa Libre, 76
Presbyterian Church, 121
priests and religious, assassination of, 17, 21, 54, 61, 98, 100, 106; *see also* Gerardi Conedera, Juan; Grande, Fr Rutilio; Jesuits; Romero, Oscar
privacy and information technology, 156
promises, 180, 182, 184-5
prosecutors, public, 65, 66, 71-6
'protective shield', aid workers as, 269
Protestant churches, 47, 56, 121
Psalms: 22, 170; 68.5, 139
psychoanalysis, 113
psychology: effect of disappearances, 117, 199-202; false memory, 179; military use, 110
Puebla Conference, *see* Bishops, Third Conference of Latin American

Q'echí, 61
Quanta Cura (1864), 260, 261-2
Quiché, *see* El Quiché
quilts, commemorative, 169

Rabinal, Baja Verapaz, 13, 129, 130
race analysis, 246, 248
Rachel's lament, 6, 161, 170, 174
radicalization of politics, 241
radio station, Salvadoran church, 50, 92
Rahner, Karl, 46, 94-5
Ramos, Bishop Joaquin, 56
Ranke, Leopold von, 253
rape, women blamed for, 166
Reagan, Ronald, US President, 47, 263
reason and 'flight from memory', 182
reception of work by audience, 250
recessions, economic, 262-3
recognition, dangerous, 162
recollection, work of, 183-4, 192n31
reconciliation, 6, 175-93; conversion

and, 189, 192; eschatological
   aspect, 192; forgetfulness and,
   188; at Jubilee, 168; and justice,
   188, 190–3; and memory, 6, 184,
   188, 190–3; political interest in,
   188; rushed, 191; *see also* REMHI
   project (recovery and
   reconciliation)
recovery, 5, 116–17, 119, 125–6;
   definitions, 116
recrimination, 192
redemption paradigm of Christianity,
   242
redress, memory and, 179, 180, 184,
   185, 190
re-education in Guatemala, 106
refugees, 23, 32, 168
relativism, 187
religious, murders of, *see under* priests
REMHI (Recovery of Historical
   Memory) project, 5, 6, 103–17;
   abridged report in English, 103n1,
   109–10; Case 5449, Guatemala
   City, 1979, 70n32; catharsis of
   testifying, 35, 106, 121, 125; and
   CEH report, 33, 104–5, 111–12;
   and commemorations, 34–5, 105,
   126; communities rebuilt, 34–5,
   106, 113; on crucifixions, 206n44;
   on disappearances, 6, 197, 198–9;
   healing through, 35, 123–6;
   history of, 104–6; and indigenous
   peoples, 34, 108, 117; massacre,
   definitions of, 106n6; media
   coverage, 126–7; and memory, 5,
   105, 113–15, 175, (dangerous),
   162, 164, (restoration of
   collective), 35, 36, 111, 126;
   methodology, 33–4, 107, 125–6;
   on methodology of perpetrators, 5,
   110–11, 162; and monuments,
   126; mourning enabled by, 113,
   123–6; naming of victims and
   perpetrators, 5, 105, 110; numbers
   of massacres and victims, 13, 21;
   ODHAG's role, 31, 33; pastoral
   programme, 125–6; on
   perpetrators, 5, 105, 108–9,
   110–11, 162; power and recovery,
   116–17; protagonists, 106–10;
   recommendations, 43, 111–13;
   recovery and reconciliation, 5,
   34–5, 105, 106, 111, 113,
   116–17, 125–6; report at
   Washington Holocaust Museum,
   11–12; and structural injustice,
   117; on truth, 105, 162, 175; on
   violence against women, 107–8;
   see also under Gerardi Conedera,
   Juan (BIOGRAPHY)
reparations, 111, 129
repentance: by Church for supporting
   powerful, 168; and dangerously
   remembering, 166, 167, 173; *see
   also* conversion
Reproaches, Good Friday liturgy, 170
resistance, poetics and politics of, 168,
   173
resurrection, 173, 186; of martyrs in
   people, 40–2, 45, 78, 83, 100
retribution, 192
Rettig Report (Chilean National
   Commission on Truth And
   Reconciliation), 196n10, 200n26
Revelo, Bishop, 55
revenge, 192
Reverte, Dr José, 66–7
revolutions, years of (1848 1nd 1968),
   261–4
Rich, Adrienne, 167
Ricoeur, Paul: hermeneutics of action,
   249–52, 260; on memory, 179,
   183, 184, 191
Rieger, Jorge, 273
Río Negro, Baja Verapaz, 129, 130
Ríos Montt, General Efraín, President
   of Guatemala, 42, 62n9, 69, 74,
   112, 129
Ríos Montt, Mario, Auxiliary Bishop
   of Guatemala City, 67, 73, 74
Rivera Damas, Mgr, Archbishop of
   San Salvador, 47, 48, 49, 149n23
Rockefeller, Nelson, 47
Rodriguez, Oscar, Archbishop of
   Tegucigalpa, 43
Romero y Galdames, Oscar Arnulfo,
   Archbishop of San Salvador:
   advisers, 52, 81; apostolic visitors
   examine, 49; assassination, 2–3,
   37, 50, 92, 193, 264, (public
   reaction), 90, 92; attractive
   qualities, 50–2; on Beatitudes, 53;
   bishops' divisions over, 49, 55,
   92, 96; boycotts state occasions,
   48–9; canonization process, 55;
   challenging quality, 38, 52, 55–6,

57; commemoration of martyrdom, 38, 41, 82, 96; conservatism, 47-8, 51, 92; 'crucified people' concept, 18, 98; and families of disappeared, 23, 25; Gerardi's situation compared, 31; Good News to poor, 26-9, 30, 38; and Grande's death, 15-17, 48-9, 92, 99; and human rights, 22-30, 135; on idols of society, 3, 27-8, 54-5, 95; and John Paul II, 49-50, 92; on law's partiality to powerful, 139; legacy, 38-42; Louvain address, 'The Political Dimension of Faith', 25, 26-30; on martyrdom, 29-30, 44-6, 54, 83, 95, 240; on national security, 3, 28, 54-5; pastoral letters, 81n1, (third, 'The Church and Popular Political Organizations)', 23-4, (fourth, 'The Church's Mission Amid the National Crisis)', 24-5, 54; and Paul VI, 49; on persecution as sign of Church, 98; personality, 16, 50-2; and the poor, 12, 14, 25, 26-9, 38, 41-2, 51, (conversion to), 15-18, 26, 48-50, 92, 99, (learns from), 3, 25, 26, 29, 39, 50-1, (loved by), 57-8, (and preferential option for), 27, 28, 52-4, 57, (proclaims Good News to), 26-9, 30, 38; on priests' deaths, 54, 98; radio broadcasts, 92; refuses military protection, 54; resurrection in the people, 40-2, 45, 83, 100; retreat, final, 44-5; on right to life, 140; sermons and writings, 22-30, (*see also* homilies *below*); on soteriological meaning of suffering, 99; tomb, 16, 38, 57-8; universal Christian, 39-40, 56-8, 92; and Vatican II, 24, 175; 'voice of the voiceless', 3, 24, 49, 56, 89; Westminster Abbey statue, 44, 56, 57, 92; willingness to die, 30, 45, 83, 240; witness, 22-30
HOMILIES, 52, 92; 15 May 1977, 45; 13 Nov 1977, 57; 22 Jan 1978, 52; 5 Feb 1978, 50; 16 Apr 1978, 52; 11 May 1978, 53; 3 Sep 1978, 26; 17 Dec 1978, 52; 11 Mar 1979, 54; 12 Apr 1979, 57; 15 Jul 1979, 54, 98; 22 Jul 1979, 54; 6 Aug 1979, 53; 12 Aug 1979, 95; 9 Sep 1979, 57; 16 Sep 1979, 57; 23 Sep 1979, 53; 11 Nov 1979, 57; 27 Jan 1980, 99; 17 Feb 1980, 53; 11 Mar 1980, 98; 16 Mar 1980, 22-3

Rönner, Lucila Diaz, 229
Rueben, Debra, 272

sacraments, presidency of, 238-9
Sacramentum Mundi, 93-4
'sacred, the', and human rights, 157
Sacred Congregation for the Doctrine of the Faith, 244n17, 260
SAE (Secretariat of Strategic Analysis, Guatemala), 75, 77
Sahakok, Alta Verapaz, 131-2
Samaritan, parable of, 271
San Salvador: Archdiocesan Office for Human Rights, 2; cathedral, 49; Divine Providence Hospital, 50; Passionist Sisters' retreat centre, 44-5; processions to commemorate Romero, 38, 41
Sánchez Olvera, Alma Rosa, 219
Sandinistas, 197, 217, 266, 267
Santa Cruz del Quiche, 18-22
Santa Fe documents, 47, 263
Saturday, Holy, 173
savagery of killings, 13-14, 33, 206n44
Scarry, Elaine, 171
Scilingo, Adolfo, 108-9
Sebastián, Luis de, 153
Secretariat of Strategic Analysis, Guatemala (SAE), 75, 77
Segundo, Juan Luis, 242, 243, 245n21
Semmelroth, Otto, 93-4
Sendero Luminoso, 209n50
Sepúlveda, Juan Ginés de, 144
sexism, structural, 213, 221, 237; *see also* kyriarchy
sexual revolution, 1960s, 262
Sherman, Sylvia, 272
Shoah, *see* Holocaust
Sieder, Rachel, 117
Siglo XXI (newspaper), 69
signs of the times, 100
silence: dangerous memory and breaking of, 162, 166, 173; about disappeared, 198; Guatemalan

culture of, 5, 118, 119, 120; on Holocaust, 162; recovery of women from, 164
Simon of Cyrene, 7, 271
Simon Peter, see Peter, St
sin, Church's denunciation of social, 151
sin-redemption paradigm of Christianity, 242
sisterhood, feminist ethic of, 247
slavery; in Americas, 138, 143, 164, 166, 168-9; Israelites' memory of, 141-2, 186
Smith, Dennis, 78-9
Sobrino, Fr Jon, SJ, 81; on 'anti-kingdom', 96; on Christians murdered in El Salvador, 56, 96; and 'crucified people', 98; on martyrdom, 90, 93, 97-100; on 'principle of mercy', 88; on Romero's legacy, 38, 39-40, 56; on solidarity, 273
social sciences, 241-2, 253, 254, 259
Solidarity (Polish movement), 265
solidarity, 265-73; as accompaniment, 265-6, 267, (from a distance), 7, 269-71, 271-2, (physical, on the spot), 7, 267-9, 271, 272; anamnestic, 165, 178; biblical models, 7, 271-3; within community, 265; and crucified peoples, 149, 165, 265; dangerous memory involves, 165; effect on First World, 268-9, 269-71, 272-3; feminist ethic of, 247; Gerardi's, with poor, 12; as long-term commitment, 7, 266-7, 267-8, 271; with martyrs, 83; Medellín and, 233, 235; missionary activity and, 267; Peter's following Jesus as act of, 204, 269n7; praxis, 265-71; 'protective shield' principle, 269; Romero's, with poor, 12, 18, 38; as 'tenderness of the people', 265; theology of, 265, 271-3
Solís Oliva, Juan Carlos, 73
soteriology, 94, 99-100, 164
Soto, Alvaro de, 128n14
south/north polarization, 148, 149-50
South Africa, 266; Truth and Reconciliation Commission, 164, 173

Spain: embassy in Guatemala 20; conquest of Hispaniola, 142-6; trials of Latin American human rights violations, 69n30, 129, 196n10, 197n12
street children, 195n3
structures, unjust, 14, 31, 53, 68, 117, 266; Gerardi on, 32-3; Romero on, 27-8; see also sexism, structural
student movement, 1960s, 219, 241, 262
Suarez, Hugo Banzer, President of Bolivia, 195n6
Suffering Servant, 23, 36-7, 99
Syllabus of Errors, 260, 261-2
Synod on the Family (1980), 62

Tabasco, Mexico; Feminist Congress (1915), 215
tapestries to commemorate AIDS victims, 169
Téllez, Dora María, 217
Tepeyac, Brown Virgin of, 223
Tertullian on martyrs, 30, 56, 83
textile workers' rights, 270
theodicy, 155
Thailand, 96
Thatcher, Margaret, Prime Minster of Britain, 263
theology: black, 246; of dangerously remembering, 6, 161-74; doing of, praxis, 4, 7, 81-9, 225, 240, 241, 242, 245, 249; human rights' significance in, 134-58; *intellectus fidei, intellectus amoris*, 88; justification of human rights infringements, 144; kyriarchal elites and, 4, 218; 'New World', 240-64; and philosophy, 241; place of, 85, 86-8; and social sciences, 241-2, 253, 254; of solidarity, 265, 271-3; see also Ellacuría, Fr Ignacio (theology); feminist theology; liberation theology; martyrdom (theology of)
'Theology in the Americas' conference (Detroit, 1975), 246
'Third World' as euphemism, 148
Thornton, Lawrence; *Imagining Argentina*, 172
time, 187, 188, 255-60
Todorov, Tzvetan, 114

Tokyo, 262
tolerance, ideology of, 151
Tomuschat, Christian, 11-12
Torah, 185
Torres, Camilo, 269
Torres, Sergio, 214n3
torture, 13-14, 19, 69, 171-2, 198, 200n26, 206n44
Traba, Marta; *Mothers and Shadows*, 201
trade, world, 267, 270
trade unions, 91, 92, 149, 265
'Triple A' (Argentine Anti-Communist Alliance), 195
truth: effect of telling, 35, 69, 105, 121, 125; Ellacuría and, 82; and memory, 11, 12, 162, 172, 175; New World theology and, 241, 242; privileging victims' over regimes', 162
Truth and Reconciliation Commissions, 179; Argentinian, 108, 196n9; Chilean, 196n10, 200n26; South African, 164, 173; *see also* CEH; REMHI
Tuñón Pablos, Esperanza, 215
Tuyuc, Rosalina, 115n20

UCA (Central American University), 51; *see also* Jesuits
underdevelopment and dependency, 148, 247
undesirables, social, 195n3
unemployment, youth, 263
unions, 91, 92, 149, 265
United Nations: arms production controlled by Security Council members, 155; Commission for Human Rights, 63, 77; Guatemalan Historical Clarification Commission, *see* CEH; Guatemalan Verification Commission (MINUGUA), 77; Salvadoran Commission on the Truth, 1-2, 12-13; and women's issues, 222
United States of America: Church aligned with, in 1980s, 263; Civil Rights movement, 243; Congress, and aid to *contra*, 270; consumption, 149; Declaration of Independence, 176; and El Salvador, 12, 82n2; embassy in San Salvador, 12, 204n38; fundamentalist Protestant churches, 121; grass-roots campaigns on aid to *contra*, 270; and Guatemala, 82n2; and history, 176-7; and liberation theology, 47, 263; military advisers in Latin America, 111, 113n17; and Nicaragua, 268-9, 270, 272; riots, 1968, 262; slavery, 138, 143, 164, 168-9; solidarity workers in Latin America, 269; women, 166, 168, 237, 246-7; *see also* African-Americans

Universal Declaration of Human Rights (1948), 134, 138, 147
Urioste, Monseñor Ricardo, 47-8, 50-1
URNG guerrillas, 13, 33, 105, 115
Uruguay, 195, 197n12

Vargas Valente, Virginia, 214-15, 218, 226, 231
'Vasco de Quiroga' Michoacano Center for Research and Education (CEMIF), 214n4
Vatican Commission for Religious Relations with Jews, 175
Vatican Council II, 61, 213, 240, 260, 262; Medellín conference and, 46, 91; Romero and, 24, 175
vengeance, 192
Ventura, Francisco Arnulfo, 204n38
Verapaz, Alta and Baja, 42, 55, 61; massacres, 106, 129, 130-1, 131-2
Veterans' Peace Convoy, 269n4
victim mentality, avoidance of, 107, 191
Vielman, Carlos, 65-6
Vietnam War protests, 262
Villagrán, Major Andrés, 73-4
Villanueva, Fr Faustino, 21
Villanueva, Obdulio, 75, 80
violence: every-day, 68, 116, 195n3; structural, 53, 103-4; *see also* massacres; savagery; *and under* women
Virgil; *lacrimae rerum*, 174
Virginia Declaration of Rights (1776), 134n1
Vitoria, J., 145

voice of the voiceless, 90–1; Gerardi, 19, 65, 79; Romero, 3, 24, 49, 56, 89

Walker, Alice, 169
wars, twentieth-century, 147
Washington DC; Holocaust Museum, 11–12
wealth: as modern idol, 54, 57, 95, 151; disparity of, 19, 25, 68, 79, 91, 148, 149
Westminster Abbey, 44, 56, 57, 92
wholeness, God's vision of, 218
Wiesel, Elie, 11, 12, 14, 163
Wild Goose Worship of Iona community, 169n17
Witness for Peace (WPF), 268–9
womanist theology, 247
women: Benjamin and, 164n7; black, 166, 168, 237, 246–7; Cuban, 220n18, 227–8; exploitation, 263; families of disappeared, 112, 116, 201–2; grassroot, 231, 238; Hispanic American, 246–7; human rights, 213, 214, 225–6, 227; indigenous, 206n44, 222, 237; and kyriarchal Church structures, 218, 221, 231–2, 238–9; lament, 170; multiple structures of oppression, 216–17, 219–20, 223; need for preferential option, 219–20, 225–6; oppression as 'secondary', 220n18, 221; rape blamed on, 166; recovery from silence, 164; violence against, 107–8, 124, 166, 206n44, 231, 237, 270; workers' rights, 270; *see also* feminism; feminist theology
Women Church, 168
work brigades, 270
workers' rights, 270
World Council of Churches, Commission of Faith and Order, 222
WPF (Witness for Peace), 268–9
Wyschogrod, Edith, 179

Yad Vashem, Jerusalem, 175
Yucatán Feminist Congress (1916), 215

Zacamil, 51–2
Zeizzig, Leopoldo, 74, 80